Bradt

Slow
Dorset

Local, characterful guides to Britain's special places

Alexandra Richards

ROTATION
PLAN

Edition 1

...vel Guides Ltd, UK
...quot Press Inc, USA

CHAPTER KEY

Portland
Bill

SUGGESTED PLACES TO BASE YOURSELF

These bases make ideal starting points for exploring localities the Slow way.

① **The Blackmore Vale** (pages 7–39) An unspoilt agricultural area ideal for farm stays, near Shaftesbury with its abbey ruins and photogenic Gold Hill.

② **Sherborne** (pages 47–53) Two castles, an abbey and an historic town centre perfect for pottering huddle at the edge of the Blackmore Vale.

③ **Dorchester** (pages 61–7) Dorset's historic county town lies at the heart of Thomas Hardy country near Maiden Castle, England's largest Iron Age hillfort.

④ **Cerne Abbas** (pages 75–6) A tiny village showcasing a jumble of architectural styles, while naked and proud on a nearby hillside is the iconic Giant chalk carving.

⑤ **Lyme Regis** (pages 101–8) An ancient seaside town at the heart of the Jurassic Coast and prime fossil-hunting territory.

⑥ **The Bride Valley** (pages 113–22) Idyllic rolling hills, woodland and thatched villages on the River Bride's route to the sea; visit charming Abbotsbury and extraordinary Chesil Beach.

⑦ **Isle of Purbeck** (pages 151–89) Stroll the peninsula's heaths, enjoy an exhilarating horseride along Studland Beach, soak up the atmosphere of ruined Corfe Castle and take a nostalgic trip on the Swanage Railway.

⑧ **Wimborne Minster** (pages 220–4) An appealing riverside town close to the National Trust Kingston Lacy Estate, Cranborne Chase and Poole Harbour.

⑨ **Poole Harbour** (pages 198–208) Beach polo in summer on Sandbanks, one of Britain's finest stretches of sand, and Brownsea Island a boat ride from Poole.

⑩ **Christchurch** (pages 213–19) Take a boat up the River Stour, and stride out across the wild Hengistbury Head from this delightful town with its magnificent medieval priory church.

A Dorset Gallery

Hop on one of the lovingly restored trains of the Swanage Railway for a truly Slow journey through the Isle of Purbeck, skirting around the base of magnificent Corfe Castle before chugging onwards to the coast. (AR)

Head to Henley Farm to glimpse shy badgers in their natural habitat. (AR)

Falconer Allan Gates and his birds are a regular sight on Mere Downs; try your hand at this ancient country sport. (AR)

Canter along deserted stretches of white sand at Studland Beach and Nature Reserve. (NS)

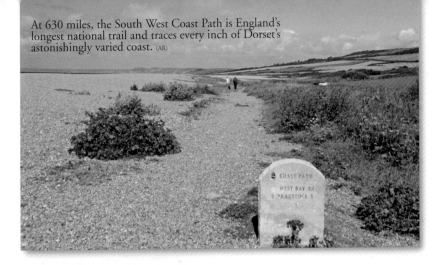

At 630 miles, the South West Coast Path is England's longest national trail and traces every inch of Dorset's astonishingly varied coast. (AR)

COAST PATH
WEST BAY 5¼
B BRADSTOCK 3

Dorset days

These activities give you a taste of the best Dorset has to offer.

Whether on a tour or on your own, fossil hunting in Lyme Regis is an exciting way to get a feel for the Dorset coast's rich geological history. (NS & AR)

Local foraging expert John Wright leads fascinating courses on hedgerow, mushroom and seashore foraging. (AR)

Hambledon Hill provides almost aerial views of the verdant Blackmore Vale. The Iron Age hillfort here seems to have been abandoned around 300BC, possibly in favour of nearby Hod Hill. (AR)

An inspiration for Enid Blyton, Brownsea Island provides the perfect secluded spot for forest walks and wildlife spotting. (AR)

Rural landscapes

Get off the beaten path and explore the dramatic vistas and natural wonders that define the Dorset countryside.

Cheerful bluebells carpet Dorset's woodlands in spring. (AR)

St Catherine's Chapel stands in the dramatic landscape of Abbotsbury, with Chesil Beach and the Fleet in view. (AR)

Established by Benedictine monks in the 11th century, the colony of 600 swans at Abbotsbury Swannery comprises the only ones in England not owned by the Queen. (NS)

Historically, North Dorset has been prime farming country, and its fine agricultural heritage is visible throughout the region. (AR)

In the village of Knowlton, a 12th-century ruined church stands in the centre of a Neolithic henge, a striking amalgam of pagan and Christian symbols. (NS)

Maiden Castle is the largest Iron Age hillfort in Britain – its terraced ramparts, which rise to almost 90 feet, enclose an area the size of 50 football pitches. (KJ)

Thatching in Britain is believed to date back to the Bronze Age, and a qualification as Master Thatcher requires a seven-year apprenticeship. (NS)

A visit to the now-ruined village of Tyneham is a moving experience – it was evacuated in 1943 to be used as an army training facility, later bought by the military. (AR)

Dating from the 4th century, the Roman Town House in Dorchester is the only fully exposed Roman site of its kind in the country. (AR)

Maypole dancing is a delightfully traditional and colourful sight at Dorset country fairs and celebrations. (AR)

History and traditions

Dorset is awash with history – take the Slow route and uncover its ancient secrets.

The workings of Sturminster Newton Mill, one of 50 mills that once operated on the River Stour. (NS)

DORSET
ANY PERSON WILFULLY INJURING ANY PART OF THIS COUNTY BRIDGE WILL BE GUILTY OF FELONY AND UPON CONVICTION LIABLE TO BE TRANSPORTED FOR LIFE
BY THE COURT
7&8 GEO 4 C30 S15   T FOOKS

The bridge at Sturminster Newton is one of several in Dorset to carry a stern 19th-century warning to would-be vandals. (NS)

Local hunts have long been a part of rural life in Dorset; the county was once home to prized royal hunting grounds. (AR)

The Dorset Heavy Horse Centre cares for these gentle giants in need, and offers a number of activities for visitors, including wagon rides. (AR)

The gardens of Minterne House in the Cerne Valley were laid out in the 18th century and are a delight at any time of year. (AR)

With an overhanging thatched roof, leadlight windows and a rose-filled garden, this cottage orné at the entrance to Gaunt's House in east Dorset is the quintessence of rural tradition. (AR)

Houses and gardens

From thatched cottages to grand estate houses, Dorset showcases a range of architectural and garden styles.

Part of one of the wealthiest Cistercian monastic estates in the country, Forde Abbey became a private house in 1649 and features 30 acres of beautiful gardens. (AR)

Durdle Door is a natural limestone arch on the Jurassic Coast, near Lulworth Cove. (AR)

The supremely characterful resort of Lyme Regis lies on the South West Coast Path and has a sheltered beach, quaint buildings and excellent fossil hunting. (AR)

Near Lulworth Cove lies the dramatic Man o' War Bay. (AR)

By the sea

The southern part of the region offers some of the most dramatic coastline in Britain – chalk, limestone and sandstone cliffs contrast with the cosier hinterland and cheerful bustle of picturesque seaside towns and beckoning sandy beaches.

Starkly white against the sea and sky, the chalk stacks of Old Harry Rocks on the Isle of Purbeck mark the most easterly point of the Jurassic Coast. (AR)

This pond or 'mere' in Ashmore gave the village its name; at 700 feet above sea level, it is the highest village in Dorset. (AR)

The village of Cerne Abbas offers a delightful mixture of architectural styles, from medieval to Georgian. (AR)

A Saxon hilltop town founded by King Alfred the Great in AD880, Shaftesbury is a treat to explore, with cobbled, timeless Gold Hill sloping down abruptly from the town centre. (AR)

Many of Dorset's villages grew up around the agricultural industry and proudly show traces of their farming past, like this sheep washing pool in the centre of Winterborne St Martin. (AR)

The narrow streets of Lyme Regis town centre provide excellent pottering territory. (AR)

A Purbeck view over the village of Corfe Castle, where many of the houses are built from the local grey limestone, some of which was recycled from the ruins of the castle. (AR)

Largely built in 1302, Stour Provost Church has gone through many renovations – the font is made of Purbeck stone and dates from the 15th century. (AR)

The original stained-glass windows of Moreton Church were destroyed by a World War II bomb, their unusual engraved replacements are exquisite. (AR)

Towns and villages

Overflowing with quintessential English rural architecture, many of Dorset's towns and villages retain their original charm.

The dainty church is the focal point of the tiny village of Little Bredy in the unspoilt Bride Valley. (AR)

With its golden hamstone exterior and striking fan-vaulted stone roof, Sherborne Abbey is the resplendent centrepiece of the town. (AR)

See a true working farm at Modbury Organic Farm and pick up a few delicious supplies from the shop, such as fresh milk and cream from their friendly Jersey cows. (AR)

Dorset Cream Teas

Food and drink

Get into the local rhythm and experience true Dorset hospitality.

Devon doesn't have the monopoly on delicious cream teas... (AR)

Inside the Hall and Woodhouse brewery, which produces the rustically named Badger ales. (AR)

Don't miss a slice of Dorset's famous apple cake – or try your hand at making your own. (SSim)

Lobster pots like these at Mudeford Quay are a common sight in an area renowned for its seafood, which includes freshly caught lobster or crab. (NS)

Author

Alexandra Richards (www.alexandra-richards.com) grew up in Dorset, where she developed a love of rural life, the natural world and outdoor pursuits. During her studies at the University of Durham she spent a year on Réunion Island in the Indian Ocean, teaching English, practising her French, getting to grips with Creole and travelling the region. Later Alex evolved into a freelance travel writer and photographer and has written four editions of the

Bradt guidebook *Mauritius, Rodrigues and Réunion*. In 2004, she undertook a writing/photography assignment travelling to Australia on a cargo ship via the Suez Canal, and has divided her time between Dorset and Australia ever since.

Author's story

I was fortunate enough to grow up in the tiny North Dorset village of Stour Provost and, as the first child born there for 25 years, I'm told my arrival was quite an event. It was a magical place for a childhood – I spent hours making camps, picking blackberries, riding ponies and fishing in our stretch of the River Stour, always accompanied by an assortment of pets, including a sheep named Perky. In those days the village was the domain of dairy farmers and farm workers, and the odd self-appointed squire; it was all rather *Vicar of Dibley*. The school run had to be timed with military precision to avoid being stuck behind the cows crossing the lane for milking; on a Saturday, the hunt would come charging over the hill, resplendent in their pink, hounds baying; village cricket and the church flower rota were serious business; and the pub was where all the big decisions were made. I have spent my life surrounded by colourful Dorset characters, some of the most genuine people you could wish to meet, and I was delighted to interview a few of them for this book.

Being based in Australia for the last few years, I've been returning to Dorset as a visitor with a new-found appreciation for its history, landscapes and culture; and writing this book gave me a reason to delve into corners of the county I didn't know particularly well. For instance, I'd never really appreciated the Jurassic Coast – my memories of it were of school art trips and being made to sketch Durdle Door from a windy clifftop. Returning there while researching this book I could see why our scatty art mistress thought the limestone arch a worthy artistic subject and I felt immense relief marvelling at it, photographing it and not having to draw it – art was never my strong suit.

I must confess I was once one of the protective Dorset folk who referred to visitors as 'grockles', lamented the summer influx of 'townies' and bemoaned ramblers trampling over our land, but having returned home with fresh eyes and written this book, I can't wait to share it with anyone who wants to experience Slow Dorset.

First published April 2012
Bradt Travel Guides Ltd
IDC House, The Vale, Chalfont St Peter, Bucks SL9 9RZ, England
www.bradtguides.com
Published in the USA by The Globe Pequot Press Inc,
PO Box 480, Guilford, Connecticut 06437-0480

Text copyright © 2012 Bradt Travel Guides
Maps copyright © 2012 Bradt Travel Guides Ltd
Photographs copyright © 2012 Individual photographers (see below)
Illustrations copyright © 2012 Alice Jones (see below)
Series editor: Tim Locke
For Bradt: Anna Moores

ISBN: 978 1 84162 393 1

British Library Cataloguing in Publication Data
A catalogue record for this book is available from the British Library

Front cover artwork Neil Gower (www.neilgower.com)
Illustrations Alice Jones (www.alice-jones.co.uk)
Photographs Alexandra Richards (AR); Katherine Jones (KJ); Neal Sullivan (NS);
Sue Simkins (SSim)

Maps Chris & Ingrid Lane (www.artinfusion.co.uk)

Typeset from the author's disc by Artinfusion Ltd
Production managed by Jellyfish Print Solutions; printed in Europe

Acknowledgements

I would like to thank all those who took the time to show me around their businesses, among them farm shops, museums, B&Bs, hotels, campsites, restaurants, nature reserves, cider orchards and breweries. They include Karen Venn from Norburton Hall, Elizabeth and Tony Edwards from Sea Fret B&B, Kevin Reid at Summer Lodge and Rose Grant from Cider by Rosie. I would also like to thank those who gave me memorable experiences to write about in this book, including but not limited to Helen and Stuart at Studland Stables, Allan and Alison Gates at Mere Down Falconry, Dr Colin Dawes (fossil-hunter), Monkey World, the Kingcombe Centre, and the Dorset Wildlife Trust. My sincere thanks to John Wright, who showed me the delights of foraging and took time out of his busy schedule to contribute to this book.

Joanne and the team at Positive PR pointed me in the right direction when it came to local businesses and answered all manner of questions. My thanks also to Fanny Charles, editor of the *Blackmore Vale Magazine*, and journalist Gay Pirrie-Weir, for their support of this project, their contributions to the book and their inspirational ideas.

I am grateful to Jan and Noel Williams, Kat Jones and Paul Connor, who was kind enough to share his local knowledge and his love of cycling in Dorset. I would like to thank all my Dorset friends for their anecdotes, advice and guidance, in particular June and Alf Wallis, Dominic and Marcia Paterson, Tim and Debbie Allard, Cleo and Chris Campbell, the White family and the villagers of Stour Provost past and present. My sincere thanks to Emma and Ed at Riversdale Farm for allowing me to continue returning to my beloved family home.

Thank you to the Australians without whom this would not have been possible, in particular Chris, and to Teena, Dave, Sarah, Julian and the gang for their support. I am indebted to Neal Sullivan for assisting me with my research, for his patience and for his help with the maps and photography for this book.

I would like to thank my parents for my Dorset childhood, my late father for all the research and writing he did on rural matters and Dorset life, and my mother for the hours she spent proof-reading and reminding me of snippets about the county. My heartfelt thanks also to Baroness Sharples for her many years of help, encouragement and advice.

Local illustrator: Alice Jones Drawing is fundamental to my practice, I enjoy the focus and variety in capturing quick responses or intensive detail from landscapes, nature and people. Living in Bridport I cannot help but get inspired by my local surroundings.

CONTENTS

GOING SLOW IN DORSET

The Slow mindset
Hilary Bradt, Founder, Bradt Travel Guides

We shall not cease from exploration
And the end of all our exploring
Will be to arrive where we started
And know the place for the first time.
T S Eliot 'Little Gidding', *Four Quartets*

This series evolved, slowly, from a Bradt editorial meeting when we started to explore ideas for guides to our favourite country – Great Britain. We wanted to get away from the usual 'top sights' formula and encourage our authors to bring out the nuances and local differences that make up a sense of place – such things as food, building styles, nature, geology, or local people and what makes them tick. Our aim was to create a series that celebrates the present, focusing on sustainable tourism, rather than taking a nostalgic wallow in the past.

So without our realising it at the time, we had defined 'Slow Travel', or at least our concept of it. For the beauty of the Slow movement is that there is no fixed definition; we adapt the philosophy to fit our individual needs and aspirations. Thus Carl Honoré, author of *In Praise of Slow*, writes: 'The Slow Movement is a cultural revolution against the notion that faster is always better. It's not about doing everything at a snail's pace, it's about seeking to do everything at the right speed. Savouring the hours and minutes rather than just counting them. Doing everything as well as possible, instead of as fast as possible. It's about quality over quantity in everything from work to food to parenting.' And travel.

So take time to explore. Don't rush it, get to know an area – and the people who live there – and you'll be as delighted as the authors by what you find.

I should mention from the outset that this is not your typical travel guidebook. It doesn't attempt to cover every aspect of the county and analyse all the accommodation and eateries. Instead, it is a personal look at what I love about Dorset, highlighting the elements that I believe encapsulate Dorset-ness and the Slow approach. There are, of course, many more places that fit the bill than I could squeeze into this book, so I must apologise to those that don't get a mention. I am always open to suggestions and you can send me your ideas via Bradt Travel Guides (see page xxi).

In our fast-paced lives, where multi-tasking and time-saving devices are key to survival, the notion of travelling slowly and mindfully may seem unnatural but it is the perfect antidote to a hectic existence. This is one of a series of guides that builds on the Slow Tourism and Slow Food movements and encourages readers to take the time to explore an area thoroughly and at a relaxed pace, finding out what really makes it distinctive, rather than racing around and ticking off attractions from a glossy brochure. Slow Tourism involves seeking out special landscapes, engaging with local people, savouring the area's produce and discovering local culture and heritage; this book invites you to do just that.

Dorset does Slow very well indeed – its quintessentially English rural landscapes, bountiful local produce, even the lilting Dorset accent has an unhurried, lullaby quality. As I was wandering the county explaining that I was writing a book called *Slow Dorset*, the response was frequently, 'Hmmm, I suppose we are pretty slow around here', accompanied by an enigmatic smile. It occurs to me that my parents and I, like many Dorset folk, lived in accordance with the Slow ethos but without giving it a label. We bought our meat fresh from a farm in the village, our milk from the local dairy, and our Christmas turkey from Mr Cox in Stour Row; collecting sloes, elderflowers, blackberries and mushrooms was an annual ritual, and homemade sloe gin in time for Christmas was one of the resulting treats. My parents didn't go out to work – our home was their livelihood – and most of our friends were in the same position. Villagers out for a walk or farmers passing in their tractors used to drop in for tea at any time – weekdays and weekends did not have the same meaning that they do for so many of us now, where we work flat out and it seems only two out of every seven days actually belong to us. That is one of the things I like about going back to Dorset; many of our friends have managed to keep that lifestyle going – they can still manage their own time, they know how to go slow. While they may h ave had to swap milking cows for running holiday cottages because of the decline in farming, they are still happy to stop for tea and a chat on a Wednesday afternoon.

A wise Dorset countryman, one of nature's gentlemen, once said to me in his broad West Country accent 'I like cities, I do'. I had known him for many years and had barely heard of him setting foot outside his native Blackmore Vale, so I was shocked by this pronouncement. He continued, 'I've never been to one but I like them because they keep all the idiots in one place'. Without wanting to insult the majority of the population, I concede he has a point – a lack of large cities is one of the intrinsic qualities that makes Dorset distinctive and ideal for Slow Travel.

As I chatted with Dorset friends about the places I had seen and things I had done in my quest for suitable material for this book, many of them said, 'I've never been there' or 'I never knew that'. I hope that locals as much as visitors will find this book helps them to become better acquainted with the county and encourages them to view it with the inquiring mind of an amateur sleuth, seeking out what makes Dorset Dorset. One local lady wrote to me while I was researching *Slow Dorset*, 'I feel sure your book will be in great demand among the many of us who treasure our country ways and heritage'; if that is the case, I couldn't ask for more.

Dorset

The county of Dorset is small, but is yet so varied in its configuration as to present an epitome of the scenery of Southern England. It is a land of moods and changes that knows no monotony, and is indeed so full of hills and dales that there is scarcely a level road within its confines, save by the banks of streams.
Sir Frederick Treves, *Highways and Byways of Dorset*, 1906.

Treves's words still hold true – Dorset's geological diversity crammed into a small area has produced varied and intimate landscapes, from fertile vales and chalk downland to unspoilt heathland and a rugged coastline. Visitors need not fear monotony around these parts.

Dorset lends itself to Slow Travel, and its status as one of only seven counties in England without a motorway seems to emphasise that fact. It has no large cities and its only heavily populated area (Poole and Bournemouth) is discreetly tucked into the southeastern corner. Slow Travel conjures images of pottering about in unspoilt rural areas and Dorset is one of the most rural counties in England, with the highest proportion of conservation areas in the country, including an Area of Outstanding Natural Beauty covering 44% of it.

North Dorset is largely taken up by the **Blackmore Vale**, a landscape of lush fields defined by ancient hedgerows and dotted with tiny thatched villages. This is traditionally a dairy-farming area, although since the decline in that industry there are far fewer cows than there were when Treves wrote in 1906, 'Everywhere are there cows, for the smell of cows is the incense of North Dorset'. The Iron Age hillforts of Hambledon Hill and Hod Hill provide memorable walks, almost aerial views of the Blackmore Vale and archaeological interest. To the east of the vale is the **Cranborne Chase**, once a royal hunting forest and now a sparsely populated area offering exceptional walking, cycling and horseriding. Gentle, rolling chalk downland dominates the centre of the county, which is where the county town, **Dorchester**, is found. The west is more hilly, while the east has unspoilt heathland and the county's major conurbation incorporating **Poole and Bournemouth**. The coastline in the east has fine sandy beaches but as you head west it becomes gradually more dramatic and culminates in the ancient cliffs of the Jurassic Coast.

The **Jurassic Coast** is England's first natural World Heritage Site, joining the likes of the Great Barrier Reef and Grand Canyon as one of the wonders of the natural world. It was granted its status for its outstandingly diverse geology, capturing 190 million years of the earth's history in just 95 miles, making walking, cycling or sailing along this stretch of coast an exhilarating experience in time travel. It begins with the oldest red stone Triassic rock around Orcombe Point in east Devon, before it enters Dorset and the Jurassic period, then leads on to the younger Cretaceous period seen in the white chalk stacks at Old Harry Rocks, where the Jurassic Coast reaches its official eastern limit. The grey cliffs around Lyme Regis and Charmouth are rich in the fossils of creatures that swam in Jurassic seas some 190 million years ago. They are constantly eroded by the sea, releasing their fossils onto the beaches, where they are eagerly scooped up by delighted fossil-hunters. You don't need to be a geologist to be blown away by the Jurassic Coast and get bitten by the fossil-hunting bug.

Another striking feature on the Jurassic Coast is **Chesil Beach**, a shingle bank stretching for 18 miles between West Bay and Portland and reaching around 40 feet at its highest point. Formed by rising seas at the end of the last Ice Age, it protects a large lagoon known as the Fleet, home to a diverse population of resident and migrating birds.

As you wander around Dorset, ancient manmade additions to the landscape stand as reminders that you are walking in the footsteps of much earlier inhabitants. Just about every hill you climb has a Neolithic site lying beneath your feet and the countryside is dotted with the tell-tale lumps and bumps of ancient burial grounds. **Maiden Castle** is the largest Iron Age hillfort in Britain and lies just outside Dorchester, which is laid out along the lines of its Roman antecedent and has the best-preserved Roman town house in the country. The Saxons left their mark all over the Kingdom of Wessex, visible in towns like **Shaftesbury**, where King Alfred built an abbey in AD888. **Sherborne** has some delightful medieval buildings and a fine abbey dating from the 15th century. The origin of one of Dorset's most famous landmarks, the **Cerne Abbas Giant** or 'Rude Man', is still much debated. The 180-foot-high figure of a naked man wielding a club, incised into the chalk of the hillside, has been variously identified as Roman, Celtic and Iron Age (or even post-medieval), and has been worshipped as a fertility symbol for centuries.

Perhaps one factor that has helped to preserve Dorset's character is that significant portions of it have remained in the hands of the same few families for centuries – it is one of the last bastions of feudalism. Several large estates still exist and their villages are carefully maintained – the areas around Lulworth Cove (Lulworth Estate) and Abbotsbury (Ilchester Estates) fall into this category. In 1981, Ralph Bankes bequeathed his family's 8,500-acre estate to the National Trust. At its heart is one of Dorset's finest houses, Kingston Lacy (see page 225), and it extends all the way to the coast at Studland, with its beautifully unspoilt beach and nature reserve.

One thing that strikes me about Dorset is how happy and proud people are to live here; they consider themselves lucky to dwell in this serene corner of England and are keen to preserve its landscapes and way of life. On your travels you are likely to see the Dorset flag – a white cross with a red border on a gold background – flying outside homes and businesses. Often referred to as St Wite's Cross, it recognises the female Anglo-Saxon saint buried at Whitchurch Canonicorum.

Any Dorset journey is inevitably enhanced by the implausibly delightful place names you encounter along the way; some of my favourites are Whitchurch Canonicorum, Toller Porcorum, Tincleton and Sixpenny Handley. The River Wriggle is found in the northwest of the county and the River Piddle winds through its centre, lined by a string of villages which take their amusing names from it: Piddlehinton, Piddletrenthide, Tolpuddle, Puddletown, Affpuddle and Briants Puddle. While we are on the subject of toilet humour, the town of Shitterton, near Bere Regis, is the butt of its fair share of jokes. I must also give a mention to the village of Fishpond Bottom in the Marshwood Vale, the uncomfortably named Scratchy Bottom near Durdle Door and its more contented counterpart Happy Bottom in Corfe Mullen near Wimborne Minster.

Some practical matters

How this book is arranged

Please note, no charge has been made for the inclusion in the main text of any business in this guide.

Maps

The colour map at the front of this book shows the area covered in each of the six chapters. In turn, each chapter begins with a sketch map of the area, highlighting the places mentioned in the text. The numbers on the map correspond to the descriptions in the text, helping you to find your way around.

Accommodation

I've listed some accommodation ideas for each area, a mixture of camping, self-catering, bed and breakfast and hotel options. Each was chosen because it has a special quality, be that its location, character or service. Prices change regularly, so are not included but I have tried to give an idea in the text as to whether a place is an upmarket option or more suited to the budget-conscious. Some accommodation providers keep their prices consistent all year but many, especially those by the coast, charge peak rates in July and August.

Food and drink

I have included a cross-section of food and drink options, including farm shops, food producers, cafés, pubs and restaurants. They were selected because they use local produce, serve homemade goodies, have a special character or follow sustainable principles – or a mixture of all four.

Attractions

For attractions, activities and eateries I have listed contact details and opening hours but it is worth checking websites for any changes. I have not listed admission fees as these change regularly, although I have mentioned if admission is free. If a description does not say admission is free, you should expect to be charged.

Getting to and around Dorset

I've given some suggestions for getting to and around each area, including car-free options wherever possible and ideas for cycling and walking. For some parts of Dorset car-free is not feasible as public transport is limited and the little-known, distinctive places I have tried to highlight are often, by their nature, out of the way and harder to reach than the usual tourist haunts.

General travel information is available at www.visit-dorset.com and www.traveline.info is useful for journey planning; **bus timetables** are online at www.dorsetforyou.com. **Bournemouth International Airport** links Dorset to other domestic and European airports, while **ferries** operate between Poole and Cherbourg. Coaches and trains connect Dorset to other English cities. **South West Trains** (*www.southwesttrains.co.uk*) is the main rail operator servicing the area, with regular trains from London Waterloo to Gillingham, Sherborne, Dorchester, Axminster (for Lyme Regis), Weymouth, Poole and Bournemouth.

Local buses can be helpful, although services are limited in rural areas and may only operate on certain days of the week; timetables and Dorset-wide maps are available at www.dorsetforyou.com and the tourist information centres in each area. The *Jurassic CoastLinX53* bus is handy; it runs every two hours along the coastline between Exeter and Poole, and stops at all the key places *en route*.

Tourist information

I have listed the tourist information centres for each area at the start of the relevant chapter, along with any websites on specific areas. For general information see www.visit-dorset.com and www.dorsetforyou.com.

Making the most of Slow Dorset

Dorset's variety means it has a wide appeal – it has much to offer the lover of the natural world, the history buff, gastronome, archaeologist, hiker and adventure sports enthusiast, just to name a few. I had countless memorable experiences while pottering around Dorset researching *Slow Dorset*, and I hope you will be able to enjoy some of them too.

Walking

Dorset's varied countryside and coastline provide excellent opportunities for walking and you will find some suggestions for short and medium-length walks in each chapter.

Information on walking is available at tourist information centres and online at www.dorsetforyou.com, from where you can download guides to some of the most popular trails, including the Wessex Ridgeway and the Stour Valley Way. Waymarked with a dragon symbol, the **Wessex Ridgeway** is a ridge-top trail from Marlborough in Wiltshire to Lyme Regis, part of the Great Ridgeway, an ancient trading route between the Devon and Norfolk coasts. The Dorset section begins at Ashmore in the Cranborne Chase and runs along a chalk ridge across the centre of the county, providing strikingly unhindered views of the surrounding countryside. In contrast, the **Stour Valley Way** takes the low road, following the River Stour 64 miles from Stourhead to Christchurch, where the river flows into the sea. The Stour Valley Way is waymarked with a kingfisher symbol.

The South West Coast Path

The standout piece in Dorset's repertoire of walks is the hugely popular South West Coast Path, which combines heritage, flora, fauna, geology and spectacular coastal scenery. The UK's longest national trail, it runs for 630 miles from Minehead in Somerset to Poole in Dorset's east, tracing the coastlines of Cornwall, Devon and Dorset on the way.

The South West Coast Path website (*www.southwestcoastpath.com*) is extremely helpful for planning and its walk-finder tool can help you choose the right route for you. You can download a range of themed walks of varying lengths and levels of difficulty, including information about where to eat and drink *en route*. The path is easy to find from most coastal towns and villages or from the beach, and is waymarked by an acorn symbol.

The Dorset section offers some of the most spectacular seaside scenery and the path provides access to the entire length of the Jurassic Coast World Heritage Site, which runs from east Devon to Old Harry Rocks, off Studland. It passes through **Lyme Regis** and **Charmouth**, popular for fossil hunting. Between Charmouth and Seatown is **Golden Cap**, the highest point on England's south coast; it is a moderately steep walk up from Seatown but the reward is expansive views along the coast, and on a clear day you can see as far as Dartmoor National Park.

One of the most rewarding walks is the section of the path between **Lulworth Cove** and **Durdle Door**, two of the most spectacular features within the Jurassic Coast World Heritage Site. Durdle Door, a near perfect coastal arch of limestone rock, lies half a mile to the west of Lulworth Cove. The walk involves some moderately steep climbs along a remarkably unspoilt and photogenic section of coast.

A gentle four-mile walk leads from Studland along the cliffs to the dramatic chalk stacks of **Old Harry Rocks**, from where you can see across to another chalk formation: The Needles, off the Isle of Wight. Early mornings are the best time for this walk, when the sun casts its first gentle rays on the crisp, white rock.

The South West Coast Path provides plenty of opportunity for wildlife-watching; on a clear day you may be lucky enough to spot basking sharks, seals or dolphins, particularly around **Durlston Country Park** near Swanage. **Portland** and **Poole Harbour** are good for watching resident and migrating seabirds, and you may catch a glimpse of rare butterflies on the Isle of Purbeck's chalk downland.

The South West Coast Path works well in combination with the **CoastLinX53 bus service** (see page 131). Luggage transfers (*0800 043 7929; www.luggagetransfers.co.uk*) is a very clever idea for walkers and cyclists – the company will transport your bags between your stop-off points along the South West Coast Path and around the South West.

Horseriding and cycling

Horseriders and cyclists can feel vulnerable on Dorset's narrow hedge-lined lanes but there are usually plenty of passing places to pull into out of anyone's way. A network of **bridleways** provides interesting off-road options and is complemented by the Wessex Ridgeway (see page xi), the North Dorset Trailway (see page 2) and the Castleman Trailway (see page 194) in the east of the county.

Suggestions for cycling routes and cycle hire are given in each chapter, and suggested horse rides and stables are mentioned where applicable. The British Horse Society (*08701 202244; www.ride-uk.org.uk*) publishes *Dorset on Horseback*, which details 25 circular rides and *Bed and Breakfast for Horses*, which lists accommodation where both you and your horse can stay.

Some Dorset **beaches** are ideal for memorable horse rides along the sand, in particular Studland (see page 157), and also certain beaches around Christchurch (see page 195). From the east of the county you can ride into the unspoilt **New Forest**, while North Dorset offers excellent riding through woodland and open countryside, including in remarkable spots like the Iron Age hillfort on **Hod Hill**.

Savouring the tastes of Dorset

In 2011 a Visit Britain survey revealed that the West Country's food is the main drawcard for visitors, with 71% of foreign visitors giving the region's food as their main reason for visiting the area. Dorset is ideally suited to the growing and savouring of seasonal, traditional and local food; its fertile soils, long farming history and food heritage combine to provide a rich variety of

Dorset apple cake: a recipe

On every tea shop menu you will see Dorset apple cake, a truly local treat. Countless different recipes exist, each subtly different, but I really enjoy this slightly lemony one.

Ingredients

8 oz self-raising flour
4 oz butter
4 oz caster sugar
8 oz cooking apples – peeled, cored and diced
Grated zest of one lemon
1 medium egg, beaten
2 oz sultanas (optional)

Preheat the oven to 375°F/190°C. In a large mixing bowl rub the butter into the flour until the mixture resembles fine breadcrumbs. Stir in the sugar, apples, lemon zest and egg, and mix well. If you want to add the sultanas, you can do so now. Put the mixture into a well greased 8-inch cake tin and bake for 30–40 minutes, or until golden in colour. Serve warm or cold, with or without custard or ice cream.

tasty treats, from fish caught off the Dorset coast, to artisan cheeses, breads and ciders. A visit to Dorset would not be complete without sampling Dorset Blue Vinny Cheese (see page 30), Dorset apple cake (see above) and Moores Dorset Knob Biscuits (see page 110). And remember, Devon does not have a monopoly on cream teas – the Dorset version is just as delicious. You will find many of the county's artisan food producers and suppliers mentioned in this book, as well as the numerous local food festivals.

Self-caterers are spoilt for choice when it comes to stocking up the pantry, and a picnic is a great way to enjoy the Dorset countryside. Rather than trudging around the supermarket, you can make gathering your ingredients into a treasure hunt by calling into local bakeries, farmers' markets and farm shops. As you are exploring the country lanes, look out for handwritten signs promising free-range eggs, homemade jams, honey, gooseberries and the like, which usually sit on a wonky table next to an honesty box. For dessert you can pick up one of the local farmhouse ice creams, such as those made by Barford Ice Cream (see page 224) and Purbeck Ice Cream (see page 189).

Drinking Dorset

To wash down your Dorset meal, you could try a locally made cider, like 'Cider by Rosie' (see page 92), or beer. My retired farming friend, Alf Wallis, remembers the days when badger leg was on the menu in Dorset pubs; happily these days when you hear someone ordering a half a Badger in the pub they are after a beer from the Hall and Woodhouse Brewery (see page 34). Thanks to its temperate climate, the county even produces its own wine, available at farm shops and delicatessens. Purbeck Vineyard (see page 112) offers tours of its vineyard near Corfe Castle, tastings and cellar door sales. Furleigh Estate (see page 53) near Bridport is a dairy farm that has been transformed into a winery producing white, red, rosé and sparkling wines; cellar door sales are available by appointment for wine by the case. Wines from the Sherborne Castle Vineyard (*Wake Court Farm, Bishops Caundle DT9 5NG; 01963 323249; www.sherbornecastle.com*) are available at the castle shop (see page 53), while Melbury Vale Vineyard (*Barfoot Farm, Redmans Lane, Melbury SP7 0DB; 07730 955593; www.melburyvaleco.co.uk*) sells its wines in shops and restaurants in the Shaftesbury area.

Dorset farmers' markets
Generally, see ⓦ www.dorsetfarmersmarkets.co.uk.

Blandford second Friday of the month (Market Place).
Bridport second Saturday of the month (Bridport Arts Centre, South St).
Christchurch first Friday of the month (Saxon Sq).
Dorchester first Saturday of the month (Poundbury).
Shaftesbury first Saturday of the month (Town Hall).
Sherborne third Friday of the month (Cheap St).
Sturminster Newton fourth Saturday of the month (Station Rd).
Wareham fourth Thursday of the month (Town Hall).
Wimborne Minster every Friday (Mill Lane).

As well as farmers' markets, watch out for the Anonymous Travelling Market (*www.theatm.co.uk*), which tours the West Country and combines food, drink, crafts and music.

Foraging
Foraging is nothing new – until around 10,000 years ago all modern humans were hunter-gatherers – but in more recent times interest in foraging has waxed and waned and it is currently enjoying one of its periodic heydays. Foraging was encouraged during World War II, flourished during the hippy years and is now trendy again in our era of environmental awareness. Television shows are devoted to it, celebrity chefs espouse its virtues, and restaurant menus tempt diners with foraged delicacies, such as nettle soup, fish dishes topped with seaweed and just about anything accompanied by wild garlic.

Foraging is the ultimate rebellion against convenience food – there is nothing convenient about scrabbling through brambles, getting plastered in mud and being chased by an irate bull in the pursuit of a few morsels that have already been chewed and rejected by a grub of some description. Yet somehow it appeals to the hunter-gatherer in many of us, including me.

While researching this book I was lucky enough to spend a day foraging at the Kingcombe Centre with the charming and entertaining John Wright (see page 128), who regularly appears on Hugh Fearnley-Whittingstall's *River Cottage* television series. He was kind enough to provide some words for this book on the subject of foraging.

Tips for happy foraging
John Wright (*www.wild-food.net*)

I gave up growing my own fruit and vegetables years ago. Although it was fun and ultimately rewarding it was also unreliable and rather hard work. But my main objection to gardening is that it all takes too long. This book celebrates the concept of Slow Food but gardening, I think, is far too slow. For me instant gratification is everything. With gardening one needs to prepare the ground, sow the seed, weed, water and worry, and one day, all being well (and sometimes it isn't) you pick. Foraging however is quite a different matter – you just pick.

My foraging career began over 30 years ago when I moved to Dorset (in my village I am described as a 'relative newcomer'). An early passion for wild fungi found full expression in the fields and woods around the farmhouse I rented. 'Top field' would keep me for hours picking field mushrooms – 120 pounds one year – and 'eight-acre field' would supply a magnificently large form of the delicious shaggy parasol. St George's mushrooms in spring, puffballs in summer, field blewits and the riotously colourful wax caps in autumn, and jelly ears and velvet shanks in winter would fill my mushrooming year. Of course everyone thought I was mad and sure to poison myself.

But mad or not, I am also extremely careful and never, ever eat anything unless I am sure of its name. My best advice to anyone embarking on a mushroom hunt is to do the same. Get a couple (you really need at least two) of field guides and study them carefully. Collect just a few different species at first – no more than one or two specimens of each in case you have picked something rare – and carefully identify them by examining all their characteristics and using the advice in your books. Never jump to conclusions but always match *all* of the characteristics of your find to the description given. If the book says a species should have a ring on the stem or turns yellow when bruised it really means it – if any characteristic is missing then it must be something else and maybe a deadly something at that.

Identifying fungi is quite a tricky business but once you have a few species committed to memory you are set for life – you do not need to become an expert mycological taxonomist. My magnificent seven edible fungi are easy to identify, common and delicious: the parasol, giant puffball, horse mushroom, jelly ear, cep, charcoal burner and the hedgehog mushroom. If you only choose one then I suggest the last of these. It is the mushroom with everything – delicious, nutty texture, very common, never gets maggots and completely unmistakeable. It grows in woodland, often in substantial rings and has a 'chamois leather' cap with little spines hanging down underneath. Nothing else looks remotely like it making it the safest of all the wild mushrooms.

It would be remiss of me not to warn you of the species which causes 99% of all poisonings. The yellow stainer looks almost exactly like the field mushroom except the edge of the cap and the base of the stem turn a remarkable chromium yellow when bruised. This fades to brown after about 15 minutes. If you eat a yellow stainer you will have to cancel all engagements for a day or two before recovering completely, sadder but wiser.

Of course there are times when mushrooms are not to be found and, caught by the foraging bug, I determined to explore other wild sources of food. The Dorset farm yielded the familiar blackberries and sloes but I wondered what else might be found and bought several guides to expand my repertoire. Most edible wild plants are easy to recognise. Everyone knows, usually to his or her cost, what a stinging nettle looks like and no-one hesitates when deciding whether the nut they are looking at is a hazel nut or some deadly impostor. Wild plants are, generally, much safer than wild mushrooms. However, some very common and excellent species can be a little more challenging: fat hen, red goosefoot, sea beet and even cherry plums may have the novice forager sensibly consulting a field guide. Incidentally, and I trust I am not putting you off the whole idea entirely, the most deadly of all plant and fungal toxins is found in a very common native plant. Its leaves look like that of flat-leaved parsley and it has substantial and tasty-looking roots. It is called hemlock waterdropwort, and a plateful will have you dead in three hours.

While most people will have picked wild plants at some time or other, even if it is just blackberries, and mushroom hunting has become quite fashionable, few venture onto our rocky shores to collect that least likely addition to a dinner party – seaweed. When I started investigating seaweeds it was not with any expectation that I would actually enjoy eating any of them – their appearance, not to mention their smell, does not encourage the gourmet; and the evangelical zeal expressed in the few books I had on the subject I rejected as the misguided rantings of eccentrics. Well I seem to have taken up ranting myself and proclaim the virtues of seaweed at every opportunity.

Seaweeds are eaten the world over, with Japan being the most accepting of this unusual food. The main problem for the British, apart from a disinclination to eat anything that doesn't come in a packet, is that they just do not know how to cook it. With one exception there is no point collecting a basket of seaweed and trying to cook it like, say, cabbage – you end up with a smelly, slimy mess. Most of the half dozen or so good, edible seaweeds found around these islands require special treatment. Laver – a membranous, brown seaweed found, mostly, attached to rocks – must be boiled for ten hours (no less!) to form the sticky paste that is laverbread. This is used, notably in south Wales, to make oatmeal cakes or as a (rather sticky) sauce for lamb. The slightly fishy flavour is of the 'umami' kind found in other delights such as Marmite and Parmesan cheese. Laver, put through a papermaking process, will be familiar to many as 'nori', the stuff that little bits of fish and rice are wrapped in to make sushi. With carragheen – a small, bushy seaweed found attached to rocks or in rock pools at low tide – you do not eat the seaweed at all; it is simply boiled for half an hour to extract the incredibly slippery/slimy substance called 'carragheenan' which is used to set such things as panna cotta. Gutweed – a bright green, hairlike seaweed of upper shores – can be deep fried to form genuine (the stuff you get in Chinese restaurants is actually cabbage) crispy seaweed. Sugar kelp is dried and fried to make seaweed crisps and the other kelps are used for their flavour enhancing glutamates and removed from the dish prior to serving. The exception I mentioned earlier is dulse. The deep red, flat, fingered fronds can be cooked like any other vegetable and make an excellent 'seaweed bubble and squeak'. I do recommend you give seaweeds a try. So much of it is 'wasted' for want of knowledge and courage.

Food collected from the wild is, of course, free and I hope I have been able to convince you that it is also delicious. But collecting wild food can feed the soul as well as the body. The forager comes to truly appreciate food. Food from the supermarket is just a commodity, the origin of which we neither know nor care. When you eat food you have gathered yourself you understand it in a way not open to others. You know where it came from, how it lived, what problems it faced, how fresh it is and how jolly hard it may have been to come by in the first place. So, I entreat you, go foraging – it will be good for your Karma.

Dorset Wildlife Trust

Dorset is one of the richest counties in England in terms of biodiversity, with some precious habitats and wildlife. To assist in preserving this great asset, the Dorset Wildlife Trust (DWT) works to champion wildlife and natural places, engage and inspire people and promote sustainable living. Its 42 reserves cover many of the most important wildlife havens, including ancient woodlands, wetlands, wildflower meadows and some of Britain's rare surviving lowland heaths. The DWT has scored many notable achievements, for example in restoring coppiced woodlands by careful management and by grazing neglected grasslands so that wildlife can flourish, and in campaigning for protection of marine habitats.

Most of the DWT's reserves are open daily and there are visitor centres providing a wealth of wildlife information at Brooklands Farm, Lorton Meadows, Kingcombe Meadows and Brownsea Island nature reserves, the voluntary Purbeck Marine Wildlife Reserve and the Urban Wildlife Centre at Upton Heath Nature Reserve. More information about DWT, its reserves and opportunities to volunteer is available at www.dorsetwildlifetrust.org.uk.

A Slow learning curve

If you find the Slow way of life in Dorset appealing, there are various short courses on offer with a Slow theme.

At Dorset Wildlife Trust's Kingcombe Centre (see page 128) you can improve your knowledge of **local flora and fauna** with courses on tracking wildlife, identifying butterflies and getting to know the area's wildflowers. They also teach rural skills and crafts, including beekeeping and willow-weaving, and for hobby farmers there are sessions on livestock management.

Dorset Centre for Rural Skills (*West Farm Barn, Farrington, Blandford Forum DT11 8RZ; 01747 811099; www.dorsetruralskills.co.uk*) is a not-for-profit training centre teaching **traditional rural crafts** such as cob and lime building renovation, blacksmithing, hurdle-making and hedge-laying.

Wood-working courses are available at Guy Mallinson's Woodland Workshop in West Dorset (see page 123) and at Bodger's Barn in West Bexington (see page 115).

Talking Dorset

Although the local dialect is less spoken than it once was, I hope that as you explore Dorset you will hear traces of it and that distinctive lilting regional accent. Although I grew up in Dorset I don't speak the dialect, nor do I have a West Country accent, but I know plenty of people around the Blackmore Vale who do, particularly among the older generation and the farming community. Friends will often chat to me about 'diddicoys' or 'diddies', meaning gypsies, and when asking the whereabouts of something or someone, they will add 'to' to the end of their question, 'Where is Harry to?' The reply might be 'He's goen on'. 'Mind' is often added to statements, as in 'T'is a nice day, min', 's' is often pronounced as 'z' and 'f' pronounced 'v'.

No-one has done more for the Dorset dialect than the poet William Barnes, whose *Poems of Rural Life in the Dorset Dialect* (1844) celebrated the lives, customs and language of the people among whom he was raised. It included a glossary of Dorset terms so that more genteel readers could understand it. Barnes was also a philologist, and in his *Glossary of the Dorset Dialect with Grammar* (1863) he recorded hundreds of words and expressions that he felt were in danger of dying out. Middle-class Victorians tended to look upon the dialect as a corruption of standard English; Barnes disagreed and maintained that the dialect of the South West was the closest form of speech to the Old English spoken in Wessex at the time of King Alfred, that it was purer and closer to the lives of those who spoke it than standard English. Subsequent publications on the dialect draw heavily on Barnes's pioneering work.

At the time of Barnes and Thomas Hardy, dialect had already begun to decline; Hardy noted that shortly after the railway arrived in Dorchester, London music-hall songs had started to replace the old folk tunes of the area. The teaching of standard English in schools, increased travel, migration

Thomas Hardy

Thomas Hardy was born on 2 June 1840 in a small, thatched cottage at Higher Bockhampton, a hamlet east of Dorchester; his father was a master mason and his mother a servant and cook. The eldest of four children, Thomas was initially pronounced still born but an observant nurse realised the newborn was breathing.

Hardy's mother encouraged him to read and study, beyond the usual level for local children. He went to school in Bockhampton and then Dorchester and at the age of 16 was apprenticed to John Hicks architects in Dorchester. He practised as an architect at Hicks's London office for five years but returned to Dorset to write fiction, living first in Sturminster Newton and then at Max Gate, the house he had built in Dorchester. Hardy's first novel was rejected but in 1871 *Desperate Remedies*, set at Kingston Maurward, was published anonymously, followed by *Under the Greenwood Tree*. Over the next 25 years he wrote 12 novels, over 50 short stories and a significant amount of poetry, including *Wessex Poems*, an anthology written over 30 years and published in 1898.

When Hardy began writing about Dorset it was a little-known county beyond its seaside resorts. The Dorset countryside was immortalised in his writings as Hardy's Wessex, and although he slightly altered the place names it was easy to guess their true identities from the descriptions. Dorchester was the inspiration for the eponymous town in *The Mayor of Casterbridge* (1886), set in the county town in the 1850s, when Hardy was at school and starting his apprenticeship there. *Tess of the d'Urbevilles* (1891) was set in the Blackmore Vale, Hardy's 'vale of little dairies', and Tess was born in the village of Marlott, actually Marnhull. The publication of *Tess* and *Jude the Obscure* (1895) cemented Hardy's fame but not perhaps in the way he would have liked – many Victorians found the books' mildly racy content immoral and offensive.

Hardy married Emma Gifford in 1874 and although he later became estranged from his wife, her death in 1912 greatly affected him and was the subject of some of his finest poetry. In 1914, Hardy married his secretary, Florence Dugdale. He died in 1928 and his heart is buried alongside Emma in the churchyard at Stinsford, while his ashes are in Westminster Abbey.

Hardy aficionados can visit his birthplace at Higher Bockhampton (see page 71), his home in Dorchester, Max Gate (see page 66), and Stinsford (see page 71). A reconstruction of his study is on display at the Dorset County Museum in Dorchester (see page 65).

of people from other areas and pervasive mass media have all contributed to the loss of England's dialects. However, some Dorset words have been reincarnated and found new modern usages; for instance, dumbledore, the Dorset word for bumblebee, is now the name of a character in J K Rowling's Harry Potter books.

Dorset dialect words are often far more fun and descriptive than their standard English cousins, for example:

betwattled – confused
biggity – conceited
chattermag – magpie or a woman who talks a lot
gallybagger – scarecrow
gurt lummock – big, clumsy person
tinklebobs – icicles
wops – wasp
zennit – seven nights (a week)
zull – plough
zummit – something

Literary Dorset

Dorset's scenery and its people have long inspired writers of prose and poetry, most notably the county's favourite literary son, **Thomas Hardy** (see box, page xix). However, Dorset has many other lesser-known literary connections, which you are likely to stumble upon as you explore the county.

A friend of Hardy's, and the son of a Blackmore Vale farmer, **William Barnes** (see box, page 7), wrote pastoral poetry in Dorset dialect, giving a voice to the county's humble farming folk and immortalising their lives and the county's landscapes in his emotive descriptions. He is buried at St Peter's Church in Winterborne Came near Dorchester, where he served as rector for 24 years.

Novelist **Henry Fielding** (1707–54) was also from the Blackmore Vale, more precisely the village of East Stour, near Shaftesbury, and some of his characters are based on people he knew while living in Dorset.

William Wordsworth (1770–1850) is commonly associated with the Lake District but he and his sister, Dorothy, spent two years in the 1790s in west Dorset near Pilsdon. It was here that he started to write seriously and Pilsdon Pen is said to have soothed his sister's longing for the hills of the Lake District. Poet **Samuel Taylor Coleridge** (1775–1834), who lived in neighbouring Somerset, visited them frequently.

Robert Louis Stevenson (1850–94) wrote *Kidnapped* while living in Bournemouth; he suffered from a weak chest and was one of many at the time who came to the seaside town for its healing air.

T E Lawrence (Lawrence of Arabia) lived at Clouds Hill, a cottage between Dorchester and Wareham, when he was stationed at Bovington Camp and he finished *The Seven Pillars of Wisdom* and *The Mint* while living there. He died in 1935 as the result of a motorcycle accident near his home and is buried at Moreton. Clouds Hill is now run by the National Trust and is open to the public, and a walking trail links Bovington, Moreton and Clouds Hill, all being points associated with Lawrence (see page 59).

Lyme Regis became a literary tourism destination as early as the 1820s, after **Jane Austen** described Louisa Musgrave falling from the steps on The Cobb in her novel *Persuasion* (1818). Austen loved Lyme Regis and the surrounding area and spent a good deal of time there. The Cobb later featured in **John Fowles's** well-known novel *The French Lieutenant's Woman* (1969); Fowles (1926–2005) had moved to Lyme Regis in 1968. He was a fan of Thomas Hardy's work and Tess is reputed to have been the inspiration for his own scandalised woman.

Children's writer **Enid Blyton** made regular visits to Dorset, in particular the Isle of Purbeck, where she bought a golf club; she later purchased a farm near Sturminster Newton in the Blackmore Vale. Dorset places and landscapes were the inspiration for many of the locations in her *Famous Five* and *Secret Seven* books. The golf club featured in *Five Have a Mystery to Solve*, her farm appeared in *Five on Finniston Farm* and Corfe Castle may have been the inspiration for Kirren Castle. Blyton's Whispering Island, also known as 'Keep-away island', was based on Brownsea Island in Poole Harbour, which during Blyton's day was owned by the reclusive Mrs Bonham-Christie who shunned visitors and let the island return to nature. Blyton fans will probably enjoy the Ginger Pop Shop in Poole, dedicated to her work (see page 202).

A handy resource for me in writing this book has been *Highways and Byways in Dorset* (1906) by **Sir Frederick Treves** (1853–1923), who managed to combine a successful career as a surgeon with travel writing, and in the former capacity famously rescued Joseph Merrick, the 'Elephant Man', who had been displayed as a circus freak. He was born in Dorchester and his forthright account of his tour of Dorset makes interesting and, in parts, amusing reading.

Today Bridport is the heart of the Dorset literary community, a literary festival is held there annually and incorporates the Bridport Prize for poetry and short stories (*www.bridportprize.org.uk*).

Feedback request

There are only so many special places and aspects of Dorset life that you can focus on when limited by word counts and book length. Much as we'd like to include them all, it simply isn't possible. We've done our best to include a good mix and to check facts but there are bound to be errors (phone numbers and websites change with alarming frequency) as well as inevitable omissions of really special places. If you send an email to info@bradtguides.com about changes to information in this book we will forward it to the author who may include it in a 'one-off update' on the Bradt website at www.bradtguides.com/guidebook-updates.html. You can also visit the website for updates to information in this guide.

North Dorset –
the Blackmore Vale,
Cranborne Chase and Sherborne

1. NORTH DORSET – THE BLACKMORE VALE, CRANBORNE CHASE AND SHERBORNE

I admit to being biased when it comes to this part of Dorset, for this is where I grew up. I have travelled to many countries around the world but there is no landscape that makes my heart sing like the glorious **Blackmore Vale**, with its tapestry of verdant fields divided by neat hedges and sprinkled with beguiling villages.

The best way to appreciate the beauty of the vale is to look down on it from above, whether by taking a flight from Compton Abbas Airfield or by viewing it from the top of Hambledon Hill, Bulbarrow Hill or the Saxon town of Shaftesbury. Alternatively, you can see it up close, perhaps with a walk along the Stour Valley Way, which follows the River Stour through the vale.

The sparsely populated **Cranborne Chase**, which reaches into Hampshire and Wiltshire, offers equally exquisite landscapes and exceptional walking, cycling and horseriding. At Knowlton is a rare and intriguing sight, the ruins of a medieval church perched in the centre of a Neolithic henge.

Nestled in the wooded Yeo Valley in the northwest of the county, **Sherborne** is one of Dorset's, and perhaps England's, most appealing towns. It enchants the visitor with its blend of historic buildings, two impressive castles and imposing abbey.

North Dorset has historically been great farming country, in particular dairy farming. With the decline of the agricultural industry, many farmers have had to diversify but the area's farming heritage is obvious – in its landscapes and its first-rate local produce.

Tourists tend to bypass North Dorset and head straight for the coast, which means the area is largely unspoilt and you can expect genuine Dorset hospitality and real Dorset characters. The delightful sing-song of Dorset accents still hangs thick in the air around these parts.

Getting there and around

The areas within this chapter are easily reached from the A30 and the A303. Driving is a good option, especially if you are short of time, because public transport services are scant.

Public transport

The towns of Gillingham (pronounced with a hard 'g' at the start), not to be confused with Gillingham in Kent (pronounced with a soft 'g'), and Sherborne are on the Exeter to London Waterloo **train** line. Trains are frequent (roughly every hour), catering for those prepared to suffer a daily commute of over two hours. Most trains divide at Salisbury, with only a few carriages continuing further south into Dorset and Devon so choose your carriage carefully.

Public transport is limited in the Blackmore Vale and Cranborne Chase. However, there are hourly **buses** between Gillingham and Shaftesbury, plus less frequent services between Gillingham and Blandford Forum via Stour Provost, Marnhull and Sturminster Newton (Line 309).

To reach the Dorset coast from Gillingham by train is not as straightforward as you may think. Getting to Bournemouth involves heading up to Salisbury, changing trains, then going across to Southampton, and changing again to hop on a train to Bournemouth. The journey time is something over two hours. Similarly, travel to Wareham involves changing at Salisbury and Southampton, with a journey time of around two and a half hours.

Cycling

The quiet **rural roads** and **bridleways** of the Blackmore Vale and Cranborne Chase have excellent scope for cycling.

You can download a leaflet on cycling in North Dorset; this includes the North Dorset Cycleway and portions of the Wessex Ridgeway (*www. dorsetforyou.com*) and features seven suggested cycling routes which largely focus on the Blackmore Vale, although two venture into the Cranborne Chase and West Wiltshire Downs Area of Outstanding Natural Beauty.

The **North Dorset Cycleway** (regional route 41) is a 73-mile circular on-road route linking Gillingham, Shaftesbury, Blandford Forum and Sturminster Newton. It wends its way through classic Blackmore Vale landscapes and is relatively flat.

The **North Dorset Trailway** (*www.dorestforyou.com*) is a route for walkers, cyclists and horse riders along the old Somerset and Dorset railway line, which closed in 1966. Sections are already open with more to be developed. The longest and most popular portion is between Shillingstone and Sturminster Newton, a four-mile route which links up with the Wessex Ridgeway. Shorter sections are open around Blandford and Stalbridge.

Cycle hire

Dorset Cycle Hire High St, Stalbridge DT10 2LL ① 01963 362476. A small cycle shop, which also does cycle hire.

Walking

The Blackmore Vale and Cranborne Chase are criss-crossed by a dense web of footpaths and bridleways. A walk up one of the hills surrounding the Blackmore Vale, especially Hambledon or Bulbarrow provides breathtaking views. Both are easily accessible with car parking nearby. The Iron Age hillforts of **Hambledon** and **Hod Hill** combine superb scenery with archaeological interest, while Duncliffe Hill offers the opportunity for an easy walk in one of the vale's few remaining wooded areas. The **Stour Valley Way** (*www. stourvalleyway.co.uk*) follows almost all of the 64-mile course of the river, passing through the Blackmore Vale from its source at Stourhead. It passes the remains of the many mills that once operated on this stretch of river, and it is worth taking a detour to visit some of them, such as the ones at Sturminster Newton and Stour Provost. The paths through the vale are far less used than those around Christchurch, making for some very pleasant, peaceful riverside walks.

You don't have to stray far from Shaftesbury for some superb walking country high on the **Cranborne Chase**, at Fontmell and Melbury Downs, around the village of Ashmore and at Win Green, just over the Wiltshire border. The café at Compton Abbas Airfield is perfectly positioned for replenishing the energy stores.

Horseriding

North Dorset lends itself to being explored on horseback, as it has been for centuries.

Hill View Stables Sunnyside Farm, Cathole Bridge Rd, Crewkerne, Somerset TA18 8PA ☎ 01460 72731 ⓦ www.hillview-riding-stables.co.uk. Near Sherborne.
Pippin Equestrian Presthayes Farm, Eccliffe SP8 5RE ☎ 01747 822997 ⓦ www.pippinequestrian.co.uk. Near Gillingham, this offers riding holidays for adults and children. Facilities include an indoor school, outdoor school, mini cross-country course and 300 acres of farmland for hacking.
Redlands Equestrian ☎ 01225 424413 ⓦ www.redlandsequestrian.com. Arranges accommodation for both horse and rider in the Cranborne Chase, allowing you to take advantage of the area's excellent riding with your own horse.
The Stables at Bushes Farm Bushes Rd, Stourpaine DT11 8SU ☎ 01258 455846 ⓦ www.thestables-bushesfarm.co.uk. Provides riding for all ages and abilities in the Blandford Forum area.
Three Gates Equestrian Leigh DT9 6JQ ☎ 01963 210284. Riding near Sherborne.

Accommodation

Many of North Dorset's farms offer true countryside breaks, with good B&B and self-catering accommodation. Staying on a working farm can be a great way to get a feel for the area, which was built on the agricultural industry. There are also some enticing upmarket country house hotels and plenty of pubs. North Dorset receives fewer visitors than the coast and so tends to be less expensive, although Sherborne can be pricey. The Blackmore Vale is relatively central for exploring the rest of Dorset, so makes a good base.

Avalon Townhouse B&B South St, Sherborne DT9 3LZ ⓣ 01935 814748 ⓔ enquiries@avalontownhouse.co.uk ⓦ www.avalontownhouse.co.uk. An Edwardian townhouse with character in the town centre. The 3 en-suite rooms are thoughtfully furnished, with flat-screen TV and free Wi-Fi. Children and pets are not allowed and the rooms are upstairs, so not suitable for those with limited mobility.

Betty's Loft Moongate, 14 Hillside, Manston DT10 1EY ⓣ 01258 471152 ⓔ jane@healingandchange.co.uk ⓦ www.stayingatmoongate.wordpress. com. Jane Williams, reiki master and active member of the local community, has created an en-suite room specifically for B&B guests at her home near Sturminster Newton. It has its own private entrance and is nicely furnished. A yurt in the garden is also available for hire. There are views of farmland and Hambledon Hill. Jane practises and teaches healing therapies, and you can choose to take a treatment during your stay if you wish. The budget-conscious will be very comfortable with the prices.

Blackmore Vale Caravan Park Sherborne Causeway, near Shaftesbury SP7 9PX ⓣ 01747 851523 ⓔ mike-farrow@btconnect.com ⓦ www.blackmorevale caravanpark.co.uk. On the A30, near Shaftesbury. Caters for motorhomes and tents, and offers on-site caravans and luxury bell tents. The facilities are comprehensive and include a fishing lake and gym.

Crown Inn Crown Rd, Marnhull DT10 1LN ⓣ 01258 820224 ⓔ enquiry@ thecrownatmarnhull.co.uk ⓦ www.thecrownatmarnhull.co.uk. This thatched, 16th-century pub on the outskirts of Marnhull appeared in Thomas Hardy's writings as 'The Pure Drop Inn'. In 2009, the pub converted outbuildings into 5 elegant, spacious en-suite rooms, one of which has disabled access. The B&B packages represent good value for money.

Eastbury Hotel Long St, Sherborne DT9 3BY ⓣ 01935 813131 ⓔ enquiries@ theeastburyhotel.co.uk ⓦ www.theesastburyhotel.co.uk. A 23-room, family-run hotel on one of Sherborne's quieter streets, within walking distance of the shops, castle and abbey. Many of the building's Georgian features have been preserved and, as a result, it has plenty of character. Each room has its own individual style, with the rooms in the extension having a much more modern feel. There is a pleasant walled garden, a good restaurant (see page 53) and, importantly, a car park.

Elwood Cottages Woolland, Blandford Forum DT11 0ES ⓣ 01258 818196 ⓔ admin@ellwoodcottages.co.uk ⓦ www.ellwoodcottages.co.uk. Converted farm buildings house 3 self-catering units designed for people with disabilities. There are spacious gardens with expansive views to Bulbarrow and Ibberton Hill, an indoor splash pool and a therapy room. Reasonably priced.

Farnham Farmhouse Farnham DT11 8DG ⓣ 01725 516254 ⓔ info@

farnhamfarmhouse.co.uk ⓦ www.farnhamfarmhouse.co.uk. A B&B on a working farm in the peaceful Cranborne Chase. Has 3 well-appointed, spacious en-suite rooms, an outdoor heated pool and a natural therapies centre. Reasonably priced.

Golden Hill Cottage Stourton Caundle DT10 2JW ⓣ 01963 362109 ⓦ www.goldenhillcottage.co.uk. A cosy thatched B&B between Sherborne and Sturminster Newton run by friendly hosts, Annie and Andrew Oliver. There is one twin en-suite bedroom with its own nicely furnished sitting room. Afternoon tea and breakfast are homemade by Annie. Good value for money.

The Grange Oborne DT9 4LA ⓣ 01935 813463 ⓦ www.thegrangeatoborne.co.uk. A small hotel in a 200-year-old farmhouse just outside Sherborne. The 18 en-suite rooms are nicely furnished, some are more modern than others, and there is a good restaurant. Prices are on the high side but not exorbitant.

Grosvenor The Commons, Shaftesbury ⓣ 01747 850580 ⓔ reception@ hotelgrosvenor.com ⓦ www.hotelgrosvenor.com. A boutique hotel in the centre of Shaftesbury, which has been completely refurbished in recent years and offers a good standard of accommodation. The very modern, urban-style interior is more akin to London than Dorset and is quite unexpected given the Grade II-listed exterior and Georgian façade. There are 16 well-appointed en-suite rooms, including 3 suites, plus a restaurant and bar. There is a room suitable for those with limited mobility. Pet-friendly. One of the more expensive options in the area.

Inside Park Fairmile Rd, Blandford Forum DT11 0HG ⓣ 01258 453719 ⓔ mail@ insidepark.co.uk ⓦ www.theinsidepark.co.uk. A great option for lovers of camping and the countryside. The campsite is open from April to October, set within 14 acres of park and woodland on a farm. The site facilities are far more elegant than the average, being contained within an 18th-century stable and coach house. There is an outdoor play area, games room and shop, as well as 6 miles of signed walks through the farmland, where you are likely to encounter local wildlife. Pet-friendly. Reasonably priced.

La Fosse London House, The Square, Cranborne BH21 5PR ⓣ 01725 517604 ⓔ lafossemail@gmail.com ⓦ www.la-fosse.com. Offers 6 en-suite rooms in the centre of Cranborne village. Some of the rooms are on the small side but they are comfortable and well-equipped. There is a good restaurant and the breakfasts are hearty. Good value for money.

Museum Inn Farnham, DT11 8DE ⓣ 01725 516261 ⓔ enquiries@museuminn. co.uk ⓦ www.museuminn.co.uk. A highly regarded gastropub with rooms in the Cranborne Chase. The accommodation is spacious and elegantly furnished; dogs are welcome in some rooms. The restaurant serves sophisticated dishes prepared using local produce wherever possible. One of the area's more expensive options.

Pipers Mill Cottages Fontmell Magna SP7 0JP ⓣ 01747 838460 ⓔ info@ pipersmillcottagesdorset.co.uk ⓦ www.pipersmillcottagesdorset.co.uk. Within easy reach of Shaftesbury and the Cranborne Chase, 2 self-catering cottages, which sleep 4 or 5 people. The cottages are spacious and nicely furnished – a real home away from home. Both have a wood-burning fire. Pet-friendly. Reasonably priced.

Plumber Manor Sturminster Newton DT10 2AF ℡ 01258 472507 Ⓔ book@
plumbermanor.com Ⓦ www.plumbermanor.com. Upmarket accommodation in
an elegant country house belonging to the Prideaux-Brune family. In the main
house are 6 comfortable en-suite rooms; converted outbuildings contain another
10 rooms. Facilities include a tennis court, croquet lawn and popular restaurant.
Dogs are allowed in some rooms. One of North Dorset's more expensive options.

Stock Gaylard Yurt Holidays Stock Gaylard Estate, Sturminster Newton DT10
2BG ℡ 01963 23511 Ⓔ aclangmead@stockgaylard.com Ⓦ www.stockgaylard.
com. Luxury yurt camping on the 1,700-acre Stock Gaylard Estate, which includes
an 80-acre deer park. There is an abundance of wildlife and plenty of peace and
quiet. Local furniture maker, James Ross, crafted the yurts from ash grown on
the estate. They are grouped in threes, 2 for sleeping and one with a kitchen. Use
of the yurts and solar power minimises the impact on the environment. Guided
nature walks are available. You can eat the estate's venison and have organic food
boxes delivered to your yurt. Not your average camping experience so expect to
pay substantially more than at a typical campsite.

Stock Hill House Gillingham SP8 5NR ℡ 01747 823626 Ⓔ reception@
stockhillhouse.co.uk Ⓦ www.stockhillhouse.co.uk. A Victorian country house
hotel run to a high standard for over 20 years by Austrian chef Peter Hauser
and his wife Nita. In a quiet location on the edge of Gillingham and set in
well-maintained grounds, the hotel has an air of exclusivity and is beautifully
furnished. There is an excellent restaurant. Upmarket, and the prices reflect this.

Summerlands Farm Hermitage DT2 7BB ℡ 01963 210495 Ⓦ www.
summerlandsfarm.co.uk. In the village of Hermitage, between Sherborne and
Dorchester. A trout and carp fishing establishment, which also has self-catering,
twin accommodation. Fishing and fly-tying tuition can be arranged. The
accommodation is simple and is easily one of the cheapest options in the area.

Todber Manor Manor Farm, Todber DT10 IJB ℡ 01258 820384 Ⓔ todbermanor@
aol.com Ⓦ www.todbermanor.co.uk. Carefully maintained fishing lakes, self-
catering cottages and a small campsite for Caravan Club members. Farm buildings
have been converted to 8 comfortable self-catering cottages. The fishing
facilities are extensive, with large, well-stocked lakes and a tackle shop. No pets.
Reasonably priced.

Whistley Farm Milton-on Stour, near Gillingham SP8 5PT ℡ 01747 860962
Ⓔ info@whistleyfarm.com Ⓦ www.whistleyfarm.com. Tim and Debbie Allard
offer exceptional self-catering accommodation on their peaceful farm near in
the Blackmore Vale. The 2 3-bedroom Scandinavian-style wooden lodges are
beautifully furnished and maintained, and overlook an attractive lake where
guests can fish. Footpaths criss-cross the farm, meaning you can explore the
countryside without turning the key in your car. There is also a 4-hole pitch-
and-putt golf course. Dogs are welcome in one of the lodges. Very good value
for money, and will appeal to all, including families. See advertisement in
colour section.

Tourist information centres
Blandford Riverside House, West St, DT11 7HW ① 01258 454770.
Shaftesbury 8 Bell St, SP7 8AE ① 01747 853514.
Sherborne Digby Rd, DT9 3NL ① 01935 815341 ⓦ www.sherbornetown.com.

The Blackmore Vale

Most visitors to the West County whizz down the A303, overlooking the Blackmore Vale just beneath it and, as a result, it remains remarkably unspoilt. It lies in North Dorset and stretches just over the border into southwest Wiltshire, a wide, sheltered valley of fertile agricultural land dotted with charming, quintessentially English villages, many of which are built from warm, golden stone. The Dorset Downs and Cranborne Chase border it, with the towns of Shaftesbury (in the north) and Blandford Forum (in the south) being natural boundary markers. Hills such as Hambledon and Bulbarrow

William Barnes
Mo Richards

William Barnes (1801–86) was born at Bagber, near Sturminster Newton in the Blackmore Vale, the son of a yeoman farmer. Although best known as a poet who wrote mostly in dialect, Barnes was also a philologist. He was fluent in Greek, Latin and several modern European languages and studied the close relationship between Dorset dialect and Old English. He called for the removal of foreign-derived words from the English language, so that it might be better understood by those lacking a classical education.

There is not a language Barnes loved more than that of the Dorset folk around him. His pastoral poetry written in Dorset dialect brought to life the voices of the county's ploughmen, milkmaids and farmers, and his fondness for Dorset's landscapes, as well as its people, shines through in his poetry.

From 1835 until 1862, Barnes ran a school in Dorchester and published *Poems of Rural Life in the Dorset Dialect* (1844). From 1862 until his death, he was rector of St Peter's Church Winterborne Came and is buried in the churchyard.

Although younger than Barnes, Thomas Hardy was a fan of Barnes's work and the two became friends. Not everyone was impressed by Barnes's use of the Dorset dialect, but Hardy defended it: 'The veil of a dialect, through which except in a few cases readers have to discern whatever of real poetry there may be in William Barnes, is disconcerting to many, and to some distasteful, chiefly, one thinks, for a superficial reason which has more to do with spelling than with the dialect itself.'

encircle the vale, and provide fine vantage points over its neat fields lined by hedges, its woodland and its villages. In spring and summer the landscape is sprinkled with yellow highlights – crops of oilseed rape. Those views would once have been quite different as the vale was densely wooded and the area around Gillingham a royal hunting forest. Few pockets of woodland remain, the most notable being on Duncliffe Hill, which rises like a beacon from the flat base of the vale.

From its source at Stourhead, just over the Wiltshire border, the River Stour meanders through the vale on its way to the sea at Christchurch. A series of mills used to punctuate the water's journey through the vale, several of them are named in the Domesday Book. Of some 50 mills that used to operate on the River Stour, many are now derelict but some have been lovingly restored. Sturminster Newton Mill is still in working order and is open to visitors in the summer months.

Dairy farming used to be the lifeblood of the Blackmore Vale, prompting Thomas Hardy to use it as the inspiration for his 'vale of a hundred dairies'. Sadly, prolonged troubled times have meant many of the dairy farms have now shut up their milking parlours and had to diversify into other activities.

The Blackmore Vale Magazine – a local institution

Fanny Charles, editor of the Blackmore Vale Magazine

The phone rang. 'Where are our *Blackmore Vales*?' 'Where are you phoning from?' asked the editor 'Crossways.' Silence at the editor's end. Where on earth was Crossways? 'Where is Crossways?' The caller explained that it was a village half way between Wareham and Dorchester. 'I didn't know we delivered down there.' 'You don't – we go to Tolpuddle on a Sunday to pick the magazines up from a man who gets them from the vegetable stall in Puddletown on Saturday.' Having no idea how they got to the vegetable stall in the first place, the editor didn't have an instant answer, but said she would do her best to find out why Crossways was missing out on its weekly fix of the BVM.

That's just one example of the reach of one of the country's most remarkable weekly papers, the free *Blackmore Vale Magazine*, produced in two converted three-storey 18th-century cottages in Stalbridge, printed in Shaftesbury and distributed across most of rural Dorset, into south and west Wiltshire and parts of south Somerset.

The BVM – universally known as 'the bible' in its heartlands – was established in its present form more than 30 years ago by professional singers Ingrid and Alan Chalcraft, who acquired the magazine shortly after it was launched in the Blackmore Vale.

It was always different from other local papers. Partly it's the shape – an A4 magazine, rather than conventional tabloid or larger newspaper. But mostly it is liked for its thoughtful, well-informed blend of news, features and photos;

The silver lining for the visitor is that those resilient, ingenious Dorset farming folk have built some fantastic rural businesses, including accommodation, farm shops, niche food production and even recreational fishing lakes.

The vale's towns, in particular Shaftesbury and Sturminster Newton, draw visitors for their history and beauty but perhaps the best way to appreciate the Blackmore Vale is to get out and walk its unspoilt countryside and hike the surrounding hills for a bird's-eye view. For generations the scenery has inspired artists, such as John Constable; writers, such as Thomas Hardy; and poets, such as William Barnes. Hardy's description of the view from the hills still holds true:

Here, in the valley, the world seems to be constructed upon a smaller and more delicate scale; the fields are mere paddocks, so reduced that from this height their hedgerows appear a network of dark green threads overspreading the paler green of the grass.

① Gillingham and surrounds

Being on the main train line to London, Gillingham is the gateway to the Blackmore Vale. Today the trains are used by suit-clad commuters making their

its coverage is admirably thorough, encompassing local food as well as arts and environmental matters. Even the classified ads are fun to peruse, and rather than huddled in a lump at the back are spread throughout the paper.

The result is a publication that regularly tops 160 pages a week, has a longer shelf life than most paid-for newspapers and is one of the most successful and unusual in the country.

People will tell you that they read it from cover to cover and that they queue up for it on Friday morning. Outlets often run out of BVMs by the end of the day, and the demand for the magazine seems to be insatiable – a remarkable achievement at a time when many newspapers are suffering falling sales and distribution.

While the editorial and the advertising are why people want it, how they get their magazines is also unusual. Of course, many people have it delivered, and others pick up their BVM from a newsagent or village shop. But not every village still has a general store, so over the years the BVM deliverers have found imaginative places to leave the magazines, including pubs, garages, church porches and village halls. In one village, the magazines are left in the only 'public space' – a bus shelter. In another tiny settlement, a bundle is pushed between the posts of a fence. And then there are the unofficial distributors who drive to collect their magazines from an established dropping point and take them back to their own community.

Over the years there have been imitators and competitors, but the BVM has a special chemistry with the community it serves, that is best defined as a real sense of ownership.

daily journey to Salisbury, London or one of the cities in between but farmers June and Alf Wallis remember when the trains' cargo was quite a different one. June and Alf have been farming in Dorset all their lives and in nearby Stour Provost since 1963. They recall the days when cattle from nearby farms were loaded directly onto trains at Gillingham and the farmers' supplies of fertiliser arrived by train and they collected it from the station in their tractors. The station, and the town, must have had quite a different character in those days.

Gillingham gets a bit of a bad rap, largely because its neighbour, Shaftesbury, is considered far more attractive. Both towns have seen a great deal of new housing development in recent years, but Shaftesbury has done a better job of maintaining its charm. Gillingham wasn't always the ugly sister, however, as in the 19th century John Constable felt it a worthy artistic subject and painted the bridge, the mill and the entrance to the town. Of these, the most recognisable scene today is **Gillingham Bridge**, which lies three quarters of the way down the high street; Constable's depiction of it is in London's Tate Britain.

Before you rush off to Shaftesbury the **Gillingham Museum** (*01747 823234; www.gillinghammuseum.co.uk; open Mon, Tue, Thu & Fri*) is worth a look. It is located near the Gillingham library, opposite Waitrose supermarket on the Wyke Road and within walking distance of the train station. The museum tells the story of area's inhabitants, from Neolithic settlement to the present and reminds us that the Gillingham area was once a busy royal hunting forest, and that in 1210 King John is said to have rewarded two huntsmen for killing wolves here. The 1790 manual fire engine on display is the only surviving one of its kind. Also on show are reproductions of John Constable's paintings of the area.

There are some pleasing villages around Gillingham, notably Silton and **Milton-on-Stour**, which has sturdy stone farmhouses and a bridge over the river, which rises in nearby Stourhead.

Silton

The village of Silton is worth visiting for its 15th-century **church of St Nicholas**, thought to stand on Saxon foundations. The interior walls carry a distinctive, dainty, stencilled decoration but the church's most striking feature is a highly theatrical 17th-century memorial to Sir Hugh Wyndham (1602–1684), with him flanked by his two weeping wives. Wyndham was a judge of the court of common pleas and was one of 22 judges who sat in the Fire Court, set up in 1667 to hear cases relating to property damaged in the Great Fire of London. Wyndham bought the Manor of Silton in 1641, on the site of the present Manor Farm, just south of the churchyard.

In a field behind the church is the **Wyndham Oak**, one of Britain's oldest trees. It is said Sir Hugh Wyndham used to rest under the oak and admire the view, so it must have been a substantial size by the 17th century. It is thought that the tree may have been used for hangings following the Monmouth

Mere Down Falconry

Manor Farm, Mere BA12 6HR ℗ 01747 824913 Ⓦ www.meredownfalconry.co.uk.

Just over the border into Wiltshire, at the base of the Mere Downs, falconer Allan Gates carefully tends to his much-loved birds of prey: hawks, owls and falcons. He is a regular sight at local country shows, flying his birds over the heads of delighted spectators, while his wife Alison runs the ferret-racing part of the enterprise. For a truly memorable experience, you can have a go at flying Allan's birds under his expert supervision.

Of the various interactive experiences on offer, my pick is the full-day introduction to falconry. You spend the morning meeting and learning about the birds and flying them short distances near the aviaries, and after lunch you take a couple of them up onto the Mere Downs and fly them over the wide valley.

I accompanied Allan, his German short-haired pointer and two of his Harris hawks up onto the downs, where we flew the birds over the bowl created by the crescent-shaped hills. The views back towards Gillingham and the Blackmore Vale were breathtaking, providing a suitably impressive backdrop for these marvellous birds. The hawks and the dog hunted as a team, the dog flushing out prey and the birds watching keenly from above, and although we didn't catch anything that day that didn't seem to dull their enthusiasm. The majesty and power of these birds in flight is something to behold, but just as fascinating is Allan's relationship with them: they are clearly bonded to him but maintain that wild, instinctive spirit. Allan told me each bird very much has its own personality and he gives them the jobs to which they are best suited and, from what I saw, they enjoy their work.

A lot of time and effort goes into training these birds. Allan sometimes spends an evening in front of the television with a bird sitting on his arm, getting it used to the glove and food rewards. (Alison is a very tolerant wife.) He even delicately repairs any damaged feathers they may have. Allan learned from one of the best falconers around, Merv Brown, who farmed in the Blackmore Vale village where I grew up, Stour Provost.

Falconry is an ancient countryside tradition practised in various countries around the world and is believed to date back to at least 3,500BC in the Middle East. The equipment used has barely changed since falconry began; you feel like you are stepping back in time as you stand on the hills and watch the birds soaring on the thermals over the valley and then swooping back to land on your glove with pinpoint accuracy. As Allan explained to me, many common expressions come from falconry, including 'under the thumb', referring to the bird's leash being tightly held.

Allan is doing a superb job of keeping this countryside pursuit alive. As well as half- and full-day flying experiences, he offers two-hour family handling sessions and occasionally runs special events such as owl night flights. He tells me the owls are particularly popular with the children.

Rebellion, although this has not been confirmed. To visit the oak today is to be in the presence of plant majesty, its gnarly, split trunk and branches like witches' fingers attest to its momentous age. Personally, I wouldn't sit Wyndham-like beneath it as it doesn't look as robust as it must once have been. Should it finally give up the ghost, it will not be lost altogether because in the 1970s the residents of Manor Farm planted an acorn from the ancient oak in the same field as its ancestor so that it can one day take over the mantle.

Food and drink

Buffalo Inn Lydford Lane, Gillingham SP8 4NJ ① 01747 823759. A traditional country pub on the Wyke side of Gillingham serving unpretentious but tasty pub food. You won't leave hungry – the portions are huge. Open daily for lunch and dinner. Thursday is trivia night.

Lagan Farm Shop Orchard Park Garden Centre, Shaftesbury Rd, Gillingham SP8 5JG ① 01747 835544. The farm shop at the garden centre stocks rare-breed lamb and beef plus a small selection of locally grown vegetables. Its casual café is a popular meeting point for locals. Free Wi-Fi. Open Mon–Sat 09.30–17.30, Sun 10.00–16.00.

Stock Hill House Gillingham SP8 5NR ① 01747 823626 ⓦ www.stockhillhouse. co.uk. An upmarket restaurant in this elegant country house hotel. Austrian chef Peter Hauser produces exceptional dishes, including Austrian specialities and using local produce where possible. Open for lunch and dinner. Reservation recommended.

② Stourhead House and Gardens

Stourton BA12 6QD ① 01747 841152 ⓦ www.nationaltrust.org.uk. Garden open 09.00–18.00 all year, house opening times vary; National Trust.

Just over the Wiltshire border, the 2,650-acre Stourhead estate is one of the area's key attractions. As the name indicates, it is here that the River Stour rises. The house is a Palladian mansion brimming with antique furniture and artwork, and evokes the lives of its former residents, the Hoare family, who made their fortune in banking. The 18th-century gardens are magical, inspired by the great landscape painters of the 17th century and grand tours of Europe. A magnificent lake constitutes the centre piece, fed by the infant River Stour, which shimmers with the reflections of autumn colours

The Gillingham and Shaftesbury Show

Turnpike Showground, Motcombe SP7 9LP ® www.gillshaftshow.co.uk.
One of the highlights of the Blackmore Vale calendar is the annual agricultural show, held on the third Wednesday in August at Motcombe, between Gillingham and Shaftesbury. It has all the best features of an agricultural show: livestock classes, dog classes, equestrian classes, heavy horses, the local hunts, agricultural trade stands, local food producers and handicrafts. Locals spend many months preparing their entries for the fiercely contested jam, cake, vegetable, embroidery and art classes.

as the leaves change hue. Classical temples, romantic bridges and mysterious grottoes create a dreamy atmosphere; the European influence is clear with a mini Pantheon and a Temple of Apollo among the features.

Nearby is King Alfred's Tower, a 160-foot folly built in 1772 in honour of the Saxon king by Stourhead's then owner, Henry Hoare II. The woods around the tower offer memorable walks and when the tower is open in summer you can walk to the top for superlative views of the surrounding countryside.

③ Shaftesbury

'Welcome to Shaftesbury, a Saxon Hilltop Town': the sign seems to sum it up, but there is more to this place because it shows immense skill in combining functionality, history and beauty. It stands on a greensand promontory at 700 feet, overlooking the Blackmore Vale; its centre is compact, packed with enticing, independent shops and easy to explore on foot. It was founded by King Alfred the Great around AD880 and is one of four Dorset towns named in the Burghal Hidage, which recorded Alfred's plan to provide fortified safe havens for local people at times of invasion. Although many of the town's buildings are Georgian and Victorian, constructed from distinctive local greensand stone, traces of its Saxon origins can be seen around the site of the abbey. Key to the town's beauty is the picture-perfect Gold Hill, a cobbled street lined with tiny cottages.

Thomas Hardy had plenty to say about Shaftesbury, referred to as 'Shaston' in his writings and it appeared in both *Jude the Obscure* and *Tess of the d'Urbevilles*. He described it as 'one of the queerest and quaintest spots in England', 'breezy and whimsical' and said 'beer was more plentiful than water'. It is certainly quaint and, thanks to its hilltop position, has a tendency to be breezy. Mercifully, the water supply is now far more reliable than it once was and although there is a healthy population of pubs serving local ales, I doubt beer is more plentiful than water. On a dull day, the town is often shrouded in cloud and this, combined with its cold greensand stone, has given it a reputation as a rather dreary, melancholy place. Catch it on a fine day and you will be amply rewarded by this queer, quaint, whimsical town that so fascinated Hardy.

The appealing town centre is an easy walk from the car parks at the top and bottom of the High Street, and buses stop outside the Town Hall, in the very centre of town. The **Town Hall** is a Georgian building whose battlements seem designed to project a serious, castle-like image; the weekly **street market** takes place here on Thursdays. Next to the Town Hall is the diminutive **St Peter's Church**; built in the late 15th century, it is the oldest church in Shaftesbury.

Just behind the Town Hall is the much-photographed, much-painted **Gold Hill**. This impossibly steep, cobbled street with its row of attractive cottages and pastoral Blackmore Vale backdrop is a local celebrity. The highlight of its career was appearing in the 1973 Hovis bread commercial directed by Ridley Scott, which featured a boy pushing a bicycle up the hill. A mildly comical statue of a Hovis loaf sits next to the Town Hall, a reminder of that pinnacle of Gold Hill's fame. Along one side of Gold Hill a formidable stone wall is all that remains of the walls that once encircled Shaftesbury Abbey. At the top of Gold Hill is a café, where you can sit and pity the poor folk walking up the steep incline, before you decide whether to venture down and back up again. Also at the top of the hill is a super little bookshop, **Gold Hill Books** (*01747 851571*), which has one of the largest collections of Dorset books I have seen, and nearby is **Gold Hill Museum** (see page 16). As you potter about the hill, don't be surprised if you hear the odd bleating sheep (although I never have) as apparently a tenant's right to keep six sheep was bestowed on all households on Gold Hill and that permission remains in place today.

A narrow alleyway (Park Lane) leads from the top of Gold Hill to Park Walk, which has pleasant public gardens, breathtaking views across the Blackmore Vale and the **Abbey Museum and Garden** (see page 16). With the abbey ruins behind and the unspoilt countryside in front, the gardens are an ideal place to sit and ponder the history of the place and how it might have been when King Alfred ruled the roost around these parts.

Shaftesbury Abbey was built by King Alfred around AD888 on the site of a pagan temple; it was the first religious house solely for women and Alfred's daughter, Aethelgifu, was the inaugural abbess. The remains of Saxon King Edward the Martyr were brought to the abbey after his murder at Corfe Castle in AD978 (see box, page 167); his shrine and the promise of associated miracles attracted streams of pilgrims. The abbey thrived and became one of the largest in the country, with around 350 inhabitants and large tracts of land in Dorset, Wiltshire and beyond. It attracted royal visitors, including King Canute who died here in 1035. In 1491 Henry VII stayed at the abbey, as did Catherine of Aragon in 1501 on her way to marry Prince Arthur, elder brother of Henry VIII. After 650 years of continuous worship, the abbey closed in 1539 as part of Henry VIII's Dissolution of the Monasteries and soon fell into disrepair. The ruins are visible within the Abbey Museum and Garden, while the ramparts on Gold Hill are all that remain of the outer walls.

King Alfred the Great

Alfred is the only English king to be known as 'The Great', an epithet bestowed for his valiant defence of his kingdom against a formidable enemy, for securing peace with the Vikings and for his educational and legal reforms.

He was born in AD849 in what is now Wantage, Oxfordshire, fifth son of Aethelwulf, king of the West Saxons. In AD871, at the age of 21, he succeeded his brother Aethelred as King of Wessex.

Viking armies had been raiding England since around AD790 and had taken much of the north; in AD870 they attacked the last remaining independent Anglo-Saxon kingdom, Wessex. After turning to guerrilla tactics to defeat the Danes in several protracted battles, Alfred negotiated a partition treaty with them in AD886, whereby the areas between the rivers Thames and Tees became Danish territory and Alfred took charge of an extended Wessex, which now included West Mercia and Kent.

To protect his kingdom, Alfred established a navy and built a series of well-defended settlements across southern England, fortified market places or 'burhs', where residents could seek shelter. Settlers received plots in return for manning the defences in times of war. The programme was recorded in the Burghal Hidage, a document detailing the building and operation of Wessex and Mercian burhs according to their size, the length of their ramparts and the number of men needed to garrison them. This network of burhs, with strong points on the main river routes, ensured that no part of Wessex was more than 20 miles from the refuge of one of the settlements.

Alfred believed strongly in education, learnt Latin in his late thirties and was patron of the Anglo-Saxon Chronicle, a patriotic history of the Anglo-Saxons. He lamented that much of the population could not understand Latin and so arranged the translation into Anglo-Saxon of a series of important books he thought 'most needful for men to know'. He also advocated justice and order and significantly reformed Anglo-Saxon law.

Alfred reigned until his death in AD899 and was buried in Winchester, capital of Wessex.

The views from Park Walk are rivalled by those from **Castle Hill**, which is within walking of the abbey ruins. Head along Abbey Walk then turn left when you reach Bimport; after a short distance, a lane on your right leads to Castle Hill, once the site of a Saxon fort. The views across the Blackmore Vale to the Somerset and Wiltshire border are topped off by King Alfred's Tower in the distance. Thomas Hardy described the scene as 'as sudden a surprise to the unexpected traveller's eyes as the medicinal air is to his lungs'.

Aside from Gold Hill, some of the best-preserved greensand cottages, with tiny doors and thatched roofs, are found at the top of town in Bell Street and at the bottom of town in **St James**, an area at the base of Gold Hill. In St

James look out for a u-shaped collection of worker's cottages set back from the road, known as Pump Court and still with the pump at its centre.

You will see plenty of references to the Grosvenor family in and around Shaftesbury, for they owned much of the town until less than a hundred years ago. In 1820, Earl Grosvenor (later Marquis of Westminster) bought the 'Property of Shaftesbury' (the 400 premises large enough to have voting rights) in order to control elections in the borough. The Grosvenors grew very wealthy and were responsible for much of the development in the town, and it is for that reason that it has an estate village character; the keen-eyed will spot many cast-iron windows of similar design and uniform rows of workers' cottages. The family also alleviated one of the town's greatest problems, a lack of water, when in the mid-1800s the marquis provided a well and a steam engine to pump free water to the residents. In 1918 Robert Grosvenor's great-grandson sold his Dorset estates, and Shaftesbury was again put up for sale. It was bought by a Londoner, then resold to a consortium of three men of the town: the doctor, the innkeeper at the Grosvenor Arms and the manager of a grocer's shop. They subsequently held the 'sale of Shaftesbury' in which, over three days, most tenants bought their own houses and shops.

Shaftesbury Abbey Museum and Garden

Park Walk, SP7 8JR ① 01747 852910 Ⓦ www.shaftesburyheritage.org.uk.

This small museum sits on the site of the abbey and gives a feel for what life would have been like for the women who lived there. It is best visited in decent weather, as you can explore the excavated foundations of the abbey in the walled garden. The foundations are all that remain as much of the stone was taken for building elsewhere, and a small herb garden commemorates the nuns' extensive use of herbs; the commanding statue of King Alfred was made as recently as 1989. Indoor exhibits include a model of the abbey church as it would have been in the 11th century. The free audio guide provides an excellent commentary as you explore at your own pace.

Gold Hill Museum

Gold Hill, SP7 8JW ① 01747 852157 Ⓦ www.goldhillmuseum.org.uk. Open Apr–Oct 10.30–16.30; free admission.

This small museum in a cottage at the top of Gold Hill was once a doss house for the drovers, jugglers and traders who came to Shaftesbury's markets and fairs. Exhibitions cover archaeology and local history. The industries on which the town was built are given due attention: the agricultural industry, lace-making and the production of Dorset buttons. Also on display is the Byzant,

Stoate and Sons Stoneground Flour

Cann Mills, Shaftesbury SP7 0BL ① 01747 852475 ⓦ www.stoatesflour.co.uk.
Open Mon 08.30–13.00, 14.00–17.00, Wed–Fri 08.30–13.00, 14.00–17.00.
The Stoate family began milling in the West Country in 1832 and in 1947 took over this mill about a mile south of Shaftesbury on the A350 to Blandford. Their mill is powered largely by the River Sturkel, a tributary of the Stour, and the flour is ground using French burr stones. They produce a range of organic and non-organic flours, including spelt, rye and wholemeal.

You can buy Stoates flour direct from the mill or from farm shops, health-food shops and bakeries across the South West. Several good local bakeries use Stoates flour, such as Long Crichel Bakery and Leakers in Bridport.

Paul Merry runs artisan bread- and pastry-making courses at the mill, which include a mill tour (*01747 823711; www.panary.co.uk*).

an exotic 18th-century wooden totem which was processed annually to nearby Enmore Green to secure the town's right to water from that area; Enmore had the closest spring and it wasn't until 1830 that Shaftesbury secured its own water supply.

Food and drink

The annual **Shaftesbury Feastival** (*www.shaftesburyfeastival.co.uk*) showcases the many fine artisan food producers in the area. It is the brainchild of local food personality Charlie Turnbull and combines food stalls, events and entertainment, including maypole dancing.

Greenhouse Restaurant Grosvenor Hotel, The Commons ① 01747 850580 ⓦ www.hotelgrosvenor.com. A trendy restaurant serving elaborate creations. Open for lunch and dinner daily.

La Fleur de Lys Bleke St, SP7 8AW ① 01747 853717 ⓦ www.lafleurdelys.co.uk. An upmarket restaurant at the entrance to the town. Open Mon–Sat for dinner and for pre-booked lunches Wed–Sun. Reservation recommended.

Salt Cellar Gold Hill Parade, SP7 8JW ① 01747 851838. This café's greatest asset is its location, right at the top of Gold Hill. If you have climbed the hill, you will have earned tea and cake here, or you can just sit and watch others struggling up the hill. Light lunches are available. The food is cooked to order, so you can expect a bit of a wait especially at busy times. Open Mon–Sat 09.00–17.00, Sun 10.00–17.00.

Turnbulls 9 High St, SP7 8HZ ① 01747 858575 ⓦ www.turnbulls.co.uk. A popular deli and café at the top of the High Street. Owner, Charlie Turnbull, is an international cheese judge and there is a huge choice of cheese on sale alongside a range of local produce.

Ye Olde Two Brewers 24 St James St, SP7 8HE ① 01747 855477. A traditional pub at the bottom of Gold Hill. The dining room and large garden have stunning views of the Blackmore Vale. Open daily, closed Sun dinner.

④ Duncliffe Wood

A visit to Duncliffe is perhaps the best way to gain an impression of what Blackmore and Gillingham would have been like when they were royal hunting forests. As the many farms grew up in the area, the land was cleared but on Duncliffe Hill remains a pocket of well-preserved woodland, cared for by the Woodland Trust. The Domesday Book records a wood here, which was traditionally coppiced. Much of the ancient oak, ash and hazel was felled in the 1950s and replanted with Norway spruce, oak, larch and beech. Today, the Woodland Trust manages it in such a way as to encourage a greater mix of native broadleaf species.

A footpath and bridleway lead through the 228-acre wood to the top of the hill (690 feet), which provides far-reaching views of the surrounding farmland. As you walk through the woods, perhaps you will be struck, as I always am, that the hedges and the woodland are just the kind where you would expect to meet the wildlife characters from a children's book. In fact, if you take the walk on a summer's evening you are likely to catch a glimpse of many of them – the local roe deer, badgers, pheasants and foxes. Butterflies are also abundant, including silver-washed fritillary, white admiral and purple hairstreak.

Duncliffe Wood lies off the A30 between Shaftesbury and East Stour, near the village of Stour Row.

⑤ East Stour and West Stour

The importance of the River Stour is evident in this area, with a string of villages named after it. This is an area of small farms, watched over by Duncliffe Hill. The small communities of East Stour and West Stour lie on the A30 between Shaftesbury and Sherborne. Both villages were mentioned in the Domesday Book but now have a noticeable amount of modern development, East Stour in particular. Thankfully it also has handsome original farms and the short, squat **church**, which was rebuilt in 1842 on the site of an earlier one. Henry Fielding, author of *Tom Jones*, lived in the old rectory which has now been demolished; Church Farm stands on the site. As you enter East Stour from Shaftesbury you pass the marvellous **Udder Farm Shop**, which has breathed new life into the area (see box, opposite).

From East Stour the A30 continues through West Stour, providing views back across the fields towards Stour Provost, where the River Stour flows.

The Udder Farm Shop

Manor Farm, East Stour SP8 5LQ ① 01747 838899 ⑩ www.theudderfarmshop. co.uk. Open Mon–Fri 09.00–18.00, Sat 08.30–18.00, Sun 10.00–16.00.

This fabulously named large farm shop (see advert in colour section) sells a wonderful array of local produce and is a great place for self-caterers to stock up. There is an on-site butcher, a delicatessen and a large selection of gifts with a local flavour. The café has become the definitive place in the area to meet up with friends. It serves excellent light lunches and delicious cakes, has views of Duncliffe Hill, an outdoor children's play area and wheelchair access.

The shop is the brainchild of local farming personalities Brian and Jane Down. I have known Brian and his family since I was born – they used to farm the land adjoining ours in Stour Provost, although their farm is in East Stour on the A30. For years I only ever saw him on a tractor and I suspect he only ever saw me on a pony. His grandfather came to Manor Farm in 1938 and it has remained in the family. In the 1990s, when my father was the European correspondent for a Canadian newspaper, he interviewed Brian and his father, Jim, for an article about the approaches of the different generations to farming. Brian had spent some time on a very progressive farm in New Zealand in the 1980s and returned full of ideas to modernise Manor Farm, some of which met with a lukewarm reception from his father. Like so many father-and-son farming teams they figured out their own *modus vivendi*, supported by a shared love of their piece of the Blackmore Vale. I thought it only right that all these years later I interview Brian about his latest venture and ask what Jim makes of it.

It was 2005 when Brian, like so many dairy farmers, came to the realisation that diversification was the only way forward. If nothing else, it would make the bad years easier to bear and with any luck provide an asset he and Jane could leave to their children. The East Stour village shop had closed, leaving a significant gap in the local community, and they came up with the idea of a farm shop. They were determined the project should benefit the community as much as possible, employing local labour as well as providing a service. It seems apt that the company they used to build the frame of the Udder Farm Shop barn was the same rural firm that built Brian and Jim's milking parlour in 1994.

They have created a hugely successful enterprise selling a tempting array of locally made products. Brian finally gave up milking 18 months after the Udder Farm Shop opened but you can't stop a farmer doing what comes naturally so he continues to run beef cattle. Much of the beef you see in the Udder Farm Shop butcher's corner is Brian's, and the pork is supplied by his uncle.

I asked who had come up with the name, Brian took the credit and said they settled on it when Jane refused to wear the T-shirt bearing his first-choice, 'The Crazy Cow'. As for Jim's reaction, he initially had some reservations about the farm shop but he got behind the project and helps out where he can. No-one can deny the Udder Farm Shop has really put East Stour on the map.

The Ship Inn, a handsome coaching inn built in 1750, is a good starting point for walks across the fields to Stour Provost.

Food and drink

Kings Arms Inn East Stour Common, SP8 5NB ℗ 01747 838325
Ⓦ www.kingsarmseaststour.com. On the A30 between Shaftesbury and East Stour, this is a popular pub with locals, especially for its Sunday lunch carvery. It offers a choice of traditional pub food or more upmarket meals. At the time of publication, the pub was offering £5 lunch main courses mid-week. The dining room has been extensively renovated. It is clean and modern but has lost much of its country pub character. Open daily for lunch and dinner.
Ship Inn West Stour SP8 5RP ℗ 01747 838640. A traditional coaching inn, which has been tastefully refurbished in recent years. The menu is diverse and uses local ingredients wherever possible. The bulk of the parking is across the road, so do take care when crossing as visibility is poor. Open daily 11.30–23.00.

⑥ Stour Provost

I grew up in this tiny community, which is little more than a single street lined with conspicuously picturesque golden limestone houses, some of them thatched, and a smattering of farms. When I came into the world in 1977, I was the first child born in the village for 25 years and something of a novelty. The pace of life has remained pretty slow ever since, although the character of the village has altered. When I was growing up at Riversdale Farm, Stour Provost still had a village shop and a pub but they are long gone. There were several working dairy farms and it was not uncommon to see herds of cows, including our own small family of beef cattle, being walked through the village to pastures new. These days most of the farms are farms in name only, bought by Londoners who use them as weekend pads. A few diehard locals remain and the village still has that small community feel but it is a smarter, more sophisticated version of its former self, without a single cowpat on the street. For the visitor it offers unabashed architectural beauty, an ancient church and tranquil walks along the River Stour.

Stour Provost's history has helped to preserve its character because until less than a hundred years ago the village as a whole was owned by one entity. From the 11th century until 1467 it was owned by the nuns of the Saint Léger de Préaux Abbey in Normandy, and was known as Stour Préaux. During the wars with France, Henry V rescinded the title of various French-held lands in England, including the village, and Henry VI gave it to Eton College. Edward IV subsequently gave it to King's College, Cambridge, which owned much of the village until 1925, when it began to sell the houses to individuals.

St Michael and All Angels Church was largely built in 1302, probably on the site of an earlier Saxon church, but has undergone alterations over the centuries. An avenue of pollarded lime trees leads to the small church; sadly it is not usually left open but you can get the key from one of the church wardens. The interior is modest but with some elaborate stained glass, while the font is Purbeck stone and dates from the 15th century. Adjacent is **Church House**, a fine 16th-century building. The thatched cottage known as **Mundy's**, which lies towards the bottom of the main street, was a house for 'poor orphan children and other poor of the parish' in the 18th century.

The River Stour runs at the base of the gardens of the houses on the west side of the street. At Riversdale Farm (my childhood home) is an oxbow which was used as the local swimming pool until the 1960s, and known as Lucky Dip. At the opposite end of the village, at the end of Mill Lane, is the **Mill House**. A footpath runs through here so the mill, its waterwheel and the millpond can be seen close up. The Domesday Book of 1086 records a mill here; the present waterwheel was made in 1886, fell into disuse and was restored in 1988 by the owners of the house, the Llewellyn family, and run to provide electricity to the house.

A **circular walk** takes you from the mill across fields to the village of **Fifehead Magdalen** and from there across fields to **West Stour**, where you can stop off for refreshments at the Ship Inn (see opposite). From the Ship Inn a footpath leads directly back to the other end of Stour Provost, taking you through fields and over a footbridge (ideal for Pooh Sticks) and arriving in Stour Provost near Riversdale Farm. From there you can simply walk up The Street back to the centre of the village.

⑦ Marnhull

Thomas Hardy enthusiasts seek out Marnhull, which Hardy referred to as Marlott, for it was here that the eponymous heroine of *Tess of the d'Urbevilles* was born and raised. The historic, partly thatched Crown Inn on the edge of the village was the Pure Drop Inn in the novel. I fear that visitors expecting a village barely changed since Hardy's day will be disappointed; it is a large scattered community with much new development. It certainly isn't the prettiest village around but is perhaps not quite as bad as Sir Frederick Treves makes out in *Highways and Byways in Dorset* (1906):

> It is a disappointing village, prim and stiff, with houses mostly of slate and stone, together with many villas of the Brixton and Camberwell type. It is as little rustic as a place on the edge of the Blackmore Vale could be. Its long listless street crowns a modest height above the River Stour.

There are, however, plenty of attractive, old buildings in the local, creamy white limestone, quarried at nearby Todber. Particularly handsome are the village's stone farmhouses, such as **Senior's Farm**, adjacent to the church, which dates from 1500, and **Chantry Farmhouse** (formerly Pope's Farm) on the road to Stalbridge. The **church of St Gregory** is largely 15th-century and its tall tower can be seen from miles around. Within the church is the alabaster figure of a recumbent knight flanked by his two wives, which dates from the

John Constable and the lawyer's wife

The late K J Richards (this is adapted from an article written by my father for a Canadian newspaper, Farm and Country, in which he wrote a regular column on European rural affairs; he was an author, farmer, film director and entrepreneur)

When we first moved to Riversdale Farm in Stour Provost some of the more ancient locals referred to the place as 'Tinney's', yet none of them knew quite why. They were right, a man called John Pern Tinney did once own the farm and John Constable's painting of *Stratford Mill* used to hang above the fireplace. The story I stumbled across played out in a Dorset village tucked away in the Blackmore Vale, and combined the agony and the ecstasy of an artist, the stubborn possessiveness of a house-proud wife and the intermediacy of a wise friend.

Stour Provost consists of a village street, almost unchanged since Constable's time, and a lane leading down to the farm. Tinney, a small town lawyer, had become the proud owner of *Stratford Mill*, now more commonly known as *The Young Waltonians*, in part payment for a law suit that he had successfully undertaken on behalf of John Fisher, Dean of Salisbury Cathedral. Fisher was Constable's closest friend and perhaps the first to realise the genius of the temperamental painter. Many in the Establishment had little time for Constable's landscapes and his canvasses regularly returned unsold from exhibitions. With a family to support he was approaching middle-age increasingly riven and in despair.

The picture must have reached the farm in early summer 1821, for on 19 July Dean Fisher wrote: 'King George IV crowned this day! My dear Constable, your picture is hanging up in a temporary way at Tinney's till his new room is finished. It excites great interest and attention'. For Mrs Tinney, probably no great connoisseuse of the arts, it quickly became the most treasured possession in her home.

Slowly but surely, and in no small measure due to Fisher's patronage, Constable's work began to find recognition and in its exhibition of 1825 the Royal Academy agreed to find a space for one of his larger canvasses. The picture

1470s. Treves (and many other writers) recorded a memorial to parish clerk John Warren, who died in 1752, which is sadly no longer visible:

Here under this stone lie Ruth and old John,
Who smoked all his life and so did his wife,
And now there's no doubt,
But their pipes are both out
Be it said without joke
That life is but smoke
Though you live to fourscore,
'Tis a wiff and no more.

Constable chose to show was *Stratford Mill*, and he wrote to Tinney requesting its loan for the period of the exhibition. Tinney, who had begun to fancy himself as a patron of the arts and had already made offers for further works by the painter, readily agreed, although it can be assumed that Mrs T was more than a little vexed to see her best room denuded of its much-admired decoration. Nevertheless, *Stratford Mill* took the stage to London.

Later that year Constable was approached to give his support to the first exhibition of the newly formed Scottish Academy and again wrote to Tinney asking him to lend the painting for the purpose. This was too much for Mrs T. Quite a few angry words must have been exchanged between the lawyer and his wife in front of the fireplace and this time she prevailed. Sharpening his quill and with his wife's shadow cast from spluttering candles above his shoulders, Tinney penned a letter to Constable, 'With respect to the beautiful picture which is the principal ornament of our house, Mrs Tinney says she will not consent to its being again removed as it was last year for so a long a time ... I hope you will not think her unreasonable.'

Constable did think the lady unreasonable and exploded into an artistic fury that must have shaken his studio to its foundations. His reply to Tinney marked the end of a friendship and the end of the lawyer's brief sway as a collector of contemporary art; Constable cancelled the arrangements under which he had agreed to sell further canvasses to Tinney.

Dean Fisher acted as intermediary and with a series of wise letters calmed the fiery Constable, who eventually accepted, 'My name (though looked for) will not appear at the opening of the noble institution in Edinburgh – I should have liked to have struck a blow in that quarter – but I must submit to circumstances'. Without the calming influence of the dean, Constable would surely have severed an ear, as well as disposed of his reason.

Stratford Mill remained with Tinney for his lifetime and was doubtless the object of minute adjustments and daily dustings by the obstinate Mrs T.

His case would do the anti-smoking lobby no good at all, as he lived to 94 years of age.

Marnhull was reportedly famous for bull-baiting until 1763, when it was banned because of the hooligan behaviour of supporters. The annual contest, held on 3 May, saw bulls brought from the surrounding area but rivalry was so intense it often led to violence, which spread from Marnhull to outlying villages.

Food and drink
The village is well equipped with village shops and 2 pubs.

Blackmore Vale Inn Burton St, DT10 1JJ ℡ 01258 820701
🌐 www.theblackmorevaleinn.co.uk. Fresh home-cooked pub food, including traditional dishes like hommity pie. Open daily for lunch and dinner.
Crown Inn Crown Rd, DT10 1LN ℡ 01258 820224. This thatched, 16th-century pub appeared in Thomas Hardy's writings as 'The Pure Drop Inn' and it oozes history with its chunky beams, wonky walls and original flagstone floor. Popular with locals, the pub gets busy at weekends. Open daily for lunch and dinner.

⑧ Hinton St Mary

As you travel along the B3092 from Marnhull to Sturminster Newton you pass through the village of Hinton St Mary. The best of the village lies away from the main road, towards the River Stour, with cottages built from the local creamy-coloured stone, and a handsome 17th-century manor house. On the river are the remains of **Cut Mill**, sadly burned down by vandals in 2003. The building dated from the 18th century but in the light of a significant archaeological discovery made barely half a mile away it is likely there had been a mill on this site since Roman times. In 1963, a local blacksmith digging a post hole unearthed the mosaic floor of a Roman building, at its centre was an early depiction of what is believed to be the head of Christ. This extraordinary mosaic is now in the British Museum.

Dike and Sons Superstore

Stalbridge ℡ 01963 362204 🌐 www.dikes-direct.co.uk.

Tucked away in the village of Stalbridge is something you don't see very often: a family-run, independent supermarket. This isn't a corner shop with supermarket aspirations, Dikes is large, well-stocked and offers plenty of variety. Despite the presence of the big supermarkets in surrounding towns, Dikes is still a firm favourite with locals and it is a mutually beneficial relationship because the store supports local farmers and small businesses. It has over a hundred local suppliers, meaning food miles are kept to a minimum, and makes its own sandwiches, pizzas and salads. Manager Andrew Dike told me this has given them a huge advantage in recent harsh winters; when heavy snowfalls meant the big supermarkets were unable to replenish their empty shelves, Dikes was still able to source its local produce, and became the place to stock up for Christmas.

The Dike family have had a shop in Stalbridge since 1851 and Andrew represents the fifth generation.

Cut Mill is on a beautiful portion of the River Stour and is popular with fishermen. Just south of the mill the River Divelish joins the Stour. From Cut Mill a pleasant walk leads along the River Stour to Sturminster Newton Mill.

⑨ Sturminster Newton

Sturminster Newton, known to locals as Stur, has been the nucleus of life in the Blackmore Vale for centuries. Although there is much new development on the outskirts of Stur, the town centre, and the market place in particular, is overflowing with a variety of historic buildings and architectural styles, including 17th- and 18th-century thatched cottages, Georgian stone houses and 19th-century brick buildings. **Church Street** and **Tanyard Lane** have some particularly pretty houses. Prominent in the market place are the well-worn stone remains of a 15th-century **market cross**, which was reportedly shaped like a mushroom until 1540 when it was smashed by thieves. A Monday market is held here and features local foods, crafts and clothing.

In a quaint 16th-century thatched building in the town centre is **Sturminster Museum** (*Old Market Cross House; 01258 817116; www.sturminsternewton-museum.co.uk; open Easter–December Mon, Thu, Fri 10.00–15.00, Sat 10.00–12.30, Jan–Mar Mon, Fri, Sat 10.00–12.30; free admission*), where the history of the livestock market and local dairy farming features heavily.

The Station Road livestock market, once the largest in Britain, was central to the vale's important agricultural industry until it closed in 1997. As I grew up in nearby Stour Provost, the Stur Monday market was very much part of my childhood and I recall the sadness that swept the area when it was announced it would close. The historic market had originated from a royal charter of 1219 and there was a fear that Stur would lose its identity when the market was demolished and a seven-acre gaping hole left in the town. However, ten years after the market closed, and thanks to a committed band of locals, **The Exchange** (*01258 475137; www.stur-exchange.co.uk*) opened on the site and its art exhibitions, theatre, cinema and community activities now draw crowds from around the vale just as the market once did. It is an impressive facility for a small country town and the complex in which it stands also houses a much-needed medical centre and shops. Just as the concept of the new community centre was a local one, so was the building of it. The committee engaged an architect from Shaftesbury and a local builder, while Stur's blacksmith, Ian Ring, created the delightful wrought-iron balustrade on the staircase.

At the bottom of town is **Harts of Stur** (*Station Rd, DT10 1BD; 01258 472240; www.hartsofstur.com*), affectionately described by locals as Stur's answer to Harrods. This family-run shop has been operating since 1918 and stocks a huge range of kitchenware, hardware and clothing.

At the southern end of town a handsome six-arched 16th-century stone

Sturminster Newton – a blend of old and new

Jane Williams, owner of Betty's Loft B&B

Stur is a charming little town which honours its history and embraces the future. Newcomers and visitors often remark on the welcoming atmosphere of the town and it is impossible for locals to 'pop in to town quickly' because there are always friends to greet and snippets of news to share.

The old and the new mix well here. The pretty little museum right in the middle of town is fascinating but only a short walk away is a gleaming new hall and arts centre called The Exchange. I love many things about The Exchange. I will always meet somebody I know and perhaps join them in a cuppa while we pick out what we will book from the variety of cinema, theatre and music on the programme. I love the fact that the whole centre *is* an exchange – it's like a bring-and-buy sale of goodwill. Everybody comes with something to offer, whether it's their time, their advice, ideas or energy, and in return they get entertainment, stimulation, a feeling of belonging. To explain how all this came about, I need to go back a few years to the closure of the livestock market.

When a market town loses its market the silence is deafening. Instead of clatter, gossip and laughter there's a gaping hole. In many small country towns, the livestock market is the reason for being. Stur's market bell rang for the last time in 1997. Big blank fences went up and sadness hovered over the site and the town like bereavement. Would Stur go the way of so many small market towns with their empty shops and loss of purpose? Absolutely not! In stepped a group of residents who formed SturQuest, a community group with enormous vision, patience and tenacity. The town was determined to meet the challenge of life after livestock and to be a part of planning its own future.

Ten years to the day after the market closed, and after extraordinary community efforts in lobbying, negotiation and fund-raising, The Exchange opened its doors:

bridge spans the River Stour; a 19th-century plaque warns would-be graffiti artists, 'Any person wilfully injuring any part of this county bridge will be guilty of felony and upon conviction liable to be transported for life'. From the bridge you catch your first glimpses of **Sturminster Mill** (*01747 854355; open Apr–Sep Mon, Thu, Sat & Sun 11.00–17.00*), 250 yards upstream. When the mill is open, volunteers are on hand to show you around, explain its workings and recount its history. The Domesday Book records a mill on this site but the present one dates from the 17th and 19th centuries. Until 1991 it was a working mill, producing flour and animal feed, but now holds just three milling weekends per year.

The River Stour is wide here and it is easy to see why generations of artists, including John Constable, have been inspired to paint the mill. On a summer's day the water seems to drift unhurriedly towards its destination, lilies provide colourful decoration and cows graze nonchalantly in the adjacent fields. The within were a hall for concerts, cinema, theatre and banquets, plus half-a-dozen other rooms and spaces for almost any activity you could wish for, from pannier markets to exercise classes and a gallery and bar.

Within weeks the place was buzzing. I am a therapist, and one wet weeknight in November I remember taking my regular meditation group in a small room there and every other room was booked – there was a family history group, foreign language class, bowls, belly-dancing, a Chamber of Trade meeting and a gallery full of people enjoying an exhibition of sculpture and art. All this, midweek in a country town of 3,500 inhabitants! The venue has not just acted as a replacement for a tired old hall; it has rejuvenated the town, given it another reason for being and encouraged visitors from all over Dorset and beyond.

There is one thing I love above all and that for me captures the spirit of this resilient little town. When the market closed its doors a local farmer managed to retrieve the big market bell complete with signals for cattle, sheep, pigs and so on. He didn't know what he was going to do with it, but among the destruction and chaos he needed to salvage an icon of a treasured way of life. The bell now sits proudly at The Exchange to call theatre-goers in for the start of a performance but was first rung there at its opening ceremony, ten years after it had last rung at the market, by a ten-year-old boy, born on the day the market closed.

It is a joy to be part of this kind of community and that is the key – there is so much to be a part of, to be engaged with. People have been consulted and plans have taken into account how we live here, so things flow.

Newcomers are attracted to the town because of its beautiful setting, snuggled into the Blackmore Vale on the Stour; they travel many a mile to the annual Cheese Festival, celebrating the area's great reputation for quality produce, and they stay because it immediately feels like home.

scene is best appreciated from the fields opposite the mill, which you can reach across the bridge over the weir, and where a footpath leads along the river towards Hinton St Mary in one direction and Fiddleford in the other.

Sturminster Newton is proud of its literary connections. Dorset poet and author William Barnes (see box, page 7) was born just outside Sturminster Newton, was christened in the church of St Mary and went to school in the town. Thomas Hardy lived in the town with his wife Emma while writing *Return of the Native* (1876–78).

The livestock market, dairy farming, button- and candle-making brought great prosperity to the town and surrounding area, particularly from 1863 when the Somerset and Dorset Railway opened and the area's milk, cheese and other produce could be sold further afield. The railway closed in 1966 but parts of it now form the **North Dorset Trailway**, a cycle and footpath which links Sturminster Newton to surrounding villages (see page 2).

Fiddleford Manor

DT10 1HD ① 0117 9750700
Ⓦ www.english-heritage.org.uk.
Open 10.00–16.00, closed bank
holidays; free admission.

This medieval manor a mile
east of Sturminster Newton
on the A357 is one of the
oldest buildings in Dorset. In 1355 it passed through marriage to William
Latimer, later sheriff of Somerset and Dorset. The great hall and solar, which
are open to the public, are thought to have been built for Latimer in around
1370. The arched timber braces of their ceilings are spectacular and give an
impression of what a medieval Dorset house may have been. The riverside
setting is beautiful.

Food and drink

Three years after the closure of the livestock market, Stur suffered another body
blow in 2000: the closure of the Sturminster Creamery, a major employer in the

Olives Et Al

1 North Dorset Business Park, Sturminster Newton DT10 2GA ① 01258 474300
Ⓦ www.olivesetal.co.uk.

Small businesses often have intriguing stories behind them and Olives Et Al is
right up there with the quirkiest that I've heard. When someone told me an ex-
army officer and a former ballerina had set up a company making marinated
olives, I had to find out more.

Giles Henschel came out of the army in 1991 and was living on a houseboat
in London with his new wife, Annie, a former ballerina and flight attendant.
They weren't exactly sure how they were going to earn a living but decided
that a long-overdue 'gap year' was in order. They embarked on a year-long
adventure that would be the inspiration for Olives Et Al, motorbiking through
the Mediterranean, Middle East and North Africa. Giles told me that there was a
common thread – wherever they were offered great local hospitality, they were
offered great local olives. No matter the religion, the political instability or the
standard of living, the olive was ubiquitous, prepared with its own local twist.
They collected recipes from countries as diverse as Spain, Greece, Turkey, Syria
and Libya, and worked on olive plantations as they went.

From what Giles tells me, their return to England brought them down to earth
with a jolt. They had sold everything before they went abroad, and so ended up
sharing a bedsit in Southampton with one of Giles's old army chums. One day
Giles suggested to Annie that rather than spend another evening worrying about

town. It had come into existence in 1913 as the initiative of a co-operative of local farmers, who sought to supply fresh milk and cheddar cheese to the area. Today, Stur's cheese-making history is celebrated via the town's annual **Cheese Festival**, one of the largest in England (*www.cheesefestival.co.uk*).

Fiddleford Inn Fiddleford DT10 2BX ℗ 01258 475612 ⓦ www.thefiddlefordinn. com. A traditional pub on the outskirts of Sturminster Newton serving pub fare at reasonable prices. Open daily 12.00–23.00.

Minsturs Bath Rd, DT10 1AT ℗ 01258 471808 ⓦ www.minsturs.co.uk. Tearooms within an elegant interior design, antique and art shop. Serves a tempting range of homemade cakes and Dorset cream teas. Tea is taken indoors or in the courtyard. Open Mon–Sat 10.00–17.00, Thu until 19.00 and Sun 11.00–15.00.

Plumber Manor DT10 2AF ℗ 01258 472507 ⓦ www.plumbermanor.com. Fine dining in elegant surroundings at this well-respected small hotel. Open for dinner daily and lunch Sun.

⑩ Holwell

Some people may wonder why I've included Holwell – there are three reasons: a church, a post box and a bakery.

the future, they set up their tents, drink wine, eat olives and pretend they were travelling again. Giles's plan was only foiled by the jar of olives he had picked up at the supermarket, which tasted nothing like those they had had on their adventure. It seemed that the only way to get decent olives was to buy them and ferment them themselves. Giles bought olives in bulk and, using the recipes they had collected, fermented them in the only vessel they could find that was large enough – the bath. Friends, even those who claimed they had never liked olives, raved about them and persuaded Giles and Annie they should sell them. They took a batch to a rural living show in Bath in 1993 and sold out. Within a year, Giles and Annie were selling olives via mail order and producing them for a large London retailer.

Today they marinate over 1½ million olives per week and the Olives Et Al range has grown to include oils, marinades, dukkahs, kiln-roasted nuts and other snacks. They remain true to the lessons they learnt on their travels: use the finest ingredients, tried and tested methods and no artificial colours, flavourings or preservatives. The olives are naturally ripened, come from trusted olive farmers, and are brought back to Dorset to be fermented. As Giles pointed out, 'it takes time, care and attention to produce a good quality product' and while the recipes may be exotic, Dorset know-how is at the heart of this business.

You will see Olives Et Al products in farm shops and delis throughout the West Country. They also have a shop at their headquarters on the edge of Sturminster Newton and a café/deli at Poundbury called The Potting Shed (see page 68).

Dorset Blue Vinny cheese

Woodbridge Farm, Stock Gaylard DT10 2BD ☏ 01963 23133
Ⓦ www.dorsetblue.com.

Dorset has many fine food traditions and one of the best known is Dorset Blue Vinny cheese. The Davies family makes this unpasteurised farmhouse cheese at their farm just outside Sturminster Newton, along with a range of fresh soups.

There was a time when the manufacture of Dorset Blue Vinny cheese was virtually ubiquitous throughout the county's farmhouses. It was a by-product of butter-making, using the milk after the cream had been skimmed off.

The production of Dorset Blue Vinny ceased with the introduction of the Milk Marketing Board, as the farmer's wife was no longer able to set aside milk for making cheese. Michael Davies revived the tradition in the 1980s. During the time of milk lakes and butter mountains, Michael began to question his commitment to early mornings and milking; he had originally trained as a cheese maker and thought it might be time to put those skills to use. According to his daughter Emily, 'he was truly one of the first to diversify and value-add – the buzzwords of today'. The family produced its first Dorset Blue Vinny in 1982, matured in the farmhouse pantry; it turned the walls, cornflakes and marmalade blue.

The 24-hour process of making this cheese begins with the milk from their herd of Friesian cows, which graze the lush pastures of the Blackmore Vale. Once the milk has been brought up to temperature they hand-skim the cream from the milk, then add skimmed milk powder to raise the fat content back up to give it a creamy, subtle character. A penicillin promotes the blueing of the cheese. Once the milk has hardened, it is cut into small pieces and left overnight. The resulting whey is drained off and the curd cut into blocks, ground, salted and packed into moulds. After a few days, the moulds are transferred to the ripening room where they stay for between three and five months, and are turned and spiked according to whether the blue needs to develop.

Holwell isn't a particularly pretty village and it's very spread out; divided into two halves, one part medieval and the other, known as Barnes Cross, mostly 19th century. Its layout is not conducive to a sense of community, one resident told me 'if you want a social life, don't live in Holwell'.

The **church of St Lawrence** is in the older part of the village, down a dead-end lane lined with Holwell's most appealing houses. It is largely 15th century and outside it are an unwelcoming set of stocks. The church is usually only open on service days but I was lucky enough to visit when the warden was mowing the graveyard. He let me into the church and we got chatting; it turned out he was my old school bursar – Dorset is a small place. He explained that the churchyard is a nature reserve; he only mows a narrow path through the graveyard because churchyard seed beds can be up to 600 years old and leaving the grass wild supports the local ecology. Many other Dorset churches are now treating their churchyards similarly. Inside the church I found a delightful, authoritative, historic wall hanging entitled 'A table of kindred and affinity'. A handy document, it provides clear guidelines as to which relatives one should not marry. There are two lists, one for men and one for women, and I was relieved to see that 'grandmother' topped the list for men but surprised that mother came in at number ten, below wife's mother's sister!

Tucked away on a quiet lane, bashfully shunning the fame its title could bestow, is the oldest Royal Mail **pillar box** in use in Britain. Made between 1853 and 1856, it is cast with Queen Victoria's cipher and the tiny letter slot is vertical. The box is at the Barnes Cross end of the village, not far from the turning to the church, outside Barnes Cross Cottage.

Food and drink

Bee Shack Naish Farm DT9 5LJ ℡ 01963 23597. ⓦ www.honeybuns.co.uk. The rustic café of the Honeybuns Bakery (where Emma Goss-Custard bakes superb cakes using locally sourced ingredients) serves tasty treats, many of which are gluten-free, and light lunches in informal surroundings in the farm's former chicken shed. All proceeds from the café are used in their BeeGreen project – building nest boxes and bat boxes, tree planting, team veggie plot & polytunnel, hedge laying and improving the nature reserve. Children can explore the nature reserve or meet Freddie, their very friendly Shetland pony. Open from 11.00 to 16.00 on the first Sat of each month between Apr and Dec.

⑪ Hazlebury Bryan

This very scattered and confusing village consists of seven tiny hamlets, each with its own name. Hazlebury Bryan is one of those deliciously descriptive Dorset village names, so it is rather deflating to learn that the older part of the village, including the church, lies in the area known as Droop. The **church of St Mary and St James** is charming, a simple golden stone building by a large pond. It is of mainly 15th-century construction; the wooden door and wagon roof date from that period, and are well preserved.

The **Red Barn Village Stores and Post Office** (*01258 818303; open daily*) is a handy resource for the community, stocking an eclectic mixture of grocery, deli, bakery and household goods. Fresh fish can be ordered and there is a post office service on Monday mornings.

Some 150 yards from Thyme after Time farm shop and café is the 35-acre **Alners Gorse Butterfly Reserve**, one of Dorset's few remaining areas of common land and open to visitors on foot. The area of wet grassland, scrub and woodland is being restored after years of neglect, and is grazed by Fell ponies. It supports an important population of butterflies and moths; the Blackmore Vale is the only area of Dorset where the brown hairstreak is found; other species you may see include grizzled skipper, silver-washed fritillary and white admiral.

Food and drink

Thyme after Time Woodrow Dairy DT10 2AH ⓣ 01258 818004
Ⓦ www.thymeaftertime.co.uk. Bubbly Dorset lady, Margot Annelle Finlay, has
put her heart and soul into her super little farm shop and café, where she also
operates a catering business. The café has a genuinely homely feel; even the
plates were hand-painted by her family. She buys local ingredients and turns
them into tasty cakes, pies, jams, chutneys and cordials, and offers a good choice
of light lunches, all served in generous (farmer) portions. Margot's motto is
'Dorset born, Dorset fed', a twist on the saying 'Dorset born, Dorset bred, strong
in the arm, thick in the head'. Local artwork and books on Dorset are on sale. Open
Tue–Fri 09.00–16.30, Sat 10.00–13.00.

⑫ Blandford Forum

Blandford is hailed as one of the finest Georgian rural market towns in
England, and occupies an enviable position in a wooded valley on the banks
of the River Stour. Much of the original town was destroyed by a devastating
fire in 1731, which began in a tallow chandler's (candle maker's) shop on
the site now occupied by the Kings Arms. Over 450 people lost their homes
and at least 14 townsfolk died; the town museum (see opposite) has a useful
model showing the extent of the damage. Memorably named local architects
and builders John and William Bastard were engaged to design and rebuild
the town: the elegant, coherent Georgian town centre is the
result. Its uniformity gives it a very different feel to other
Dorset towns.

The **church of St Peter and St Paul** (*open Mon–Fri
09.30–12.00*) dominates the town centre, a simple,
classical building built on the site of its
medieval predecessor. Ironically, its most
recognisable feature, the wooden cupola
on its tower was not part of the original
design. The Bastard brothers intended
a steeple to be built but apparently
the money ran out and they had to
make do with the cupola, which was added
in 1758. By all accounts, the Bastard brothers were not impressed with this
deviation from their plan. The interior is unashamedly grand, with Portland
stone columns supporting a vaulted ceiling. The ornately carved wooden
Mayor's Chair was made in 1748.

In front of the church is the **Fire Monument** designed by John Bastard and
dated 1760, known as the Bastard's Pump. It was intended to provide water for
fire fighting in the event of a further fire. The inscription acknowledges, with
just a touch of hyperbole, 'the divine mercy that has since raised this town, like
the Phoenix from its ashes to its present beautiful and flourishing state'. John
Bastard signs himself off as 'a considerable sharer in the great calamity'.

Opposite the church, marked with a plaque, is the house that was built for John and William Bastard following the fire. Along with the Town Hall and the former Greyhound Inn (with a hare and a hound painted above the entrance), it is one of the town's finest buildings. A few buildings survived the fire, including the Ryves Almshouses of 1682 in Salisbury Street and the Old House of 1660 in The Close. Most of East Street escaped unscathed as it had been rebuilt in brick after an earlier fire in 1713.

Today's Blandfordians can see the lighter side of the 'calamity': a paving stone in front of the Town Hall bears the inscription, 'Recipe for regeneration: take one careless tallow chandler and two ingenious Bastards', words drafted by the Blandford poetry group for the Millennium project.

The Georgian market place comes into its own on Thursdays and Saturdays, when it hosts a bustling food and bric-a-brac market. Blandford is justifiably proud of its Georgian heritage and a **Georgian Fayre** (*01258 480333; www.georgianfayre.co.uk*) is held on the May Day Bank Holiday every other year in the town centre, when people dress in period costume and enjoy cultural presentations, stalls and a funfair.

Blandford has strong military links, with Blandford Camp lying just outside the town. Guided tours of Blandford Forum are organised in the summer months by the Blandford and District Civic Society, and can be booked via the Blandford Tourist Information Centre.

Blandford Town Museum

Beres Yard, Market Pl, DT11 7HQ ① 01258 450388 Ⓦ www.blandfordtownmuseum.org. Open Apr–Sep Mon–Sat 11.00–17.00, closing an hour earlier Oct–Apr; free admission.

The assistant curator of this outstanding local museum, Jack Greaves, told me 'we have just about everything, from palaeontology to music'. Particularly interesting is the model of the town following the fire of 1731, clearly showing the devastation caused and the few areas which survived. More unusual exhibits include a reproduction of the 19th-century forge used to service the local Portman Hunt horses, and a cobbler's shop. Behind the museum is a small Victorian garden; the shop sells plants grown there, along with honey products from bees kept by one of the museum staff. A dedicated team of volunteers keeps the museum running and as Jack said, 'they restore your faith in human beings after all the bad things that are happening in the world'.

Jack also pointed out to me the metal doors on the outside of the building. In 1788 a band of smugglers was apprehended near Sixpenny Handley and their loot taken to Blandford and put into an excise store. The following night some unsavoury characters broke into the store, grabbed the tea and liquor and rode through the town handing it out to the townspeople.

The Blandford Fashion Museum

Lime Tree House, The Plocks, DT11 7AA ① 01258 453006
Ⓦ www.theblandfordfashionmuseum.co.u. Open Mon, Thu–Sat.

Within an attractive red-brick house, the costume collection dates from the 1730s to the 1970s and was begun by the late Betty Penny MBE. There is a resources room for students studying fashion and textiles, a tearoom and a small shop, while enthusiastic volunteers are on hand to show you around.

Hall and Woodhouse Brewery

The Brewery, Blandford St Mary DT11 9LS ① 01258 486004 ⓦ www.hall-woodhouse. co.uk. Tours Jan–Nov Mon, Tue, Thu–Sat 11.00.

The badger logo of the Hall and Woodhouse Brewery is a familiar sight around Dorset, as are its quirkily named beers, among them Fursty Ferret, Pickled Partridge and Poacher's Choice (all sold under the name Badger rather than Hall and Woodhouse).

Hall and Woodhouse is run by the fifth generation of the Woodhouse family and has a formidable history. A Dorset farmer, Charles Hall, founded a brewery at Ansty in 1777, providing beer to the troops during the Napoleonic Wars. In 1847 Robert Hall, the founder's son, went into partnership with George Woodhouse. The badger was adopted as the brewery's trademark in 1875 and in 1899 the brewery moved to its present site, where it has been brewing ever since. It has developed into a successful independent brewery with a network of 240 pubs across the south of England. In 2011, in order to keep pace with its own growth, the company began building a new brewery adjacent to the one it has been using for over a hundred years.

The visitor centre tells the story of the brewery and guided tours are available, ending with a tasting. I enjoyed a tour of the brewery with head brewer, Toby Heasman. It was an assignment for which I felt particularly under-qualified as I have never been a beer drinker; in fact I can barely tolerate the smell of it. The tour turned out to be an experience full of surprises and lessons learned.

Firstly, Toby didn't fit my image of a head brewer at all; I had envisioned a short, round, balding chap in overalls but I was greeted by a tall, slim, dapper gentleman in his early thirties, wearing chinos and a tweed jacket, who told me he had a degree in brewing and had studied for a further five years to become a master brewer. I was fascinated by the highly complex process and the antique machinery that is still in use in some sections of the brewery. Many of the techniques used here have barely changed over the past 250 years, and the water has been supplied by the same wells since 1899.

The family-company culture is delightfully evident throughout the brewery, and a roll of long service shows an amazing number of local people who have been with the company for over 30, and even 40, years. This is just as well for Toby because one of the earlier Woodhouses coined the company motto 'never trust a thin brewer' and Toby has a fair way to go before he acquires a trustworthy shape.

Needless to say, I was a little apprehensive when tasting time came but even I, with a totally uneducated beer palette, could discern the subtle differences between the beers (with a few hints from the experts).

Shepherds' huts

Shepherds' huts are making a comeback. These wheeled huts are thought to have been used to shelter farm workers in fields around England since the 16th century. The huts typically contained a small stove, a straw bed over a cage where lambs could be kept and a basic medicine cupboard with a range of potions to treat both shepherd and sheep.

Today, people are buying them to use as garden decorations, artist studios, children's cubby houses or guest accommodation. Alf Wallis of Stour Provost (*01747 838783*) carefully crafts shepherds' huts as they would have been made many years ago but with a touch of luxury. They are encased in tin on the outside and the interior is lined with wood, they have dainty windows and the layout can be tailored to the buyer's requirements.

A well-stocked shop on site sells Hall and Woodhouse beer, plus wine and soft drinks. You can sample the brewery's Badger beers in the numerous Hall and Woodhouse pubs dotted around Dorset.

The Royal Signals Museum

Blandford DT11 8RH ℗ 01258 482248 Ⓦ www.royalsignalsmuseum.com. Open Mon–Fri 10.00–17.00 all year and Sat–Sun Feb–Oct 10.00–16.00.

This high-tech, interactive museum tells the story of military communications through the ages. It lies within Blandford Camp Military Base, two miles northeast of Blandford Forum. Fascinating displays on codes and code-breaking include the story of the Special Operations Executive (SOE) in World War II and the ENIGMA cipher machine, while exhibits on courageous female spies who assisted the Allied Forces in World War II, such as Violette Szabo and Odette, prove how true was that era's warning poster 'Keep mum, she's not so dumb'. Motorcycle enthusiasts will enjoy the collection of military motorcycles from 1914 to the present; also look out for the exhibit on the role of animals in war.

Food and drink

Crown Hotel West St, DT11 7AJ ℗ 01258 456626. A Hall and Woodhouse pub within a large Georgian red-brick building at the far western end of the market place. The restaurant and beer garden are nicely laid out and the food is of a good standard.

Georgian Tea Room 7 Georgian Passage, East St, DT11 7DX ℗ 01258 450307. A small café serving reasonably priced cakes and light lunches. Open Mon–Sat 09.00–16.30.

Half Crown Café 9 Market Pl, DT11 7AF ℗ 01258 459293. In the centre of town. Serves light lunches and locally made cakes. Open Mon–Sat.

⑬ Stourpaine

The busy A350 runs through the village of Stourpaine but there are some attractive, quiet spots away from the road, in particular near the Holy Trinity Church. Here you will find dainty cottages, some thatched, with flower-filled gardens; the smell of roses and other flowers hangs in the air on a summer's day. Just north of the church is a crossroads; the turning to the left leads to the **Trailway**, a foot, cycle and bridle path which runs to Shillingstone (2½ miles) and Sturminster Newton (5½ miles). To the right of the Trailway is a track leading to a footpath running through woodland beside the River Stour and up onto Hod Hill.

In 2010, Stourpaine suffered a loss that has been felt by many villages around the country – its post office and village shop closed. A year later, thanks to village spirit and 'The Pub is the Hub', they re-opened at the White Horse pub on the main road. The Pub is the Hub (*www.pubisthehub.org.uk*) is a scheme initiated in 2001 by Prince Charles, champion of preserving rural ways of life; his venture encourages local people, breweries and pub owners to provide essential services, like a village shop, within rural pubs.

Stourpaine did just that and villagers now have access to a well-stocked little shop and a postal counter open two days a week, rather than having to travel into Blandford. The shopkeeper told me locals are very supportive of the shop and it has breathed new life into the community. A letter from the Prince of Wales's office in support of the move has pride of place on the wall of the shop, and in May 2011 Prince Charles and the Duchess of Cornwall visited the White Horse to see the changes for themselves.

The Great Dorset Steam Fair

Tarrant Hinton ℗ 01258 860361
Ⓦ www.gdsf.co.uk.

From modest beginnings in 1968, the Great Dorset Steam Fair has grown into the largest steam and vintage fair in the world, attracting over 200,000 visitors over five days. It is held on a 600-acre site just outside the village of Tarrant Hinton, near Blandford Forum.

The focus is heritage machinery: 200 working steam engines are on display, some of them hard at work sawing wood, hauling loads or driving ploughs and threshing machines. You can also expect classic cars, military vehicles, tractors, heavy horses, and country crafts and pursuits in addition to the steam-driven funfair and a huge modern one.

Food and drink

White Horse Shaston Rd, TQ1 4TS ℗ 01258 453535. A popular pub on the main
A350, which serves traditional food and local beers. There is a village shop at one
end. Open daily for lunch and dinner.

⑭ Child Okeford

Child Okeford is a large, scattered village with some good 18th- and 19th-
century houses and farm buildings, and several modern housing developments
on the outskirts. Its principle attraction is that it lies in the shadow of
Hambledon Hill and is a good starting point for walks up it to view the Iron
Age hillfort on the summit.

In the 1560s the village vicar, William Kethe, composed the well-known
hymn, *The Old Hundredth* ('All People that on Earth do Dwell'). A Bible from
his era (1568) is on display in the church, although the church would have
looked rather different in his day; while the tower is 15th century, the rest dates
from the mid-1800s.

Gold Hill Organic Farm

DT11 8HB ℗ 01258 861916 Ⓦ www.goldhillorganicfarm.com. Open Wed–Sat 10.00–
16.00, Sun 10.00–14.00.

Gold Hill was one of the first organic farms in Dorset, started over 25 years
ago. The farm shop sells an inviting variety of organic meat, dairy products and
vegetables, which are picked the same morning. Some of the farm buildings
have been converted to house local businesses and it has developed into a small
complex with arty shops and a café, and regularly hosts travelling markets.

The **Cake Tin** (*01258 861119*) serves café food and patisserie in a casual
setting within the farmyard, with many of the ingredients coming from the
farm. **The Art Stable** (*01258 863866; www.theartstable.co.uk*) specialises
in contemporary and modern British paintings, prints and sculpture. **Meg
Morton Interiors** (*07952 089075; www.mortoninteriors.co.uk*) sells French-
inspired furniture.

⑮ Hod Hill

Hod Hill (owned by the National Trust; free access) stands unassumingly
beside its more celebrated neighbour, Hambledon Hill, yet Hod's hillfort is
larger: 54 acres versus Hambledon's 30. Its multiple ramparts protected an Iron
Age village of over 250 roundhouses, the footprints of many of which are still
visible as depressions in the ground. The Romans, led by Vespasian, captured
the Celtic settlement of the Durotriges tribe around AD44 and built their own
camp in the northwest corner. By that stage, they had already taken Maiden
Castle, near Dorchester.

There is a small car parking area at the base of Hod Hill; to reach it take the
Child Okeford and Hanford turning from the A350. Several paths begin here;
one leads through woodland and along the River Stour to Stourpaine, while

a bridleway leads to the top of Hod Hill. A steep walk up rewards you with glorious views of the surrounding countryside and a fabulous archaeological juxtaposition: the rigid lines of the Roman fort and the softer, more organic ones of the earlier settlement; a fine place to contemplate life for the original inhabitants when they saw the mighty Roman army advancing across the countryside. These days it is remarkably peaceful on top of the hill, the only sound is the breeze and the occasional shriek of a buzzard circling over the vale, while livestock graze nonchalantly, oblivious of the many layers of history beneath them.

Hod Hill is a rich chalk grassland site with a colourful carpet of wildflowers. Cowslips are prolific in spring, followed by milkwort, horseshoe vetch, rock rose and common spotted orchids. It is a popular butterfly-watching spot thanks to its populations of Adonis blue, chalkhill blue, marsh fritillary and grizzled skipper.

⑯ Hambledon Hill

The view from Hambledon Hill is one to soothe the soul and replenish the energy stores, which is just as well as the walk to the summit is one to tire the legs. The hill juts out into the Blackmore Vale, providing a natural viewing platform over the tapestry of small fields and villages.

Archaeologists flock to Hambledon Hill – although its earliest occupation was Neolithic, it is best known as an Iron Age hillfort. The site seems to have been abandoned around 300BC, possibly in favour of nearby Hod Hill. When I was walking on Hambledon Hill recently, photographing the view towards Shaftesbury, a group of archaeologists on a guided tour came up behind me and I heard several shrieks of excitement. It was the end of a particularly hot and dry spell and the weather had exposed the outline of a Neolithic enclosure, which even the tour leader had never seen before.

Hambledon Hill is where the Dorset Clubmen were routed by Cromwell in 1645 during the Civil War. Armed only with clubs, about 2,000–4,000 farmers and yeomen banded together to protest at the plundering by the armies traversing Dorset. They were not in favour of either the king or the parliament, they had simply lost patience with troops from both sides trampling their crops, stealing their livestock and ransacking their barns. Their motto made their grievance clear:

If ye offer to plunder or take our cattle, be assured we'll give you battle.

Cromwell attacked with a thousand men; a dozen farmers were killed and some 300 taken prisoner in Iwerne Courtney Church, where Cromwell rebuked them before releasing them.

Of various starting points for walks up Hambledon Hill, a particularly good one is from just behind the Cricketers pub in **Iwerne Courtney** (also known as Shroton) because of the promise of a hearty meal on your return.

Food and drink

The Cricketers Main St, Iwerne Courtney (Shroton), Blandford Forum
① 01258 860421 Ⓦ www.thecricketersshroton.co.uk. A popular family-run
pub, opposite the village green and backing onto Hambledon Hill – the perfect
spot from which to explore this huge prehistoric hillfort. A good selection of
traditional pub food, with daily deliveries of fresh fish, meat and local produce.

Cranborne Chase

The B3081 from Shaftesbury takes you up onto the hills of the Cranborne
Chase for sweeping panoramas of the Dorset and Wiltshire countryside. **Win
Green** (National Trust) lies just over the Wiltshire border; it is the highest
point in the Cranborne Chase and draws an assortment of walkers, model
aircraft enthusiasts and kite-flyers. The hill is crowned by a clump of trees
growing on a Bronze Age bowl barrow.

Cranborne Chase was once a royal hunting ground, hence the 'Chase' part
of the name, and originally covered the area between Shaftesbury, Salisbury,
Ringwood, Wimborne and Blandford Forum. An impressive line-up of
monarchs hunted here, including King John, Henry VIII and James I. In those
days much of the area would have been wooded but today it is characterised
by open downland with pockets of woodland. The land remained in royal
ownership until James I handed the estate to Robert Cecil, First Earl of
Salisbury and the royal hunting lodge became Cranborne Manor, which
remains at the heart of the estate. In the 18th century, the chase's remoteness
attracted smugglers, who hid contraband here.

The unspoilt Cranborne Chase draws walkers, cyclists and horse riders, as
well as archaeologists, who come in search of the **Dorset Cursus**, a Neolithic
cursus monument spanning 6¼ miles of chalk downland. A cursus consists of
large, parallel linear banks with external ditches, perhaps used as a processional
route or as part of ceremonial competitions. The Dorset Cursus, the longest
known example of its kind, crosses a river and three valleys, and runs close to
Knowlton and its Neolithic henge topped with the ruins of a medieval church
(see page 45).

En route to the village of Cranborne from Shaftesbury the road sneaks briefly
into Wiltshire again around Tollard Royal and the Rushmore Estate. This well-
managed estate incorporates a popular golf course, preparatory school and the
Larmer Tree Gardens (*Tollard Royal, Wiltshire SP5 5PT; 01725 516971; www.
larmertreegardens.co.uk*). Opening times for the garden vary; a popular music
festival is held here every July (*www.larmertreefestival.co.uk*).

⑰ Fontmell and Melbury Downs

The unclassified upper Blandford road from Shaftesbury takes you through
the village of **Melbury Abbas** and up onto Fontmell and Melbury Downs,

which open up before you in a burst of bucolic beauty. The quintessentially English rolling hills with patches of woodland provide inspiring views and walks on the western edge of the Cranborne Chase. Many locals escape here to walk the dog, or just admire the scenery.

At 720 acres, Fontmell and Melbury Downs is the National Trust's largest chalk downland site, and in summer the area is awash with wildflowers, birdlife and butterflies, including the Adonis blue and chalkhill blue. Access to the walks above Melbury Abbas is from small car parks on Spread Eagle Hill; take care along this road as visibility is poor and traffic moves at high speeds. It is an easy, mostly level walk of three miles along the hill top to **Melbury Beacon**, erected in 1588 to warn of the invading Spanish Armada. The walk skirts around the edge of the Blackmore Vale, providing far-reaching views across the fields and villages. Buzzards can often be seen drifting on the currents that swirl around the bowl formed by the hills, and skylarks provide a tuneful accompaniment to a walk. On the opposite side of the road, another walk leads along the base of Melbury Down, with Compton Abbas Airfield on the hilltop above.

The Dorset Wildlife Trust manages 148 acres on **Fontmell Down**, above the village of Fontmell Magna. A variety of wildflower species grow here, including nine different orchids and the rare early gentian, while 35 species of butterfly have been recorded on the reserve. Glow worms are plentiful in summer and winged residents include sparrowhawks, green woodpeckers and yellowhammers. Evidence of Bronze Age habitation is visible in the form of two cross dykes, which were probably used as territorial boundary markers. On the flatter land on top of Fontmell Down are traces of a Bronze Age field system, most easily seen when the sun is low in the evening.

⑱ Ashmore

As you enter Ashmore, the highest village in Dorset, you might feel transported back to an earlier era. It is a tiny village, with 17th- and 18th-century stone houses huddled around a village pond, which some believe is of Roman origin.

One of the major problems for hilltop settlements like Ashmore was that of water supply. The chalk drained the water away, so to preserve water the hilltop settlers dug 'dew ponds' and lined them with clay to retain water. Ashmore's **dew pond** is one of the few remaining in the area. It rarely dries out but when it does tradition has it that villagers bake cakes and eat them in its bed. The farmers haul out the hundreds of cartloads of silt that have accumulated on the bottom, and lay them on their land.

The pond is the venue for the village's annual **Filly Loo** festival, held to celebrate the summer solstice. This is rural tradition at its best: a Green Man kicks off the dancing to folk music, which continues throughout the evening. At dusk the celebrations reach their climax with the 700-year-old Abbots Bromley Horn Dance. This is a torchlit procession with six men wearing antlers and four other colourful costumed characters: Maid Marion, a bowman, a hobbyhorse and a fool. It is accompanied by a haunting solo flute melody. The celebration finishes with everyone joining hands around the pond for a final torchlit dance.

Food and drink

Compton Abbas Airfield SP5 5AP ① 01747 811767. An informal café and restaurant with indoor and outdoor seating overlooking the runway and with superb countryside views. Open daily 09.30–17.00.

⑲ Compton Abbas Airfield

Ashmore SP5 5AP ① 01747 811767 Ⓦ www.abbasair.com. Open daily.
This family-run grass airfield is near Ashmore, high on Spread Eagle Hill, overlooking Shaftesbury. It has a tremendous sense of community and a very welcoming atmosphere, and houses almost 50 aircraft, many of which are owned by syndicates made up of local people. It was first utilised as an airfield in 1960 by the farmer who owned the land; he used it to fly his Tiger Moth and then opened the runway up to others. The current owners bought the site in 1988 and the airfield is now managed by their two young, accomplished daughters, Laura and Emma Hughes.

The light-aircraft experience flights and trial flying lessons are an unforgettable way to see the South West's countryside, and you will usually get a chance to take the controls. For a bit of nostalgia, you can take a flight in the resident Tiger Moth and, if you get a taste for flying, you can study for your pilot's licence here. Film-maker Guy Ritchie, who owns an estate nearby, is one of the airfield's alumni. If you don't fancy taking to the skies, watching the light aircraft from the airfield restaurant is a very enjoyable way to spend a couple of lazy hours. The outdoor seating is right beside the grass runway and there are far-reaching views across to Shaftesbury and beyond.

⑳ Sixpenny Handley

The name of this village is derived from two medieval 'hundreds', 'Sexpena' and 'Hanlega'. Over the years, local folk and the highways authority have reduced it to the memorable 6d Handley, and it sometimes appears on signposts as that.

It is a large village with considerable new development. Although some older buildings remain, including the 13th-century church, much of the village was destroyed by fire in 1892. It is an active community with all the ingredients that keep a village alive: a pub, village shop and thriving, local butcher. There is more to the village shop than you might expect: it is also a post office and tearooms.

John Clarke who runs **W S Clarke** (*55 High St, SP5 5ND; 01725 552328*) is the fourth generation of his family to run this butcher's shop. Unusually it still has an abattoir at the back of the shop.

Food and drink

Roebuck Inn 22 High St, SP5 5NR ① 01725 552002. A red-brick building in the centre of the village. The landlord of the Roebuck Inn told me he recognises its important role in serving the community; it holds a popular quiz on Sunday afternoons and serves take-away fish and chips on Friday nights.

Sixpenny Handley Village Shop 24 High St, SP5 5ND ① 01725 552241. The village shop houses a small tearoom serving homemade cakes.

㉑ Cranborne Estate and Cranborne village

The seemingly endless acres of fertile farmland and woodland that you see in this area have been the property of just one family since the early 1600s, when the lordship of Cranborne was granted to Sir Robert Cecil, later the first Earl of Salisbury. At the heart of the estate is Cranborne Manor, the home of the current Viscount Cranborne, the eldest son of the Seventh Marquis of Salisbury.

Adjacent to the manor is the village of Cranborne, where (unusually for Dorset) most of the buildings are brick. The village is centred around an attractive square; in 1748, a fire destroyed many of the older buildings – the north side is 18th century and the south side Edwardian. Cottages with doors painted in the ubiquitous Cranborne blue colour belong to the estate. At the superb **Cranborne Village Stores** (*1 The Square, BH21 5PR; 01725 517210*) you can buy game and rare-breed meat from the estate, while locals catch up on gossip.

The predominance of red brick belies Cranborne's true age. The village, which lies on a winterborne (a stream which flows only in winter) called the Crane, dates from Saxon times. There was a Benedictine Abbey here from circa AD980 until the Dissolution of the Monasteries in 1539. Until the 18th century Cranborne was a thriving market town on the main route from Salisbury to Poole but in the 1750s the Great Western Turnpike from Salisbury to Blandford was built, bypassing Cranborne, and its trade declined. Thomas Hardy described it as 'a decayed market town' but it has a pleasant feel today and is unmistakably an estate village.

The **church of St Mary and St Bartholomew** dates from the 12th century; the faded wall-paintings are 14th century and the tower 15th century. On the wall a memorial commissioned by Lady Norton for her grandson, John Elliot, features a statue of a boy with a skull on his knee. According to the inscription he was a very promising boy who had made 'an almost supernatural progress' in his studies, and who died suddenly at school on 2 February 1641; reputedly he died by choking on a fish bone.

Cranborne Manor Garden

BH21 5PP ℗ 01725 517248 ℗ www.cranborne.co.uk. Open Mar–Sep Wed 09.00–17.00.
A quintessentially English formal garden surrounds the manor house (which is not open to the public). One of Dorset's finest, it was partly laid out by 17th-century gardener John Tradescant, and more recently it owes its splendour to Lady Salisbury, also a noted gardener. The walled garden and yew hedges are particularly fine, and there is a rather fun Sundial Garden, where a sundial stands sentinel on a mound surrounded by parterres. Various statues and sculptures catch the eye as you wander, and the garden runs down to the River Crane, a winterborne, where a mass of spring bulbs flower in April and May.

On site are a well-stocked garden centre, a shop and a good café.

Food and drink

La Fosse London House, The Square, BH21 5PR ℗ 01725 517604. A small restaurant which punches above its weight, serving excellent, creative British dishes made using locally sourced ingredients. Open Mon, Fri, Sat dinner and Sun lunch.
Mary's Tearoom Cranborne Garden Centre BH21 5PP ℗ 01725 517248. A pleasant, informal café within the attractive walled garden that houses the garden centre. Light lunch options include some of the speciality meats from the Cranborne Estate and ingredients from the manor garden. Open daily.

㉒ Edmonsham House

Edmonsham BH21 5RE ℗ 01725 517207. House open Apr–Oct Wed afternoon, Easter Sun and bank holidays; garden is also open Sun afternoons during the same period.
The owner, Julia Smith, gives guided tours of her home, an Elizabethan building with Georgian extensions. The six acres of attractive grounds are typical of a country house of this size, with colourful herbaceous borders and a fine walled garden. An unusual feature lies within the grounds – the site of a **medieval cock-fighting pit**. The grand Victorian stable block will be the envy of most horse owners and the octagonal Victorian dairy is built over an underground stream, with louvered windows in order to keep it cool.

Dorset Heavy Horse Farm Park and Rescue Centre

Edmonsham, near Verwood BH21 5RJ ℗ 01202 824040 ℗ www.dorset-heavy-horse-centre.co.uk. Open Apr–Oct daily 10.00–17.00.
The centre does valuable work caring for heavy horses in need: wonderful creatures, they really are gentle giants. At the other end of the scale, there are miniature ponies as well as kunie kunie pigs, alpacas, sheep and goats. Before you visit, check the daily schedule on the website; there is plenty to entertain the children, including wagon rides, pony rides, pony grooming, rabbit and guinea pig handling, and feeding the farm animals.

㉓ Hare Lane Pottery

Hare Lane, near Cranborne BH21 5QT ℡ 01725 517700 ⓦ www.jonathangarratt.com.

On the B3078 between Cranborne and Alderholt are the thatched cottage and farm buildings where Jonathan Garratt creates wood-fired earthenware pots for houses and gardens. Jonathan takes a truly Slow approach to his art, stripping the process right back to basics. A local farmer delivers freshly dug clay from his farm, which is just one mile from the pottery. Jonathan then carefully cleans and rolls the clay by hand to filter out impurities and prepare it for use. It is a laborious process but he explained to me that you simply cannot buy clay like it. He sculpts the clay to create his unusual pieces and then fires them in the African-style wood kiln he built himself in one of his barns.

Jonathan's wife, Trisha, showed me the very simple but effective equipment Jonathan uses for the process, describing the set up as 'utterly Heath Robinson'. It certainly seems to be, but produces some striking pots, many of which are highly sculptural. His designs are inspired by prehistoric and traditional pots from Europe, West Africa and the Far East. Trisha explained that some of these influences can be traced to Jonathan's early life: he spent the first two years of his life in Africa, where his parents were working, and later studied ceramics while a schoolboy at Eton and read archaeology at Cambridge. Jonathan's creations are dotted in a higgledy-piggledy fashion around the 18th-century farmyard, amidst a colourful array of plants. Wood-fired earthenware was once common throughout Europe but is now very rare; the pots are distinctive and personal, unlike anything you will see on the high street.

㉔ Moors Valley Country Park and Forest

Horton Rd, Ashley Heath BH24 2ET ℡ 01425 470721 ⓦ www.moors-valley.co.uk. Open 08.00–dusk; free admission but car parking is charged.

This 1,000 acres of forest, woodland, grassland, heath and lakes is run as a countryside recreation facility and is a joint venture between East Dorset District Council and the Forestry Commission. It is home to plentiful wildlife but the emphasis is on family fun: you can walk, cycle (bike hire is on site) or catch a narrow-gauge steam train around the park, while more adventurous activities include a high-ropes course, orienteering, segway and an 18-hole golf course. Coarse fishing is available from June to March; you can buy a day ticket or season ticket from the visitor centre, anyone over 12 years of age will need to show a valid Environment Agency rod licence. Wheelchair access is good, and dogs are allowed. You can take a picnic or use the restaurant.

㉕ Wimborne St Giles

This small, peaceful community is the estate village at the centre of the Earl of Shaftesbury's 9,000-acre landholding. The ancestors of the Ashley-Cooper family arrived here in the 15th century and reminders of them can be seen all around, although the manor house, St Giles House, is hidden by trees. Facing the village green is a row of **almshouses** and **St Giles Church**. The almshouses were built in 1624 by Sir Anthony Ashley and were intended to house 11 poor people; an inscription above the door reads, 'he hath delivered me out of all trouble'. The church has been through several incarnations. In 1732, the Dorset architects responsible for rebuilding Blandford Forum after the 1731 fire, John and William Bastard, were commissioned to build a church on the site of an earlier, disused one. In 1908 it burned down in a fire accidentally started by workmen repairing the lead roof and the Shaftesburys called in renowned architect Ninian Comper to conduct the restoration. The result is a magnificent and colourful interior, far more elaborate than that of most village churches. An ornate rood screen carved in dark wood separates the altar from the nave. Prevalent are impressive tombs of various members of the Ashley-Cooper family, including Sir Anthony Ashley who has the unglamorous claim to fame of being the first person to grow cabbages in England. The seventh earl (1801–85) improved the lot of working children through a series of reforms and founded the Great Ormond Street Hospital for Children; he was offered burial in Westminster Abbey but declined and is buried here.

Towards the other end of the green are the remains of the **village stocks**, behind iron railings and protected by a small roof.

㉖ Knowlton Church and Neolithic Earthworks

BH21 5AE. Always open; free admission; free parking 150 yards away; English Heritage.
At **Knowlton**, on the B3078 south of Cranborne, you can visit two monuments in one: a ruined medieval church stands in the middle of a Neolithic henge; it is a magical, almost eerie, sight, and is said to be haunted by a ghostly horse and rider galloping through the rings, a nun who kneels within the church and the ringing of a non-existent bell. In the snow, the site resembles a decoration on top of a tiered Christmas cake. On a deeper level, it represents the transition from pagan to Christian worship – it is thought the church was built to symbolically destroy the power of the Neolithic rings.

The henge is circular with a substantial ditch around it and is just one part of a complex of Neolithic earthworks in the area. The clump of trees 200 feet to the east of the henge stands on the Great Barrow, the largest individual barrow in Dorset. The church is 12th century with a 15th-century tower; it was abandoned after the roof collapsed in the 18th century. Not many people visit Knowlton, so you may well have the site to yourself, making it all the more atmospheric.

㉗ Horton

On a hill on the edge of the scattered, low-lying village of Horton is **Horton Tower**, a triangular, turreted brick structure 140 feet high. Local landowner Humphrey Sturt built this folly in 1750, possibly as a vantage point from which to watch the hunt when he became too old to ride to the hounds. It is said there was a fireplace halfway up the tower. Although the tower can be seen from miles around and a bridleway runs nearby, it stands on private

Long Crichel Bakery

Long Crichel BH21 5JU ⓣ 01258 830852 ⓦ www.longcrichelbakery.co.uk. Open Tue–Fri 09.30–17.00, Sat 09.00–13.30.

This traditional bakery produces delicious handmade organic breads and cakes baked in a wood-fired oven. They use organic flour from the Stoate and Sons mill near Shaftesbury (see page 17) and organic milk and cream from a local dairy farm. They produce eight different kinds of sourdough bread, croissants, brioche and patisserie, as well as jam and delicious muesli, which is toasted in the wood-fired oven. The bakery sells these products, plus local cheese and honey, and organic beer, wine and cider. You can find their baked goods in farmers' markets or order direct from the bakery to have them delivered to your home.

land and is not open to the public. The tower was the location for the cockfight in the film *Far from the Madding Crowd*; in recent years it has found a new purpose, as a discreet mobile phone tower.

The Duke of Monmouth was reportedly captured in Horton in 1685 after his failed rebellion. Following his defeat at the Battle of Sedgemoor, Monmouth disguised himself as a shepherd and headed towards Poole, where he planned to catch a boat to Holland. Monmouth was crossing the Cranborne Chase when he was recognised by an old woman, who reported him. A search ensued and he was discovered hiding in a ditch under an ash tree, now known as Monmouth's ash (although it's unlikely to be the same tree).

㉘ Chettle

Chettle is a remarkable place, the very essence of an English rural idyll, with lovingly maintained thatched cottages and the obligatory manor house and church. It is something of a rarity, being one of only a handful of villages still owned by the manor house, and that is what has helped to preserve it. Thanks to the Bourke family and their predecessors at Chettle House (the elegant Queen Anne manor at the heart of the community), this village, with a population of just 90, has fared much better than others of a similar size.

Chettle has avoided the sad fate of many small villages, where outsiders buy up the houses as weekend homes driving up property prices, leaving the village empty except on weekends, and where the village shop and post office close and the young local people can't afford to buy in their own area. Chettle doesn't have that problem because outsiders can't buy houses here. The 42 farms and cottages are owned by the Chettle Estate and rented out to people who actually live and work in the village, at a rate far below market value. Priority is given to families of those who work on the estate; because of these kinds of policies

Chettle has even managed to keep its shop. The village's distinctive story is the subject of a book *Enduring Village*, published in 2008.

Chettle House (*DT11 8DB; 01258 830858; www.chettlehouse.co.uk; open Easter Sun, Apr–Oct first and second Sun of the month 11.00–17.00*) was built in 1710, designed by architect Thomas Archer for George Chaffin MP, to replace the Elizabethan manor house on the site. It has a striking English Baroque exterior with rounded corners, one of Archer's trademarks. The house was bought by the Castleman family in 1846 and their descendants, the Bourkes, own and live in it today. Its interior is grand but restrained; the entrance hall features a beautifully carved oak staircase adorned with family portraits. The gardens are similarly elegant but understated, with colourful herbaceous borders lining the croquet lawn. Refreshments are available in the tearooms in the basement. Nearby is the small **church of St Mary**, which dates from the 16th century although it was largely rebuilt by the Castlemans in the 19th century.

><><><><

Food and drink

Castleman DT11 8DB ① 01258 830096 ⓦ www.castlemanhotel.co.uk. Like the rest of the village, the Castleman is managed by a member of the Bourke family, in this case Teddy. The dining room is elegant, with high ceilings and tall windows overlooking the garden. Local ingredients are used to produce tasty but unfussy dishes. Open daily for dinner and Sun for lunch.

Sherborne and around

This ancient town marking the boundary of the Blackmore Vale has much to offer the visitor, including two castles, a splendid abbey and a charming town centre. Allow at least one full day to explore.

㉙ Sherborne

Sherborne is attractive, and knows it. If Sherborne were a woman, she would be an incredibly pretty, popular socialite who relishes the envy she generates in everyone else. She has an impressive aristocratic pedigree spanning hundreds of years and exudes a refined sense of style. In most towns and villages in the Blackmore Vale you will see a farmer fresh from his tractor (which may be parked around the corner) or a woman in well-worn jodhpurs and wellies popping into the bank or the grocer, but this doesn't seem to happen here. I get the impression Sherborne would frown upon such activity because it is the sort of place where you get dressed up and slap on some makeup to go shopping.

That impressive aristocratic pedigree is embodied in its finest buildings, Sherborne Abbey, Sherborne Old Castle and Sherborne Castle (built by Sir Walter Raleigh), which are all open to the public. A stroll around the town centre with its medieval buildings is enough to gain an appreciation for the town's history; it dates back to the Saxons, who named the town 'scir burne', meaning the place of the clear stream, and made it the capital of Wessex. Today it is a vibrant market town and a centre of learning, thanks to its three private schools, Sherborne Boys, Sherborne Girls and Leweston.

With its compact centre and abundance of buildings of architectural interest, the town is best explored on foot. The tourist information centre stocks helpful booklets on the town and surrounding area, including the excellent *Official Guide to Sherborne*. Guided walks leave from the tourist office at 11.00 on Fridays between July and September, and take around 90 minutes.

Cheap Street

The name of Sherborne's main shopping street is misleading, for it is crammed with upmarket shops, art galleries, antique shops and eateries. Refreshingly, many of them are small, independent shops. Be sure to look above the tempting shop windows to appreciate the blend of architectural styles, with many buildings dating from the 16th century. Some 19th-century shop fronts survive, as well as grand houses built for merchants made wealthy by the silk-throwing and cloth-, glove-, button- and lace-making industries that existed in Sherborne until the 19th century.

Just above the junction with Long Street, is **The Conduit**, a hexagonal stone structure that was originally the monk's *lavatorium* or washhouse; it was moved here in 1539 following the closure of the monastery to form a small market house. It is mentioned in Thomas Hardy's *The Woodlanders* as the place where Giles Winterborne, who was seeking work, stood in the market place 'as he always did at this season of the year, with his specimen apple tree'.

The Conduit has been used variously as a water supply, a police station, a bank and a reading room. At Christmas it houses a nativity scene, one of many festive features which draw visitors from miles around at that time of year.

Near The Conduit, an alleyway leads to the abbey, with the 15th-century **Bow Arch** spanning the gap above, from where it is believed 12 local Monmouth rebels were hanged in 1685 following their unsuccessful rebellion. It is along here that you will find the **Sherborne Museum** (see page 51).

Henry Willis Antique Silver (*38 Cheap St, DT9 3PX; 01935 816828*) is within a wooden, jettied building dating from around 1490, The Shoemaker's House. It is worth popping in to browse the lovely, shiny items inside and to see the preserved square of wattle and daub in the wall, which is now visible behind glass.

The small, **independent shops** along Cheap Street contribute to the town's bygone-era flavour. Among them are the **Toy Box** (*7 Cheap St, DT9 3PT; 01935 817913*), an old-fashioned toy and sweet shop, and **The Chocolate Musketeer** (*16 Cheap St, DT9 3PX; 01935 815139*), a family-owned handmade chocolate shop. **The Swan Gallery** (*51 Cheap St, DT9 3AX; 01935 814465*) is a family-run business selling fine watercolours, oil paintings, antique maps and prints, including a section devoted to antique prints and maps of Dorset. It stands at the entrance to **Swan Yard**, a small pedestrianised shopping area converted from stables.

At the top of the hill Cheap Street leads into **The Green**. On the corner stands **Julian House**, a 16th-century stone-built hospice with mullioned windows. Beside it is the 16th-century **George Inn**, Sherborne's oldest surviving inn.

Markets are held in Cheap Street on Thursday and Saturday, and there's a farmers' market on the third Friday of each month (09.00–13.00).

Sherborne Abbey (Abbey Church of St Mary the Virgin) and around

Ⓦ www.sherborneabbey.com. Free guided tours Tue 10.30 and Fri 14.30.

The centrepiece of Sherborne is undoubtedly its abbey, a glorious spectacle of architecture and history. Resplendent in its golden hamstone, it stands proudly on a perfectly groomed lawn platform, surveying the goings on of the town. In front a memorial commemorates George Winfield Digby of Sherborne Castle, one of the principle financiers of the abbey's Victorian restoration.

The land on which the abbey stands has been consecrated for over 1,300 years. In AD705 King Ine divided the Diocese of Winchester in two, created a new seat at Sherborne and appointed Aldhelm, Abbot of Malmesbury, as the first bishop of the West Saxons. The Cathedral of Sherborne served Aldhelm and 26 succeeding Saxon bishops until the bishop's seat was moved to Old Sarum (near Salisbury) shortly after the Norman Conquest. The abbey became the church of a Benedictine monastery until 1539, when it was dissolved as part of King Henry VIII's Reformation. The building as it stands today was largely the work of Abbot Ramsam (1475–1504).

Perhaps its most striking architectural feature is its superb **fan-vaulted stone roof**, the earliest in England. In his book, *England's Thousand Best Churches*, Simon Jenkins proclaims, 'I would pit Sherborne's roof against any contemporary work of the Italian Renaissance'. Another highlight is the **engraved glass reredos** (1968) by Lawrence Whistler in the Lady Chapel. St Katherine's Chapel contains most of the abbey's surviving medieval glass and is where Sir Walter Raleigh attended services, while the rear choir stalls feature ornate 15th-century misericords.

Fascinating tombs and monuments are dotted about the abbey, vestiges of various periods in its history. The north choir aisle contains Saxon tombs believed to be those of two kings of Wessex, Ethelbald and Ethelbert, elder brothers of Alfred the Great. In the south transept is an impressive marble monument to John Digby, Third and Last Earl of Bristol, dated 1698 and featuring a rather troubling skull and crossbones. In the north transept, within the Wykeham Chapel, a monument honours Sir John Horsey, who bought the abbey estates from the Crown during the Reformation and then sold the abbey back to the people of Sherborne as their parish church. The monument of 1564 has him lying next to his son, both wearing armour of about a century earlier. Horses' heads, looking like chess pieces with enigmatic expressions, adorn the top of the monument.

Today, the abbey holds regular classical music concerts and performances, in particular during the annual Sherborne Abbey Festival held over five days in May. It is also a memorable and extremely popular venue for a Christmas service.

Behind the abbey, occupying some of the former monastic buildings, is **Sherborne Boys' School**, which was founded in 1550 as King Edward's School. The handsome stone buildings may look familiar, as the school has been used as a location for various films, including *The Guinea Pig*, *The Browning Version* and *Goodbye Mr Chips*.

Not far from the abbey, past the almshouse, is the shop of **Edward Oliver** (*The Old Stables, Trendle St, DT9 3NT; 07947 468674; www.edward-oliver. co.uk*), who restores furniture. Housed in 18th-century stables, it makes for fun browsing.

The Almshouse of St John the Baptist and St John the Evangelist

Half Moon St, DT9 3LJ ℗ 01935 813245 ⓦ www.stjohnshouse.org. Open May–Sep Tue, Thu, Fri & Sat 14.00–16.00.

In front of the abbey is this monastic-looking almshouse, built between 1440 and 1445 and extended in 1864, when additions included the cloister and the Victorian railings. Now a residential home for the elderly, it has been providing assistance to local people for over 500 years. In 1437, Henry VI granted a licence for a home for 'twelve pore feeble and ympotent old men and four old women' to be cared for by a housewife whose duty was to 'feeche in and dyght to the victaill wash wrying make beddys and al other things do'. When new residents first arrived they had to bring their few possessions with them and surrender them to the house on their death. They also swore to obey the rules of the house and could be evicted for serious misdemeanours; daily religious services were compulsory. Residents were required to wear uniform; for women in Victorian times this was a red cape and black bonnet, while the men were dressed in black.

Inside, a chapel features fine medieval stained-glass windows and a vivid triptych (circa 1480), a three-panelled altar piece of oil on wood depicting five of the miracles of Christ. For a small fee, you can take a guided tour of the main areas, chapel and gardens. Aside from the chapel, other highlights include the uniforms worn by earlier residents, copies of the royal licence and foundation deed, a solid wooden chest requiring five separate keys, and a letter from Sir Walter Raleigh to the Almshouse Master and a collection of 18th-century pewter plates.

Sherborne Museum

Church Lane, DT9 3BP ℡ 01935 812252 ⓦ www.sherbornemuseum.co.uk. Open Mar–Dec Tue–Fri 10.30–16.30, Jan–Mar Tue & Thu 10.30–12.30.

Between Cheap Street and the abbey, this museum is dedicated to the history of the town and the surrounding area. It covers prominent buildings, such as Sherborne Castle and the abbey, as well as giving an insight into the life of local agricultural workers and tradesmen.

In the early 1400s the monks of Sherborne Abbey wrote and illuminated the **Sherborne Missal**, the largest and most ornately decorated English medieval service book to survive from the Middle Ages. The original is held in the British Library but a digital copy can be viewed at the Sherborne Museum. Other highlights include a scale model of the old castle before it was seized, a wall-painting from 1480, a costume collection and a fully-furnished Victorian doll's house. The majority of the items on display were donated by local residents.

Castleton Waterwheel Museum

Oborne Rd, DT9 3RX ℡ 01935 389535 ⓦ www.castletonwaterwheelmuseum.org.uk. Open once or twice a month May–Oct, but see website for dates.

The focal point of the museum is a 26-foot waterwheel, which was used to supply water to the town from 1869. Its use led to a 50% reduction in deaths from water-borne diseases. Having fallen into disrepair, it was restored to full working order by volunteers and re-installed in 2008.

The museum also displays other examples of Victorian engineering, including a Hindley steam engine like that originally used to supplement the water supply provided by the waterwheel. Also on display are the remains of a waterwheel from nearby Nether Cerne Manor, built near Gillingham in 1819 and one of the oldest all-iron waterwheels in England. Access is from Oborne Road, down a lane 100 yards from the Castleton/Long Street/Newland junction.

Sherborne Old Castle

Castletom DT9 3SA ℡ 01935 812730 ⓦ www.english-heritage.org.uk. Open Apr–Oct daily 10.00–16.00.

This atmospheric ruin lies to the east of the town, in the grounds of the new Sherborne Castle, and is all that remains of the original, which was destroyed by Cromwell's troops during the Civil War. It reportedly took 16 days for Cromwell's men to bring the castle down in 1645; only the imposing gatehouse, parts of the keep and the outer walls survive, surrounded by a moat. The entrance passes over a modern bridge with the piers of the medieval one beneath it. It is a serene spot with fine beech trees, views of the surrounding countryside and the town. It oozes history and mystery, conjuring images of medieval banquets and battles.

The castle was built in the 12th century by Roger de Caen, Bishop of Salisbury and Chancellor of England. In 1592, Queen Elizabeth I gave the castle, which was already deteriorating, to explorer Sir Walter Raleigh. Raleigh initially tried to modernise the castle but gave up and built a home (Sherborne Castle) in the deer park opposite; he kept the old castle for ceremonial use.

Sherborne Castle

New Rd, DT9 5NR ☎ 01935 812072 ⓦ www.sherborne castle.com. Open Apr–Oct Tue–Thu, Sat–Sun.

Having decided that Sherborne Old Castle was not fit for habitation, Sir Walter Raleigh built this Elizabethan mansion on the other side of the River Yeo in 1594. Raleigh and his wife enjoyed their new home for less than nine years before his execution during the reign of James I. In 1617 the estate, with its two castles, was purchased by Sir John Digby and has remained in the family ever since. At its core is the house built by Raleigh with polygonal turrets in each corner. It was extended in a similar style (more turrets) by various Digbys through the generations, giving it its rather unusual shape. During World War I the house was used by the Red Cross as a hospital, and in World War II as the headquarters for the commandos involved in the D-Day landings.

The interior presents a parade of styles from different eras: Tudor, Jacobean, Georgian and Victorian. The furniture, art and family memorabilia give it a very human touch. There is a lot to take in, so it is just as well that there are guides on hand to explain each room. The slightly comical ostrich with a horseshoe in its mouth, which you can see depicted all around the building, has been the heraldic symbol of the Digby family since 1350. The 18th-century library is striking, with formidable-looking busts tucked into recesses between the highly decorative bookcases. The green drawing room has Raleigh's arms on the ceiling and three beautiful 17th-century fireplaces.

The spectacular gardens were created in 1753 by Capability Brown with a 50-acre lake fed by the River Yeo as their centrepiece. Around the lake are sweeping lawns, majestic old trees and colourful flower borders, while the remains of Old Sherborne Castle in the distance, provide a romantic backdrop. Exploring the grounds is like being lost in a Jane Austen adaptation. I, for one, was certainly hoping that Mr Darcy would ride up on his powerful, grey gelding to invite me to a sumptuous picnic by the lake, and perhaps a lifetime as Mrs Darcy. As you walk around the lake in the direction of Sherborne Old Castle you come to '**Raleigh's seat**', a large stone seat where the adventurer reportedly used to sit to survey the estate and keep an eye on the road below, the main route to Dorchester. Raleigh's role in popularising tobacco in England is well documented and legend has it that a servant happened upon

Sherborne Castle Country Fair

Ⓦ www.sherbornecountryfair.com.

Sherborne Castle plays host to an annual country fair, usually held in early June. It was started by a small group of volunteers in 1996, with the aim of raising money for local charities, especially those working with children, and to date has raised over three-quarters of a million pounds.

It makes a thoroughly entertaining day out, showcasing country pursuits and crafts, including Morris dancing, rare breed shows, heavy horses, gun dog trials, falconry and local hunts and their hounds. A more unusual inclusion on the schedule is the dragon-boat racing on Sherborne Castle lake. The food hall, crammed with delicious local produce, is another highlight.

Sir Walter smoking his pipe at the stone seat and, thinking his master was on fire, threw a pitcher of beer over him to extinguish the flames. Raleigh's ghost reportedly walks the castle grounds and sits on the stone seat gazing longingly across the estate.

Both the castle and its gardens are open to visitors; you can visit both or just the gardens. The gardens provide a beautiful, peaceful spot to enjoy a picnic or to walk the dogs around the lake. There is a good tearoom in the former nursery building and the estate produces wine, on sale in the gift shop.

Food and drink

Eastbury Hotel Long St, DT9 3BY ℗ 01935 813131. Home-grown and local is the culinary theme at this boutique hotel; the menu tells you exactly which producers supplied the ingredients. Creative dishes, beautifully presented.

The Grange Oborne DT9 4LA ℗ 01935 813463. A fine-dining restaurant just outside Sherborne. Open daily for lunch and dinner.

Olivers 19 Cheap St, DT9 3PU ℗ 01935 815005. Casual café with long tables and a back room with unusual 2-person booths.

Swan Inn Swan Yard, Cheap St, DT9 3AX ℗ 01935 817022. Tucked away in a pedestrian alleyway off the main street. A light and fresh country-style interior, a real fire in winter and a walled garden create a pleasant atmosphere. A varied and creative menu, including some tasty desserts and cakes for afternoon tea. Open Mon–Thu 09.30–18.00, Fri–Sat 09.30–22.00.

Three Wishes 78 Cheap St, DT9 3BJ ℗ 01935 817777. A popular café/bistro priding itself on using local ingredients in its carefully presented dishes. On the menu is the 'Sherborne Stodger', a bun containing dried fruit and spices. Open Mon–Sat 09.30–17.00, Sun 11.00–15.00, Thu–Sun 18.30–21.00.

Town Mill Bakery 1 The Green, DT9 3HY ℗ 01935 813264. Seating is at school-like long tables and it is self-service, making for an informal, friendly atmosphere. On offer are freshly baked breads, cakes, pizzas, homemade soups and the like.

My Orcha'd in Linden Lea

The following poem by Dorset dialect poet William Barnes is considered to be an unofficial Dorset anthem. It was set to music by Ralph Vaughan Williams.

'Ithin the woodlands, flow'ry gleaded,
By the woak tree's mossy moot,
The sheenen grass bleades, timber-sheaded,
Now do quiver under voot;
An' birds do whissle auver head,
An' water's bubblen in its bed,
An' ther vor me the apple tree
Do lean down low in Linden Lea.

When leaves that leately wer a-springen
Now do feade 'ithin the copse,
An' painted birds do hush ther zingen
Up upon the timber's tops;
An' brown-leav'd fruit's a-turnen red,
In cloudless zunsheen, auver head,
Wi' fruit vor me the apple tree
Do lean down low in Linden Lea.

Let other vo'k meake money vaster
In the air o' dark-room'd towns,
I don't dread a peevish measter;
Though noo man do heed my frowns,
I be free to goo abrode,
Or teake agean my hwomeward road
To where vor me the apple tree
Do lean down low in Linden Lea.

㉚ Sandford Orcas Manor House

The Manor House, Sandford Orcas DT9 4SB ① 01963 220206. Open Easter Mon 10.00–17.00, May & Jul–Sep Sun & Mon 14.00–17.00.

Sandford Orcas is an appealing stone village three miles north of Sherborne, just inside the border with Somerset. The manor house was constructed in the mid-16th century from local hamstone, on the site of an earlier house; it is little altered and a rare example of the small Tudor manor houses that were once dotted throughout the countryside. Tudor architects got away with things that would simply look ridiculous today, like the stone monkeys that crouch on the gables. It was built for William Knoyle and only two families, the Knoyles and the Meldycotts, have owned it since then. When the house is open, you are likely to be shown around by one of the Meldycotts.

The entrance is impressive, passing through a gatehouse to reveal the atmospheric house; inside, the hall has fine wood panelling and there is some original stained glass. The house is reputed to be haunted by a litany of ghostly characters, somewhat suspiciously most of the ghost stories originate from the 1960s when the then tenant, Colonel Claridge, opened it to the public to raise funds, leaving one to wonder whether the ghost stories may have been an attempt to boost ticket sales.

The typically English gardens are also open and contain fine hedges, terracing, herbaceous borders and mature trees; the roses put on a colourful show in earlier summer.

Adjacent to the house, the medieval **church of St Nicholas** contains a memorial to William Knoyle dated 1607. He is depicted as a knight with his two wives and 11 children, four of whom are shown dead and wrapped in red swaddling clothes. It seems the four children he had with his first wife did not survive.

DORCHESTER AND THE PIDDLE AND FROME VALLEYS

WAREHAM

A351

A31

A35

Winterborne Tomson

River Frame

Monkey World Ape Rescue Centre **(20)**

Clouds Hill

Bere Regis **(15)**

(16) Shitterton

River Piddle

(18) Bovington Tank Museum

(19)

Winterborne Stickland

Winterborne Houghton **(23)**

Milton Abbas **(22)**

Bulbarrow Hill **(21)**

A354

Tolpuddle **(14)**

Athelhampton House **(13)**

A35

Moreton

(17)

Mill House Cider Museum **(7)**

A352

Hardy's Cottage

Higher Bockhampton

Stinsford **(6)**

Kingston Maurward

Buckland Newton **(11)**

Cerne Abbas and its giant **(9)**

Piddletrenthide **(12)**

Piddlehinton

Wolveton House **(2)**

A35

WEYMOUTH

A354

Minterne Magna **(10)**

A37

A352

Godmanstone **(8)**

DORCHESTER **(1)**

(3) Poundbury

(4) Maiden Castle

Winterborne Abbas **(5)**

Winterborne St Martin

A35

A356

N

0   4 miles
0   5km

56

2. DORCHESTER AND THE PIDDLE AND FROME VALLEYS

A t the heart of Dorset is an unspoilt landscape of rolling chalk downland, wooded hills and river valleys. The area is sparsely populated, its chalk hills with their short springy grass being relatively inhospitable farmland compared to the fertile, neighbouring Blackmore Vale. Visitors tend to bypass the area in favour of the Dorset coast, yet it has much to offer those who want to slow down and really get to know what lies at the centre of the county.

Strings of villages huddle in clusters along the river valleys, like those along the **River Frome** and the evocatively named **River Piddle**. In the east the Frome and Piddle valleys lead into water meadows and from there to an area of heathland, which spreads towards the Isle of Purbeck and Poole Harbour. The chalk hills hold a large water table, which means there are many seasonal rivers that flow depending on the level of the water. The area has 15 villages with names pre-fixed by 'Winterborne', indicating they lie on a stream which only runs in winter.

Dorchester, the county town, and the surrounding area have a strong sense of history, having been settled since around 4,000BC. Dorchester still bears the imprint of Roman occupation, including the only fully exposed and best-preserved Roman town house in Britain. It also has arguably the most comprehensive museum in Dorset, the Dorset County Museum.

Just outside Dorchester is **Maiden Castle**, the largest Iron Age hillfort in Britain. It is one of several prehistoric sites in this area, along with Maumbury Rings and Badbury Rings. Dorset's past inhabitants have left their mark all over this part of the county. It seems chalk hills do have their uses – you can make enormous carvings in them which last for centuries and glisten white for all to see. That is precisely what someone (no-one knows quite who or when) has done at **Cerne Abbas**, where the chalk carving of a naked, club-wielding, 180-foot giant dominates the landscape.

Dorchester and the surrounding countryside inspired one of Dorset's most famous sons, author Thomas Hardy, who was born in a tiny hamlet near Dorchester in 1840 and later moved into the town. In this part of the county are innumerable reminders of Hardy's work and thankfully much of the landscape has changed little since his day. The various sites for aficionados to visit include the cottage where he was born.

Getting there and around

Unless you have all the time in the world, a car really is the best way to reach the delightful hidden places in this area. The main roads are good (the A35 running east to west and the A352 running north to south) but getting away from them and exploring is where the real fun is. Dorchester is straightforward to negotiate by car, there is plenty of parking and the town doesn't usually feel crowded.

The Dorchester tourist information centre stocks a leaflet entitled *Discover the heart of Hardy's Wessex*, which includes a Hardy trail linking together sites where he lived, places he wrote about and the church at Stinsford where his heart is buried. Parts of the trail are designed to be walked, such as Dorchester to Hardy's birthplace at Higher Bockhampton, but most of it follows the road and can be covered by car.

Public transport

Travelling to Dorchester via public transport is relatively easy. London Waterloo to Weymouth **train** services (South West Trains) call at Dorchester South Station, while Bristol to Weymouth services (Wessex Trains) call at Dorchester West. A **National Express bus** service runs from London Victoria to Dorchester via Bournemouth.

Getting beyond Dorchester and out into the villages and more remote points of interest is less straightforward. However, regular **bus services** are available between Dorchester and some of the main attractions, including Maiden Castle (Dorset Town Services 1 and 2), Cerne Abbas (bus 216, Damory Coaches), Milton Abbas (bus 311) and Bovington Tank Museum (bus 103). A useful service is the 387 operated by Damory Coaches, which runs from Dorchester to Poole via Athelhampton House, Tolpuddle and Bere Regis (Monday to Saturday only). Bus 31 will take you to Bridport via Poundbury, Martinstown and Winterborne Abbas.

Hardy's Cottage at Higher Bockhampton is not well served by public transport: the closest bus stop is on the A35, but you need to walk across the busy road and then onwards to the cottage. Two buses have this as a request stop: bus 387 and 183/184 (Weymouth–Salisbury). A simpler solution is a **taxi** from Dorchester, which is inexpensive.

Cycling

The unspoilt countryside and relatively quiet roads make for some very pleasant cycling country. National Cycle Network (NCN) **Route 2** covers 30 miles between Lyme Regis and Dorchester, taking you through the West Dorset countryside. The route passes through the Marshwood Vale, around Bridport and through the beautiful Bride Valley. It runs close to the Hardy Monument and Maiden Castle on the approach to Dorchester. The *Cycling in West Dorset* leaflet is available from tourist information centres and can be used in conjunction with OS Explorer maps 116 and OL15. Various branches allow you to detour to see local sites of interest, such as Abbotsbury. NCN **Route 26** begins in Dorchester and runs 28 miles north to Sherborne, passing Cerne Abbas *en route*.

Guided mountain-biking is available from The Kingcombe Centre (*Lower Kingcombe, Dorchester DT2 0EQ; 01300 320684; www.king combe.org – see page 128*). Cycling holidays are based at the centre and they can arrange local and on-site accommodation.

Cycle hire

Cycloan, Dorset Cycle Hire 49 London Rd, Dorchester DT1 1NF ℗ 01305 251521
Ⓦ www.cycloan.co.uk. Guided cycle tours, cycle hire and repair.
Dorchester Cycles 31 Great Western Rd, Dorchester DT1 1UF ℗ 01305 268787
Ⓦ www.dorchestercycles.co.uk. Trailer bikes for towing small children are also
available for hire. Closed Sun.

Walking

The town of **Dorchester** lends itself to being explored on foot and The Walks, following the Roman town walls, are a good place to start. The town crier, Alistair Chisholm, offers guided walks of the town, including a Thomas Hardy tour (see box, page 69).

The prehistoric site of **Maiden Castle** offers a memorable short stroll, as well as the chance to soak up thousands of years of history and some breathtaking views of the countryside.

The **Cerne Valley** is criss-crossed by footpaths and bridleways that can tie in with a memorable walk up Giant Hill to get a closer look at the chalk carving.

For those with an interest in **Lawrence of Arabia**, a themed trail starts at the Bovington Tank Museum and takes in Clouds Hill and Moreton. A leaflet on the trail is available from local tourist information centres (such as Wareham) and online (*www.dorsetforyou.com*).

If you want to walk in quintessential **Hardy country**, the obvious starting point is Hardy's Cottage, and the walk into Thorncombe Wood and Duddle Heath ('Egdon Heath' in Hardy's writings), or along the river from Lower Bockhampton to the church at Stinsford. The 212-mile trail known as the **Hardy Way** links together many of the key sites.

Bulbarrow Hill lies on a section of the Wessex Ridgeway and has superb views of the Blackmore Vale. You can easily reach it from car parks on the hilltop and along the Ridgeway or combine it with a longer walk, such as starting from Ibberton beneath the escarpment, climbing steeply to the top, then from Bulbarrow dropping down through Woolland. Just to the south, there's a beautiful stroll from Milton Abbas to Milton Abbey; the best longer walks around the village lie to the north, including Hilton and Winterbourne Houghton.

The **Dorset Jubilee Trail** runs 90 miles from Forde Abbey on the Somerset border across Dorset to Bokerley Dyke on the Hampshire border and takes in several places mentioned in this chapter, including Moreton, Bere Regis and Milton Abbas.

Accommodation

Dorchester is a handy base if you are travelling by public transport, but there are also some lovely out-of-the-way villages with good accommodation which will really allow you to experience what this unspoilt area has to offer. **Cerne Abbas** is one such place and well positioned for exploring Dorchester, Sherborne, the Blackmore Vale and even the coast. For those with an interest in Hardy, **Higher** and **Lower Bockhampton** will appeal. The Landmark Trust lets out two beautifully restored properties in this area, Wolveton House and Woodford Castle.

Abbots B&B 7 Long St, Cerne Abbas DT2 7JF ① 01300 341349 ⓔ info@ abbotsbedandbreakfast.co.uk ⓦ www.abbotsbedandbreakfast.co.uk. 5 clean and comfortable rooms in the centre of the village. Rooms are equipped with TV and tea- and coffee-making facilities. Reasonable value for money.

Dorset Resort Bere Regis BH20 7NT ① 01929 472244 ⓔ resort@ dorsetgolfresort.com ⓦ www.dorsetgolfresort.com. Located south of Bere Regis at the East Dorset Golf Club at Hyde. Within easy reach of the coast but away from the summer crowds. You can take advantage of 3 9-hole golf courses, coarse fishing lakes and an indoor bowling green here, and non-golfers are welcome too. It has spacious and well-appointed Swiss chalet-style wooden cabins (sleeping up to 8), each with sauna and fireplace, and which are in a secluded setting backing onto woodland: deer sightings are common. Half board (dinner and breakfast) packages are available, as well as self-catering.

Field Farmhouse Godmanstone DT2 7AE ① 01300 341384 ⓔ info@ fieldfarmhouse.co.uk ⓦ www.fieldfarmhouse.co.uk. Very well-appointed self-catering accommodation off the A352 just south of Godmanstone, close to Cerne Abbas. The farm buildings have been thoughtfully converted to 2 self-catering cottages (one sleeps 5, the other sleeps 2 and they inter-connect for large parties), and there are 2 en-suite B&B rooms at the end of the farmhouse. Self-catering guests have the option of staying on a B&B basis, and there is a conveniently located farm shop next door. Reasonable value for money.

Fox Inn Ansty, near Dorchester DT2 7PN ① 01258 880328 ⓦ www.anstyfoxinn. co.uk. 11 comfortable en-suite rooms in one of Dorset's most popular pubs. In a handy location for visiting the Blackmore Vale and Dorchester areas, and it has a good restaurant.

Greenwood Grange Higher Bockhampton DT2 8QH ① 01305 268874 ⓔ info@ greenwoodgrange.co.uk ⓦ www.greenwoodgrange.co.uk. Upmarket self-catering accommodation within a few hundred yards of Hardy's cottage. There are 17 cottages, which sleep from 2 to 12 people, in and around buildings constructed by Hardy's father in the 19th century. The facilities are exceptional: tennis courts, indoor pool, badminton, croquet and games room. Dogs are allowed in some cottages.

Heathcote House Milborne St Andrew DT11 0JG ① 01258 837219 ⓔ enquiries@
heathcotehouse.co.uk ⓦ www.heathcotehouse.co.uk. Grade II-listed village house
with 3 beautifully decorated en-suite rooms. Drawing room with a cosy fire.
Prices are average.

New Inn 14 Long St, Cerne Abbas DT2 7JF ① 01300 341274 ⓔ jeremy@
thenewinncerneabbas.co.uk ⓦ www.thenewinncerneabbas.co.uk. At the time of
writing there were plans to refurbish the interior of this 16th-century coaching
inn and expand the 6 en-suite rooms to 11. The existing Woodpecker room is
full of period features, including chunky dark beams. Pets are allowed in 2 of the
rooms.

River Cottage at Athelhampton House and Gardens Dorchester DT2 7LG
① 01305 848363 ⓦ www.athelhampton.co.uk. A thatched self-catering cottage
in the grounds of the house. It is nicely decorated and has 3 en-suite bedrooms.
A small private golf course is available for use. You pay a slight premium for the
location.

Wolveton Gatehouse Dorchester DT2 9QN ① 01628 825925 ⓔ bookings@
landmarktrust.org.uk ⓦ www.landmarktrust.co.uk. The Landmark Trust lets out
part of the gatehouse of the privately owned medieval and Elizabethan Wolveton
House. It is a stately building full of character and the guesthouse sleeps up to
6 people. Wolveton House, but not the gatehouse, is open to the public between
June and September (see page 67).

Woodsford Castle Dorchester DT2 8AS ① 01628 825925 ⓔ bookings@
landmarktrust.org.uk ⓦ www.landmarktrust.co.uk. An unusual thatched castle,
which dates from 1370. The castle was in the same family for 600 years, until it
was taken over by the Landmark Trust, which now lets it out. The castle sleeps 8
and dogs are allowed.

Yalbury Cottage Lower Bockhampton DT2 8PZ ① 01305 262382
ⓦ www.yalburycottage.com. Within walking distance of Hardy's cottage. 8 light
and airy en-suite rooms, priced towards the expensive end. The building dates
back 300 years but the rooms are modern, with everything you may require; and
there is a popular restaurant (see page 74).

Tourist information centre

General information ⓦ www.westdorset.com ⓦ www.dorchesterdorset.com.
Dorchester Antelope Walk, DT1 1BE ① 01305 267992.

Dorchester and around

You may be tempted to assume that **Dorchester**, being Dorset's county town,
is large, crowded and surrounded by new, soulless housing developments. That
is not the case. Dorchester is full of old-world charm and with just 18,000

inhabitants is a very manageable size. The countryside and villages around it are unspoilt and it only takes a brief look at a road atlas to see that many of Dorset's archaeological and historical attractions are in this area, including the hillfort at Maiden Castle. As for new housing developments, they don't come any more remarkable than Poundbury, the community designed in the 1990s by HRH Prince of Wales.

Dorchester is the heart of **Hardy country**: aficionados come here to pay homage to the author. High on the list of Hardy haunts to visit are his birthplace at **Higher Bockhampton** and his former home at **Max Gate** in Dorchester.

① Dorchester

The town is populous, tho' not large, the streets broad, but the buildings old, and low; however, there is good company and a good deal of it; and a man that coveted a retreat in this world might as agreeably spend his time, and as well in Dorchester, as in any town I know in England.

I am inclined to agree with Daniel Defoe's description in his *A tour thro' the Whole Island of Great Britain* (1724–26).

Dorchester as you see it today has been forged over a long and fascinating history. One of the great pleasures of wandering around the town is the chance to trace portions of that history by visiting sites of Neolithic, Roman, medieval and more recent importance. The Dorchester area has been inhabited since Neolithic times, circa 4000BC, with settlements based around what later became the Iron Age hillfort of Maiden Castle to the southwest of the town (see page 68). When the Romans arrived in AD70 they laid out what is now the town of Dorchester, which they called Durnovaria, in their usual cruciform manner surrounded by a wall. The basic structure of the town remains unchanged. Today, pleasant avenues lined with lime, chestnut and sycamore trees, trace the line of the town walls. Known as **The Walks**, the avenues were laid down in the 18th century and to wander along them is an enjoyable way to get a feel for the town. As you explore, it may strike you that Dorchester does not look as old as you may expect. That is because much of medieval Dorchester was lost in five devastating fires between 1613 and 1775 but the rebuilding left us streets of handsome 18th-century houses.

A good place to start any visit to Dorchester is the **tourist information centre** on Antelope Walk. It is well stocked with books and brochures, the staff are helpful and can provide leaflets on walks around the town and in the area.

Dorchester has a surprisingly long and varied list of museums, some devoted to themes that have little to do with the area, such as the Tutankhamun

Exhibition and the Terracotta Warriors Museum. Of the town's museums, two really stand out as worth visiting, the **Dorset County Museum** (see page 65) and **The Keep Military Museum of Devon and Dorset** (see page 65).

The clues pointing to Dorchester's Roman origins were certainly not lost on Thomas Hardy. In his novel *The Mayor of Casterbridge*, Hardy based the fictional town on Dorchester, which he knew well, being born and raised in the area. His description of Casterbridge may as easily have been a description of Dorchester: 'Casterbridge announced old Rome in every street, alley and precinct. It looked Roman, bespoke the art of Rome, concealed the dead men of Rome.' Dorchester's Roman origins are even more evident today than they were in Hardy's time, for Hardy would not have seen the most striking proof of Roman occupation, **The Roman Town House** (*01305 221000; www.romantownhouse.org*). The house, which dates from the 4th century, was found in 1937 during the building of a new County Hall and is the only fully exposed Roman town house in the country. It is perhaps surprising (and certainly refreshing) that you are able to walk freely around the ruins and that no entry fee is charged. Parts of the ruins are protected by roofs and glass walls but the basic structure, mosaic floors and underfloor heating are clearly visible. An audio guide is available through your mobile phone, or there are display panels for the less technically minded. The items found during the excavation of the town house are on display in the Dorset County Museum (see page 65). The only disappointing aspect of the ruins is their location, backing onto the County Council's rather unlovely offices.

Not far from the Roman town house, on the banks of the River Frome, is **Hangman's Cottage**. This very pretty thatched building in the traditional Dorset style is believed to have been home to the town's executioner. In 1856, at the age of 16, Hardy was present at the execution of Martha Brown, and the memory of this public hanging, on top of the north-facing main entrance to the prison only 150 yards downstream from Hangman's Cottage, stayed with him. Town crier Alistair Chisholm told me some Hardy scholars link the event to the ultimate fate of Tess of the d'Urbervilles. Thomas Hardy's short story *The Withered Arm* features the hangman's cottage on this site and, Alistair told me, the association has remained to this day with stories of hangman's ropes being found in the roof in the late 19th century.

Near Hangman's Cottage is **John's Pond**, part of the intricate drainage system of the water meadows which enabled low-lying areas to be flooded in winter to stop the ground freezing and allow fertile silt to settle. The name is reportedly in memory of a hapless prisoner, who, having managed to escape the nearby gaol on a dark night, fell into the pond and was drowned.

Dorchester's **high street** is inviting, brimming with character, points of interest and some decent shops. On the south side of High West Street are the only timber-framed buildings surviving in anything like their original state. The black-and-white building now housing a restaurant (*6 High West St – see page 67*) is where **Judge Jeffreys** ('The Hanging Judge') lodged during the trials of those who took part in the Monmouth Rebellion of 1685 (see below). The trials, known as the **Bloody Assizes**, were held in the Oak Room (now a tearoom – see page 67) of the **Antelope Hotel**. Judge Jeffreys, whose deadly zero-tolerance policy made him highly unpopular, is said to have had a secret passage leading there from his lodgings.

The **Shire Hall**, built in 1797 of Portland stone, contains the **Old Crown Court** (*Stratton House, 58–60 High West St, DT1 1UZ; 01305 267992; open Mon–Fri 10.00–12.00 & 14.00–16.00*), where the Tolpuddle Martyrs were tried in 1834 (see box, page 81). Inscribed on the outside of the building, at a level for stage-coach passengers to read, are the distances to the nearest towns. The court is owned by the Trades Union Congress (TUC) and was restored as a memorial to the martyrs in 1956. At selected times in summer you can take a guided tour of the cells as well as the court – call for tour times.

St Peter's, at the junction of South Street and High Street, is the town's only surviving medieval church. The church was restored by the Dorchester architect John Hicks in 1856, along with his 16-year-old assistant, the future author Thomas Hardy, who trained as an architect. The plans Hardy drew for the church are on display in the south chapel. Outside the church is a statue

Judge Jeffreys and the Bloody Assizes

In May 1685, the Duke of Monmouth set sail from Holland, where he had exiled himself, bound for Lyme Regis. Monmouth, a Protestant, intended to overthrow the Roman Catholic King James II. Lyme Regis was strongly Protestant; Monmouth gathered supporters and marched towards Somerset. Monmouth was defeated on 6 July at the Battle of Sedgemoor and executed shortly thereafter. Following the Monmouth Rebellion, Judge Jeffreys held his infamous 'Bloody Assizes', a series of trials which began in Winchester then moved through Salisbury, Dorchester, Taunton and Wells. The 'hanging judge' sentenced 292 Monmouth supporters to death and around 800 to be transported to the West Indies. After the hangings, the heads of some of the executed were impaled on church railings, and left there for several years as a warning of the penalty for treason.

While presiding over the trials in Dorchester, Judge Jeffreys lodged at 6 High West Street (now a restaurant). The trials were held on 5 September in the Oak Room of the Antelope Hotel (now a tearoom).

In 1688, when King James II was overthrown by William of Orange, Judge Jeffreys was imprisoned in the Tower of London. He died a year later, aged 44, of kidney disease.

erected in 1888 to the Dorset dialect poet **William Barnes** (see box, page 7), who lived in Dorchester from 1837 until 1886. Barnes was a rector of nearby Winterborne Came and a great friend of Thomas Hardy. Dorchester couldn't possibly have a statue of Barnes without one of Hardy too; the Hardy one is at the western end of High West Street, near the top-of-town roundabout. Opposite St Peter's Church is the **Corn Exchange** of 1848. The rather playful clock tower was added in 1864.

A quiet retreat within the town is the flower-filled **Borough Gardens** on Cornwall Road, where the colourful bandstand and clock provide a Victorian feel.

Grey's Bridge on London Road leads over the River Frome and towards Poole and Bournemouth. The bridge is one of several in Dorset bearing a sign that warns any person damaging it is liable to be transported for life. During World War II fear of invasion resulted in Royal Engineers drilling holes in the stonework, ready for explosives. No invasion took place but in 1942 several bombs fell on the water meadows and riverbank, killing ten cows and a horse, injuring several people, and damaging nearby houses.

The Dorset County Museum

High West St, DT1 1XA ℡ 01305 262735 ⓦ www.dorsetcountymuseum.org.
Open Jan–Oct Mon–Sat, Nov–Mar Tue–Sat.

The fetching mock-medieval-style building (1884), with high ceilings and fine cast iron work inspired by the Great Exhibition of 1851, provides a fitting backdrop for the exhibits. Its collections comprehensively cover Dorset's social history, literature, archaeology, geology and natural history. The Jurassic Coast exhibition, complete with fossilised dinosaur remains, is bound to be a hit with children, while Dorchester's early history is well represented with finds from digs of Iron Age, Roman, Anglo Saxon and medieval sites. The floor of the Victorian Hall, the museum's magnificent main gallery, is one of the few places in England where you can actually walk on a Roman mosaic floor, this one coming from Roman town houses excavated in and around Dorchester. There are fascinating finds from Maiden Castle (see page 68), including the skeleton of a member of the Durotriges tribe of Iron Age Britons with a Roman ballista bolt lodged in his spine. Hardy fans will enjoy the reconstruction of Hardy's study at Max Gate, his Dorchester home (see page 66).

The Keep Military Museum of Devon and Dorset

Bridport Rd, DT1 1RN ℡ 01305 264066 ⓦ www.keepmilitarymuseum.org. Open Apr–Sep Mon–Sat 09.30–17.00, Oct–Mar Tue–Fri 10.00–16.30.

The museum occupies the imposing former gatehouse of the Dorsetshire Regiment barracks, built in 1879 from Portland stone. The regiments of Devon and Dorset have a history spanning over 300 years. Here you can follow their story right up to 2007, when the Devon and Dorset Light Infantry was disbanded and absorbed into The Rifles.

I found this a highly emotive museum, dedicated to the many West Country folk who have left their beloved towns, villages and farms to serve their country in a faraway land. During World War I they were joined by many of the area's finest horses. The **Queen's Own Dorset Yeomanry Horses** are best known for their 26 February 1916 charge of the Senussi forces at Agagia in Egypt. Despite being outnumbered almost three-to-one, the Yeomanry charged across the desert in the face of rifle and machine-gun fire. They lost half their horses and a third of their men but won the ensuing battle and captured General Jaafa Pasha. On the ground floor of the museum is a life-size model of 2nd lieutenant Blaksley on horseback, carrying the original sword he used in the battle. On 3 March 1916 he wrote to his mother: 'I was within 30 yards of the enemy when my horse came down, shot through the heart. He was, I think, the nicest horse I have ever ridden, a well known hunter in the Blackmore Vale.' For me, this was perhaps the starkest illustration of what a shock it must have been for both soldier and horse to be plucked from the tranquillity of Dorset and sent to a battlefield in northern Africa.

The museum is brilliantly laid out and has some gems that you may not expect to see tucked away in Dorset, such as Hitler's desk. From the roof there are breathtaking 360° views of Dorchester and the surrounding countryside.

Maumbury Rings

On the southern side of town, Maumbury Rings (*www.maumburyrings.co.uk; free access*) acts almost as a physical representation of a timeline charting the area's history. The rings began life as a Neolithic henge around 2,500BC. Just over 2,500 years later the Romans turned the site into an amphitheatre and held gladiatorial conquests here. During the Middle Ages it was a venue for bear-baiting and when the Civil War came, it became an artillery fort. In the 17th and 18th centuries Maumbury Rings was again used as an amphitheatre, drawing excited crowds to its public executions or 'Hanging Fairs'. The site continues to host public entertainment today, although the violent displays of the past have been replaced by more genteel activities, such as choral recitals, plays and Dorchester's Arts Festivals. You can visit the Rings and walk along the banks, although the views are very urban. Finds from excavations of Maumbury Rings can be seen at the Dorset County Museum (see page 65).

Max Gate

Alington Av, DT1 2AB ① 01305 262538 ⓦ www.maxgate.co.uk. Open 1 Apr–30 Oct Wed–Sun and Bank Holiday Mon 11.00–17.00; National Trust.

Max Gate, on the eastern peripheries of town near the A35, was the home of Thomas Hardy from 1885, when he was aged 45, until he died in 1928. The house is now in the care of the National Trust. Construction of the house was a family affair – it was designed by Hardy and built by his brother. It was here that the author wrote *Tess of the d'Urbevilles, Jude the Obscure, The Woodlanders* and much of his poetry, and entertained other literary figures of the day, including Robert Louis Stevenson, Rudyard Kipling and T E Lawrence. Hardy had no children with either of his wives (Emma and Florence) but had a number of pets, including a dog called Wessex, who are buried in the garden. The house provides a rare glimpse into Hardy's personal life, as many of his letters were destroyed upon his death, in accordance with his will.

Food and drink

A large weekly market is held opposite the Brewery Square development (Weymouth Avenue) every Wednesday and includes a farmers' market.

No 6 6 North Sq, DT1 1HY ℗ 01305 267679. French restaurant which uses Dorset ingredients. Uncharacteristically for a French restaurant there is a good selection of vegetarian dishes. Open Tue–Fri lunch and dinner, Sat dinner. Reservation recommended.

Oak Room 5b Antelope Walk, DT1 1BE ℗ 01305 250760. A traditional tearoom in the oak-panelled room which served as Judge Jeffreys' court during the Bloody Assizes. Open Mon–Sat.

Potter's Café 19 Durngate St, DT1 1JP ℗ 01305 260312. Centrally located in a quirky, creaky building and with a courtyard garden for sunny days. On offer is a variety of lunch dishes, delicious cakes (including gluten free) and homemade smoothies. Generous portions, reasonably priced. Not open for dinner.

Prezzo 6 High West St, DT1 1UJ ℗ 01305 259678
Ⓦ www.prezzorestaurants.co.uk. This Italian restaurant's big draw card is the incredible Judge Jeffreys's building which houses it. The notorious 'hanging judge' lodged here when he presided over the Bloody Assizes in 1685.

Sienna 36 High West St, DT1 1UP ℗ 01305 250022 Ⓦ www.siennarestaurant. co.uk. A tiny, upmarket but friendly restaurant, this comes with impressive enough credentials: a Michelin star and 3AA rosettes. Widely acknowledged as the best place to eat in Dorchester. Uses seasonal, local produce to great effect. Open Tue–Sat lunch and dinner.

② Wolveton House

Wolveton, near Dorchester DT2 9QN ℗ 01305 263500 Ⓦ www.hha.org.uk. Open Jun–Sep Mon, Tue, Thu 14.00–17.00.

This fine medieval and Elizabethan manor to the north of Dorchester is the home of the Thimbleby family, and was the home of The Lady Penelope in Thomas Hardy's *A Group of Noble Dames*. The house has magnificent carved oak panelling, ornate ceilings, grand fireplaces and stone stairs. There is also an impressive collection of art and furniture. The house can be visited at certain times (best to check the website as these can vary) and the gatehouse is available for letting through the Landmark Trust (see page 61).

③ Poundbury

Poundbury is the well-known western extension of Dorchester, constructed on Duchy of Cornwall land as an initiative of Prince Charles. The development was designed in accordance with the Prince's town-planning theories, outlined in his 1989 book, *A Vision of Britain*. Building began in 1993 and is due to be completed in 2025, the target being a total of 2,500 dwellings and a population of about 6,000.

Unsurprisingly, given its high profile, Poundbury has attracted its fair share of critics. However, the theories behind it seem sound. Aiming to create an integrated community of shops, businesses and housing, it comprises many thoughtfully designed buildings – the architecture is largely traditional and incorporates period features. The streets are planned with people rather than cars in mind, with narrow roads and wide pavements. The most alluring parts of Poundbury are the oldest ones, at the Dorchester end.

Just to the north of the development lies a much older Poundbury: **Poundbury Hillfort**, a middle Bronze Age enclosure dating from around 1500BC. As well as the relatively simple ramparts of the roughly rectangular fort, the channel of the Roman aqueduct which supplied water to Durnovaria is clearly visible as a terrace in the hillside. The aqueduct cut across the northern and eastern sides of the hillfort's outer defences. On the northern side of the fort, the ramparts slope steeply down to the River Frome and there are good views of Dorchester and the surrounding countryside. It may be much smaller than Maiden Castle, but it is relatively easy to access.

Food and drink

A farmers' market is held in Pummery Square under the Brownsword Hall on the morning of the first Saturday of each month.

Octagon Café 4 Pummery Sq, DT1 3GW ① 01305 261555. In an octagonal building on the edge of the square. Serves breakfast, lunch and snacks. Open Mon–Sat 08.30–17.00.

Olives Et Al @ The Potting Shed Poundbury Farm Way, DT1 3RT ① 01305 216788 ⓦ www.olivesetal.co.uk. Deli and licensed café run by Dorset company Olives Et Al (see page 28). As you would expect, there is a great range of local produce and freshly made lunches. Open daily.

④ Maiden Castle

Free to access, this magnificent earthen fortification around two miles southwest of Dorchester is the largest Iron Age hillfort in Britain. The terraced ramparts, which rise to almost 90 feet, enclose an area the size of 50 football pitches. Although it is best known as an Iron Age settlement, the hilltop was first inhabited much earlier, some 6,000 years ago, in the Neolithic period.

Guided tours and walks around Dorchester

Ⓜ 07773 286197 Ⓦ www.thomas-hardy-explorer.co.uk.

Dorchester's town crier, Alistair Chisholm, offers entertaining guided tours and walks around Dorchester and the surrounding area. Some of the most popular are evening ghost walks (focusing on Judge Jeffreys and the Bloody Assizes), Thomas Hardy tours and guided visits to Tolpuddle to trace the story of the martyrs.

Alistair has been Dorchester's town crier since 1997 and has been national champion town crier seven times. His enthusiasm for Dorchester, which he describes as 'the small town with the big story', is wonderfully evident.

Maiden Castle was a bustling settlement populated by the Durotriges tribe. In AD43, the Romans, led by Vespasian, attacked and the Durotriges, armed with only slings and stones, were massacred. A war cemetery excavated near the east gate revealed 34 defenders buried there, one with a Roman ballista bolt in his spine. His remains, along with other finds from the site, are in the Dorset County Museum (see page 65).

The Romans built a temple on the hilltop, the foundations of which are still visible in the northeast sector. However, they had no real use for an oversized hillfort, so they abandoned the site and established Durnovaria, now Dorchester.

It is a short but steep walk from the car park at the base of the fort to the hilltop. It is only by walking around the site that you can get an appreciation of the scale and complexity of the ramparts and the area they protected. It is easy to imagine how petrified the Durotriges must have been as they saw the advancing Roman armies, and how formidable those ramparts must have looked to the opposition.

⑤ The South Winterbornes

The area has two clusters of villages with the 'winterbourne' (or winterborne) prefix to their name, indicating they lie on a stream which flows only in winter. The South Winterbornes are those just west of Dorchester and the North Winterbornes are those near Blandford.

The winterbourne near Dorchester rises above Winterbourne Abbas and joins the River Frome at West Stafford, passing through Winterbourne Steepleton, Winterborne St Martin, Winterborne Monkton and Winterborne Came. The spelling of 'Winterborne' has never been consistent, but traditionally Winterbourne Abbas and Winterbourne Steepleton retain the 'u'.

Attractive **Winterbourne Abbas** is rather spoilt by the A35 running through it. Just west of the village a small Bronze Age stone circle on the edge of a beech wood is known as **Nine Stones**. The canopies of the beech trees cast dappled light over the stones but their proximity to the busy main road is unfortunate.

Winterbourne Steepleton has stone or stone and flint cottages with thatched roofs, mostly dating from the 17th and 18th centuries. The delightful little St Michael and All Angels Church is Saxon and Norman; a rare Saxon sculpture of a flying angel hangs on the north wall of the chancel. In 2011 work began to restore the mill in the village; it retains its mill wheel but had become overgrown by weeds. The rather fine Steepleton Manor is now a retirement home.

Winterborne St Martin, also known as **Martinstown**, is an adorable village, with the stream running down the main street alongside the houses, which are reached by small footbridges over the water. Not surprisingly it won the title of Dorset's Best Kept Large Village in 2007 and 2010. The village still has a post office, pub, village shop and **Stevens Farm Shop**, which has good views of the valley. In the centre is the **Church of St Martin**, which dates from the 12th century and has a 15th-century tower. Inside is a square Purbeck marble font dating from around 1125. Nearby a seasonal stream, or winterbourne, crosses under the road, just in front of the Brewers Arms, which was built as a girls' private school in 1848. If you follow the path upstream past the Brewers Arms you will see the stone **sheep washing pool**, that was used to wash the sheep before sale, as a higher price could be achieved for clean fleeces. It may look simple but it was certainly effective as it was in use as recently as the 1960s. Today, the stream outside the pub is the venue for the village's annual yellow-plastic **duck race**, held in May.

From the centre of the village it is an easy walk to **Maiden Castle**. The round distance is 3½ miles, although this can be extended by walking around the ramparts of the hillfort. As you walk, look out for the many prehistoric mounds known as tumuli or barrows (set up as tombs and landmarks in the Bronze Age) around the Winterbornes and particularly concentrated around Winterborne St Martin. The best known of the barrows in the area is Clandon Barrow, which was partially excavated in 1882. The finds, which included an urn, a copper dagger, a bronze ring and a gold plate are held in the Dorset County Museum.

Food and drink

Brewers Arms DT2 9LB ① 01305 889361 ⓦ www.thebrewersarms.com. A traditional, dog-friendly pub in the centre of the village, built in 1848 as a school. If you stop at the pub be sure to head up the lane along the stream for a look at the sheep washing pool. Open for lunch Tue–Sun, dinner Tue–Sat.

Stevens Farm Shop DT2 9JR ① 01305 889216 ⓦ www.stevensfarmshop.co.uk. Has a range of local produce, handmade gifts and a café. Norman and Liz Barnes have farmed here for over 35 years. It is a great one for the children because of the notable array of farm animals close to the shop – when I visited the varied beasts included cows, goats, pigs and chickens. The café serves roast lunches every Sun.

⑥ Higher Bockhampton, Stinsford and surrounds

The hamlets of Higher Bockhampton and Stinsford just east of Dorchester are best known for their links to Thomas Hardy, who was born in a small, highly picturesque cottage in Higher Bockhampton (see below). He was christened in the **Church of St Michael** in Stinsford and attended services there as a child.

Although he was famously agnostic, Hardy loved this little church. It was in Stinsford that his grandfather founded a small band, who accompanied services from the church's wooden gallery. Hardy's father and Thomas also played with the group, Thomas playing the violin. A tablet within the church commemorates the family's participation. Hardy remembered Stinsford and the band with great affection as 'Mellstock' in his novel *Under the Greenwood Tree*.

Hardy's parents, sister and first wife, Emma, are buried in the churchyard. The Hardy family graves are on the left as you enter from the car park. Hardy's heart is buried alongside Emma but his ashes are in Poet's Corner within Westminster Abbey. Also buried in the graveyard is Cecil Day Lewis (1904–72), poet laureate and detective novelist.

Hardy's Cottage

Higher Bockhampton DT2 8QJ ① 01305 262366 Ⓦ www.nationaltrust.org.uk. Open Mar–Oct Thu–Mon 11.00–17.00; National Trust.

It is fortunate that Thomas Hardy was born in a picture-perfect thatched cob cottage with flower-filled garden, for this must be one of the most photographed addresses in Dorset. The cottage, now held by the National Trust, is nestled at the base of Thorncombe Wood, a five to ten minute walk from the car park. The most direct route is along a fairly level but rough track or there is a pretty, slightly longer and steeper path, through the woods.

The cottage was built by his great-grandfather and was Hardy's home, on and off, from his birth in 1840 until he married Emma Gifford in 1874. Visiting it gives you an appreciation for how quiet, secluded and reflective Hardy's young life must have been. You have the chance to wander the tiny rooms, negotiate the perilously steep staircase and see where he wrote *Under the Greenwood Tree* and *Far from the Madding Crowd*. The cottage has altered little since he lived here and described it in his earliest surviving poem, *Domicilium*:

Red roses, lilacs, variegated box
Are there in plenty, and such hardy flowers

As flourish best untrained. Adjoining these
Are herbs and esculents; and farther still
A field; then cottages with trees, and last
The distant hills and sky.
Behind, the scene is wilder. Heath and furze
Are everything that seems to grow and thrive
Upon the uneven ground. A stunted thorn
Stands here and there, indeed; and from a pit
An oak uprises, Springing from a seed
Dropped by some bird a hundred years ago.

The art of thatching

With Edward Taylor, Master Thatcher

A thatched cottage with a rose wandering around the door is one of the quintessential images of English rural living, and with chocolate-box cottages around every Dorset corner thatch is very much part of the landscape and culture.

Thatching is one of the oldest ways of protecting houses from the elements, and in Britain is believed to date back to the Bronze Age. Not all of the thatched properties you see in Dorset are old, however: many new building projects include houses that are thatched in order to blend in with the surroundings and clear the planning authorities.

Dorset Master Thatcher, Edward Taylor, better known as 'Spike', has been working in the thatching trade since he left school. Before he could call himself qualified, he had to complete a seven-year apprenticeship. According to Spike, the ancient craft takes this long to learn because numerous styles, techniques and materials are used, which vary from county to county.

Spike works mainly with combed wheat reed and water reed. Today, much of the water reed used in England is imported from other countries where it is cheaper to produce but local alternatives can be found. Spike grows several varieties of thatching straw, which can be seen on the roofs he creates. He told me reed is still cut at Abbotsbury and used on the Ilchester Estate buildings, including the 14th-century Tithe Barn, which is by far the largest thatched building in the area. It is fascinating to contemplate that the barn must have been re-thatched by many hands over the centuries yet always with reeds from the same stretch of land.

Spike explained to me that thatching wheat is cut with a reaper/binder and the sheaves (bundles) are 'stooked' up in the fields. It is at this point that I began to realise thatching has its own language of ancient technical terms, so Spike had to translate – eight sheaves make a stook, 16 make a stock. The sheaves are left in the stook for two weeks to dry slowly and evenly, and then put into the rick before going on the threshing machine or reed comber. Here, the short

Kingston Maurward Gardens and Animal Park

DT2 8PY ① 01305 215003 Ⓦ www.kmc.ac.uk. Open daily 10.00–17.30.

Kingston Maurward House lies between Stinsford and Lower Bockhampton. The house was built in 1720 in the classic Palladian style for George Pitt, cousin of William Pitt the Elder, who became prime minister in 1766. During World War II it was occupied by American servicemen and the estate used as a fuel depot for the D-Day landings. Today, Kingston Maurward is a well-regarded agricultural college. The gardens are open to the public and showcase a number of different horticultural styles, including Arts and Crafts and Japanese, and its large lake is a haven for wildlife. The animal park is popular with children, and spring brings the chance to see lambing.

straws, leaf and flag are combed out and the grain and chaff removed. The long stems are kept perfectly straight. Finally, the straw is trussed up and bundled, ready to use.

Laying the thatch is tough physical work and often a battle with the elements. The primary tool is a legget, which is used to coerce the material into position, a process known as 'dressing'. A 'spar', a branch of split hazel wood tapered to a point at each end and twisted into a V shape, is used to staple the thatch into place. Each course overlaps the one below it, providing a continuous depth of straw over the entire roof. The ridge is where the thatcher can really leave his mark; Spike favours the traditional pointed end, which has been used for centuries.

Most of Spike's tools have been made by local blacksmiths and his legget heads cast at Bridport Foundry. He scours the antique farm machinery section at country fairs, looking for the original tools of his trade, now prized above some of the newer versions. He even coppices his own hazel, to make traditional fixings for the thatch – spars, ledgers, liggers and sways.

Spike points out that qualifying and working as a Master Thatcher is not for the faint-hearted: the few men who carry on this ancient craft do so for the love of it and are fiercely proud.

While we all love the look of a thatched roof, people are divided as to whether they would want to live under one. Beauty doesn't come cheap: the roof needs to be re-thatched about every 25 years and the ridge needs to be replaced around every ten years. Depending on the roof and the materials used re-thatching can cost around £25,000; on top of that there is usually an insurance premium because of a perceived fire risk. Thankfully, the undeniable charm of a thatched roof means that they will remain part of the rural landscape, just as they have for the past 4,500 years.

Edward Taylor ① 01297 489528, 07966 209561 Ⓦ www.thatching.biz.

Food and drink

Yalbury Cottage Lower Bockhampton DT2 8PZ ① 01305 262382 ⑩ www.
yalburycottage.com. A highly regarded restaurant in this small, thatched hotel.
The menu changes daily according to the produce available. The 3-course farmers'
market Sunday lunch is very popular. Reservation recommended.

⑦ Mill House Cider Museum and A Dorset Collection of Clocks

33 Moreton Rd, Owermoigne DT2 8HZ ① 01305 852220 ⑩ www.millhousecider.com.
Open Tue–Sun and public holidays.

This museum (north of the A352) provides an insight into traditional cider-
making and includes displays of antique cider-making equipment. In October
you can see apples being transformed into cider using 19th-century machinery.
You can even bring your own apples and put them through the museum's
crusher and press to make apple juice or cider. Some villages pool their apples
and take them to the museum by the trailer load to produce a communal
supply. Also on site are a shop selling West Country produce and a garden
nursery specialising in seed potatoes.

Adjacent, a separate clock museum houses an extensive collection including
over 30 grandfather clocks. They are beautifully displayed and will delight
anyone with even a passing interest in timepieces.

North from Dorchester towards the Blackmore Vale

The A352 runs north from Dorchester to Sherborne and North Dorset.
Between Dorchester and Minterne Magna the road runs parallel to the River
Cerne and takes you through the pretty villages of the Cerne Valley. It is along
this road that you will see one of Dorset's most distinctive sights, the **Cerne
Abbas Giant**.

⑧ Godmanstone

With a bar measuring just 20 by 10 feet, **The Smith's Arms** at Godmanstone
once claimed (among many others) to be the smallest pub in England. It is
visible from the A352 as you pass through Godmanstone: a thatched 15th-
century building of mud and flint, backing onto the River Cerne.

Tradition has it that King Charles II stopped at a blacksmith's forge in
Godmanstone and requested a glass of porter. The blacksmith responded, 'I
cannot oblige you Sire, as I have no license.' The king reportedly granted one
on the spot and The Smith's Arms came into being.

In 1982 the licensee of the Nutshell at Bury St Edmunds challenged The
Smith's Arms's claim to be the smallest pub. The rival landlords decided to

settle the matter with a football match, which the Nutshell won. The Nutshell has subsequently lost the title to even tinier competitors.

The Smith's Arms operated as a pub for many years but a sign on it now announces that it has closed indefinitely. It is still worth stopping off to admire it from the outside.

⑨ Cerne Abbas and its giant

Travellers along the A352 are treated to a very unusual and surprising sight – the 180-foot tall chalk carving of a naked man known as the **Cerne Abbas Giant**. He is also known as 'The Rude Man', for reasons (actually one very obvious reason) which become apparent when you look at him from the roadside viewpoint. I strongly suspect that the postcards of the Rude Man in his birthday suit are the county's best-selling postcards.

The giant is a Scheduled Ancient Monument in the care of the National Trust although his origins are uncertain.

AJ.

Some believe that he represents the Roman god, Hercules, and is over 1,500 years old. This theory is supported by the fact he is brandishing a club and a recent discovery indicating he once carried a cloak over his left arm. However, there is no known record of the carving prior to 1694 and it has been suggested that the giant is more recent, perhaps a caricature of any one of a number of historical figures – Oliver Cromwell is one candidate. Whatever the truth, he has been worshipped as a fertility symbol for centuries and appears to be highly effective in this regard, at least as far as the local population is concerned: in 2010 it was revealed that North Dorset has the highest birth rates in the country, with women having an average of three children. There is a picnic area 200 yards from the giant viewpoint on the road towards the village of Cerne Abbas. This is the place to park if you want to tackle the walk up the hill to get a closer look at the giant as the walk begins just near the picnic area, at Kettle Bridge.

The Benedictine abbey founded in AD987, around which the village of **Cerne Abbas** grew up, was largely destroyed after the Dissolution of the Monasteries in the 16th century. Little remains of the abbey, save the ruins at **Abbey Farm** at the top of Abbey Street, near the duck pond. The house was built around two walls and a Saxon doorway from the abbey, and with much other surviving stonework reset into its walls. To the right is the gate into the graveyard and if you follow the wall to your right you will come to **St Augustine's Well**. Also known as the Silver Well, this is another of the few relics remaining from the days of the abbey. According to legend, **St Augustine of Canterbury** (died AD604) visited Dorset and met some shepherds in the then uninhabited Cerne Valley. He asked if they would prefer beer or water to quench their thirst. When they replied 'water', the saint struck the ground with his staff and the spring started to flow. Some cynical folk have suggested that the Benedictine monks of Cerne Abbey fabricated the story to attract pilgrims.

Cerne Abbas is a delightful village with a mixture of architectural styles evoking different eras from medieval to Georgian. It has only around 800 permanent residents but is well-equipped with tearooms and pubs to cater for the many tourists who come to marvel at the giant. On Abbey Street, opposite the **Church of St Mary the Virgin**, is a row of wonderfully wonky wooden houses dating from around 1500. The church itself was built by the abbey. It dates from the 15th century, although the chancel is earlier being circa 1300, and there were various additions in the 17th and 18th centuries.

Food and drink

Abbots Tea Rooms 7 Long St, DT2 7JF ℗ 01300 341349
Ⓦ www.abbotsbedandbreakfast.co.uk. Light lunches are on offer, as well as the usual cream teas. Open 10.00–16.30, closed Mon Oct–Easter.
New Inn 14 Long St, DT2 7JF ℗ 01300 341274
Ⓦ www.newinncerneabbas.com. The restaurant within this 16th-century coaching inn is full of beams and character. The restaurant specialises in local fish and game prepared to a high standard. Main courses start at around £12. Open for lunch and dinner daily, but with a bar menu only on Sun evenings.
Royal Oak 23 Long St, DT2 7JG ℗ 01300 341797 Ⓦ www.royaloakcerneabbas. co.uk. This charming ivy-covered pub dates from 1540 and serves traditional pub food, including some excellent game dishes. Popular with walkers and dog owners. I was told that the previous landlord reported a ghostly presence at the pub, although the current landlord has yet to see any evidence of a haunting. Open for lunch and dinner daily.

⑩ Minterne Magna

As you travel north from Cerne Abbas towards Sherborne on the A352, you pass through the pretty village of Minterne Magna. The church here, **St Andrew's**, is based on an original Saxon church now incorporated into the chancel. The nave and chancel were built in the early 15th century, while the north chapel was added between 1610 and 1620. Next door to the church is the entrance to **Minterne Gardens** (see below).

Minterne Gardens

DT2 7AU ℗ 01300 341370 Ⓦ www.minterne.co.uk. Open Mar–Nov 10.00–18.00.
Although the house is only open by appointment, visitors can walk around the impressive gardens of this private home. You will need to leave your car in the car park opposite St Andrew's Church and walk across the road to enter the gardens, which were landscaped in the 18th century in the manner of Capability Brown. The owner at that time, Robert Digby, reportedly used to visit the family home at Sherborne Castle whenever Brown was working there

and pick his brain for ideas. Keen gardeners will enjoy walking the 1½ miles of paths, which wind through the garden and criss-cross the stream. Himalayan rhododendrons and azaleas feature heavily in the design, so it is particularly colourful from March to June. In April and May, bluebells and wild garlic add soft colour and a woodland perfume. The garden's appeal is greatly enhanced by its location, in a wide valley where sheep graze nonchalantly below a band of woodland.

The Piddle Valley and Bere Regis

The River Piddle (also known far less amusingly as the River Trent) rises near the church in the village of Alton Pancras and flows towards Wareham, entering the sea at Poole Harbour along with the River Frome. The name Piddle is thought to derive from the Saxon meaning clear water. Many of the villages it passes through are named after the river, creating some of the best village names in existence: Puddletown, Tolpuddle, Piddlehinton, Piddletrenthide, Affpuddle, Briantspuddle and Turnerspuddle. All but two of those names now contain 'puddle' rather than 'piddle'. The reason for that is up for debate. A popular story tells that the villages were renamed prior to a visit by Queen Victoria to avoid offending her sensibilities but there is no firm evidence of this. A more prosaic theory is that the names were altered in response to a request from the post office.

⑪ Buckland Newton

Just above Alton Pancras on the B3143 is the scattered village of Buckland Newton and the hamlets which surround it. It is largely an agricultural community within a landscape of pastureland and gentle hills. Between Buckland Newton and Alton Pancras is the tiny hamlet of Henley, which is where you will find Old Henley Farm with its unmissable **badger-watching** opportunities.

Badger and Wildlife Night Watch
Old Henley Farm DT2 7BL ① 01300 345293 ⓜ 07860 759996
ⓦ www.badgerwatchdorset.co.uk. Booking essential.
A hugely rewarding way for anyone interested in wildlife to spend an evening. Viewing of the badgers is from two hides (each can take up to 12 people) positioned in front of the farm's badger setts. You arrive at 18.30 for an 18.45 start, which means you have a good chance of seeing the shy creatures in daylight. The evening I went was warm and sunny – lovely weather for badgers and even better for badger watchers. We only had to wait about 20 minutes before the first badger appeared from the hedgerow. She poked her head out and cautiously sniffed the air, then waddled down towards the hide, where she snuffled around in the grass, just a few yards

from us, hoovering up tasty morsels. At one point she appeared to be having a battle with a particularly stubborn worm as she dug in her heels and tugged tenaciously on what looked like a piece of elastic; it finally gave way and she staggered backwards with her reward. Throughout the evening we saw four or five different badgers merrily going about their business, oblivious that they were taking part in a thrilling reality show for the viewers within the hide. As darkness fell, soft lights came on under the hides allowing us to continue watching the wildlife. We saw rabbits (of course) and bats, and the sightings book in the hide showed visitors have also seen foxes, deer and barn owls.

Henley Hillbillies
Old Henley Farm, DT2 7BL ① 01300 345293 ⓜ 07860 759996
ⓦ www.henleyhillbillies.co.uk.
As well as badger watching, Old Henley Farm offers daytime activities which are more 'Extreme Dorset' than 'Slow Dorset'. Thrill seekers can career around a track on quad-bikes, mini maveriks and hovercrafts. Clay shooting, archery and crossbows are also on offer.

Food and drink
Gaggle of Geese DT2 7BS ① 01300 345249 ⓦ www.thegaggle.co.uk. Gaggle of Geese is proof that the pub can be the hub of the community. Owners Emily and Mark see providing a venue for village events as central to their role. They host the village fête, school Christmas lunch and, of course, the village skittles team. In May and September they hold a poultry auction to raise money for charity. The menu has some old favourites, as well as more adventurous creations. Mark uses local produce whenever possible, including meat from his mother's farm at Lower Wraxall. Open for lunch and dinner daily. Take-away available.

⑫ Piddletrenthide and Piddlehinton
Piddletrenthide and its neighbour Piddlehinton are appealing villages, with stone and flint-banded cottages. Stretched along the river valley, **Piddletrenthide** gets its memorable name from the fact that it is on the River Piddle and was assessed for 30 hides in the Domesday Book. A hide was a unit used to measure land value in order to calculate tax, and was originally the amount of land that could be ploughed in a year using one plough and an eight-ox team. The area thus varied with soil quality and a 'hide' could range from 60 to 180 acres. Piddletrenthide has a good village shop and, at the northern end of the village, a fine **church** with a splendid tower dated 1487.

The name of the river was a marketing gem waiting to be exploited. In 2002 a micro-brewery was set up in Piddlehinton, **The Piddle Brewery** (*www. dorsetpiddlebrewery.co.uk*), which now markets a series of beers with names like

Piddle in a Bottle, Jimmy Riddle and *Silent Slasher*. You will see their beers in pubs and shops throughout the county.

⑬ Athelhampton House and Gardens

Athelhampton DT2 7LG ℡ 01305 848363 ⓦ www.athelhampton.co.uk. Open Mar–Oct Sun–Thu 10.30–17.00, Nov–Feb Sun 11.00–dusk.

A beautiful manor house, dating from the 15th century, this is now privately owned by the Cooke family. Thomas Hardy was a frequent visitor and referred to it in his writings as 'Athelhall'. Its sumptuously furnished rooms include the Great Hall (built in1485) with its vast fireplace and stained-glass windows. On the second floor is a gallery displaying the work of the artist Marevna, who lived at the house from 1948 to 1957. In the East Wing an intimate 50-seat **cinema** shows films on Sunday afternoon and Monday evening, making a rather grand cinematic experience; you can buy refreshments in the Great Hall before taking your seat.

The Grade I-listed gardens were largely laid down in the late 19th century and feature perfect topiary pyramids and colourful herbaceous borders. Also in the garden, which is bordered by the River Piddle, are a 15th-century dovecote, a 19th-century toll house and a self-catering cottage sleeping six (see page 61), as well as a pleasant restaurant open for lunch, morning and afternoon tea.

Like all big, old houses Athelhampton Hall has a ghost story, although its story involves a rather unusual haunting: it is reportedly haunted by a phantom monkey who lived as a pet in the hall in the 15th century. It is said the unfortunate primate was accidentally imprisoned in a secret passage and starved to death.

Food and drink

Poachers Inn Piddletrenthide DT2 7QX ℡ 01300 348358 ⓦ www.thepoachersinn. co.uk. A pleasant restaurant in a 17th-century pub, which serves unpretentious meals. Has a nice riverside garden. Open daily for breakfast, lunch and dinner.

⑭ Tolpuddle

The small village of Tolpuddle has secured its place in history thanks to the actions of six farm labourers in 1834, now known as the Tolpuddle Martyrs (see box, page 81). The labourers spoke up about their intolerable poverty and took an oath of mutual support, essentially forming an early trade union. This did not go down at all well with the local landowners; the farm labourers were charged with swearing an illegal oath and were transported to Australia. Public outcry eventually led to their pardon and they returned to England.

The village has become a place of pilgrimage for its links to the trade union movement. The Trades Union Congress (TUC) holds an annual festival at Tolpuddle in honour of the martyrs on the third Sunday in July. The festival, which attracts as many as 10,000 people, culminates in a procession through the village by representatives of various Trade Unions, accompanied by marching bands. The festival also involves live music, speeches by prominent socialists and stalls selling local produce.

On the west side of the village are six memorial cottages built by the TUC in 1934 to commemorate the 100th anniversary of the martyrs' transportation and to provide accommodation for retired agricultural trade unionists. In the centre of these is the small **Tolpuddle Martyrs Museum** (*DT2 7EH; 01305 848237; www.tolpuddlemartyrs.org.uk; open Apr–Oct Tue–Sun, Nov–Mar Thu–Sun; free admission*), devoted to the martyrs and the history of the trade union movement. This interesting and well laid-out little museum evolved from a library intended for residents of the cottages but which soon became a depository for artefacts, documents and memorabilia relating to the martyrs. Over the years, it developed into the Tolpuddle Martyrs Museum.

When I visited the museum, there was an elderly gentleman wearing a TUC cap sitting on a bench in the sunshine just outside the cottages. His name, it transpired, was Ernest (Ernie) Chaffey. Ernie and I got chatting and it turned out he lived in one of the six TUC cottages. Ernie told me proudly that in 51 years of working as a farm labourer he had only had one day unemployed, and that was a bank holiday which happened to fall between the end of one job and the start of another. Ernie explained that he had worked for over 30 years on a 3,000-acre dairy farm near Dorchester, during which time he lived in a farm worker's cottage on the estate. When he retired he had to move out of the cottage and, even after all those years of hard work, Ernie had no home of his own. He was lucky enough to be allocated one of the TUC cottages. Ernie mused, 'I suppose I could have gone into a retirement flat, but I have the wife and the dog to consider and I don't think we would have liked it'. It was obvious to me that this man was not meant to be confined to a flat. Even as we spoke, I could see his eyes scanning the rolling fields and I suspect he was longing to be back in the tractor seat. We talked about farming and the changes it has seen in Ernie's lifetime. These days all of Ernie's agricultural attention and energy is focused on the garden at the back of the cottage, where vibrantly healthy vegetables stand to attention in neat rows.

The village of Tolpuddle has a pleasing blend of brick and cob cottages, many of them thatched. Some newer houses have been added but thankfully in a similar architectural style to the old ones. At the centre of the village is a small green, on which stands the largest sycamore in Dorset. This is the tree under which the martyrs used to meet but it seems it was there long before the martyrs came along – the National Trust has dated the tree as having started its life in the 1680s. Next to the tree is a thatched shelter dedicated to the martyrs, erected as part of the 100th anniversary celebrations in 1934. A new sycamore was planted in 1984 to replace the old one when the time comes.

St John's Church is a striking stone and flint building. Although the original

The Tolpuddle Martyrs

In the 1830s life was tough for farm labourers in Dorset. Increased mechanisation of farming practices in the early part of the 19th century meant landowners became less dependent on labourers and lowered the average agricultural wage. Labourers in Dorset had traditionally been poorly paid in comparison with their counterparts in the rest of England and eventually wages in the county fell to just seven shillings a week. It became impossible for a labourer to support his family.

In 1833, a group of farm labourers from Tolpuddle made representation to their local landowners and employers for an increase in wages. This request was met by a decree that wages would be reduced further to six shillings a week.

Under the leadership of George Loveless (a respected Methodist lay preacher), some of the aggrieved labourers organised themselves into a 'Friendly Society of Agricultural Labourers', effectively an early trade union. The group would meet either under what has now become known as the 'Martyrs Tree' on the village green or in the cottage of group member John Standfield.

Local landowners, led by James Frampton of Moreton House, were determined to quash any uprising, particularly given what had happened to their French counterparts during the French Revolution.

On a cold February morning in 1834, police arrested six members of the group: George Loveless and his brother James, Thomas Standfield and his son John, James Hammett and James Brine. These men were tried at Dorchester Assizes, and found guilty of unlawful assembly and administering an illegal oath. Forming a union had been made legal in 1824, but they had made the mistake of swearing an oath which meant they could be tried under the Mutiny Act of 1797. Sentencing them to transportation to Australia for a period of seven years, the judge noted he wanted to make an example of them. At the trial, George Loveless reportedly said: 'if we have violated any law, it was not intentionally. We have injured no person or property. We were uniting to preserve ourselves, our wives and our children from utter degradation and starvation.'

The public outcry at the martyrs' harsh treatment, driven by a fledging trade union movement, was so great that it led to pardons being granted in March 1836. It was three years before the martyrs were brought back to Dorset. During their absence, their families were sustained by the trade union movement. The martyrs returned first to Essex, where land had been set aside for them, but several later migrated to London in Ontario, Canada. The only martyr to remain in Tolpuddle was James Hammett, who returned to England a year later than the others and worked as a builder. He died in Tolpuddle in 1891 and is buried in the churchyard.

church dates from the 12th century it has been altered and restored over the years, most significantly in 1855. In the graveyard is the grave of the only one of the Tolpuddle Martyrs who returned to live in the village, James Hammett, who died in 1891.

Food and drink

The Martyrs Inn DT2 7LG ℗ 01305 848249 Ⓦ www.themartyrsinn.co.uk. Serves traditional pub food. The beef comes from a farm just 5 miles away. Morning coffee, lunch and dinner daily.

⑮ Bere Regis

Bere Regis is one of those towns that used to suffer from having a main road running through it, but it has now been by-passed. Much of the town was destroyed in a series of fires, the worst of which occurred in 1788, and as a result it is largely a mixture of 18th century and more modern buildings. The one exception is the marvellous **Church of St John the Baptist**, which dates from 1050.

The uninspiring approach to the church from the car park in town takes you through an estate of modern houses and does not do the church justice, but do persevere. The church bell ringers were in full swing when I visited on a sunny evening in May. A 16th-century tower in flint and stone sets an impressive note, and inside it is even better. The nave has a magnificent 15th-century carved oak ceiling with figures of the Apostles looking down from above. Much of the wood is painted and gilded: coin-operated lights highlight the ceiling to really bring out its colours and detail. The central bosses depict Cardinal Morton, his shield of arms, a Tudor rose and a golden cord symbolising the marriage he arranged between Henry VII and Elizabeth of York in 1486, so ending the Wars of the Roses. A small amount of the 1050 church survives at the northeast end of the nave. Just inside the door at the edge of the nave are 12th-century capitals with some curious carvings: the head of a monkey, a king and two people apparently with toothache.

There is a slab in the floor over the entrance to the Turbeville vault, which reads '1710 Door of the sepulchre of the ancient family of the Turbevilles'. The manor house at Bere Regis was the home of the Turberville family from the 13th century to the 18th century, when that branch of the family became extinct. It was the fall of the powerful Turbervilles which inspired Thomas Hardy's *Tess of the d'Urbervilles*.

While you are in the church look out for the Bere Regis funeral bier – the September 1898 model. A sign tells that it could be hired as a burial board by Bere for 2/6d, Kingston for 5/- and other parishes for 10/-; that's respectively 12½p, 25p and 50p in today's money.

Food and drink

Pampered Pigs Pantry Rye Hill Farm House, Rye Hill BH20 7LP ℗ 01929 472327. Animal welfare is a priority for this free-range farm, which raises traditional breeds of cattle, pigs and sheep. The meat is available in the farm shop, along with organic groceries. Visitors can take a walk around the farm or stop in at the café. Open daily.

Royal Oak West St, BH20 7HQ ⓣ 01929 471203 ⓦ www.theroyaloakhotel.co.uk. A 16th-century coaching inn in the centre of Bere Regis. Decent pub food is served in the pleasant bar area, beer garden or courtyard. Good vegetarian options.

⑯ Shitterton

You won't be surprised to hear that the hamlet of Shitterton, near Bere Regis, is best known for its name, which appeals greatly to those with a fondness for lavatory humour and ranks at number nine in *Rude Britain: The 100 Rudest Place Names in Britain*. While some prudish folk leave out the 'h', many of the residents are proud to tell you precisely where they live and even emphasise the 'sh'. In a broad Dorset accent, the name has even more of a ring to it.

The most irritating thing about living in Shitterton was, until recently, the lack of a road sign, which played havoc with home deliveries. Due to frequent theft of Shitterton's sign by souvenir hunters, the council gave up replacing it. In July 2010, after nearly three years without a sign, residents banded together to purchase a slab of Purbeck stone and have it engraved with the hamlet's name. Of some 50 Shitterton households, well over half contributed and the local council chipped in too. It would take a highly committed souvenir hunter to make off with the 1½-ton slab of Purbeck stone which now announces, rather grandly, the hamlet's name.

Shitterton is far more comely than its name may indicate. It was protected by the Bere River from the fires that destroyed Bere Regis, so still retains some older, mostly thatched buildings. A pretty stream runs through Shitterton, although it loses some of its charm when you learn the origin of the hamlet's name, which apparently means stream used as a public convenience.

The Frome Valley

⑰ Moreton

The small village of Moreton is firmly on the Lawrence of Arabia trail, for it was in **St Nicholas's Church** that Lawrence's funeral took place on the afternoon of 21 May 1935. It was well attended, including by Sir Winston Churchill, Robert Graves and Siegfried Sassoon. Lawrence is buried in the cemetery to the south of the village; his grave is at the far end on the right. The headstone records Lawrence's real name, although he had changed his name by deed poll to T E Shaw in 1923 to escape his celebrity status (see box, page 85).

Regardless of its connections to Lawrence of Arabia, St Nicholas's Church is fascinating. The original church was demolished in 1776 and replaced by a Georgian, Gothic building, thanks to the Frampton family (cousins of T E Lawrence), who lived in Moreton House behind the church.

The church's best-known feature is its unusual engraved windows by Laurence Whistler. The windows were installed in 1955 and 1974–84. A German bomb destroyed the original stained-glass windows on 8 October 1940, along with the north wall of the church. The theme of the replacement windows is light: one depicts candles, another lightning, one the sun, and the effect of the clear glass is striking. You are so accustomed to not being able to see the view from a church, yet this one allows you to see the sky and trees outside and lets light flood in. Near the church is Moreton Tearooms, a convenient lunch or tea stop.

Food and drink

Moreton Tearooms ① 01929 463647 ⑩ www.moretontearooms.co.uk. In an attractive former schoolhouse near the church, with a large outdoor walled patio area. The menu is more sophisticated than your typical tearooms, with lunches such as local game stew. There are displays on the life of T E Lawrence. Open daily 10.00–17.00.

⑱ Clouds Hill

Near Wareham BH20 7NQ ① 01929 405616 ⑩ www.nationaltrust.org.uk. Open Mar–Oct Wed–Sun; National Trust.

This unassuming former forester's cottage, now owned by the National Trust, is where T E Lawrence (Lawrence of Arabia; see box opposite) lived between 1923 and 1935. At that time, he was using the pseudonym T E Shaw to escape the fame he had acquired in the Middle East.

Lawrence first rented the cottage in 1923 while stationed at Bovington Camp with the Tank Corps, and bought it in 1925 from his cousins, the Framptons, the landlords of the Moreton Estate. It was here that Lawrence completed *Seven Pillars of Wisdom* and *The Mint.*

The interior has been recreated to appear as it was when Lawrence lived there. The house is deliberately spartan – Lawrence wrote: 'nothing in Clouds Hill is to be a care upon the world. While I have it there shall be nothing exquisite or unique in it. Nothing to anchor me'. The cottage served as Lawrence's retreat, where he read, wrote and listened to music, so it is fitting that his collection of music and books remains. An exhibition provides further insight into Lawrence's extraordinary life.

In 1935, Lawrence left the RAF and retired to Clouds Hill. A few months later, at the age of 46, he was involved in a fatal accident on his Brough Superior motorcycle close to the house.

⑲ Bovington Tank Museum

Bovington BH20 6JG ① 01929 462359 ⑩ www.tankmuseum.org. Open daily.

The tank museum adjoins Bovington Camp, home of the British Army's Armour Centre. As the name indicates, the museum tells the story of the tank from its invention in 1915 to the present day. The first thing to strike you about this museum is its size – it is vast. You will need to allow at least three hours to get around. A useful large café overlooks the arena.

Lawrence of Arabia

Thomas Edward Lawrence, also known as Lawrence of Arabia, was born in Wales on 16 August 1888. From the age of eight he lived in Oxford, where he later read Modern History at Jesus College.

In 1911, Lawrence worked as an archaeologist in Syria, where he gained knowledge of the Arab culture and language. He made several further trips to the Middle East until the outbreak of World War I.

In 1914, he joined the British Army and was posted to Military Intelligence in Cairo. In June 1916, he was sent to investigate the Arab revolt in the Hejaz, where he formed a bond with the local Arab leader, Amir Feisal. Feisal's troops were committed but ill-disciplined and Lawrence planned to harness their passion by focusing on guerrilla tactics to disrupt the Turkish Army's activities. He led Bedouin tribesmen in guerrilla raids against the Turkish Army, which eventually contributed to British and Arab forces taking Damascus. Lawrence lived the life of a Bedouin, eating what they ate, wearing Arab dress and riding a camel, which earned him an almost mythical status among the Arabs who fought with him.

He returned to Britain in 1918 as Colonel Lawrence and lobbied unsuccessfully for Arab independence. Lawrence attempted to escape from the public eye by changing his identity and in 1922 enlisted in the RAF as Aircraftman Ross. His alias was soon discovered and he was forced out of the RAF.

In 1923, as T E Shaw, he joined the Tank Corps and was stationed at Bovington Camp. He didn't much care for army life and purchased nearby Clouds Hill as a retreat. In 1925, Lawrence rejoined the RAF, and after a spell in Karachi, was posted to Plymouth, where he lobbied successfully for faster rescue boats. He spent the rest of his career developing and testing high-speed rescue boats, which formed the basis of the air-sea rescue service.

Lawrence retired to Clouds Hill in 1935, where, only a few months later, he was involved in a serious collision on his Brough Superior motorcycle. He died six days later in the military hospital at Bovington Camp. Lawrence's mother arranged for his body to be buried at Moreton Church, in the family plot belonging to his cousins, the Framptons of Moreton House.

You can walk the 6¾-mile 'Lawrence of Arabia Trail' tracing his life in the area. It starts at the Bovington Tank Museum and takes in Clouds Hill and Moreton. A leaflet on the trail is available from local tourist information centres (such as Wareham) and online (*www.dorsetforyou.com; under 'walking in Purbeck'*). If you want to know more but don't fancy the walk, the Wareham Town Museum has a display devoted to Lawrence, as does the Moreton Tearooms.

Front-of-house manager, Alan Tubbs, told me that the collection of tanks is one of the biggest and most varied in the world. Alan went on to explain that it was Rudyard Kipling who pressed for the creation of a museum after a visit to Bovington in 1923, when it held a small selection of tanks that had survived World War I. The museum opened to the public in 1947.

Almost 200 vehicles from 26 countries are on display, each with a story to tell. They include 'Little Willie', the first tracked vehicle, which was developed in 1915 by the Landships Committee, which had been established by First Lord of the Admiralty, Winston Churchill, to tackle the problems of trench warfare.

The World War I trench experience is particularly moving, taking you from the recruiting office to the front line in the boots of a young soldier. When I visited I was lucky enough to see the Battlegroup Afghanistan exhibition, revealing the work of the Royal Armoured Corps in that area. The reconstruction of a forward operating base provides an insight into what life is like for troops on the frontline.

On weekdays during the school summer holidays (and at some other specific times) live tank displays take place on the Kuwait Arena and are a big hit with children. Tank ride experiences were postponed at the time of writing but are set to return.

⑳ Monkey World Ape Rescue Centre

Near Wool BH20 6HH ☏ 01929 462537 ⓦ www.monkeyworld.org. Open daily except Christmas Day. See advert in colour section.

In a 65-acre park between Bere Regis and Wool live some unlikely Dorset residents: over 240 rescued and endangered apes and monkeys call Monkey World home. As well as making a perfect day out for children and adults, this is first and foremost a rescue centre: every one of the animals at Monkey World is there because it needs to be. The centre has about 60 chimpanzees living in four social groups, plus orang-utans, woolly monkeys, squirrel monkeys, capuchins and more. One of the highlights for visitors is a walk-through **lemur enclosure**, which allows you to get up close to these curious creatures.

New Yorker Jim Cronin started the rescue centre in 1987, on the site of a derelict pig farm near Wool. There was a good degree of scepticism in the local community and beyond, but Jim had a vision and the energy and enthusiasm to bring it to life. He met his wife Alison when she visited in 1992. She had a background in biological anthropology and animal behaviour and had been working on the rescue of bears. Jim and Alison married in 1996 and, together with Jim's right-hand-man, Jeremy Keeling, continued to rescue primates. Their work and the centre drew international acclaim and touched a wide audience through the television shows *Monkey Business* and *Monkey Life*. Sadly, Jim died suddenly of cancer in 2007 at the age of 55, a year after he and Alison were awarded the MBE for services to animal welfare. Alison, Jeremy and their team continue the centre's valuable work and the realisation of Jim's vision.

Monkey World was one of the world's first primate rescue centres. Initially its mission was to provide homes for chimpanzees rescued from a miserable life as props for beach photographers in Spain. By necessity, that mission expanded to rescuing primates from circuses, laboratories and the entertainment industry worldwide. Monkey World now works to assist governments around the world to stop the smuggling and mistreatment of primates. The centre also runs important captive-breeding programmes for endangered species, including orang-utans, golden-cheeked gibbons and woolly monkeys.

In January 2008, Monkey World completed the largest primate rescue in history, when 88 capuchin monkeys were rescued from a medical research laboratory in Santiago, Chile. They had been living in solitary confinement in small cages, some for as long as 20 years.

Like the capuchins, many of the rescued primates who arrive at Monkey World have been kept in unnatural conditions, neglected or suffered cruel treatment. They arrive in poor condition, with physical and psychological problems. As you wander around Monkey World, it is a joy to see the rehabilitated animals living in large enclosures with plenty of stimulation and good company. Watching the antics of Monkey World's primates is bound to bring a smile to any visitor's face. The keepers are a devoted bunch, and hold regular, informative talks. Guided tours are available by appointment and you can even get married here.

Monkey World does not receive government funding: it depends on donations and funds raised by opening the rescue centre to the public. By visiting you are helping to support the valuable work conducted here. If you are as moved by the centre's animals as I was, you may wish to consider primate adoption. In exchange for a small fee, you can 'adopt' a particular primate. Monkey World will send you a photograph of your chosen primate, an adoption certificate, three editions of the centre's newsletter and free entry for a year. Adoption also makes a great gift – I recently gave my mother adoption of a young orang-utan and she was delighted. (I suppose that makes the orang-utan my step brother!) Further details are available on Monkey World's website.

Bulbarrow Hill, Milton Abbas and surrounds

At 902 feet, **Bulbarrow Hill** is the third highest point in Dorset and affords far-reaching views over the Blackmore Vale and towards Somerset. It can be reached on foot from the much-photographed village of **Milton Abbas**, passing Milton Abbey School *en route*.

㉑ Bulbarrow Hill and Woolland Hill

At any time of year the views from Bulbarrow and Woolland Hill are breathtaking. Up here you can see five counties, namely Dorset, Somerset, Wiltshire, Hampshire and Devon. Standing out on the horizon are King

Alfred's Tower near Stourhead in Wiltshire and Duncliffe Hill (see page 18). In summer the patchwork fields of the Blackmore Vale are every shade of green and yellow, while in winter the bare trees stand like skeletons silhouetted against a frosty backdrop. They are views which have been delighting visitors for hundreds of years, at least. Renowned Dorset historian, Reverend John Hutchins, described the view from Bulbarrow as 'surpassing imagination'. In his *Highways and Byways in Dorset*, Sir Frederick Treves (1853–1923) poetically portrayed it as a waving valley of green fields stretching for miles, 'with trees in lines, in knolls, in avenues, in dots; a red roof, the glitter of a trout stream, the trail of a white road, and at the end blue-grey hills so far away that they seem to be made of sea mist'.

Ever-popular with paragliders and model aircraft enthusiasts, **Bulbarrow Hill** has on its promontory Rawlsbury Camp, an Iron Age hillfort with discernable traces of its twin embankments. Also on the summit are two tall masts which served as radio location posts during World War II. As one of Dorset's grandest viewpoints, this makes a highly rewarding objective for walks; the well-signposted Wessex Ridgeway runs along the road between Bulbarrow Hill and Ibberton Hill.

There is a car park and local nature reserve at nearby **Woolland Hill**, one of the largest remaining fragments of chalk heath in Dorset at over ten acres. This rare habitat enables acid-loving plants, such as heather, to grow in an alkaline area. Profuse bird and butterfly life includes stonechats and meadow brown butterflies.

㉒ Milton Abbas and Milton Abbey

Milton Abbas is typically described with a combination of over-used phrases, including 'chocolate-box' and 'picture-postcard'. With its two neat rows of pleasingly uniform white cob thatched cottages on either side of a wide road, it is hard to imagine a village more deserving of those descriptions. It did not evolve but was deliberately planned in the 18th century as an estate village for the nearby Abbey House. The cottages were designed to house two families and there was a good deal of overcrowding and poverty. Most of them have since been converted to single dwellings. Some house names point to the identity of their original inhabitants: baker, blacksmith and brewery. On the main street there is also a pub, almshouses, a post office and a church. The almshouses, dated 1674, were moved from the original estate village of Middleton.

The Benedictine Abbey at Milton Abbas was founded circa AD934 by King Athelstan, grandson of Alfred the Great, and became one of the richest in the West Country with estates of over 14,000 acres. Following the Dissolution of the Monasteries in 1539 the abbey was sold. In 1752, it was bought by Joseph Damer (Lord Milton and later Earl of Dorchester). Damer demolished many of the monastic buildings and built a grand Gothic mansion, **Abbey House**, adjacent to the abbey church.

Damer drafted in famed landscape designer Capability Brown to design gardens worthy of his new home. Damer and Brown felt that the town of Middleton was spoiling the view from the big house, so Damer set about demolishing it in order to replace it with an ornamental lake. The only obstacle was what to do with the townspeople, but Damer found a straightforward solution. He commissioned the building of one of the first model villages in order to house the displaced Middletonians. After all, they would still be needed to run the house and the estate. Capability Brown assisted with the design of the new village and Milton Abbas was built in 1780, just one mile from the original town of Middleton. When the last residents of Middleton refused to leave the town, Damer opened the sluice gates of the new dam and flooded the area. Unfortunately for Damer, one of those residents was a lawyer, who sued and won.

Abbey House is now part of **Milton Abbey School**, one of Dorset's many fine private schools. It is easy to see why Damer thought it the perfect spot for a house, nestled in a natural amphitheatre of wooded hills. The lawns in front of the house make an idyllic spot for playing cricket, which is precisely what you will see the schoolboys doing on a summer's day.

Every two years the villagers hold a **fair** with an 18th-century flavour to celebrate the rebuilding of the village. The main street is closed to traffic, and residents and stall holders dress in 18th-century costume. The day includes traditional music and dancing, local craft stalls and a farmers' market.

Milton Abbey Church

You can take the estate road in to see the church. Additionally, a public footpath crosses the estate – from the bottom of Milton Abbas, walk down to the junction, turn right and the signposted path soon goes off on the left. To give it its full and rather convoluted title, the Abbey Church of St Mary, St Sampson and St Branwalader is now the chapel of Milton Abbas School and occupies a spectacular location next to the mansion with expansive views of the valley. It comprises a chancel, tower and transepts; the nave was never built and the chapels have been demolished. As it stands today it is large but were it complete it would be enormous. What remains dates largely from the 14th and 15th centuries; the original buildings were destroyed by fire in 1309 after lightning struck the spire.

Joseph Damer married Caroline Sackville, daughter of the first Duke of Dorset. After her death in 1775 the Italian sculptor, Carlini, was commissioned to make a monument to her. In the north transept of the abbey, the white marble carving depicts Caroline Damer lying on a sofa with her grieving husband beside her.

Oxford Sandy and Black Pigs at Ansty

Broadclose, Ansty DT2 7PN ℗ 01258 880143.

When David Norman and his wife Jenny started breeding Oxford Sandy and Black pigs in the late 1990s there were only around a hundred of these animals in existence. Like many native breeds they were dangerously close to extinction. The Oxford Sandy and Black is one of the oldest British breeds and, David told me, the breed was saved by the perseverance and sheer bloody mindedness of a few individuals who formed a breed society in 1985. David is the breed's British Pig Association representative.

David explained that the exact origin of the breed is unknown but it is believed to have developed some two centuries ago in Oxfordshire. They are an excellent multi-purpose pig producing succulent pork, bacon and ham.

Some of David and Jenny's prize-winning herd are bred to end up as hog roasts and sausages. A firm favourite for those who are lucky enough to have tasted the sausages is the pork and marmalade variety. David and Jenny sell most of their sausages by word of mouth from their home next to the Fox Inn at Ansty: if you would like to try some, contact them at the above address.

A story that is often repeated in connection with the Abbey Church is that of John Tregonwell, son of the owner of the house, who in 1588 and aged five is reputed to have fallen 60 feet from the top of the church tower. As was customary at the time, he was wearing several petticoats, which acted as a parachute and he landed on the ground unharmed. He went on to become the High Sheriff of Dorset. Whatever the accuracy of the story, it does conjure up an intriguing image.

The **Chapel of St Catherine** overlooks the Abbey Church. It was once reached by a set of grass steps leading from the garden of the house but the steps are no longer used. The chapel was part of King Athelstan's original construction, although what remains today dates largely from the 12th century and later restoration work.

Food and drink

Fox Inn Ansty DT2 7PN ℗ 01258 880328 ⓦ www.anstyfoxinn.co.uk. Popular and well-known pub near Milton Abbas. The menu features a good selection of traditional dishes with a creative twist and there is a carvery on Sunday.

Hambro Arms DT11 0BP ℗ 01258 880233 ⓦ www.hambroarms.com. A traditional pub in the centre of Milton Abbas, almost camouflaged among the white thatched cottages. The restaurant and bar have plenty of character, with wooden beams and an open fire. Local and seasonal produce are used where possible. Open for lunch and dinner daily.

㉓ The North Winterbornes

Referred to as the North Winterbornes to differentiate them from those southeast of Dorchester, these villages sit at the base of a valley just south of the Blackmore Vale. As their names indicate, they lie near a stream which only runs in winter: Winterborne Houghton, Winterborne Stickland, Winterborne Clenston, Winterborne Whitechurch, Winterborne Kingston, Winterborne Tomson (also known as Anderson) and Winterborne Zelston. The River Winterborne joins the River Stour near Sturminster Marshall to continue its journey to the sea at Christchurch.

All of the villages are rewarding to potter around, with a mixture of thatched cottages and more modern houses. Winterborne Whitechurch is the only one to suffer from having a main road passing through it and is larger than its relatives; the others are relatively unspoilt.

Winterborne Houghton and **Winterborne Stickland** are within striking distance of Bulbarrow Hill and Woolland Hill (see page 87), both of which command spectacular views over the Blackmore Vale. Winterborne Houghton feels remote and almost disappears into the hill at whose base it sits. It is within a thatched cottage in this village that local character Rosie Grant produces her much-loved cider (see box, page 92). Winterborne Stickland is slightly larger and has managed to hold on to its post office, village shop and school.

Winterborne Tomson consists of Tomson House, a farm and a few cottages. It has a strangely shaped (Norman apsidal) church, St Andrew's, which looks rather like an upturned boat. The small weatherboard belfry, resembling a dovecote, dates largely from the 12th century but has undergone various renovations along the way. Services are rarely held in the church now but it is usually open to visit. Inside you will find total simplicity: whitewashed walls, 18th-century oak pews, screen and pulpit, installed by Archbishop of Canterbury, William Wake, who had grown up in the village of Shapwick. The church was saved from dereliction in the 1920s when it was carefully restored: prior to that it was being used as an outbuilding by the neighbouring farm.

The Dorset Red Post

On the A31, between Bere Regis and Wimborne Minster, not far from Winterborne Tomson, is a distinctive, bright red signpost. In fact it is one of three in Dorset painted that colour, the other two being near Evershot and north of Sherborne.

The sign was erected for the benefit of illiterate guards escorting prisoners as they were marched from Dorchester Gaol to Portsmouth for transportation to Australia. It was intended to mark the turning to get to the substantial barn at Botany Bay Farm, where they would spend the night secured. The barn burnt down in the 1930s and only the base of the walls remain.

Cider by Rosie

If you see bottles of Cider by Rosie in the shops you may be tempted to assume, like I did, that the name (playing on the title of the Laurie Lee book) and the label with its cartoon drawing of a cheery, rosy-cheeked woman in an orchard next to a thatched cottage are just clever marketing. For once, that is not the case. This craft cider is lovingly made by Rose Grant ('Rosie') from apples grown in her own orchard in the small village of Winterborne Houghton. And, yes, she does live in a beautiful thatched cottage (with a fabulously colourful garden), just like the one on the label.

Now in her seventies, Rose has been making cider and selling it commercially since 2003. Essentially it was a retirement project that snowballed – 'it enlivens my retirement', Rose told me. Cider by Rosie is sold in pubs, farm shops and markets around Dorset. It is a true craft cider, with nothing added, not even sugar or water: the drink is simply the result of the natural fermentation process.

To make her cider, Rose uses over 20 varieties of apples gathered over a whole season from her orchard and others around Dorset. According to Rose, the blend of the correct apple varieties is vital to producing a good quality cider. The apples are harvested between September and December and pressing takes place from November to January in the former farm buildings at her cottage. There is around a ten-week window of intense work during some of the coldest months of the year. I asked Rose if she hires any help: 'I have had young men come and help but they usually only last a few days because it is such hard work'. Even more amazing, is that not only does Rose produce the cider almost single-handedly, she delivers it to the pubs herself. 'If I was completely retired I would just potter about at home reading and gardening. Making, selling and delivering cider gives me a chance to get out and visit the pubs and see the beautiful Dorset countryside at the same time'.

Rose is passionate about orchards and traditional cider-making and she has made it her mission to bring real cider back to Dorset. The demise of cider-making began when cider ceased to be used as payment for farm workers: many orchards were ripped up and replaced with more profitable beef and cereal crops. Somerset, however, as Rose explained, never lost its cider-making tradition. Rose spent her teenage years living in Somerset and it was there that she was first introduced to cider. Rose believes the revival is well under way, 'all the young are drinking it – cider is the new lager', she told me. Rose may well be right – the last Bath and West Show had 400 entries in its champion cider competition, a prize Rose's cider has won several times. Rose recommends cider to accompany fish and chips – it counteracts the greasiness, she says.

Rose is a retired electronic engineer, who worked both in the RAF and private industry. Her engineering background undoubtedly shapes her approach to cider-making. She uses traditional and antique machinery, which she has carefully restored, including a beautiful French apple press built in the 1920s. To assist with the physically challenging tasks and increase efficiency, Rose has erected systems of pulleys and lifts, which even she describes as Heath Robinson. The process is very precise and scientific, and I can see how it would appeal to a former engineer. According to Rose, however, it isn't just about the science; you also have to have a feel for it.

Making her own alcohol has long been a hobby for Rose. For a while she dabbled with making country wines, the odd beer and cider to compete with the chaps at work. Her cider came into its own in 2002, the year of the Queen's Golden Jubilee. The village needed to raise money to put on a party to celebrate the milestone and various fundraising events were organised. Rose had around 30 jars of homemade cider lurking in her utility room so put on a cheese and cider tasting to raise some funds for the party. She was delighted with how well received her cider was. It was the villagers' enthusiasm that spurred her on to increase production to a level that would allow her to sell it commercially.

The whole village has become involved in Rose's revival of the cider tradition. In May, the villagers crown the Queen of the May and bless Rose's orchard for the coming season. They carry the young queen, a teenage girl from the village, around the orchard on a throne made from a rocking chair and hazel twigs bedecked with flowers.

It is hard to imagine a better example of Slow and local produce than Rose's cider, made the traditional way in her own home. More information, including where to buy Cider by Rosie, is available at www.ciderbyrosie.co.uk.

The Marshwood Vale
and West Dorset

N

4 miles

5km

0

0

DORCHESTER

A356

to Weymouth

A35

Little Bredy

Valley of Stones

Abbotsbury

Abbotsbury Swannery

Evershot (18)

Bride River

Eggardon Hillfort (20)

Kingcombe Centre (19)

A356

Puncknowle (8)

Litton Cheney (9)

BEAMINSTER (17)

A3066

B3157

West Bexington (7)

A3066

Broadwindsor Craft and Design Centre (15)

A356

Whitchurch Canonicorum (16)

BRIDPORT (5)

Burton Bradstock

CREWKERNE

Pilsdon Pen (14)

Morecombelake (3)

(4)

West Bay

A30

B3162

Guy Mallinson Woodland Workshop (13)

Lambert's Castle

A35

Seatown

B3165

Coney's Castle

Charmouth (2)

Golden Cap

Forde Abbey (12)

CHARD

LYME REGIS (1)

A3052

94

3. THE MARSHWOOD VALE AND WEST DORSET

West Dorset is endowed with one of the most enticing sections of the **Jurassic Coast World Heritage Site**. The Jurassic Coast stretches 95 miles from east Devon along the Dorset coastline to Old Harry Rocks in the Isle of Purbeck and records 185 million years of the earth's history. At its heart, just inside the Dorset border lies the supremely characterful resort of **Lyme Regis**. Lyme, as it is often known, is a popular holiday destination for its quaint buildings, sheltered beach and fossil hunting. From here you'll find a choice of excellent walks, notably a particularly beautiful stretch of the South West Coast Path which incorporates Golden Cap, the highest point on the south coast.

The market town of **Bridport** has a rich food culture and its myriad food and drink producers, farm shops and restaurants are showcased each June during the annual Bridport Food Festival. Bridport's harbour, **West Bay**, marks the start of **Chesil Beach**, a shingle bank which stretches 18 miles east to Portland and protects a natural lagoon known as **The Fleet**. The coastline between West Bexington and Abbotsbury has a rugged, untouched appeal. A journey inland through the unspoilt Bride Valley is equally rewarding.

As you travel inland between Lyme Regis and Bridport the roads turn quickly to narrow lanes winding through farmland dotted with hamlets and villages – this is the picturesque and unspoilt **Marshwood Vale**. For exhilarating views over the vale and towards the coast, you can't beat a walk up **Pilsdon Pen** or **Lewesdon Hill**, the two highest points in Dorset.

At Lower Kingcombe is the Dorset Wildlife Trust's **Kingcombe Centre**, the best-preserved lowland meadow in southern England. The centre offers a range of courses and activities, such as beekeeping and foraging, or you can simply enjoy seeing the countryside as it would have looked many years ago.

Getting there and around

Drivers will find the West Dorset coast easy to access, with most of the places described in this chapter easily reached from the A35, which in turn links up with the A303.

Public transport

Local tourist information centres stock a useful leaflet entitled *Jurassic Coast: explore without your car*, which suggests car-free routes.

There is no mainline train station in this part of Dorset but London Waterloo to Exeter services (South West Trains) call at Axminster in Devon, from where you can pick up a **bus** to Lyme Regis. Alternatively, you can get a **train** from London to Dorchester and then hop on a bus. The hourly number 31 bus is useful: it links Dorchester and Axminster rail services to Bridport and Lyme Regis.

The **Jurassic Coast bus** (CoastLinX53) runs every two hours along the coastline between Exeter and Poole, and stops at all the key places in West Dorset, including Lyme Regis, Bridport, Burton Bradstock and Abbotsbury.

Inland, services to places described within this chapter are very limited, although there are regular buses between Bridport and Beaminster.

By boat

Travelling by boat along the Jurassic Coast can give you a real appreciation of the area's geology and the multi-layered cliffs that run along the coastline. West Dorset's two harbours, Lyme Regis and West Bay, both have a slipway for public use; visiting craft are welcome but there is a long waiting list for the moorings that are let on an annual basis. Lyme Regis Sailing Club (*www.lymeregissailingclub.co.uk*) offers temporary membership for visitors. Further information about using the harbours is available at www.dorsetforyou.com, while general information about exploring the Jurassic Coast by boat is available at www.jurassiccoast.com.

You can take **fishing, sightseeing and diving trips** from both Lyme Regis and West Bay. Lyme Bay RIB charter (*07971 258515; www.lymbayribcharter.co.uk*) operates a **water taxi** between Lyme Regis and West Bay, and Jurassic Coast cruises departing from Lyme Regis. For a bit of variation you can take the CoastLinX53 bus from Lyme Regis to West Bay and then the water taxi on your return trip. The Lyme Regis Pleasure Boat Company (*07765 501539*) offers **self-drive hire boats** from the harbour in Lyme Regis, if you prefer to explore the coast at your own pace.

Cycling

West Dorset offers some very special cycling country, if you don't mind a few hills. The roads along the coast can get pretty crowded in summer but at least there are no big towns or cities to negotiate.

National Cycle Network (NCN) **Route 2** covers 30 miles between Lyme Regis and Dorchester, taking you through the Marshwood Vale, around Bridport and across the Bride Valley, then close to the Hardy Monument and Maiden Castle on the approach to Dorchester. The *Cycling in West Dorset* leaflet is available from tourist information centres and can be used in conjunction with OS Explorer maps 116 and OL15.

The **West Dorset Pedal** is a series of five shorter routes uncovering West Dorset's finest food and arts. Available from tourist information centres is a leaflet pack containing the routes and describing eateries, farm shops, art galleries and attractions along the route.

Guided mountain-biking is available from the Kingcombe Centre (*Lower*

Kingcombe, Dorchester DT2 0EQ; 01300 320684; www.kingcombe.org). Cycling holidays are based at the centre and accommodation can be arranged. Check with the Kingcombe Centre for dates and availability.

Cycle hire
The following all offer cycle hire and repair:

Bikenutz 5 South St, Axminster, Devon EX13 5AD ℗ 01297 631202 ℗ www.bike-nutz.co.uk.
Bspoke 51 South St, Bridport DT6 3NY ℗ 01308 421211 ℗ www.bspokeonline.co.uk.
Revolutions Grove Works, West Rd, Bridport DT6 5JT ℗ 01308 420586 ℗ www.revolutionsbikes.co.uk.

Walking
Some long-distance trails pass through West Dorset, including the South West Coast Path and the Wessex Ridgeway. Rather lesser known is the **Dorset Jubilee Trail**, which runs 90 miles from Forde Abbey on the Somerset border across Dorset to Bokerley Dyke on the Hampshire border. The route incorporates the Iron Age hillfort of **Pilsdon Pen** for views of the Marshwood Vale and the Dorset Wildlife Trust's reserve at the **Kingcombe Centre** (see page 128). A walk to the top of **Golden Cap** near Seatown will take you to the highest point on England's south coast for breathtaking views, which on a clear day can even include Dartmoor; immediately inland it's interestingly hilly enough for some hugely satisfying round walks linking up with Golden Cap itself.

One of the most rewarding areas for walking is around **Abbotsbury**, where within a few miles you can walk up onto the hillsides immediately north of the village for glorious views, and climb up the hill to St Catherine's Chapel, explore the swannery and head out to the end of Chesil Beach (which itself is painfully slow progress for walking but worth contemplating from this point).

Accommodation

The West Dorset coast has an abundance and variety of accommodation. If you are after peace and tranquillity during the summer months, consider looking beyond Lyme Regis for a place to lay your head. The area between Burton Bradstock and Abbotsbury has some good, quieter options. There are also some nice places to stay inland, including some good B&Bs.

Abbey House Church St, Abbotsbury DT3 4JJ ℗ 01305 871330 ℗ info@theabbeyhouse.co.uk ℗ www.theabbeyhouse.co.uk. Guesthouse accommodation in an historic building overlooking the millpond and the Tithe Barn, with 4 en-suite rooms and one with separate private bathroom, all decorated in country style. One room has a sitting area – handy for longer stays. The garden has good views of St Catherine's Chapel. Reasonable value for money.

Abbotsbury Tearooms and B&B 26 Rodden Row, Abbotsbury DT3 4JL ① 01305 871143 Ⓔ atr@uwclub.net Ⓦ www.abbotsbury-tearooms.co.uk. A 17th-century cottage in the village centre, on the corner opposite the turning to the swannery. The 3 en-suite rooms are thoughtfully decorated in a country style. My pick of the rooms would be the one with a bath. Owner Lyn, who has lived in Dorset all her life, makes every effort to ensure her guests are content. The gardens are the perfect place to sit on a summer's evening after a day exploring the coast. Good value for money.

Abbots House The Street, Charmouth DT6 6QF ① 01297 560339 Ⓔ stay@ abbotshouse.co.uk Ⓦ www.abbotshouse.co.uk. A beautifully restored home in the centre of Charmouth. 3 well-appointed rooms with bathrooms complete with double-ended roll top baths and flat-screen TV. At one end of the house is a 1-bedroom self-catering cottage. The garden has a model train running around it. One of the more upmarket options, and priced accordingly.

Acorn Inn 28 Fore St, Evershot DT2 0JW ① 01935 83228 Ⓔ stay@acorn-inn. co.uk Ⓦ www.acorn-inn.co.uk. This 16th-century coaching inn has a pubby feel in the main areas but the 10 en-suite rooms are finished in the style of a luxury hotel, which is perhaps unsurprising as it shares the same owners as Summer Lodge (see page 100). In the evenings, guests and locals enjoy the bar and restaurant. Reasonably priced.

Alexandra Hotel Pound St, Lyme Regis DT7 3HZ ① 01297 442010 Ⓔ enquiries@ hotelalexandra.co.uk Ⓦ www.hotelalexandra.co.uk. An elegant 24-room hotel in an enviable position on a hill overlooking the Lyme Regis seafront and with a pleasant lawn on which to relax. An upmarket and expensive Lyme Regis option.

The Bay Hotel Marine Parade, Lyme Regis DT7 3JQ ① 01297 442059 Ⓔ info@ lymebayhotel.co.uk Ⓦ www.lymebayhotel.co.uk. Hotel, bar, bistro and café right on the seafront. Clean, modern, trendy 1- and 2-bedroom suites with kitchenette. All but one of the suites has a sea view. There is no parking here but the hotel has a lock-up garage on Coombe Street. Considering its location, this hotel is reasonably priced.

Bridge House Hotel 3 Prout Bridge, Beaminster DT8 3AY ① 01308 862200 Ⓔ enquiries@bridge-house.co.uk Ⓦ www.bridge-house.co.uk. A very inviting combination of history and modern comfort. The 14 rooms of this 13th-century former priest's house have been finished to a high standard. There is an excellent restaurant (see page 125). Pet friendly. An upmarket option for the area and the price reflects this.

Bridge House Hotel 115 East St, Bridport DT6 3LB ① 01308 423371 Ⓔ info@ bridgehousebridport.co.uk Ⓦ www.bridgehousebridport.co.uk. A family-run hotel in a Georgian building on the edge of town. The 10 en-suite rooms are cosy and full of character. Pet-friendly. Prices are mid-range.

Downhouse Farm Downhouse Lane, Higher Eype DT6 6AH ① 01308 421232

Ⓔ nikki@downhousefarm.org Ⓦ www.downhousefarm.org. A 500-acre organic farm on a hillside with spectacular views of the coast, within walking distance of the beach and close to the South West Coastal Path. There are a limited number of camping pitches in a small field with access to water, a toilet and shower. It may lack the facilities and entertainment of some campsites but it also lacks the crowds. Wholesome food is served in the café. Access is down a very narrow lane. Good value for those on a tight budget.

Eggcup Tearooms Vurlands Farm, Coast Rd, Swyre DT2 9DB Ⓣ 01308 897160. On the B3157 between Burton Bradstock and Swyre, and close to Abbotsbury, this farm has 5 spots for caravans in the field behind the tearooms and views of the Bride Valley; you have to be a Caravan Club member to stay here. Good value.

Fernhill Hotel Charmouth DT6 6BX Ⓣ 01297 560492 Ⓔ mail@fernhill-hotel. co.uk Ⓦ www.fernhill-hotel.co.uk. An AA 3-star hotel between Lyme Regis and Charmouth. Very thoughtfully refurbished inside, with relaxing public spaces and 10 pretty rooms, including a studio for families. Owners Jo and Rob pride themselves on their friendly service and their focus on local and green living. They employ local staff and source local produce for their restaurant (see page 108). There is an emphasis on relaxation and health, with an outdoor pool, holistic therapies and wholesome, homemade food. Guests also have access to 36 acres of woodland and fishing ponds. Unusually for this area, there is plenty of parking. In many ways the hotel exceeds expectations with nice touches like remote control lights and fans in rooms, making it good value for money.

Golden Cap Holiday Park Seatown DT6 6JX Ⓣ 01308 422139 Ⓔ holidays@ wdlh.co.uk Ⓦ www.wdlh.co.uk. Campsite in a great location around 100 yards from Seatown Beach. A good starting point for the walk up Golden Cap. There is a shop, which is handy as it is a fair walk to the village of Seatown.

Hensleigh House Hotel Lower Sea Lane, Charmouth DT6 6LW Ⓣ 01297 560830 Ⓔ info@hensleighhouse.co.uk Ⓦ www.hensleighhouse.co.uk. A small, friendly hotel around 300 yards from Charmouth Beach. There are 6 simple but comfortable en-suite rooms and a conservatory restaurant serving breakfast, cream teas and dinner. The hotel has parking and Lyme Regis is a short bus ride away. For the budget-conscious this is a great option, being fantastic value for money all year round. Pet friendly.

Higher Kingcombe Lodge Toller Porcorum DT2 0EH Ⓣ 01300 320537 Ⓔ info@ higherkingcombelodge.co.uk Ⓦ www.higherkingcombelodge.co.uk. Farm buildings in a quiet rural setting near the Dorset Wildlife Trust's Kingcombe Centre have been converted to B&B accommodation. The 7 en-suite rooms have a simple, modern feel. Coarse fishing is available in the 8 lakes. A very affordable option.

Highlands End Holiday Park Eype DT6 6AR Ⓣ 01308 422139 Ⓔ holidays@ wdlh.co.uk Ⓦ www.wdlh.co.uk. Quietly located on a hill above Eype, this site has views of the coast. Caravan holiday homes and camping are available. Prices are typical of the area, with a hefty supplement in peak season. Extensive facilities, including a bar/restaurant and indoor pool (payable for campers). Eype Beach is dog friendly, even in summer.

Manor Hotel Beach Rd, West Bexington DT2 9DF ① 01308 897660
ⓦ www.manorhoteldorset.com. Located 400 yards up the hill from West
Bexington Beach. The hotel was extensively refurbished in 2011 and now has 13
nicely decorated en-suite rooms, many with sea views. One of the more expensive
options in the area. The rooms are upstairs so not suitable for those with limited
mobility.

Norburton Hall Shipton Lane, Burton Bradstock DT6 4NQ ① 01308 897007
ⓔ info@norburtonhall.com ⓦ www.norburtonhall.com. The kind of self-
catering accommodation travellers always hope to find and seldom do. This
16th-century property, which was originally a farm, is in a quiet village location
about a 20-minute stroll from Burton Bradstock Beach. Owner, Karen Venn, has
thoughtfully converted parts of her beautiful home and outbuildings to provide
4 self-contained units, which sleep between 2 and 10 people. Modern facilities
and a touch of luxury are combined with period charm. Guests receive a very
warm welcome and Karen is always happy to share her extensive knowledge
of the local area. She is a great proponent of the Slow Food and Slow Tourism
movements: every effort has been made to follow sustainable living principles
and Karen even provides a compost bin for guests. If the crowds at the local
beaches get too much, there are 6 acres of well-maintained gardens at the hall
in which to relax. Given its location, oodles of character and exceptionally well-
appointed accommodation, Norburton Hall is very good value for money.

Sea Fret B&B Coast Rd, Puncknowle DT2 9DQ ① 01308 897435 ⓔ enquiries@
seafret.co.uk ⓦ www.seafret.co.uk. Standing alone on a hill on the coast road
near Swyre, this B&B has stunning views of the sea, seen to full effect from the
upstairs sitting room, which is glass on all sides. The 2 ground floor bedrooms are
suitable for those with limited mobility. Owners Elizabeth and Tony Edwards are
extremely friendly and accommodating, while their small alpaca herd provides
added interest. Small pets are welcome. One of the most reasonably priced B&Bs
in the area.

Summer Lodge Country House Hotel Restaurant and Spa Summer Lane,
Evershot DT2 0JR ① 01935 482000 ⓔ summer@relaischateaux.com ⓦ www.
summerlodgehotel.com. A very elegant 24-room hotel in the heart of this lovely
village. The property was home to the Earls of Ilchester from 1789 and retains the
feel of a fine country house or shooting retreat thanks to luxurious furnishings
and artwork featuring handsome horses and gun dogs. As well as rooms and
suites, the hotel offers sophisticated self-contained cottages in the village. In
1893, Dorset author and architect, Thomas Hardy, designed an extension to the
house, which now contains the drawing room. You can indulge yourself in the
spa, which has a range of relaxing treatments, an indoor pool and sauna. One
guest told me she planned to spend the day admiring the hotel's garden rather
than pay to visit a garden open to the public. The service is excellent and there is
a very good restaurant (see page 127). One of Dorset's most upmarket hotels,
so expect to pay accordingly.

Lyme Regis to Bridport and West Bay

① Lyme Regis and surrounds

Somehow it doesn't look real: with its rows of houses of every shape and size huddled together along the seafront beneath open fields and woodland, Lyme Regis looks more like a painting in a children's book, or perhaps a model town. You might half expect to see an oversized adult bending down peering through the windows of the cottages.

Lyme Regis snuggles up against the Dorset/Devon border, on the River Lim. The Jurassic blue-grey cliffs on either side of the town are filled with layers of fossils, making the beaches of Lyme Regis excellent for fossil hunting. The narrow, twisting (and in parts steep) streets lead down through the town to the attractive seafront and the manmade harbour protected by the ancient breakwater known as **The Cobb**.

The town centre

The town is best explored on foot as the centre is compact, packed with small shops, eateries and art galleries, and there is little room for cars. At the northern end of the seafront you will find the **tourist information centre**, which, as well as the usual brochures on accommodation, eateries and activities can provide tide times – essential if you plan to go fossil hunting. Nearby is the bright white **Marine Theatre** (*Church St, DT7 3QA; 01297 442394; www.marinetheatre.com*), an active, traditional seaside theatre with regular performances and events.

Nearby, the eccentric tower of the **guildhall** almost encroaches onto the narrow road; tucked away behind it is the **Lyme Regis Museum** (*Bridge St, DT7 3QA; 01297 443370; www.lymeregismuseum.co.uk; open Easter–Oct daily, Oct–Easter Wed–Sun*). The museum is within a quirky turreted brick building built in 1901 and, like the town, is a warren full of hidden corners to be explored. As you would expect, it has good exhibits on local geology and fossils, and Lyme's literary connections. The museum runs a regular programme of activities, such as guided walks, rock pooling and fossil hunting, which can be booked in advance. Look out for the medieval bridge nearby spanning the river.

The seafront and The Cobb

The beach to the east of Lyme Regis Museum (Back Beach) is excellent for rock pooling. Above the beach you can see the retaining wall that was installed after people complained of skeletons poking out of the cliff from the graveyard at **St Michael's Church**. In the churchyard is the **grave of Mary Anning** (see page 106), while inside the church, on the left, is a stained-glass window commemorating her. It is a beautiful building with two Norman pillars in the entrance.

Lyme Regis is perhaps at its most enchanting viewed from **The Cobb** at sunset, when the sun illuminates the hills above the harbour and you can see the geological layers within the cliffs, stacked like a deck of cards. Sheltering behind the breakwater is a colourful array of fishing and pleasure boats. The Cobb has been protecting the harbour and the town from erosion since the 13th century. It was originally made from huge boulders inside oak walls and detached from the land at high tide. It was joined to the land in 1756 and rebuilt in Portland stone in the 1820s, as the gently tilting serpentine wall that you see today.

It may look like a tiddler of a harbour but in its heyday Lyme Regis was a major port – the second largest in Dorset in the 14th century. Ships from Lyme Regis traded all over the world until the 20th century. Attached to the front of The Cobb's buildings, near the aquarium (see opposite), is a venerable toll board dated 1879 and entitled 'Rates of Merchandise'. It lists the amount of tax levied on imports and exports to and from the harbour with incredible detail, such as 'for every barrel of salted beef, cod, herring … 4d', 'for every Hogshead of Ale, Beer or Porter … 6d', 'for each horse, mule, cow or ox … 6d'.

The Cobb has seen its fair share of drama, real and fictional. It was at The Cobb that James Scott, Duke of Monmouth, landed with his followers in 1685, intent on taking the throne from his uncle, James II. Monmouth, the son of King Charles II, chose Lyme Regis because the West Country was strongly Protestant. A month after they landed, Monmouth and his followers were defeated at the Battle of Sedgemoor in Somerset. Following the trial known as the 'Bloody Assizes', presided over by the notorious Judge Jeffreys (see page 64), 292 Monmouth supporters were executed. A dozen of them were hanged, drawn and quartered on the spot where they had disembarked in Lyme Regis.

You won't be in Lyme Regis for long before finding mention of its connection with John Fowles's *The French Lieutenant's Woman*, the story of a romance between Sarah Woodruff and Charles Smithson, a fossil hunter. Fowles was

Cruises and fishing trips

At the shore end of The Cobb you can arrange fishing trips, self-drive hire boats, Jurassic Coast cruises or a water taxi to West Bay (see page 96). Harry May's (*07974 753287*) mackerel-fishing and deep-sea fishing trips come highly recommended by locals. If you fancy getting in some sea time, a mackerel-fishing trip is a pleasant way to spend an hour pottering around the bay. On a deep-sea fishing trip your catch is likely to be cod, conger and skate. Sailing lessons are available from Lyme Regis Sea School (*01297 442644; www.lrss.org.uk*) and the Lyme Regis Sailing Club (*www.lymeregissailingclub.co.uk*) offers temporary membership for visitors.

living in a farmhouse in Lyme Regis when he wrote the book. The Cobb is the setting of the dramatic opening scene of the film, when Sarah, played by Meryl Streep, is standing alone looking out to sea. Lyme Regis's other literary claim to fame involves Jane Austen, who stayed in the town in 1803–04. The Cobb features in her novel, *Persuasion*, which describes Louisa Musgrove falling from the steps.

On The Cobb, within a building dating from 1723, is the small, unpretentious **Lyme Regis Aquarium** (*01297 444230; www.lymeregismarineaquarium.co.uk; open mid-Feb to Nov daily 10.00–17.00*), run by the Gallop family since 1958. It contains a modest collection of species found in the local waters and children will enjoy helping to hand feed the mullet. It is perhaps useful to know that you can download a discount voucher from the aquarium's website. Alongside the sea creatures is a display of photographs showing films being shot in Lyme Regis, including *The French Lieutenant's Woman* and *Persuasion*. Mr Gallop proudly told me that the aquarium was used as a make-up room during the making of the latter.

Along the seafront (Marine Parade) is a string of pastel-coloured wooden **beach huts**, well-equipped and well-used. The slightest bit of sun has holidaymakers throwing open their doors. Like magicians pulling rabbits from hats, they reach into their hut and produce with a flourish a never-ending supply of deckchairs, beach games, umbrellas and, of course, the all important tea-making paraphernalia, and if this prospect tempts you, beach huts are available for daily, weekly or seasonal hire from the council (*01297 445175; www.lymeregistowncouncil.gov.uk*).

As well as the pebble beach, there is a manmade sandy one, known as **Front Beach**. Lyme Regis is busy in summer and the area around Front Beach is where it shows. The sand is barely visible beneath the sun worshippers, the restaurants are buzzing and the shops are crowded with souvenir hunters.

The **Langmoor and Lister Gardens** above the seafront provide a chance to step back from the crowds and admire the views of The Cobb and the coastline.

The Town Mill Complex

Mill Lane, DT7 3PU ① 01297 443579 ⓦ www.townmill.org.uk. Mill tours Easter–Oct
Tue–Sun 11.00–16.00, Nov–Easter Sat–Sun 11.00–16.00, plus weekdays during
school holidays.

Around a cobbled courtyard at the Town Mill Complex, restored mill buildings
house small shops showcasing local art, crafts and produce (including a potter,
a cheesemonger and a tearoom). The tour of the working watermill is certainly
worthwhile, with its volunteer millers overflowing with enthusiasm and
knowledge about its workings and its history dating back to the 11th century.
Powered by the River Lim, the mill continues to produce a small amount
of stone-ground flour, which is available in the mill shop. It also generates
electricity, which powers the site.

Dinosaurland Fossil Museum

Coombe St, DT73PY ① 01297 443541 ⓦ www.dinosaurland.co.uk. Open mid-Feb to
Nov 10.00–17.00, opening hours Dec–Feb vary so it is best to check beforehand.

The museum, which is in a former 18th-century chapel, has impressive
displays of fossils from the local area and beyond, and interesting facts about
their origins. There are dinosaur displays (good for children) and a rather
odd display of taxidermy of British animals. If you choose to search for fossils
without doing a fossil-hunting tour, a visit to the museum will help you
understand their formation.

Fossil hunting around Lyme Regis

Made from soft clay layered with a few hard
bands of limestone that formed on
the bottom of the sea during the early
Jurassic period, some 190 million years
ago, the grey cliffs of the Lyme Regis
area regularly offer up some valuable clues
about life on earth in geological ages past.
The Jurassic fossils within the cliffs are derived
from sea creatures that lived when dinosaurs roamed the land. Landslides and
waves cause fossils to fall from the cliffs onto the beach below, making the
beaches prime fossil-hunting territory.

You may like to consider heading out with an expert on a guided fossil tour.
It can certainly help you to get the most from your fossil-hunting expedition
and give you a greater understanding of how they are formed.

I was lucky enough to go fossil hunting with Dr Colin Dawes. I arranged
to meet him at his home in Broad Street, one of the oldest (and allegedly
most haunted) houses in Lyme Regis. I was delighted that he looked exactly
as I would imagine a fossil hunter to look, with bushy sideburns, a safari vest,
a bushman's hat and carrying a long staff and a hammer. Having heard the
various ghost stories associated with the house, I was quietly relieved when

we headed out to Back Beach (at the Charmouth end of town) and it wasn't long before Colin had found several fossils to show me, each with its own fascinating story.

Colin's other favourite fossil-hunting haunt is Monmouth Beach, west of The Cobb. If you walk around half way to the headland you will come across the 'graveyard of the ammonites', a ledge of limestone packed with the internal moulds of football-sized ammonites, which happens to lie on the Dorset/Devon border. The spiral-shaped ammonites are intriguing to admire but you should not attempt to extract them; to do so would be dangerous and damage this amazing site.

Colin explained to me that there is no reason why people should not take small fossils home from the beach. The large ones should be left alone but by collecting the small ones we are preventing them from being washed out to sea.

On the way back from Back Beach we stopped off at St Michael's Church to see Mary Anning's grave (see page 106), a site of pilgrimage for anyone, like Colin, who is interested in geology and palaeontology.

One of the joys of a tour with Colin is that he is vastly knowledgeable on a range of topics. He studied zoology, was a lecturer at the Royal Veterinary College, is a keen ornithologist and enjoys metal detecting. He now divides his time between fossil hunting and metal detecting as he relishes any opportunity to 'add something to our knowledge of history'.

Colin gave me some tips for a productive and safe fossil-hunting trip. Fossil hunting is usually most productive after stormy weather or rough seas, as cliff falls are frequent and the shingle is rapidly turned over, exposing new fossils. Landslides are common, so it is important to stay away from the cliffs when searching the beaches. Sturdy footwear will help you to negotiate the rocks, which are slippery when covered in seaweed. You will also need to keep an eye on tide times – you don't want to get stranded. The best time to collect is 1½ hours either side of tide times. You will see some fossil hunters carrying hammers. These are not essential fossil-hunting equipment but if you do decide to hammer at a rock, wear eye protection and watch out for flying splinters.

Fossil tours

Guided fossil tours are available from Lyme Regis Museum ☏ 01297 443370, Lyme Fossil Shop ☏ 01297 442088, Brandon Lennon Ⓜ 07944 664757, Dr Colin Dawes ☏ 01297 443758 Ⓦ www.fossilhunting.tv, and Charmouth Heritage Coast Centre ☏ 01297 560772.

Food and drink

By the Bay Marine Parade, DT7 3JH ☏ 01297 442668 Ⓦ www.bythebay.co.uk. Smart, modern restaurant and wine bar in a prime position overlooking the beach. The menu is creative with the emphasis on seafood.

Mary Anning – ground-breaking fossil hunter

A female fossil hunter, dealer and palaeontologist who unearthed some of the most significant geological finds ever made, Mary Anning (1799–1847) was ahead of her time. Her discoveries were key to a fundamental shift in scientific thinking about the history of the Earth, and challenged religious views.

Mary was born into a humble family of religious dissenters in Lyme Regis. She and her brother, Joseph, were the only survivors of ten children born to Richard Anning, a carpenter and cabinetmaker, and his wife Mary. At the age of 15 months, Mary survived a lightning strike, which killed three others; local legend had it the lightning turned her into a bright and observant child. Mary attended a Congregationalist Sunday School where she learned to read and write. Congregationalist doctrine emphasised the importance of education for the poor, unlike the Church of England at the time. However, the family's position as dissenters against the Church of England caused them further discrimination than did poverty alone.

Richard Anning taught his children how to look for and clean fossils that had been hidden within the cliffs at Lyme Regis. They sold the 'curiosities' they collected on the seafront to the wealthy tourists who flocked to Lyme Regis in the summer.

Richard died in 1810, when Mary was 11 years old, and she supplemented the family's meagre income by continuing the fossil trade. Waves and landslides exposed new fossils, especially during winter, which needed to be collected quickly before they washed out to sea. It was a dangerous living – landslides, treacherous tides and ferocious seas. In 1833, Mary narrowly avoided being killed by a landslide that buried her constant companion, a terrier named Tray. It has been suggested that Mary was the inspiration for the well-known tongue-twister 'she sells seashells on the seashore', written by Terry Sullivan in 1908.

Mary taught herself geology and anatomy and she, and her family, made some important discoveries. In 1811, Mary's brother Joseph found a skull protruding from a cliff. Over a period of months Mary painstakingly uncovered an almost

Cobb Arms Marine Parade, DT7 3JF ☎ 01297 443242. A popular pub at The Cobb end of the seafront. Gluten-free dishes available. Dogs are welcome.

Good Food Store 21 Broad St, DT7 3QE ☎ 01297 442076. A deli, bakery and organic produce shop, which also has a café. Good, wholesome, local food. Open daily 08.30–17.00 in summer and closed Sun in winter.

Harbour Inn 23 Marine Parade, DT7 3JF ☎ 01297 442299. A deceptively large pub just behind the beach. There is a small outdoor seating area bordering the beach. Serves the usual pub fare and plenty of seafood dishes, including pretty good fish and chips. Open for lunch and dinner daily.

Hix Oyster & Fish House Cobb Rd, DT7 3JP ☎ 01297 446910 ⓦ www.hixoyster andfishhouse.co.uk. Lyme's best-known and most exclusive restaurant, owned complete 17-foot-long skeleton of a 'crocodile'. The specimen was bought by the local lord of the manor, who sold it to William Bullock for his Museum of Natural Curiosities in London. The find caused quite a stir and brought Mary to the attention of scientific circles. The specimen was later named *Ichthyosaurus*, the 'fish-lizard'.

In 1828, Mary made another important discovery – the first complete skeleton of a flying reptile recorded in England. It was named *dimorphodon* after its two kinds of teeth and appears to have been a fish eater.

The Anning family had established themselves as fossil hunters but remained very poor. In 1820 one of their patrons, Lieutenant-Colonel Thomas James Birch, organised an auction of specimens he had purchased from them. The sale raised £400, which he donated to the Annings, and the publicity cemented Mary's fame.

Mary's gender and social class meant she could not fully participate in the scientific community of the day. As a woman, she was not eligible to join the Geological Society of London and rarely received due credit for her work. However, she was visited by and corresponded with eminent scientists of the time and her opinions were valued. In 1838, Mary was given an annuity raised by members of the British Association for the Advancement of Science and the Geological Society of London.

From humble beginnings she had gained the respect of the scientific community and captured the imagination of the public. She may not have been eligible to join during her lifetime but her death was recorded by the Geological Society. In 2010, the Royal Society included Anning in a list of the ten British women who have most influenced the history of science.

She died from breast cancer aged 47 and is buried in the churchyard of St Michael's in Lyme Regis, along with her brother, Joseph. A stained-glass window within the church, commissioned by the Geological Society of London, commemorates her life. On the wall of the Lyme Regis Museum is a blue plaque dedicated to her. The museum is believed to be on the site of Anning's home and her first fossil shop.

by celebrity chef Mark Hix. Great if you want to treat yourself or someone else, especially if you like fish. At the end of the gardens above the seafront, it has sweeping views over the bay and the service is very good. There is no parking here but you can drop people off and park nearby.

Millside Restaurant and Wine Bar 1 Mill Lane, DT7 3PU ℗ 01297 445999 ⓦ www.themillside.co.uk. The owners describe themselves as champions of local ingredients, which they turn into dishes with flair. They make their own bread, pasta and cakes using local organic flour. Closed Sun evening and Mon.

Mill Tea & Dining Room The Town Mill, Mill Lane, DT7 3PU ℗ 01297 445757 ⓦ www.teaanddiningroom.com. It may look simple but this place has a great reputation and awards to match. Chef Anthony McNamara has an impressive CV, having worked in top London restaurants and as private chef to prime ministers and celebrities. His cuisine (traditional British food, cooked from scratch) draws on his childhood growing up on the family farm in Ireland. Open Tue for dinner, Wed–Sat 11.00–16.00 and for dinner, Sun for lunch.

Pilot Boat Inn 1 Bridge St, DT7 3QA ① 01297 443157 ⓦ www.thepilotboatinn. co.uk. Unassuming pub right in the centre of Lyme Regis. Traditional pub fare at reasonable prices. Plenty of vegetarian options. Open daily 11.00–23.00.

River Cottage Park Farm, Trinity Hill Rd, Axminster, Devon EX13 8TB ① 01297 630313 ⓦ www.rivercottage.net. Dinner at Hugh Fearnley-Whittingstall's River Cottage (Park Farm) is an experience to remember. You will need to book in advance (see box opposite).

The Terrace 8–10 Bridge St, DT7 3QA ① 01297 444110 ⓦ www.theterrace.co.uk. Gift shop and café with a terrace overlooking the sea.

Town Mill Bakery 2 Riverside Studios, Coombe St, DT7 3PY ① 01297 444754 ⓦ www.townmillbakery.com. Bread, pastries and pizzas, made on site. Well known for their sourdough breads and use of local produce. Long, wooden tables reminiscent of school mealtimes and the open bakery provide a casual atmosphere. Popular for breakfast.

② Charmouth

Smaller than Lyme Regis, Charmouth is billed as the quieter of the two, although the beach can feel pretty crowded in the summer. The bulk of Charmouth is about half a mile back from the sea, spread along either side of the main street, which runs between the coast and the A35. You can drive down to the seafront, where there is ample parking close to the beach. The seafront is decidedly low-key – there is no fancy esplanade lined with shops, amusement arcades and hotels; instead there is a pebble beach, fossil-rich cliffs, a café and the **Charmouth Heritage Coast Centre** (*Lower Sea Lane, DT6 6LL; 01297 560772; www.charmouth.org/chcc*). If you plan on collecting fossils, or simply want to know more about the Jurassic Coast, the centre is worth a visit. The interactive displays and fossil touch table will appeal to most children, and there is a video microscope for you to examine your fossil finds on your return. Displays on the coastal wildlife of the area, including two marine rock pool aquariums, add another dimension. The centre provides a large and varied programme of events, including fossil hunting, ammonite-slice polishing and rock pooling.

During the summer a large **flea market** is held in a field on the edge of Charmouth every Monday, at Manor Farm Park.

Food and drink

Fernhill Hotel DT6 6BX ① 01297 560492 ⓦ www.fernhill-hotel.co.uk. An elegant restaurant, good service and delicious food combine to make a meal here a very pleasant experience. The owners describe their food philosophy as 'we buy local

River Cottage and Hugh Fearnley-Whittingstall

When I mentioned Dorset to an Australian friend recently she said, 'Oh, that's where God lives'. I was quite chuffed, thinking she was describing Dorset as God's own country, such is its beauty. She then clarified that she was talking about 'Hugh', that is to say television personality Hugh Fearnley-Whittingstall. I was surprised on a number of levels, firstly that the scruffy but likeable Hugh should attract such blasphemous praise and secondly that his back to basics food philosophy has such wide appeal, even on the other side of the globe.

Dorset and Hugh have been inextricably linked since 1998, when he moved into the original River Cottage to start growing and rearing his own food. River Cottage has in fact moved to a farm (Park Farm) just a smidgeon over the Devon border but I believe Dorset still has a fair claim to Hugh. The River Cottage principles remain unchanged: less dependence on the outside world, food integrity, and the consumption of local, seasonal produce. The message is nothing new – it is the way my family and most of our Dorset farming friends have been living for years – but it is highly relevant in today's world of ready-made mush (I hesitate to use the word 'meals').

River Cottage HQ at Park Farm is the venue for courses inspired by the philosophy of the original River Cottage, including foraging, curing, gardening, bread-making and butchery. You can also enjoy an entertaining dinner at Park Farm, where you get to mingle with fellow guests over canapés, then potter around and draw inspiration from the flourishing fruit and vegetable garden and elaborate chicken enclosure, before sitting down to eat. Dinner is at two long tables and each course is accompanied by a talk from the chef, who explains the detail behind the dish. When I went I was struck by the convivial and collegiate atmosphere, although a little intimidated by the serious foodies who took notes throughout the evening. I began to worry that there was going to be an exam at the end of the meal – thankfully not.

River Cottage also has a Canteen and Deli in Axminster, where they sell local and organic food and drink.

first; free range, organic and fair-trade where possible; and ensure no GM or artificial additives are in our food'. The menu offers plenty of variety, including vegetarian, vegan and gluten-free options. Closed Sun evening and Mon.
Hensleigh House Hotel Lower Sea Lane, DT6 6LW ℡ 01297 560830 Ⓦ www.hensleighhouse.co.uk. At the top of the hill on the way to the beach, the hotel has a simple conservatory restaurant serving cream teas and dinner. Unfussy and reasonably priced. Open Tue–Sat.

③ Morecombelake

Morecombelake has long been associated with a Dorset icon, for it was here that **Moores Biscuits** (*www.moores-biscuits.co.uk*) opened their bakery in 1880. Today, this family business is in the hands of the fifth generation. Although Moores now has a factory in Bridport, the Morecombelake bakery is still active (*01308 428520; open Mon–Sat*). Bread is baked on site from Tuesday to Friday. As well as baked goods, including some excellent doughnuts which I can personally recommend, the bakery has a deli, a display of historical Moores Bakery items and a collection of paintings of the West Country by Mrs Moore. The most famous of the biscuit selection is the Dorset Knob, a savoury biscuit moulded by hand and baked three times; the whole process takes eight to ten hours.

④ Seatown and Golden Cap

A small seaside hamlet nestled between cliffs, Seatown has a shingle beach, a pub and a good campsite. On its west side is Golden Cap, which lives up to its name – the top of the cliff has a warm golden glow, which can be seen for miles around, and at 626 feet it is the highest point on the south coast of Britain. It can be reached on foot either from Seatown or from Langdon Hill Wood.

⑤ Bridport and West Bay

'A vibrant and quirky market town, whose population doubles in summer', is how Bob Smith of the Bridport District Tourism Association describes his home town. I met with Bob and Clive Edwards, a fellow member of the association, and their enthusiasm for the area in which they live and work was immediately apparent. They are rightly proud of the town's rope-making history, its market, its food culture and its arts scene. Yet, Bridport and the surrounding area have to work hard to compete with the likes of Lulworth Cove, Lyme Regis and the coastal towns over the border in Devon. To do that Bridport has had to be a little creative, which is probably one reason why it has a staggering number of events for such a small town. There is the food festival in June, the hat festival in September and the literary festival in November, to name but a few.

The **Bridport Food Festival** (*www.bridportfoodfestival.wordpress.com*), launched in 2004 by celebrity chef and local food advocate Hugh Fearnley-Whittingstall, is a fitting way to celebrate the area's local produce. The farms of the fertile Marshwood Vale and the seas off West Bay do their part to contribute, offering up delicious, natural food.

Bridport is still very much a market town, with street markets held on Wednesdays and Saturdays. The **Saturday market** is crammed with bric-a-brac stalls and attracts bargain hunters from miles around. Equally popular is the **farmers' market**, held on the second Saturday of each month in the Bridport Arts Centre.

Perhaps because it is surrounded by inspiring land and seascapes, Bridport has developed a flourishing artistic and literary community. There is a healthy population of art galleries where you can pick up a souvenir of your visit. The **Bridport Arts Centre** (*01308 424204; www.bridport-arts.com*) runs a programme of free exhibitions and is the home of the literary festival and the coveted Bridport Prize International Creative Writing Competition. The **Electric Palace** (*01308 424901; www.electricpalace.org.uk*) is considered to be one of the best entertainment venues in the region, playing host to theatre, live music, cinema and art exhibitions.

Bridport has had a **rope-making industry** since the 13th century. The town was once well known for producing hangman's ropes, hence the mildly euphemistic saying 'to be stabbed with a Bridport dagger', meaning to be hanged. You may notice the long gardens around Bridport, which were once walks used for making lengths of rope. A **net-making industry** also survives in the town, with fishing and sporting nets being made in Bridport, including the nets for the Wimbledon Tennis Championships. Information about the rope- and net-making industries, and other local history, is on display at the **Bridport Museum** (*The Coach House, 25 South St, DT6 3NR; 01308 458703; www.bridportmuseum.co.uk*).

Beer has been produced continuously since 1794 at **Palmers Brewery** (*West Bay Rd, DT6 4JA; 01308 427500; www.palmersbrewery.com*), which claims to be the only thatched brewery in the UK. The brewery is run by the founder's great-grandsons, John and Cleeves Palmer. From Easter to the end of September you can take a **brewery tour**, but will usually need to book in advance. **Palmers Wine Store** is adjacent to the brewery.

A mile from the town is **West Bay**, Bridport's harbour, where the River Brit, a tidal river, flows into the sea through the sluice gates and harbour basin. A harbour was first recorded at West Bay

in the 13th century and was known as Bridport Harbour until 1884. It was a centre of the boat-building industry until the late 19th century and many ships were built here during the Napoleonic Wars (1799–1815). West Bay has not been primped and preened to turn it into a glamorous, tourist honey-pot; instead it continues as a working fishing harbour with a 'what you see is what you get' attitude and where unpretentious fish and chip kiosks are the lunch venue of choice. Above the pebble beach tower sandstone cliffs, and the pier looks out along the coastline from the Isle of Portland to Brixham in Devon.

Mangerton Mill

Mangerton DT6 3SG ① 01308 485224 Ⓦ www.mangertonmill.com. Open Easter–Oct Tue–Sun and Bank Holiday Mon.

North of Bridport, this three-storey watermill dates from the 17th-century. Last worked commercially in 1966, it has been restored and is now a workable grist mill. A small collection of household and agricultural artefacts is arranged in a rather chaotic, grandpa's shed fashion.

Trout fishing is available and you can enjoy a pleasant walk along the River Manger.

Food and drink

Bridge House Hotel 115 East St, Bridport DT6 3LB ℗ 01308 423371 ⓦ www.bridgehousebridport.co.uk. Bob Smith, owner of the hotel, told me, 'we cook from first principles, using fresh, local ingredients'. Bob's wife is Russian and the menu often reflects her eastern European influence. The wine list is extensive and full of unusual wines you will not find in the shops. Open for lunch and dinner daily.

Bull Hotel 34 East St, Bridport DT6 3LF ℗ 01308 422878 ⓦ www.thebullhotel. co.uk. The restaurant at this hotel has a reputation for good, locally produced food and is open for breakfast, lunch and dinner. The stable yard has been converted into a relaxed cider, pizza and pie house.

Furleigh Estate Salway Ash, near Bridport DT6 5JF ℗ 01308 488991 ⓦ www.furleighestate.co.uk. A traditional dairy farm has been transformed into a vineyard producing some well-respected wines. The wines are available in local shops and restaurants, or from the cellar door by appointment.

Garden Café Downhouse Farm, Downhouse Lane, Higher Eype DT6 6AH ℗ 01308 421232 ⓦ www.downhousefarm.org. This outdoor café at the farm serves delicious homemade food. Dishes are prepared using the farm's own organic meats, vegetables and herbs. Plenty of vegetarian options. The bubble and squeak is delicious. Down a very narrow lane. Open Mar–Oct Tue–Sun 10.00–18.00.

Leakers Bakery 29 East St, Bridport DT6 3JX ℗ 01308 423296 ⓦ www.leakers. co.uk. Not a café, just a very special bakery selling their handmade bread and cakes, including the delicious Dorset cider and cheese cottage loaf. This is also where you will find the Jurassic foot loaf, in the shape of a dinosaur's footprint. G S Leaker bought this bakery in 1914 and it remained in the family until 2002: a granddaughter of the original Leakers is still responsible for baking the Dorset apple cakes. Open Mon–Sat.

Riverside Restaurant West Bay DT6 4EZ ℗ 01308 422011 ⓦ http://thefish restaurant-westbay.co.uk. Seafood restaurant on the water at West Bay, reached by crossing a footbridge over the river. More expensive than some others in the area, although the lunchtime set menu is relatively good value. Closed Mon and Sun evening.

Washingpool Farm Shop Dottery Rd, North Allington DT6 5HP ℗ 01308 459549 ⓦ www.washingpool.co.uk. On the B3162 to the northeast of Bridport is this well-stocked farm shop and licensed restaurant on a working farm. As well as vegetables and meat produced on the farm, the shop stocks a range of goodies from within a 50-mile radius. A tranquil spot for lunch close to town.

East of Bridport via the Bride Valley to Abbotsbury

As you travel east from Bridport you are heading towards some utterly captivating scenery – the Bride Valley, the start of **Chesil Beach** and the village of **Abbotsbury**. The River Bride, which in parts is more a stream than a river, rises in Little Bredy and runs along a 6½-mile course to the sea at **Burton Bradstock**. The surrounding valley is a bucolic blend of rolling hills, woodland and small stone and thatched villages that remain genuine Dorset, and not Dorset dressed up for the tourist trade, with scarcely a trinket shop in sight. Even the wildlife feels unthreatened – walking around the villages of the Bride Valley I saw a stoat, a fox and numerous rabbits all happily going about their business. If you are looking for a quieter base within easy reach of the coast, Burton Bradstock and the Bride Valley are good options.

The **Bride Valley** area provides some good walking country, some of which incorporates Neolithic sites such as the **Kingston Russell Stone Circle** and its neighbour, the long barrow known as **The Grey Mare and her Colts**.

Abbotsbury does get busy during summer but it is a delightful village, best known for its swannery.

⑥ Burton Bradstock

The village nestles at the base of the Bride Valley, at the point where the River Bride flows into the sea. Although there has been some modern development on the outskirts, photogenic thatched 17th- and 18th- century cottages remain around the Church of St Mary the Virgin. The **post office** on Mill Street does everything a local post office should do and more; it doubles as a village shop, selling a range of local produce, including cheese, meat and bread.

A pleasant shingle **beach** lies on the edge of the village, shielded by golden cliffs that regularly yield up their fossils. Apart from a National Trust car park and the popular Hive Beach Café (see page 115), there are no other facilities of note at the beach. The South West Coastal Path leads from the beach up onto cliffs and towards West Bay, or eastwards towards West Bexington.

Just outside Burton Bradstock on the Bridport road is the **Bridport and District Golf Club** (*Burton Rd, DT6 4PS; 01308 421095; www.bridportgolfclub.org.uk*), which is open to visitors on most days. The club, which was founded in 1891, is said to be the oldest in Dorset. If you play here and find you are off your game, you can always use the excuse that you were distracted by the spectacular views across Lyme Bay and Chesil Beach. Club member, Tony Edwards, and owner of Sea Fret House (see page 100), told me it is pretty challenging to play a cliff top course with swirling winds. 'It is a real test of a golfer's skills, and the sixth is a keynote hole from an elevated tee over wilderness onto a green surrounded by five bunkers with the sea and the beach waiting to catch the wilder shots. The vistas rival anything on the Med, and I feel lucky we can play on such a course at an affordable price'.

Modbury Farm Shop at Modbury Organic Farm

Modbury Farm, DT6 4NE

Ⓣ 01308 897193 Ⓦ www.modburyfarm.co.uk.

A visit to this farm shop is far more than a shopping experience. If you are in the area, I urge you to drop in. This is a true working farm. The shop is within the farmyard and, unusually for a farm shop, visitors are free to look at the animals. What better way to know where your food comes from than to see how it is produced?

A hard-working and charming couple, Julie and Tim Garry, have been running a herd of pedigree Jersey cattle here since 1987. The farm converted to organic in 2001 and, as well as being a home for happy, healthy livestock, it has become a haven for wildlife.

Julie and Tim took me on a tour of the farmyard. Our first stop was the poultry house. Tim opened the door and out rushed a colourful assortment of chickens, turkeys, ducks and guinea fowl. Among the excited feathered crowd was one who didn't quite seem to fit. Julie explained to me that the pigeon had appeared one day and begun to hang out with the farmyard birds. The tag on its leg gave it away as a racing pigeon who had gone off course (or was plain lazy). Bizarrely, the pigeon's identity crisis seemed to deepen when it developed a crush on a bantam cockerel. I witnessed this for myself – the apparently love-struck pigeon wandered around the farmyard clinging to the feathered ankles of the long-suffering bantam.

We then visited the farm's cows and calves. Jerseys have always been among my favourite breeds. With kind eyes, long eyelashes, a quizzical expression and dainty figure, they almost look like cartoon cows. While Tim milks the cows (around a hundred of them), Julie makes the cream. Julie explained to me that the cream must be made during milking, while the milk is still warm and separates more easily.

Modbury Farm's organic, unpasteurised (raw) milk and cream are on sale in the shop and I can assure you they are nothing like their tasteless supermarket cousins. This is food at its purest. The farm also produces its own Angus-cross-Jersey beef, as well as organic vegetables and honey. All of these delicious, natural foods are on sale in the shop.

Modbury Farm Shop is two miles from Burton Bradstock on the Litton Cheney Road. More information about raw milk is available on the US website www.realmilk.com.

Food and drink

Anchor Inn High St, DT6 4QF Ⓣ 01308 897228. Behind the rather average pub exterior hides a clean, comfortable restaurant divided into several small rooms, which creates an intimate atmosphere. The menu is varied and creative, with a focus on seafood. The local scallops are excellent. Open for lunch and dinner daily. Reservation recommended.

Hive Beach Café Beach Rd, DT6 4RF ℗ 01308 897070 ⓦ www.hivebeachcafe. co.uk. The name is misleading, for this is not your average beachside café. Trendy, well-known and with a reputation for superb seafood, this restaurant draws quite a crowd. So trendy is it that they now sell more lobster for breakfast than they do for lunch. The manager told me they're committed to sustainable fishing: you can even order a local fish with an identity tag which allows you to look up who caught the fish and when. Open during the day, plus Friday and Saturday evenings in summer. Opening times are dependent on the weather, so if in doubt, check. Reservation recommended.

⑦ West Bexington

West Bexington is a small settlement tucked away off the B3157 between Burton Bradstock and Abbotsbury. A lane leads down to the pebble **beach**, where there is a car park that extends over the beach. You can step straight from the car park onto the beach – one of the easiest to access and manageable for those with limited mobility.

The beach is very popular with beach fishermen, who can be seen casting their lines into the sea whatever the weather. There is a small café nearby but its opening hours are rather hit and miss. An alternative is the Manor Hotel, on the road down to the beach, which has a bar and restaurant (see below).

Opposite the Manor Hotel is **The Bodger's Barn** (*01308 485006; www. bodgersbarn.co.uk*), where Mace Bryant runs green woodwork courses (two to four days) and evening classes. The wood is supplied by local woodsmen and traditional tools, rather than machines, are used. Mace offered me a quick go at wood turning on the pole lathe. I was amazed he was happy to trust me with the contraption; after all, I had retired from woodworking at the age of nine after the enormous, square, pine coffee table I made at school received a lukewarm reception from my parents. Putting past traumas behind me, I took up Mace's offer. I found using the foot-operated pole lathe rather therapeutic, with its hypnotic rhythm and the pure and earthy qualities of the wood. Mace's courses range from bowl turning to yurt making and class sizes are limited to four people. Mace also offers longer-term programmes for people with learning disabilities or challenging behaviour.

Food and drink

Manor Hotel Beach Rd, West Bexington DT2 9DF ℗ 01308 897660 ⓦ www. manorhoteldorset.com. A very pleasant restaurant with a flagstone floor plus an outdoor eating area. The bar is open all day, making it a good spot for post-beach refreshments. The menu features local produce and the portions are generous.

Chillies from Dorset

Sea Spring Farm, West Bexington DT2 9DD ① 01308 897898
Ⓦ www.peppersbypost.biz.

Dorset is well known for its cream teas, its cheese and its apple cake. It is less well known for its chillies, yet one of the hottest chillies in the world, the **Dorset Naga**, was first grown in a polytunnel in the garden of a bungalow in West Bexington.

The Dorset Naga is the creation of Joy and Michael Michaud. The couple, who both have doctorates in agronomy, began growing chillies at West Bexington in the early 1990s and are widely acknowledged as the first commercial chilli-growers in the UK. Although the Dorset Naga is frequently referred to as the hottest chilli in the world, it is a title Joy shies away from, knowing that there may be others out there that have not yet been tested. One thing is for certain, annual tests since 2005 have consistently shown that the Dorset Naga is exceptionally fierce; it is just one of the many varieties the Michauds cultivate, ranging from mild to extra hot.

Joy explained to me that growing chillies was an interest that became a way to make their 15-acre small-holding pay for itself. The gently sloping site, reflection of sunlight on the sea and mild coastal climate made the garden of their bungalow one of the best places to grow chillies in Britain. It wasn't easy to sell chillies in West Dorset when they started so the Michauds began offering a mail-order service, which is now used by chilli aficionados, restaurants and sauce producers around the country. When you order chillies from Peppers by Post they are picked, packed and sent the same day, plus you are able to buy varieties that you just wouldn't see in the supermarket.

Joy and Michael also sell their chillies at fairs and festivals. Washingpool Farm Shop (see page 112) stocks the Michaud's chillies and the Punch and Judy Bakery in Bridport (*38–40 West St, DT6 3QP*) sells a bread made using them.

Joy and Michael also sell seeds for vegetable varieties (including their chillies), which they have tested themselves for quality. If you fancy growing your own Dorset Naga or any of the other special varieties, the website for seed purchase is www.seaspringseeds.co.uk.

Joy and Michael have really helped to put Dorset on the chilli-growing map. **The Great Dorset Chilli Festival** (*www.greatdorsetchillifestival.co.uk*) was held for the first time in August 2011 at Kingston Lacy House and it is hoped that it will become an annual event.

⑧ Puncknowle

Despite its spelling, Puncknowle is pronounced 'Punnel'. There is no agreed explanation for the 'Punck' part of the name but the second part is believed to refer to the knoll to the south of the village. On top of the knoll is a small, mysterious **stone house**. No-one is certain of its origins but its positioning high above the coast means it has long been used as a land and sea mark.

In 1794 the knoll was the site of a signal station, one of a chain along the coast, and it has been suggested the house may have been associated with it. The house is built on a Bronze Age barrow and a cremation urn, now in the County Museum in Dorchester (see page 65), was found under its foundations.

The **village** has a simple charm – narrow roads lined with thatched, stone cottages and farm buildings. Behind the high walls in the centre is the manor house, and next to it the church. Their positioning side by side is a reminder of how dominant the church and the big house were in England's rural villages. The manor is at the heart of a 2,000-acre farm, whose principal activity is dairy production.

Puncknowle has a real sense of community, as I witnessed at the Crown Inn on a Tuesday evening. There can be few country pubs so full of jovial locals on a weeknight. They explained that it was their 'Tuesday club', the night when they try to get together. The pub also has active and enthusiastic table skittles teams in the Bridport league; the aim is to knock down miniature skittles on a table by swinging a ball on a chain at a right angle so it travels around three sides of the square then hits the skittles. A couple of the locals pointed out the two rows of windows in the main bar, showing that there used to be an upstairs to this part of the pub, and told me that there are still people living in the village who were born up there. The chatter continued and I learned more about a quirky character with a broad Dorset accent whom I had met briefly earlier in the evening. Known as the Mayor of Swyre, Michael is something of a celebrity around these parts. He has never left the Bride Valley or married but he takes his mayoral duties seriously and wears a toilet chain and plug as his chain of office. Michael used to be employed helping move cattle safely around the village, but since the decline in farming he has redirected those skills and now helps escort children across the road.

Food and drink

Crown Inn Church St, DT2 9BN ℡ 01308 897711. A handsome, 16th-century inn popular with locals and visitors. Tasty, traditional pub food; fish is caught by husband Glyn and cooked by wife Jane. Closed Sun dinner Oct–Easter.

⑨ Litton Cheney

The road from Puncknowle to Litton Cheney takes the most extraordinary route – right through the centre of the farmyard of Looke Farm. Around the village several pretty stone bridges span the River Bride. Litton Cheney is another picturesque Bride Valley village with 17th- and 18th-century cottages reached by crossing the flagstones which lie over the stream running in front of them. Look out for **Mill Cottage** with its mill wheel.

The White Horse Inn is a true country pub. A resident dog sits on a bar stool, begging at the bar until it is rewarded with bar snacks or dog biscuits, and one of the part-time barmen is not far off 90 years old.

Food and drink

White Horse Inn DT2 9AT ① 01308 482539 Ⓦ www.thewhitehorse-littoncheney. co.uk. Traditional country pub drawing a good local crowd, and with a skittle alley, beer garden and boules pitch. Closed Mon lunch all year and Mon dinner in winter.

⑩ Little Bredy

At the head of the Bride Valley, Little Bredy is an idyllic hamlet in a magical setting. As I approached the village on my last visit the unmistakable Englishness of the scene struck me – the green rolling countryside, the neat hedgerows and the buzzards shrieking above.

Only cars belonging to Little Bredy's 85 residents are allowed into the community, so you will need to park and walk. Above the church is a good place to leave the car. There is a very pleasant circular walk from the church, into the grounds of Bridehead House then along the Bride River and back up the hill to the church. Bridehead House was the manor house at the centre of the estate; it stands behind the village cricket ground and can be glimpsed from the road.

With its dainty spire, the **Church of St Michael and All Angels** stands out against the deep green of the hill behind, making it look super-imposed on the scene. The church was largely rebuilt in 1850 and the spire was added to the 14th-century tower.

From the church you can walk through part of the grounds of **Bridehead House** and admire the lake, which was formed by damming the springs that are the start of the River Bride. Water tumbles from the lake down a waterfall and into the river, which passes in front of Little Bredy's cottages. From the waterfall a footbridge takes you across the river, which is small at this stage, and onto a path that runs beside the water. You will pass thatched, stone cottages built in the 19th century but in the medieval style – essentially this is an early Victorian model village. Even the village hall (once a school), which is near the church, looks like a cottage. You come to a five-acre **Victorian walled garden** (*01305 898055; open Easter–Oct Wed, Sun and bank holidays 14.00–17.00*), which belonged to the local estate. The gardens and walls are being restored by a not-for-profit community interest venture, and an experimental vineyard has been planted.

Fresh Face Furniture (*The Old Forge, Estate Yard, DT2 9H; 01308 482278; www.freshfacefurniture.co.uk*), within the estate's old forge, is a small business which restores, hand-paints and sells furniture. They can also make and paint furniture according to your requirements.

Christine McFadden Cookery Courses at Little Bredy

Christine McFadden, Dorset-based cookery teacher and food writer, runs hands-on cookery classes in Little Bredy. Christine is the author of *The Farm Shop Cook Book, Pepper: the Spice that Changed the World* and *Cool Green Leaves and Red Hot Peppers*, all three nominated for international cookbook awards.

Christine's classes make the most of Dorset's abundance of top-notch produce, but also draw on flavours and cuisines from around the world. The emphasis is very much on seasonal, local and Slow, with time allocated to in-depth study of key ingredients – from their history, provenance and cultural importance to tutored tastings and how to cook them. Topics include Spices of India, Glorious Greens, Exotic Eggs and Cooking with Herbs.

The friendly and relaxed classes are limited to a maximum of seven people, and include a recipe folder to take away, delicious refreshments and a leisurely meal to finish.

For more information or to book visit www.thedorsetfoodie.co.uk or www.littlebredy.com.

The **Valley of Stones National Nature Reserve** lies on the southeastern edge of Little Bredy and its 24 acres are pleasant for walking and horseriding. It is named for the sarsen stones that have tumbled down the valley. The stones were formed at the end of the last ice age as the tightly cemented sandstone that capped the chalk hilltops gradually fragmented under freeze/thaw conditions. The chalk grassland is home to wildflowers and butterflies, and scarce lichens and mosses grow on the sarsens. It is managed by the grazing of cattle and sheep.

⑪ Abbotsbury

Approaching Abbotsbury by road from the west is an absolute delight, as you gaze down towards Chesil Beach, which is watched over by St Catherine's Chapel. There are a few lay-bys where you can pull over and admire the view but it can all get a bit frantic if there are streams of traffic in both directions. A more relaxing option is to head up to **Abbotsbury hillfort** to take in the views at your leisure. Before you begin the descent to Abbotsbury, take the small turning on your left signed 'Ashley Close only'. It is worth the short detour to the top of the hill, where you can park and walk along Abbotsbury hillfort for practically aerial views of **Chesil Beach** and the lagoon it shields, known as **The Fleet**. The hill forms the western end of the ridgeway, which protects Abbotsbury from the worst of the weather and gives it its own microclimate. The fort would have been of great strategic importance to the Iron Age population as news of any seaward invasion could be passed to the region's other hillforts, including Maiden Castle (see page 68).

As the name indicates, Abbotsbury was the site of an abbey, built in 1044 around the Church of St Peter and populated with Benedictine monks from Cerne Abbas. It was destroyed in 1539, during the Dissolution, and some of the stone was used to build the village you see today. Near the church and Abbey House you will see other scattered ruins of the abbey, but the most obvious reminder of the monastic days is the **Tithe Barn**, which now houses a children's farm and play centre (*01305 871817; www.abbotsburychildrensfarm. co.uk*). The barn was built in the 14th century to store the tithe payments (a tenth of the harvest) paid by local farmers to the abbot and at 272 feet is the longest tithe barn in England. Its thatched roof covers only half the building but even that takes around three years to re-thatch.

One of the best views of the Tithe Barn is from Abbey House, where you can have lunch or afternoon tea in the garden (see page 122). In the corner of the garden is the Old Mill House, believed to be the only surviving Benedictine water mill in England. The **church of St Nicholas**, parts of which were built around the same time as the Tithe Barn, features some bullet holes in the pulpit. These are not the result of a violent reaction to a particularly dreary sermon, rather they were caused when the Parliamentarians expelled a Royalist garrison from the church during the Civil War.

While Abbotsbury can get very busy during the day in summer, the crowds are largely made up of day trippers who perform a mass exodus shortly after 17.00, making it a more pleasant place to stay than you might expect. The village has model looks; it is crammed with golden stone cottages, many topped with thatched roofs and decorated with window boxes full of colourful flowers. Most of Abbotsbury is owned by Ilchester Estates (see page 127) and only around 15 houses are freehold. Lyn from Abbotsbury Tearooms credits Ilchester Estates with keeping Abbotsbury beautiful because they take care of any repairs and alterations ensuring all work is in harmony with the village.

Abbotsbury caters for the steady stream of tourists it receives with an abundance of tearooms and art galleries. One of the most popular is **Marie Laywine's gallery** (*The Old Chapel, Back St, DT3 4JP; 01305 871175; www. marielaywine.com*), within a former Congregational chapel, built in 1870. In the centre of the village, outside the 19th-century Strangways Village Hall, is a helpful sign listing the various businesses. An **Abbotsbury passport ticket** (available from the attractions or local tourist information centres) allows you reduced admission prices for the three main attractions: the swannery, subtropical garden and children's farm.

St Catherine's Chapel

This lonely building dominates the village from its position high on a hill and beckons you to walk up to it for stunning views of the coastline. From Market Street in the centre of the village take Chapel Lane and follow the path up the hill, which is fairly steep in parts. The chapel was built in the 14th century and may have been used as a chantry by the monks. When they built St Catherine's Chapel they certainly meant it to last – it is constructed entirely of stone, including the roof, with walls four feet thick. It survived the Dissolution, probably because of its importance as a seamark for shipping. St Catherine is the patron saint of spinsters and once a year for centuries unmarried women have climbed up to the chapel to pray for a husband: 'A husband, St Catherine; a handsome one, St Catherine; a rich one, St Catherine; a nice one, St Catherine; and soon, St Catherine!'. I know plenty of girlfriends who have tried everything to find one of those, myself included, so a girls' trip to St Catherine's Chapel may well be on the cards. Non-denominational services are held monthly in summer and if your prayers to St Catherine bear fruit, it is good to know that you can get married here.

Abbotsbury Swannery

New Barn Rd, DT3 4JG ① 01305 871858 Ⓦ www.abbotsburyswannery.co.uk. Open mid-Mar to end Oct daily 10.00–17.00.

By far Abbotsbury's best known attraction is the swannery on the Fleet lagoon, which is home to around 600 swans (and various other canny birds who have taken up residence and exploit the very pleasant living conditions). It was established by Benedictine monks during the 1040s, when they farmed the swans for food. Sir Giles Strangways bought the swannery from Henry VIII in 1543 and it is still owned by his descendants, the Ilchester Estate, making these the only swans in England not owned by the Queen.

Clearly the swans you see here today won't end up on anyone's plate – this is a sanctuary – and you won't see swans in pens, they are free to roam. The visit begins with a video and an exhibition about swans and the swannery. You can then wander along the paths among the nesting mute swans, and hides allow you to watch the birds out on the water. On display are some rather dastardly looking old-fashioned duck traps. Children have the opportunity to help with feeding at 12.00 and 16.00. Mid-May to late June is a particularly exciting time to visit as this is when the cygnets hatch. On site are a well-stocked gift shop and a café.

Abbotsbury Subtropical Gardens

Bullers Way, DT3 4LA ① 01305 871387 Ⓦ www.abbotsburygardens.co.uk. Open daily.

Established in 1765 by the first Countess of Ilchester as a kitchen garden, this has developed into a colourful 20-acre garden filled with rare and exotic plants from all over the world. Many of the plants were first introductions to Britain, discovered by the descendants of the countess. It has notable rhododendron, camellia and hydrangea collections. Its plant centre sells some of the plants on show in the garden, and there's a good restaurant.

Food and drink

Abbey House Church St, DT3 4JJ ℗ 01305 871330 ⓦ www.theabbeyhouse.co.uk.
Teas and lunches around the enormous fireplace or on the lawn, with views of the
millpond and Tithe Barn. Open Mar–Oct 10.00–17.00.

Abbotsbury Tearooms and B&B 26 Rodden Row, DT3 4JL ℗ 01305 871143
ⓦ www.abbotsbury-tearooms.co.uk. Clean, comfortable tearooms serving
generous light lunches and good cakes. On sunny days, the garden is a nice spot
to eat. Friendly service.

The Ilchester Arms Market St, DT3 4JR ℗ 01305 871243 ⓦ www.ilchester-arms.
co.uk. This pub in the centre of the village has a restaurant and small beer garden.

Old Schoolhouse Tearooms 1 Back St, DT3 4JP ℗ 01305 871808. A traditional
tearooms, which almost has a French feel thanks to the red-and-white checked
table cloths. There is also a garden area. Good homemade light lunches and cakes,
plus a range of preserves on sale. Closed Mon Oct–Jul.

From the Somerset border to the Marshwood Vale

Once part of a wealthy monastic estate with Forde Abbey at its heart, the area
between the Somerset border and the A35 coastal road remains remarkably
unspoilt. The accurately named **Marshwood Vale** is marshy and wooded,
which has protected it from the development of large settlements; instead the
bowl-shaped valley has just a few scattered farms and hamlets. It is encircled by
hills, including Dorset's two highest points: **Pilsdon Pen** and **Lewesdon Hill**,
which make for superb walking country.

⑫ Forde Abbey

Forde Abbey, near Chard TA20 4LU ℗ 01460
220231 ⓦ www.fordeabbey.co.uk. Gardens
open daily. House open Apr–Oct Tue–Fri &
Sun 12.00–16.00.

Founded by Cistercian monks over 800
years ago, Forde Abbey became one of the
richest monasteries in the country. It was transformed into a private house
in 1649 and lies at the heart of a family-run estate. The house is surrounded
by 30 acres of beautiful gardens. If it inspires you to start your own garden
makeover, there is a small garden nursery on site. Central to the garden are its
lakes. At 12.00, 13.30 and 15.00 the centenary fountain is turned on in the
Mermaid Pond in front of the house and throws water high into the air for
15 minutes, creating a good photo-opportunity. You enter the house via the
Great Hall, one of the remaining monastic rooms, which doesn't really live
up to its name and feels rather cold and bare. Upstairs is of greater interest,
in particular the Saloon with its wall-hanging Mortlake Tapestries depicting

scenes from St John's Gospel. The tapestries were made in London around 1620 as copies of those woven in Brussels a hundred years earlier for the Sistine Chapel at the instigation of Pope Julius II; elsewhere are a fair range of family heirlooms and some evocative 18th-century bedrooms. Aside from the Great Hall, some other remnants of the house's monastic days remain: the chapel, the monks' dormitory, the cloisters and the undercroft, which now houses a restaurant.

⑬ Guy Mallinson Woodland Workshop

Higher Holditch Farm, Holditch TA20 4NL ① 01460 221102 ⑩ www.mallinson.co.uk.

Spending a few days living in a wood and creating something from it has the potential to be supremely relaxing. From April to November, Guy Mallinson, a cabinet maker, runs two- and five-day woodwork courses in woodland not far from Forde Abbey. One-day courses are available for children. The courses, which cater for all levels, range from carving a bowl to making a hide-covered coracle or a chair from a tree. On site are luxury camping facilities, as well as bodgers' shelters for hire by those who want to try out their woodworking skills in private.

⑭ Pilsdon Pen and Lewesdon Hill

Pilsdon Pen and Lewesdon Hill are the two highest points in Dorset. No-one ever seems quite sure which of the two is actually the higher, although I am reliably informed Lewesdon narrowly takes the title at 915 feet. These neighbouring hills have a lot in common: both were once Iron Age hillforts, both were once used as beacon sites to warn of impending invasion and both provide magnificent views of the Marshwood Vale. A round walk from Broadwindsor, incorporating both Pilsdon Pen and Lewesdon Hill, takes about four hours.

Pilsdon Pen is particularly easy to access and makes a brief but satisfying walk on its own. There is a car park opposite the start of the walk, on the B3164. From there it is a short, steep climb up the hillside until you reach the flat top, which was once the site of the Iron Age hillfort.

⑮ Broadwindsor Craft and Design Centre

Broadwindsor DT8 3PX ① 01308 868362 ⑩ broadwindsor-crafts.co.uk. Open daily.

Former farm buildings house this craft centre and restaurant in the village of Broadwindsor, east of Beaminster. At the heart of the centre is a large gift shop selling country-style gifts, furniture and food; in the lead-up to Christmas it sells a huge range of Christmas decorations. In the surrounding buildings, formerly the pig pens, are studios showcasing different crafts, such as glass-blowing, floristry and quilting. The **Earth Design** shop sells a range of semi-precious stones, jewellery and crystals reputed to heal all manner of ills: owner Clive was so convincing about the healing power of crystals that I was persuaded to buy two. The restaurant here serves homemade light lunches and cakes, and is a popular pit-stop for walkers tackling nearby Pilsdon Pen and Lewesdon Hill. There is plenty of free parking and the centre is accessible to the disabled. It has been part of the local farming community since 1986 and its farming links contribute to its charm; the manager, Sarah, is a farmer's wife and the day I met her she had had to rush home earlier that morning to deal with escaped cows.

⑯ Whitchurch Canonicorum

A village of farms and cottages tucked back from the coast at the southern edge of the Marshwood Vale, Whitchurch Canonicorum has a **church** with an unusual dedication – to St Candida, also known as St Wite. Within the church is the 13th-century shrine containing St Wite's remains. The three oval openings were originally designed for the sick to insert their ailing limbs into, or if they couldn't make it to the church a handkerchief was inserted and taken to them. Today the openings are used for depositing prayers hand-written on small cards, and there were plenty of them when I last visited in 2011. The shrine is a rare survival as most were destroyed during the Reformation. This is the only church in England, other than Westminster Abbey, that still contains the original medieval shrine and relics of the saint to whom it was dedicated. St Wite has not conclusively been identified: one theory is that she was a Saxon woman killed by the Danes in one of their raids on Charmouth.

Near the altar is a rather splendid shrine to 'S John Ieffrey of Catherstone, Knight', who died in 1611. The recumbent stone figure dressed in a knight's armour is in excellent condition.

Buried in the churchyard is **Georgi Ivanov Markov**, the Bulgarian dissident writer who died in London in 1978 after being stabbed by an umbrella which was used to insert a ricin pellet into his calf. His assassination was allegedly organised by the Bulgarian Secret Police with the help of the Soviet KGB. It was their third attempt to dispose of him, and several prominent KGB defectors, including Oleg Gordievskiy, have asserted that the KGB was responsible for the killing. The inscription on Markov's gravestone, which is written in both English and Russian, states that he died 'in the cause of freedom'.

Coney's Castle and Lambert's Castle

Those Iron Age folk certainly kept themselves busy, for not far from Pilsdon Pen and Lewesdon Hill are these two further Iron Age hillforts. Tucked away down narrow lanes and preserved by the National Trust, they offer fine walks and are ideal spots for a picnic overlooking the Marshwood Vale. They are perhaps at their best when wearing their spring finery in the form of a layer of bluebells. Both Coney's and Lambert's castles may have been built as border posts between the neighbouring tribes the Durotriges (eastwards) and the Dumnonii (southwest) or as status symbols for local chiefs. More recently (from 1709 to 1947), Lambert's Castle was used as the venue for a fair, with the hilltop serving as a racecourse.

Eastwards from Beaminster

⑰ Beaminster and surrounds

Beaminster, a market town since 1284, positively glows on
a sunny day thanks to the golden hamstone from which
much of the town is built. Narrow lanes of terraced cottages
converge in the market square. It is surrounded by gently
rolling hills, which provide easy walking country.

The Square is the focal point; at its centre is a covered market cross known
as the Julia Memorial. This was erected in 1906 by Vincent Robinson of
Parnham House, which lies south of the town, as a memorial to his sister, Julia.

St Mary's Church faces a row of pretty terraced cottages of assorted shapes,
sizes and colours. The community has come up with an ingenious solution
to the problem of getting an ageing population into church. A small stone
building at the end of the churchyard contains a lift allowing those with
limited mobility or in wheelchairs to avoid the steps. Volunteers are usually on
hand to guide visitors; the community has done an admirable job conserving
and restoring the church and deservedly won an award for their efforts. The
volunteer who showed me around told me proudly that they had installed
under-floor heating, when each of the original flagstones was painstakingly
lifted and replaced. Sadly the pews had to be removed due to wood rot, and
have been replaced with chairs. The tower, which dates from the 1500s, is
one of the most elaborate in the West Country: every three hours the church
clock plays the Hymn Tune known as Hanover. Within the church are large
memorials to the Strobe family who once lived in nearby Parnham House,
while the embroidery screen near the organ, which depicts nearby scenes,
was made by local ladies as part of their millennium celebrations.

Beaminster has a small, local **museum** with limited opening hours
(*Whitcombe Rd, DT8 3NB; 01308 863623; www.beaminstermuseum.org.*)

Food and drink

The small, independent shop seems to have survived better in Beaminster than
elsewhere. Around The Square are several selling locally grown food, such as **Nick
Tett Family Butchers** and **Fruit n' Two Veg**. Just around the corner, on Hogshill
Street, is **The Village Bakery** – irrepressibly quaint and old-world. On the other side
of the street is **Vicki's Pantry** (*4–6 Hogshill St*), which provides a great service to
the community selling all the essentials and local produce (such as Denhay cheese
and bacon) and has a small, inexpensive café.

Beaminster Brasserie Bridge House Hotel, 3 Prout Bridge, DT8 3AY ① 01308
862200 ⓦ www.beaminsterbrasserie.co.uk. Head chef Steve gives local ingredients
an international flavour at this elegant restaurant. Local snails always appear on
the menu – perhaps they are the ultimate Slow Food? – and might include snail

rarebit with Palmers beer. Open daily for breakfast, lunch and dinner.

Out of Town Farmshop Lane End Farm, Tunnel Rd DT8 3HB Ⓜ 07518 982148 Ⓦ www.outoftownfarmshop.co.uk. On the A3066 ½ mile north of Beaminster. A small shop on a working farm, selling home-grown meat and vegetables, plus homemade pies, cakes and preserves. Closed Sun and Mon.

Wild Garlic The Square DT8 3AW Ⓣ 01308 861446 Ⓦ www.thewildgarlic.co.uk. The restaurant of 2009 Masterchef winner, Matt Follas, is, unsurprisingly, very popular. There is a lot to like about Wild Garlic before you even get to the food, including the edible plants on the tables and the poetry playing in the restrooms. The menu is written daily, depending on what local produce is available; some ingredients are foraged, and Matt organises foraging courses with a three-course lunch. Open Wed–Sat for morning tea, lunch and dinner.

Mapperton Gardens

DT8 3NR Ⓣ 01308 862645 Ⓦ www.mapperton.com. Open Apr–Oct Sun–Fri.

Mapperton, the home of the Earl and Countess of Sandwich, lies in a gloriously bucolic landscape two miles east of Beaminster. Its garden, hidden in a narrow, steep-sided valley below the house, is fascinating for its amalgamation of three styles at the hands of three different owners. The banks, terraces and long, rectangular fish ponds date from the Elizabethan period but in the 1920s a wealthy widow, Ethel Labouchère, created an Arts and Crafts garden in the Italianate style on the highest of the terraces, into the banks of which she built little rooms, complete with fireplaces for taking afternoon tea. It's possible she was influenced, or helped, by Harold Peto, creator of the (Arts and Crafts Italianate) garden at Iford in Wiltshire. The present owner's father (Victor Montagu) bought the property in the 1950s and made several important additions to the garden, including a classical-style orangery, overlooking Mrs Labouchère's fountains and topiary, and a pergola. He also converted one of the Elizabethan fish ponds into a swimming pool of near-Olympic proportions, while in the wild, stream-fed valley below the pool he planted an arboretum with some notable specimen trees. The current owners have done an admirable

Buckham Down Fair

An annual pony and dog show, Buckham Down Fair (*www.buckhamfair.co.uk*) takes place in August just outside Beaminster. The fair is the initiative of actor and TV presenter, Martin Clunes, and his wife Philippa, on whose land it is held. Martin has made his Dorset retreat his permanent home and is very much a fixture of the local community. The Clunes family, like so many who live in Dorset, are horse and dog people. As well as a gymkhana and dog classes, the fair has stalls selling local produce, trade stands and fairground rides. This fun day out, which attracts several thousand visitors, is also an important fundraising event: since it began in 2008, the fair has raised £70,000 for local charities.

Denhay Farms

On a farm in the Marshwood Vale, Denhay produces farmhouse cheddar and hand-cured bacon. They have been making West Country Farmhouse Cheddar since 1959 using milk from their Friesian herd, and it is left to mature for around a year. Their bacon is produced with similar care, using outdoor-reared pork that is hand-rubbed with sea salt and smoked over beech logs. Denhay products are available in shops, supermarkets and online at www.denhay.co.uk.

amount to improve the planting on all three levels of the garden over the past two decades. The Jacobean manor house is open for limited periods during the summer.

⑱ Evershot

Evershot is the second highest village in Dorset, after Ashmore, although unlike Ashmore it doesn't feel particularly high. It is also where the River Frome rises, just behind St Osmund's Church in Back Lane.

Much of the village's undeniable charm derives from its mixture of architectural styles, from tiny 17th-century cottages to large Georgian houses. Although the main street is largely residential, Evershot has managed to keep its village shop, and the excellent bakery is thriving. The pavement is raised on one side of the village street; this protected pedestrians and residents of the more upmarket side of the street from the muck that collected in the road, presumably mostly donated by the local bovine population. The houses on the raised pavement side were therefore considered more desirable and expensive.

On the edge of Evershot is the heart of the vastly wealthy **Ilchester Estate**, which owns 15,000 acres of West Dorset, including Abbotsbury and Chesil Beach, and 40 acres of central London, including Holland Park. The estate is currently owned by Charlotte Townshend, a country sports enthusiast and active opponent of the ban on foxhunting. As the owner of the Abbotsbury Swannery (see page 121), she is the only person in the country, other than the Queen, who is allowed to own swans.

Food and drink

Acorn Inn 28 Fore St, DT2 0JW ① 01935 83228 Ⓦ www.acorn-inn.co.uk. A 16th-century coaching inn with good food and service, and an active skittles team.
Evershot Village Bakery 18 Fore St, DT2 0JW ① 01935 83379. Spelt and sourdough breads sell briskly, alongside a range of pizzas and sweet treats.
Summer Lodge Country House Hotel Restaurant and Spa Summer Lane, DT2 0JR ① 01935 482000 Ⓦ www.summerlodgehotel.com. This elegant hotel has a fine-dining restaurant with excellent service. Meals are taken in the conservatory, restaurant or cosy bar and afternoon tea is served daily in the drawing room.

⑲ The Kingcombe Centre

Lower Kingcombe, DT2 0EQ ① 01300 320684 ⓦ www.kingcombecentre.org. Open daily.

The marketing material gives Kingcombe the title of 'the jewel in Dorset's crown'. It certainly is very precious. The Dorset Wildlife Trust (DWT) manages almost 1,000 acres of meadows and nature reserve at Kingcombe and Powerstock. The Kingcombe site was formerly a well-managed organic farm, owned by the Wallbridge family, and is now rich in wildflowers, butterflies and birdlife. Grazing is an important element of the conservation of this land and you will see Kingcombe organic beef on sale in the area. You can simply wander and experience the English countryside as it used to be, have lunch in the café or take part in one of the many activities or environmental studies courses on offer, such as beekeeping, hedgelaying and wildlife tracking.

I spent a wonderful and informative day on a **foraging course** with John Wright, known for his appearances on television's *River Cottage*. By the end of a day foraging with him, I was surprised I had survived my childhood. As an only child and a tomboy, I spent many hours building camps in the countryside surrounding our house and was often joined by my equally tomboyish friend, Gillian, who later put her countryside training to good use and married a Devon farmer. Gillian and I collected all manner of leaves, berries, even fir cones, and held 'tea parties' – by sheer fluke it seems, we managed to steer clear of the various toxic plants that John took care to point out on his course. As he said, 'it is just as important, if not more so, to know the plants you can't eat as it is to know the plants you can'. Particularly scary was the hemlock waterdropwort, Britain's most deadly plant which seems cunningly disguised as some relation of parsley or celery.

John describes himself as one of those lucky people who has turned a hobby into a job. I had assumed he must have had some sort of botany studies background but he was actually a cabinetmaker, whose passion for mushrooms led him to become a self-taught forager. John runs a series of fascinating foraging courses, covering hedgerow, seashore, fungi and more. He maintains an interesting and helpful website (*www.wild-food.net*) and has written some lovely books on foraging, which are part of the River Cottage Handbook series, *Mushroom Handbook, Edible Seashore Handbook* and *Hedgerow Handbook*.

⑳ Eggardon Hillfort

This hugely atmospheric Iron Age hillfort, four miles east of Bridport, has superb panoramic views and is one of the most accessible hillforts in Dorset. On a clear day you can see right across Lyme Bay to south Devon, and across the Marshwood Vale to Pilsdon Pen.

The fort covers 20 acres of the hill top. Its impressive ditches and banks seem to ripple as shadows cast by the clouds drift across them. The interior contains a large octagonal earthwork, thought to be the result of tree planting by a smuggler who owned the land and used the formation as a seamark for his ships. It is certainly worth a visit for the views, the history and the serenity.

4. WEYMOUTH AND THE SOUTHERN COAST

Along this portion of the Dorset coast the huge shingle bank of **Chesil Beach** stands separated from the mainland by a lagoon, creating a strange, but entirely natural, visual phenomenon. At the beach's southeastern end are the town of Weymouth and the peninsula known as the Isle of Portland. Depending on how you look at it, **Weymouth** is either confused about what it wants to be or multi-talented, having to juggle being a working town, a port and a seaside resort. Now it can add another achievement to its CV – Olympic venue. It was quite a coup for Weymouth, and for Dorset, when the Weymouth and Portland National Sailing Academy (WPNSA) was chosen to host the sailing events for the London 2012 Olympic and Paralympic Games. Thanks to the WPNSA, the area now has world-class facilities to complement its superb sailing waters.

Linked to Weymouth by a causeway is the **Isle of Portland**, famed for its Portland stone quarries and its lighthouse, Portland Bill, which warns shipping to steer clear of Dorset's southernmost point. A highlight of the island is Portland Castle, an extraordinarily well-preserved fort built by Henry VIII in the 1540s.

Smuggling became rife along the south coast after an act was passed in 1751 which dramatically increased the tax levied on spirits. Weymouth and the surrounding area was a smuggling hot spot, with a notorious gang operating around **Osmington Mills**. The quiet waters of the **Fleet Lagoon** behind Chesil Beach were ideal for stowing contraband for collection at a more convenient time.

The **South Dorset Ridgeway** is a ridge of chalky downland running parallel to the coast from **Abbotsbury** in the west to the village of **Osmington** in the east. The ridgeway is extraordinarily rich in prehistoric sites such as long barrows, round barrows, stone circles and hillforts.

Getting there and around

Reaching Weymouth and Portland by road can be irksome, as the main route from Dorchester is very congested in the peak holiday months. It is hoped the infrastructure developments underway for the London 2012 Olympic Games will improve the situation.

If you decide to leave your car at home, Weymouth is the main entry point for the area as it has a mainline train station and connecting buses to get you to the more hidden places, including access points for the South Dorset Ridgeway such as Portesham.

WEYMOUTH AND THE SOUTHERN COAST

A356

A37

A37

A35

DORCHESTER

A35

Hardy Monument

Portesham ①

Abbotsbury

A354

White Horse

⑧ Osmington

Langton Herring

B3157

A353

Osmington Mills

② Chesil Beach

The Fleet

③ WEYMOUTH

Nothe Fort

𝒩

Portland Castle

0 ———— 4 miles

0 ———— 5km

④ Fortuneswell

A354

⑥ Church Ope

⑤ Weston

Portland Bill

⑦

Public transport

Weymouth is three hours from London Waterloo by **train** and is also connected by train to other Dorset towns: Dorchester, Wareham, Poole and Bournemouth.

The **Jurassic Coast bus** (CoastLinX53) runs along the south coast, calling at Poole, Wareham, Wool, Weymouth, Abbotsbury, West Bay, Bridport, Chideock, Charmouth, Lyme Regis, Seaton, Beer and Exeter. Other parts of Dorset are relatively easy to reach by bus: **South West Coaches** operates an hourly service between Portland and Dorchester via Weymouth (210), and **Wilts & Dorset** operates buses to Blandford (route 183). In summer the **Go-Ahead service** (Damory/Wilts & Dorset) operates between Weymouth, Lulworth and Swanage, which is handy for the South West Coast Path; it stops at Norden Park and Ride station, the starting point for the Swanage Heritage Railway to Corfe Castle and Swanage.

In Weymouth, **First Buses** (*www.firstgroup.com*) operates regular services, which are useful for getting around the town and the surrounding area, including Portland. From Easter to September there are open-top bus services from Weymouth Esplanade to Portland Bill.

Information about local bus services and how to link up with the South Dorset Ridgeway is available at www.travelinesw.com.

By boat

White Motor Boats (*01305 785000; www.whitemotorboat.freeuk.com*) operates a summer **ferry** service from Weymouth (Brewers Quay) to Portland Castle, which takes around 40 minutes. The usual boat is *My Girl*, a veteran of World War II. The ferry leaves Brewers Quay at 10.30, 12.30 and 14.30 and returns from Portland Castle at 11.20, 13.20 and 15.20.

During the summer, local boatmen operate **rowing-boat ferries** across the harbour from near the ferry terminal. This is a novel way of getting from the town to Nothe Fort and saves you the walk up to the Town Bridge.

Numerous **cruises** along the Jurassic Coast depart from Weymouth, including those aboard the world's last sea-going paddle steamer, *The Waverley* (*0845 1304647; www.waverleyexcursions.co.uk*).

Cruise operators

Ferry Step Cruises Ⓜ 07909 292667. Boat trips around Weymouth and Portland harbours.

MV Freedom 11 Redcliff View, DT4 8RW Ⓣ 01305 826199 Ⓦ www.mvfreedom. co.uk. Trips along the Jurassic Coast or around Portland Harbour in a boat specifically equipped for the disabled.

Weymouth Whitewater Ⓜ 07899 892317 Ⓦ www.weymouth-whitewater.co.uk. Rigid inflatable boat rides to Lulworth Cove, Portland or around Weymouth Bay lasting 1–2 hours.

White Motor Boats Brewers Quay DT4 8TJ ℗ 01305 785000
Ⓦ www.whitemotorboat.freeuk.com. Daily ferry service from Weymouth to
Portland and cruises along the Jurassic Coast. Also available for private charters.

Cycling

Just as driving around Weymouth can be problematic due to traffic, so
can cycling be. The most cycle-friendly routes are outlined in *Active Travel
Weymouth and Portland, A Guide to Walking and Cycling*, available from tourist
information centres and online (*www.dorsetforyou.com*).

The **South Dorset Ridgeway** offers some good off-roading with fantastic
views and a chance to stop off at the numerous prehistoric sites.

Cycle hire

Cycle Life 28 Abbotsbury Rd, Weymouth DT4 0AE ℗ 01305 781831
Ⓦ www.cyclelife.com.
Weymouth Bike Hire Ⓜ 07973 751393 Ⓦ www.weymouthbikehire.co.uk. Free
delivery and collection within the Weymouth and Portland area.

Walking

The South West Coast Path runs along this stretch, diverting inland around
Weymouth and passes above the **White Horse** near Osmington. An easily
followed four-mile circuit from Osmington works very well, through fields to
Sutton Poyntz, then up onto White Horse Hill for the high-level section on
the coast path before dropping near the White Horse itself into Osmington.

The **South Dorset Ridgeway** is part of the South West Coast Path and
runs from West Bexington to Osmington Mills. Glorious views of the Jurassic
Coast, chalk downland and river valleys are not its only draw card as this
is an area packed with archaeological delights, reminders that the land has
been inhabited for over 6,000 years. These include the Hell Stone, a highly
atmospheric chambered long barrow (see page 135). *Round-a-bout the Ridge*
is a collection of four walks taking in the archaeology and scenery of the
South Dorset Ridgeway. The nicely illustrated packs are available from tourist
information centres and can also be downloaded from the publications section
of the AONB website (*www.dorsetaonb.org.uk*).

The Visit Weymouth website (*www.visitweymouth.co.uk*) suggests numerous
walking routes in the area using local buses.

Portland is easy to explore on foot and a nine-mile path runs around the
peninsula. The fascinating southern tip around Portland Bill makes a perfect
three-mile circuit past the three lighthouses. Southwell is a useful starting point,
giving the pleasure of arriving at the Bill on foot, and taking in atmospherically
decayed old quarries with rusting cranes and derricks, and a huge blow-hole on
the east coast; follow the west coast until you're nearly level with the strikingly
hideous factory on the skyline, then head inland back to Southwell.

Accommodation

Bay View Hotel 35 The Esplanade, Weymouth DT4 8DH ℗ 0800 2982389
Ⓔ info@bayview-weymouth.co.uk Ⓦ www.bayview-weymouth.co.uk. Family-run
guesthouse opposite the beach, with 6 en-suite rooms, some with sea view. Has
free, off-street parking, which is a bonus in this area. Rates are reasonable but are
on a room-only basis.

Beach House 51 Chiswell, Portland DT5 1AW ℗ 01305 821155 Ⓔ pete@beach-
house-bandb.co.uk Ⓦ www.beach-house-bandb.co.uk. This B&B backs onto
Chesil Beach at the Portland end and is close to the National Sailing Academy.
The attractive house was built in the 1800s. 5 of the 6 rooms have en-suite
bathrooms. Not luxurious but quite comfortable. Slightly-below-average B&B
prices.

Contemporary Cottages 2 Easton Lane, Portland DT5 1BW Ⓜ 07976 152723
Ⓔ Deborah@dsare.co.uk Ⓦ www.contemporarycottage.co.uk. Offers 3 modern
self-catering units, which sleep 6 or 7; clean, fresh and modern décor. Each of the
properties has sea views. Available for short breaks and by the week.

No. 10 10 Trinity Rd, Weymouth ℗ 01305 776753 Ⓦ www.
weymouthharboursideaccommodation.co.uk. Luxurious B&B accommodation
open June to October. One guest suite with private courtyard in a Georgian
cottage overlooking the harbour. Upmarket but not overpriced.

Old Higher Lighthouse Portland Bill DT5 2JT ℗ 01305 822300 Ⓔ enquiries@
oldhigherlighthouse.com Ⓦ www.oldhigherlighthouse.com. There are a couple of
2-bedroom self-catering cottages in the grounds of the disused lighthouse, which
is now a private residence. Handy for the summer months are the outdoor heated
pool and jacuzzi. Guests also have access to the lighthouse tower observatory for
seagull's-eye views.

Old Lower Light Portland Bill DT5 2JT ℗ 01305 820553 Ⓔ obs@btinternet.
com Ⓦ www.portlandbirdobs.org.uk. Basic, hostel-style accommodation in a
former lighthouse, now a bird observatory. Aimed at birdwatchers, naturalists and
walkers, and those on a tight budget.

Osmington Holiday Park Osmington DT3 6HB ℗ 01305 837010 Ⓔ info@
osmingtonholidays.co.uk Ⓦ www.osmingtonholidays.co.uk. A newly renovated
family holiday park in a quiet location, this has nice wooden self-catering lodges
as well as caravans, a restaurant and outdoor pool. A good option if you are
trying to keep accommodation costs down.

Roundhouse Hotel 1 The Esplanade, Weymouth DT4 8EA ℗ 01305 761010
Ⓔ office@roundhouse-hotel-weymouth.com Ⓦ www.roundhouse-hotel-
weymouth.com. 6 spacious en-suite rooms with contemporary décor, in an
attractive listed building overlooking the harbour and the beach. At the expensive
end of the B&B range. Children and pets are not allowed.

Sea Shell Cottage 14 Cove St, Brewers Quay, Weymouth DT4 8TS ℗ 01305
772167 Ⓔ sales@seashellcottageweymouth.com Ⓦ www.seashellcottage
weymouth.com. Self-catering accommodation in a beautifully refurbished

150-year-old fisherman's cottage near the harbour. Sleeps up to 6 in 2 double rooms and one twin, and has a cosy courtyard. The cottage comes with a parking permit for one vehicle and is available for short breaks and week-long stays. Reasonable value if there is a group of you, but prices rise significantly in peak season. Dogs allowed.

Smugglers Inn Osmington Mills DT3 6HF ℗ 01305 833125 Ⓦ www.smugglersinnosmingtonmills.co.uk. In a quiet spot right on the South West Coast Path, this pub with rooms is perfectly located for walkers (see page 149). It has 4 reasonably priced, comfortable en-suite rooms and a good restaurant.

Tourist information centre

General information Ⓦ www.visitweymouth.co.uk.
Weymouth The Pavilion, The Esplanade, DT4 8ED ℗ 01305 785747.

West of Weymouth, including Chesil Beach

① Portesham and surrounds

The village of Portesham snuggles up against the base of the chalk hills of the South Dorset Ridgeway. **St Peter's Church**, which is largely 12th and 13th century, is reached over a flagstone across the flower-topped stream which flows gently alongside the main street. The handsome 18th-century **Portesham House** is where Vice-Admiral Sir Thomas Masterman Hardy once lived (see *Hardy Monument* below).

Standing high above Portesham on Black Down Hill, is the **Hardy Monument**. It is not, as you may at first assume, a monument to the novelist Thomas Hardy but to Vice-Admiral Sir Thomas Masterman Hardy, who served aboard Nelson's HMS *Victory* during the Battle of Trafalgar in 1805. During the battle the French and Spanish fleets were defeated but Nelson was fatally wounded. It was to Hardy that Nelson reputedly uttered his famous last words, 'Kiss me, Hardy'. Hardy spent his childhood in Portesham until joining the navy as a 13-year old captain's servant. The monument is a 72-foot Portland stone tower built in 1844. It certainly isn't a thing of beauty, looking rather like a factory chimney protruding from the hilltop: its shape was intended to represent a telescope of the type Hardy may have used at sea. Once you know that, it doesn't seem so out of place. You used to be able to climb to the top of the monument for spectacular views but at the time of writing it was closed for an extended period for restoration; however the views from the base are splendid, without the climb. The heathy surroundings make great strolling terrain, with the South Dorset Ridgeway passing the monument; bear in mind that, although the National Trust owns the monument and a small patch of land around it, the rest of the land is private.

From the Hardy Monument, you have several options for **walking**: one of the most pleasing (around seven miles) is to start from Portesham and walk up, then carry on eastwards along the well-marked track along the ridge of Bronkham Hill with its spectacularly profuse series of prehistoric tumuli, and down to Corton Farm, then back to Portesham by lanes and footpaths.

The Hell Stone

Not far from the Hardy Monument, along the South Dorset Ridgeway, is the 6,000-year-old Hell Stone, a chambered long barrow, which would have originally been covered by a mound of earth. Consisting of nine upright sarsen stones supporting a single capstone, it was restored in 1866 after collapse. Doubts proliferate about the accuracy of the restoration and it is unlikely the restorers managed to replace the stones precisely in their original position. Nevertheless, the structure oozes atmosphere and history, and is worthy of the local legend which says that the devil threw the stone from Portland while playing quoits.

><><><

Food and drink

Kings Arms 2 Front St, DT3 4ET ① 01305 871342 ⓦ www.kingsarmsatportesham. com. Pub food, reasonably priced. The large beer garden is popular in the warmer months. Open daily 11.00–23.00.

② Chesil Beach

Stand on Portland Heights or outside St Catherine's Chapel high above Abbotsbury and look out to sea and you will be treated to the most extraordinary sight – a wide, golden, shingle bank rising out of the water and running along the coastline, with a lagoon sheltering sheepishly behind it. If you saw such a thing in Dubai you might assume it was the zany creation of a capricious sheikh, but this is Dorset and Chesil Beach is all natural.

Stretching for 18 miles between West Bay and Portland, Chesil Beach is the largest of three major shingle structures in Britain. The shingle bank, which reaches around 40 feet at its highest point, was formed by rising seas at the end of the last Ice Age. Its rounded pebbles have been graded in size by strong tidal currents; they are as small as peas at the western end and the size of oranges at the Portland end. For centuries the size of the pebbles has been helping locals, mostly smugglers and fishermen, pinpoint where they are landing on the beach.

The lagoon, known as **the Fleet**, extends from Abbotsbury to Portland and contains a mixture of salt and fresh water. Home to an abundance of birdlife, wading birds can be seen all year, while brent geese from Siberia and red-breasted merganser (fish eating duck) visit in winter. The birds' ancestors must have had quite a shock back in 1942–43, when Barnes Wallis's famous bouncing bomb was tested on the Fleet in preparation for the Dambusters raids.

At the southern end of the Fleet, just before you head over the causeway from Weymouth to Portland, is the **Chesil Beach and Nature Reserve Information Centre** (*Portland Beach Rd, DT4 9XE; 01305 760579; www. chesilbeach.org*) and a pay-and-display car park with direct access to Chesil Beach. It is worth popping into the centre, which provides information on Chesil Beach, the Fleet and Portland. Telescopes inside allow you to watch seabirds feeding on the sand flats and there is live video from cameras on the bed of the lagoon. It is worth checking whether any sections of the beach are closed, as during nesting season (usually April to August) parts are off-limits to avoid disturbing the birds. Since Chesil Beach is virtually physically impossible to walk along, the South West Coast Path follows the inland side of the Fleet, midway along which **Langton Herring** makes a handy access point for walks to the water's edge.

Glass-bottom boat trips provide the opportunity to explore the Fleet and get a closer look at its bird and sealife (*The Fleet Observer, Ferryman's Way, Wyke Regis, Weymouth DT4 9YU; 01305 759692; www.thefleetobserver.co.uk*).

③ Weymouth

A bustling seaside town of around 52,000 people, Weymouth attracts thousands of holiday-makers in summer, earning it the rather dubious nickname of 'England's Bay of Naples'. It has an active harbour, constantly criss-crossed by fishing vessels and pleasure craft, and a ferry port which connects it to France and the Channel Islands. When it was announced as the venue for the sailing events of the London 2012 Olympic and Paralympic Games, work quickly began to spruce up the town, which had begun to look a little neglected. I visited in 2011, when the town and the surrounding area were busy preparing for the event and buzzing with Olympics excitement.

Plague port and royal resort
Weymouth began as two medieval ports on either side of the mouth of the River Wey. The two towns, Weymouth and Melcombe Regis, were joined in

1571 by royal charter and a bridge was later built across the harbour between them. The portion now referred to as the town centre, which lies north of the River Wey, was actually Melcombe Regis, which has a grim claim to fame, for it was here that the bubonic plague, or Black Death, entered England in 1348.

During the 18th century Weymouth, like many coastal towns, was touted as a health retreat. King George III came to Weymouth in 1789 to try out one of the first bathing machines, a hut on wheels drawn into the water by horses where one could bathe supervised by an attendant. It is said that while he bathed 'God save the King' was dutifully sung from another hut. The king visited regularly until 1810, a fact which is commemorated by a chalk carving on a hillside at Osmington depicting the monarch on horseback (see page 148). The promise of healing properties and royal patronage made Weymouth highly fashionable and rows of elegant houses sprung up along the esplanade to cater for well-to-do visitors.

The **statue of George III** on the esplanade was erected in 1809 to mark the 50th anniversary of his succession. Nearby, at the end of King Street, is the colourful **Jubilee Clock**, which was built in 1887 to commemorate 50 years of the reign of Queen Victoria. A bronze **statue of Queen Victoria** sits in front of **St John's Church**, a fine Portland stone building completed in 1854.

During World War II, Weymouth suffered heavy damage. It also featured prominently in the D-Day landings in Normandy as a departure point for many British and American soldiers. A **memorial** on the esplanade, opposite the Royal Hotel, records that 517,816 troops and 144,093 vehicles embarked at Weymouth between 6 June 1944 and 7 May 1945.

The seafront and Lodmoor Country Park

Today, handsome Georgian terraced houses and some sizeable hotels line Weymouth's seafront. The earlier terraces have iron balconies, while the later ones (1820s) have bay windows. If you can manage to screen out the amusement arcades and tacky souvenir shops you can just about imagine how the seafront was back in the 18th and early 19th centuries. In summer the long sandy beach is given over to the usual seaside entertainment, including a funfair, traditional Punch and Judy show and the ever-popular donkey rides. A colourful gypsy kiosk can be seen on the esplanade, where Romany gypsy Zara Lee will tell your fortune. Zara's family has been telling fortunes on Weymouth Esplanade for 40 years and Zara, who told me she has had the gift since childhood, took over from her parents in 2008.

A land train operates between Easter and the end of September from the town centre along the seafront to **Lodmoor Country Park**. The 350-acre park contains an RSPB nature reserve and numerous more lively attractions, such as mini-golf, a miniature railway, Weymouth Sea Life Park and Sandworld. As parking is expensive at Lodmoor Country Park, catching the land train can help to keep costs down.

One of the town's best-known attractions is **Weymouth Sea Life Park** (*Lodmoor Country Park, DT4 7SX; 01305 761070; www.sealife.co.uk; open daily 10.00–18.00*). As well as the displays of colourful fish you may expect, more unusual residents feature, such as baby crocodiles, seals, sharks, otters, rays and rescued green sea turtles. Many of the creatures have been rescued and cannot be released, or were born and bred at the park as part of its conservation work. You might like to plan your visit around particular feeding times or keeper talks (details on the website), and to take along swimwear and towels for the water rides. Admission is costly but various vouchers offer reduced rates.

For many years visitors to Weymouth have admired Mark Anderson's sand sculptures, and those of his grandfather, Fred Darrington, before him. Fred began creating them on Weymouth Beach in the 1920s, a skill he later passed on to his grandson. Mark's sand sculptures now have a more permanent home in the form of **Sandworld** (*Lodmoor Country Park, Preston Beach Rd, DT4 7SX; 07411 387529; www.sandworld.co.uk*), which he co-founded in 2011. Incredibly, the intricately detailed works are created by Mark and his fellow sculptors using nothing but sand and water. His website (*www.sculpturesinsand. com*) shows many of his and Fred's creations.

Radipole Lake

Returning towards the town centre and heading away from the esplanade along King Street you will come to the Swannery car park, where a huge open-air **market** is held on Thursdays between Easter and autumn. This is also where you will find the visitor centre for the **Radipole Lake RSPB Reserve** (*01305 778313; www.rspb.org.uk; see box opposite*), a surprising chunk of tranquillity in the centre of town. The lake, which flows into Weymouth Harbour, and the surrounding wetland are home to an impressive line-up of bird species, including rare bitterns and Cetti's warblers. You don't need to be a knowledgeable ornithologist to enjoy the reserve – the visitor centre (*open daily 09.00–17.00 or 16.00 in winter*) and handy display boards make it accessible to everyone. Simply getting away from the hustle and bustle and wandering through the wetland is a joy. Children can be entertained with specially created trails, bird events, and during the summer, family activities such as pond dipping and bug hunts, while paths make the reserve accessible to wheelchairs and pushchairs.

Around Weymouth Harbour

Weymouth Harbour is a very pleasant place to wander, divided into two distinct halves by the River Wey, as it was when it was two communities prior to 1571. On the old Melcombe Regis (north) side is **Custom House Quay**, where the buildings that were once at Weymouth's commercial shipping heart now stand at the centre of an area dominated by restaurants and shops. Being an old mariners' haunt, there is no shortage of historic pubs along this stretch.

Radipole Lake RSPB Reserve

Sarah Cookson, RSPB volunteer

The first time I visited the RSPB's Weymouth Wetlands Nature Reserve at Radipole Lake, I could hardly believe that I was still in the middle of a busy town with houses and shops on every side and the beach, amusement arcades and ice cream sellers of the tourist resort just five minutes' walk away.

The noise and bustle fell away and so did the cares. I was in Weymouth's tranquil heart, a peaceful oasis for locals and holiday makers alike. I had stumbled across a little piece of paradise with meandering paths overhung with arches of hawthorn and blackthorn, sweeping willows and buddleia adorned with butterflies and bees.

The paths led to surprising vistas over pools and lagoons, where kingfishers dived and ducks dabbled, and small nooks and stretches of the River Wey, where water vole plopped and otters played.

I could cheerfully have stayed and set up home there and, in a manner of speaking, I did. I became an RSPB volunteer; that was three years ago.

During that time, a major restoration project has been carried out, transforming the site from a perfectly respectable bed and breakfast to a five-star hotel and restaurant for wildlife, some of which are entirely dependent upon reedbeds like these, now Britain's most threatened wildlife habitat.

As well as breeding kingfishers, Weymouth Wetlands are home to bearded tits and a wide range of wildfowl and warblers, including the Cetti's. Bitterns, the UK's rarest bird species, regularly overwinter here. In 2009, a pair of marsh harriers nested on the reserve and successfully reared three young – the first breeding pair in Dorset for nearly half a century and the most urban in the country. These rare and magnificent birds of prey are back again this year, with six fledglings – what a coup!

Other creatures are thriving too – the aforementioned otters and water voles, five species of bats as well as reptiles and amphibians, butterflies and moths and a whole host of other insects and plants.

The visitor centre in the Swannery car park at the entrance to the reserve offers everything from a warm welcome to hot drinks; from all manner of wildlife-related products to information and advice from enthusiastic and knowledgeable staff and volunteers.

Upgraded paths are wheelchair and pushchair accessible and there are new pond-dipping and duck-feeding platforms.

So whether you're a dedicated wildlife watcher, want somewhere to take the family that's considerably less crowded than the esplanade or simply want a quiet walk in the 'countryside', Weymouth Wetlands is a great place to be. And I mean just be. It restores my soul on a regular basis and it's well on the way to becoming one of the country's finest urban wetlands, stuffed with breathtaking wildlife, right at the heart of the town.

From here you can watch the fishing and pleasure boats on the harbour and explore the narrow streets that lead back into the town centre. **Custom House** is a fine brick building, as is the **George Inn** which towers over its neighbours. The newly refurbished **Royal Dorset Yacht Club** (*11 Custom House Quay DT4 8BG; 01305 786258*) occupies a chapel-like

A.J.

building, which was once an institute for seamen, known as the Sailor's Bethel.

The squat stone building at the end of Maiden Street is the original **Fish Market**, built in 1855, and appropriately still sells fish. It is worth taking a short walk along Maiden Street for a closer look at the stone building on the corner of St Edmund Street. I wouldn't ordinarily suggest people take a closer look at a **public convenience**; however this one has a cannon ball lodged in the wall above the first floor window, believed to have been fired during the Civil War.

Heading towards the ferry terminal you come to the **tourist information centre** and the Pavilion, Weymouth's popular theatre. From the terminal, ferries operate between Weymouth and the Channel Islands and France. The first ferry service between Weymouth and the Channel Islands was launched in 1794 with a packet steamer service. Although the purpose was originally trade, the link led to many Dorset families settling in the Channel Islands.

In summer you can cross to the other side of the harbour via a rowing boat ferry from the ferry terminal to Nothe Gardens. Alternatively, you can take the **Town Bridge**, an opening bridge which lifts every two hours during the day to allow tall ships to pass through. The bridge is reputed to be in the same place as the wooden one constructed in 1597 after Melcombe Regis and Weymouth were united.

Holy Trinity Church, erected in the 1830s, is one of the first buildings you are likely to see if you come across the bridge and it gives its name to Trinity Road, which runs alongside the harbour. Colourful buildings stand shoulder to shoulder facing the water, where the boats are busy bustling up and down. This side of the harbour has more residential buildings than the other, giving it a homely, village-like feel. Set back from the harbour is **Tudor House** (*3 Trinity St, DT4 8TW; 01305 779711; open Jun–Sep Tue–Fri 13.00–15.45, Oct–Dec & Feb–May first Sun of the month 14.00–16.00*), one of Weymouth's few remaining Tudor buildings. It is decorated and furnished in the style of a 17th-century middle-class home and guided tours provide an insight into domestic life at that time.

Nearby Hope Square is dominated by **Brewers Quay**, the converted buildings of the Devenish Brewery. For many years they were a popular feature with visitors and housed an assortment of shops and attractions, including the **Weymouth Museum** (*www.weymouthmuseum.org.uk*), but when I last visited Brewers Quay was closed and being converted to apartments, a hotel and shops. There are plans for the museum to return there once the redevelopment is complete. Continuing along the peninsula, Nothe Gardens lead to **Nothe Fort**, part of Weymouth's 19th-century defences and now a fascinating museum (see below).

Nothe Fort

Barrack Rd, DT4 8UF ① 01305 766626 ⓦ www.nothefort.co.uk. Open Apr–Sep daily, and at specified times during the rest of the year – see website.

At the end of a promontory on the south side of the entrance to Weymouth Harbour, Nothe Fort was built between 1860 and 1872 by the Royal Engineers with the help of inmates from Portland Prison. It was part of England's coastal defences and remained in active service until 1956. It is one of the best-preserved forts of its kind.

Today it is an absorbing museum, displayed over three levels, charting its own history and Weymouth's, with particularly detailed information on the town's role in World War II. The Fort Artillery in their splendid Victorian artillery uniforms put on displays of musketry and cannon firing on alternate Sundays throughout the year and during special events.

It is great value for money and particularly good on a rainy day as much of it is under cover. In better weather, however, you can take in the views of the harbour from the picnic areas on the ramparts. The fort is wheelchair accessible and has a good café.

Lorton Meadows Wildlife Centre – Dorset Wildlife Trust

Lorton Lane, Upwey DT3 5QH ① 01305 816546 ⓦ www.dorsetwildlifetrust.org.uk.

On the northern edge of Weymouth, this is a Dorset Wildlife Trust reserve of unimproved grassland with views over Portland and Weymouth Harbour. The grassland attracts a variety of bird and butterfly species, including marbled white, common and holly blues and small and large skipper. Wildlife webcams enable you to watch resident barn owls, tawny owls, great tits and kestrels; there's also a small shop and a picnic area. Although the reserve is open all year and the Wildlife Centre is open between April and October, the Wildlife Centre opening times vary so it is best to call and check.

Boating around Weymouth

From Weymouth you can take boat trips of varying durations, including along the Jurassic Coast (see *Getting there and around*, page 131).

With superb **sailing** waters, it is unsurprising that there are numerous sailing schools in the area. Information on sailing, as well as windsurfing and kitesurfing, can be found at www.visitweymouth.co.uk. If you want to try your hand at **performance yachting**, Weymouth Sailing (*07970 122718;*

www.weymouthsailing.co.uk) offers groups of up to eight people the opportunity to have a go on a state-of-the-art yacht. Sailing is either around Weymouth and Portland or along the Jurassic Coast to Swanage.

Weymouth has one of the largest charter **angling** fleets in Britain, with turbot, brill, bass, plaice, pollack, cod and ray fishing available. A list of charter boat operators is available at www.visitweymouth.co.uk.

Festivals

Weymouth and Portland's close relationship with the sea is celebrated in the annual **Spirit of the Sea Maritime Festival**, which takes place over a week in July. It incorporates cultural events, sporting activities and entertainment, including the Dorset Seafood Festival, a sailing regatta, live music and a carnival procession (*www. spiritofthesea.org.uk*). Another favourite on the Weymouth calendar is the colourful **Beach Kite Festival**, held in May (*www.visitweymouth.co.uk*).

Food and drink

Weymouth Harbour is overflowing with eateries of varying kinds, from excellent fish and chip shops to upmarket pubs.

Crab House Café Ferry Man's Way, Portland Rd, Wyke Regis DT4 9YU ① 01305 788867 Ⓦ www.crabhousecafe.co.uk. Located at the Weymouth end of Ferry Bridge (to Portland), this unassuming little shack has earned an enormous reputation for excellent seafood. It is also an oyster farm, so the oysters are as fresh as they get. The café has views of the Fleet and Chesil Beach. Open Wed–Sun for lunch and dinner; reservation recommended.

Floods Seafood Restaurant 19 Custom House Quay DT4 8BG ① 01305 772270 Ⓦ http://floodsrestaurant.co.uk. Seafood restaurant serving catch straight from Weymouth's fishing fleet. Simple fish dishes, nicely presented. The restaurant is committed to using only sustainable fish stocks. Open daily for dinner; reservation recommended.

Homemade by Lizzie & Bekki Windspatch Bakery, Friar Wadden Rd, Upwey DT3 4EW ① 01305 816378 Ⓦ www.homemadebylb.co.uk. Lizzie and Bekki create innovative home baked and handmade goods using local, seasonal produce. Open Tue–Sat 09.30–13.30.

Mallams 5 Trinity Rd, DT4 8TJ ① 01305 776757 Ⓦ www.mallamsrestaurant.co.uk. A popular restaurant specialising in locally sourced fish, meat and game. Open Mon–Sat for dinner.

Nothe Tavern Barrack Rd, DT4 8TZ ① 01305 839255 Ⓦ www.thenothetavern. co.uk. Situated in Nothe Gardens, not far from the fort; good-quality food at a reasonable price.

Perry's Restaurant 4 Trinity Rd, DT4 8TJ ① 01305 785799 Ⓦ www. perrysrestaurant.co.uk. An upmarket option in an attractive Georgian town house overlooking the harbour.

The Isle of Portland

Despite its name, the Isle of Portland is a peninsula connected to the mainland by Chesil Beach and the A354, which runs alongside it. A place of maritime history and quarrying, Portland is a term familiar to many, either via the BBC's shipping forecast or linked to its most famous product, Portland stone.

In recent times a popular car sticker has been seen around this part of Dorset, proclaiming 'Keep Portland Weird'. Evidently it has been that way for some time, which is perhaps why it feels like you are entering another country when you cross here. Reverend John Hutchins (1698–1773), the Dorset historian, wrote 'the people are a stout, hardy, industrious race and in general better informed than most labouring people; very healthy, but not long-lived, for, though at 60 many of the men appear strong and robust, they soon drop off and there are no instances of longevity, which may be accounted for from too great a use of spirits.' By all accounts they were not a friendly bunch: Portlanders used to throw stones at outsiders, whom they called 'kimberlins', to keep them from setting foot on their island. Hutchins commented, 'the natives are jealous of strangers coming to settle in the Island and … in consequence they marry and intermarry so much among themselves that most of the Islanders are related.' They reportedly followed a bizarre marriage custom, whereby women did not marry until pregnant, at which point 'she tells her mother, the mother tells her father; her father tells his father and he tells his son that it is then the proper time to be married'. The system only broke down when non-Portlanders got the local ladies pregnant and then reneged on the deal to get married.

Stone island

The Isle of Portland has been quarried since the 17th century. In his 1793 paper on Dorset, written for the Board of Agriculture and Internal Improvement, John Claridge wrote:

> As to quarries, the whole island of Portland seems to be one mass of the most beautiful stone, chiefly used in the metropolis and elsewhere for the most superb buildings, and universally admired for its close texture and durability, surpassing any other. The raising of it, is a laborious business, sometimes employing upwards of a hundred men, to break down a large jam of it, afterwards it is divided into blocks and then conveyed in cars by horses to the shore.

Indeed there is plenty of Portland stone to be admired in the 'metropolis' today, including St Paul's Cathedral, the Bank of England and the British Museum. The island still has working quarries; those which are disused have been colonised by plants and wildlife creating mini nature reserves.

143

Thankfully Portland has come a long way since Hutchins's days, the locals no longer throw stones at outsiders and its rugged curiosity value (rather than beauty) makes it worth a visit. Portland should perhaps be more attractive than it is – after all it is surrounded by the sea, overlooks Chesil Beach and there is no shortage of beautiful stone with which to build. While there are some attractive buildings of Portland stone, the island also has many rows of boxy-looking houses and most of the villages turn their back on the sea.

The whole of Portland is a solid block of limestone, windswept and industrial in feel, owing to its many quarries, extant and defunct. Its long and fascinating history is neatly summarised in the island's museum (see page 146); finds from the Culverwell Mesolithic site indicate that it is the oldest known settlement in Britain. The peninsula is easily explored on foot, along the nine-mile coastal path.

④ The north

The drive across the causeway, shielded on one side by the vast Chesil Beach, makes a memorably strange approach to Portland. Chesil Beach is so high at this point that it resembles an enormous desert dune and you might half expect to see a camel lolloping over the hill.

The modern complex on your left as you arrive on the Isle of Portland is the **Weymouth and Portland National Sailing Academy** (*Osprey Quay DT5 1SA; 01305 866000; www.wpnsa.org.uk*), the venue for the London 2012 Olympic and Paralympic sailing events. It occupies the site of the former Royal Navy air station, and breathed new life into the area when it was founded in 1999 as a not-for-profit company to promote sailing at all levels and make the sport more accessible to a wider group of people. It has certainly achieved that and much more. The academy has superb facilities and direct access to Weymouth Bay and Portland Harbour, reputed to be some of the best sailing waters in the world.

The road climbs to the top of a hill and from just in front of the Heights Hotel there are expansive views over Chesil Beach and Portland Harbour. It isn't exactly a beautiful view – the dense mass of housing and modern harbour buildings see to that – but gives you your bearings. On Tuesdays in summer you may encounter the Portland market, near the Heights Hotel. Also nearby, on the island's highest point, **Verne Citadel** was built between 1848 and 1869 as a fort and became a prison in 1950.

Portland Castle

Liberty Rd, Castletown DT5 1AZ ① 01305 820539 ⓦ www.english-heritage.org.uk, www.portlandcastle.co.uk. Open daily most of the year but parts are closed at times for private events; English Heritage.

Overlooking the harbour and just beyond the National Sailing Academy, juxtaposed with a series of ultra-modern buildings Portland Castle, is one of English Heritage's best-preserved Tudor monuments . It was built in the 1540s by Henry VIII to protect against French and Spanish invasion after his break from the Catholic Church.

A short, squat building, designed to make it less of a target, it has a rounded wall facing the sea to deflect incoming artillery. Its surroundings are unexceptional – modern buildings tower over it – but once you are inside the castle walls it is a different story. The castle is built of Portland stone, which seems to be tough stuff as it remains in superb shape. One doubts the modern buildings around it will fare as well over the next 550 years.

The other reason Portland Castle is well preserved is that it saw less battle action than Henry VIII had perhaps anticipated. During the Civil War the Parliamentarians and Royalists alternately occupied the Castle. In the 19th century it became a private house. During World War I it was used as a sea plane station, and during World War II it was used as a base in preparation for the D-Day landings.

You are free to wander through the castle at your own pace (the audio guides are helpful) and browse a series of exhibits on its history. The rooms overflow with atmosphere, especially the Great Hall, and the enormous fireplaces the size of a modern apartment's kitchen transport you back to the time of Henry VIII. This is a great castle for firing up the imagination of children, who will enjoy the arrow slits, canons and life-sized model of Henry Tudor.

⑤ From Fortuneswell to Weston

Above the rugged cliffs of West Weares is **Tout Quarry** (*Tradecroft Industrial Estate, DT5 2LN; 01305 826736; www.learningstone.org; open daily; free admission*), an abandoned stone quarry, which has been turned into a sculpture park with a difference. You can wander through it on foot, look at the sculptures carved into the rock and you may see local stonemasons at work. Stone-carving courses are available; details are on the website.

St George's Church, off Weston Road, is 18th century and replaced the Church of St Andrew above Church Ope Cove, although St George's is now itself redundant. Built from Portland stone, the nave exudes residential rather than ecclesiastical style, but the tower was apparently inspired by St Paul's Cathedral. The church is usually kept locked but the large churchyard contains some interesting graves, including that of the unfortunate Benjamin Scriven, chief officer of the SS *Porto Alegro*, who 'was accidentally shot by the steward' in 1875.

⑥ Church Ope and around

Church Ope Cove is a small pebbly bay on the east side of the island, which can only be reached on foot. You can park opposite Pennsylvania Castle (a large private house) and follow the path down the steep hill, through the ruins of the medieval **Church of St Andrew**. Dating from the 12th century, it was abandoned in 1756 and is Portland's earliest surviving building. The path takes you through woodland, then eerily through the middle of the plant-covered ruins and between the gravestones.

On the hillside above Church Ope Cove are the ruins of **Rufus Castle**, also known as Bow and Arrow Castle. What little remains of the structure is almost entirely covered by a shroud of vegetation. The castle is believed to have been built by Richard, Duke of York between 1432 and 1460 as a coastal defence against the French during the final stages of the Hundred Years' War.

Not far from Church Ope Cove on the way to Portland Bill is a viewpoint at **Cheyne Weares** with views as far as St Aldhelm's Head near Swanage, and a different perspective on the ruins of Rufus Castle.

HM Portland Prison (now a young offenders' institution) in the village of The Grove, was established in 1848 to provide labour to quarry the island's stone. Artefacts and photographs from the prison's early days make an interesting display at the Portland Museum.

Portland Museum

217 Wakeham, Portland DT5 1HS ℗ 01305 821804 Ⓦ www.portlandmuseum.co.uk.
Open Jul–Aug daily, Sep–Jun Tue–Sun.

The museum is built around two tiny 17th-century cottages and a small garden above Church Ope Cove. For a little island, Portland certainly has a big history and this museum covers it from Jurassic fossils, through prehistoric inhabitants to the more recent maritime links, prison and Portland stone. The displays on finds from archaeological digs on the island are fascinating and include information on the important Mesolithic site at Culverwell. There are some interesting items from the days when the Romans inhabited the island, including a beautiful duck brooch inlaid with blue and cream enamel, and the sarcophagi in the garden of the museum. The museum's director drew my attention to the rare Iron Age ingots, which date from around 500BC, while other highlights are the displays of historic photos and paraphernalia from the island's prison. A recent addition to the museum is the fossil of a freshwater turtle, unearthed on the island in 2010.

⑦ Portland Bill and surrounds

Portland Bill is a narrow promontory, which forms the most southerly part of the Isle of Portland. Before you reach Portland Bill's lighthouses, you will pass the **Culverwell Mesolithic site** (*open first Sun of month, May–Aug, or by appointment through 01305 861576*), which provides evidence that Portland has been inhabited for 8,000 –8,300 years, making it the oldest known site of permanent residence in Britain. A stone floor is the earliest known use of Portland stone for building purposes. You can learn more about the site and see some of the items found here at the Portland Museum (see page 146).

Of the three lighthouses on the promontory, one is still operational. The red-and-white striped **Portland Bill Lighthouse** (*DT5 2JT; 01305 861233; www.trinityhouse.co.uk; open Easter–Oct daily, Oct–Mar Sun only*) was built in 1906 and is 115 feet high. It guides vessels bound for Portland and Weymouth through the strong currents and acts as a marker for ships navigating the English Channel. Inside is a visitor centre with information on the Isle of Portland and the Jurassic Coast, as well as live footage of birds nesting on nearby cliffs. Tours of the lighthouse are also available and include walking the 153 steps up to the light itself.

One of the disused lighthouses, built in 1788, has been transformed into the **Portland Bird Observatory and Field Centre** (*The Old Lower Light, Portland Bill DT5 2JT; 01305 820553; www.portlandbirdobs.org.uk*), with basic hostel-style accommodation. The other, **Old Higher Lighthouse**, is a private residence but also offers guest accommodation (see page 133).

Water-based activities around Portland

Portland's reputation as a sailing venue is assured thanks to the Olympics, but it is also popular for other watersports, including windsurfing, canoeing and diving. Waterskiing is permitted in specially designated areas. Portland is also popular for sea fishing. The best source of information is Weymouth Angling Centre (*01305 777771*).

Watersports providers
Breakwater Dive Centre ℗ 01305 860269.
Portland Dive Centre ℗ 01305 820870.
Portland Harbour Authority ℗ 01305 824044.
Weymouth Sailing Centre ℗ 01305 776549.
Windtek ℗ 01305 787900. Windsurfing sales and school.

Don't mention the 'R' word!
Whatever you do while on Portland, don't mention the 'R' word. The use of the word is taboo because rabbits have long been associated with bad luck, instead locals refer to them as 'underground mutton', 'long-eared furry things' or 'bunnies'. The superstition is thought to derive from quarry workers, who would see rabbits rising from their burrows immediately before a rockfall and blamed them for increasing the likelihood of landslides.

Jurassic Safaris – 4x4 tours

☎ 01305 772324 ⓦ www.jurassicsafari.co.uk.

Husband and wife team Gary and Carol Fry offer 4x4 tours from Weymouth along the Dorset coast. Tours start from two hours and cover different areas, such as the Isle of Portland, the Purbeck Hills or Golden Cap. Gary and Carol have lived in Dorset all their lives and have devised routes that take you off the beaten track, along country lanes and ancient byways. This means you are likely to see some good wildlife, as well as great views. The trusty Land Rover makes easy work of the off-roading and gives the whole experience a real 'safari' feel.

Food and drink

There is a shortage of enticing eateries on Portland, although there are a couple with good views and decent food.

Blue Fish Café 16–17a Chiswell DT5 1AN ☎ 01305 822991
ⓦ www.thebluefishrestaurant.com. Friendly, unpretentious restaurant that serves excellent seafood. Easily the best on Portland and probably one of the best in Weymouth.

The Heights DT5 2EN ☎ 01305 821361 ⓦ www.heightshotel.com. It doesn't look like much from the outside, and the bistro has a bit of a chain restaurant feel, but it does have superb views over Chesil Beach and Weymouth Bay. The food is good and the service friendly.

Lobster Pot Restaurant Portland Bill DT5 2JT ☎ 01305 820242
ⓦ www.lobsterpotrestaurantportland.co.uk. Next to Portland Bill Lighthouse with sea views. Good, simple fare, including comforting Dorset cream teas. Open daily 09.30–17.30.

East of Weymouth

Leaving Weymouth and heading east you are welcomed back into wild, unspoilt Dorset. Inland lies gentle chalk downland, river valleys, farms and scattered villages, while the coast features austere cliff faces.

⑧ Osmington and Osmington Mills

Although just four miles from Weymouth, Osmington seems a world away from the bustling town. Its narrow street is lined with thatched cottages and the backdrop of verdant hills leaves you in no doubt that you have re-entered rural Dorset. To the north of the village of Osmington is the **White Horse**, a depiction of George III on horseback, carved into the chalk hillside. It was created in 1808 in honour of the king, to commemorate the summers he had spent in the Weymouth area. Sadly, due to ill health, the king never returned to see it completed. At 279 feet long and 327 feet high, the carving is clearly visible from the A353 to the east of Weymouth. A walk from Osmington or the nearby village of Sutton Poyntz allows a closer view.

On the coast is **Osmington Mills**, which has a rugged coastline and spectacular views towards Portland. The South West Coast Path runs along the top of the cliffs here, dipping down to the **Smugglers Inn**, a very popular pub with an inviting garden. It is easy to see why this building, parts of which date from the 13th century, has a long association with smugglers: its location is perfect for bringing contraband ashore – right on the coast at the bottom of a gulley. In the 18th and 19th centuries it was home to one of the area's most notorious smugglers, Emmanuel Charles; a file on the inn's history available at the bar makes interesting reading.

Jordan Hill Roman Temple

Ⓦ www.english-heritage.org.uk. Open daily; free admission.
On a hill between Weymouth and Osmington, off the A353, are the foundations of a 4th-century Romano-Celtic temple. All that remains of the building are the stone foundations in the form of a square, but there are fine views of the coast and the Osmington White Horse from the site. Built during the Roman occupation of the area, the temple would have served the local farming and fishing communities, and would have been visible from the sea.

Excavations of the site located a large cemetery to the north of the temple, where more than 80 skeletons were found, some originally in wooden coffins, others in stone cists. Various personal objects were buried with them, including pots, combs, jewellery, arrowheads and an iron sword; some are now on display in the County Museum in Dorchester (see page 65).

Food and drink

The Smugglers Inn Osmington Mills DT3 6HF Ⓣ 01305 833125 Ⓦ www. smugglersinnosmingtonmills.co.uk. A perfect stop-off for walkers on the South West Coast Path (with Burning Cliff above Ringstead Bay to the east and Black Head to the west) this large pub has lots of separate eating areas and a huge beer garden on either side of the stream, and its menu offers plenty of variety. There is a fee for the car park but you can redeem it at the bar for orders over £5. Dogs are welcome in the garden. Gets very busy in summer.

Screen Bites Film Festival

Gay Pirrie-Weir

Screen Bites, the UK's only food film festival, started life as an add-on to Dorset Food Week at the end of October, as affordable entertainment in village halls during the evenings of the countywide celebration. An entirely local initiative, Screen Bites brings films from all over the world to tiny communities in Dorset and highlights the vibrant culinary and cultural life of the county.

The festival was dreamt up in 2005 by two journalists, a film-maker and photographer and his opera-singer wife – appropriately over Sunday lunch. The American Robert Golden had recently completed a second set of short documentary films focusing on the specific food traditions of 13 areas in Europe. The quartet decided to run three or four evenings of food-themed feature films, each complemented by one of Robert's *Savouring Europe* series. They invited Dorset food producers to come along and offer samples of their wares. By the time Food Week 2005 arrived, the project had been named Screen Bites and ten venues chosen for films and tastings to be held over seven days. Sturminster Newton-based Olives Et Al had agreed to sponsor the festival, a sponsorship that has continued.

Screen Bites was so popular that over the following years it grew, linked up with Purbeck Film Festival and the National Trust's Barrington Court, commissioned foodie silk banners from a special-needs school at Cranborne, ran Edible Playground projects with local schools and appeared on television's *Ready Steady Cook*. Dorset Cereals took up the Edible Playground idea, creating gardens for both Chelsea and Hampton Court flower shows. The Chelsea courtyard garden won its section, and was then transported to a school in Bridport. The Hampton Court garden won the overall championship, and is now productively installed at a school in Wyke Regis near Weymouth.

The Screen Bites Festival runs each year in October and early November, visiting village halls all around Dorset and over the borders into Somerset and Wiltshire. More than 70 food producers have taken part in the festival and new ones join each year. They go along to the village halls and set up stalls, often providing hot meals for the audience, and always offering tastings of food and drink, which is also on sale, creating a mini farmers' market at each Screen Bites evening.

Various speakers have entertained audiences, with talks about bread-making, olive preparation, growing chillies, making cider and matching beers with biscuits. Dame Harriet Walter, who has a house in Dorset, has supported Screen Bites by coming along to talk about her roles in Louis Malle's *Milou en Mai* and *Morris: A Life with Bells On*.

Local restaurants also get involved, offering meals for winners of nightly draws. The website (*www.screenbites.co.uk*) provides a lasting directory of food production and Dorset eateries serving locally sourced produce, as well as the annual festival programme.

5. ISLE OF PURBECK

One glance at the map tells you that the Isle of Purbeck is not actually an island, but a peninsula of some 60 square miles bordered to the south and east by the English Channel and to the north by Poole Harbour and the River Frome. Nevertheless, I wouldn't be surprised to wake up one morning to the news that residents of the Isle of Purbeck are lobbying for independence from the rest of Britain. And I for one wouldn't blame them. The people who live here will proudly tell you how lucky they are to dwell in this unspoilt corner of England. When extolling the virtues of the peninsula, locals may tell you that it inspired some of Enid Blyton's stories and that it has its own microclimate. Both claims are evidently true: Blyton was a regular visitor to the area from 1931 and the Isle of Purbeck does indeed have one of the highest sunshine records in England.

The peninsula is dissected by the **Purbeck Hills**, a chalk ridge which runs westward from the sea near Old Harry Rocks across the Isle of Purbeck to Lulworth Cove, and whose shape hints at the origin of the name 'Purbeck' – supposedly from the Saxon 'pur', meaning bittern or snipe, and beck meaning 'beak'. **Purbeck marble** has been quarried from the Isle of Purbeck's coastal plateau, especially the area between Swanage and **St Aldhelm's Head**, since Roman times and can be seen in many of England's grandest buildings.

Wareham, a pleasing ancient market town within Saxon earthen defences, marks the obvious gateway to the Isle of Purbeck and Poole Harbour. In the centre of the peninsula the towering ruins of **Corfe Castle** constitute one of Dorset's most-visited landmarks. **Swanage** is a seaside resort with all the associated entertainment, while **Studland Nature Reserve** provides sandy, unspoilt beaches and heathland. Off the coast from Studland the chalk stacks known as **Old Harry Rocks** mark the eastern end of the **Jurassic Coast**. The military training area around East Lulworth encompasses the fascinating deserted village of **Tyneham**, which can be visited when the firing ranges are not in use. Nearby are some of the Dorset coast's most photogenic landmarks, **Lulworth Cove** and **Durdle Door**.

You'll chance across plenty of opportunities here for Slow Travel, including a ride through the peninsula on the **Swanage Steam Railway**, and ideal country for cycling and **walking**. The South West Coast Path traces the outline of the peninsula and footpaths and bridleways criss-cross the hills. For me, the highlight has to be **horseriding** along Studland Beach as the sun is setting, illuminating the pale faces of Old Harry Rocks.

ISLE OF PURBECK

BOURNEMOUTH

POOLE

Studland Bay

Old Harry Rocks

⑧ SWANAGE

⑨ Durlston Country Park

⑦ Studland

B3351

Swanage Railway

Harman's Cross

Langton Matravers

③ Arne RSPB Reserve

⑤ Corfe Castle

⑩ Worth Matravers

St Aldhelm's Head

WAREHAM

A351

A351

⑥

④ Blue Pool

Margaret Green Animal Sanctuary

Kimmeridge

① WAREHAM

⑪

② Wareham Forest

A351

River Piddle

A352

B3070

⑫ Tyneham

A35

⑬ Lulworth Castle

River Frome

B3071

⑭ Lulworth Cove

Durdle Door

4 miles

5km

N

0

0

Getting there and around

The Isle of Purbeck is easily accessible by car: the A351 runs along the spine of the peninsula between Wareham and Swanage and minor roads branch off it. Crowds are drawn to Swanage and Studland in summer and the roads can become congested. Leaving the car at Norden to catch the Swanage Railway heritage service to Swanage is therefore a popular option.

Purbeck District Council publishes *Car free days in South Purbeck by foot, bus, train and boat* and *Car free days out in North Purbeck*, which can be downloaded from www.dorsetforyou.com. It suggests a series of car-free routes taking in some of the highlights of the area.

Public transport

Three handy entry points to the Isle of Purbeck – **Wareham**, **Wool** and **Bournemouth** – have mainline **train stations** with connections to London. From Wareham you can access the main attractions by **bus**, including Corfe Castle, Swanage and Lulworth Cove. The Wilts & Dorset Purbeck Breezer (route 50) links Bournemouth, Sandbanks, Studland and Swanage, crossing from Sandbanks to Studland on the **chain ferry** (see below); during the spring and summer months most buses on this route are open-topped, making for a very pleasant journey to the peninsula. For West Lulworth the closest mainline station is Wool.

The CoastLinX53 **Jurassic Coast bus** (see page 131) stops at Wareham and link buses (routes 40 and X43) provide access to Corfe Castle and Swanage.

A memorably vintage way to travel is by the **Swanage Railway** (see page 177), a heritage train service between Norden, Corfe Castle, Harman's Cross, Herston and Swanage. In the summer, many families heading to the beach opt to leave their car at the Norden Park and Ride and catch the train to Swanage. Another great use of this train is to walk from Swanage to Corfe Castle along the Purbeck Ridge and then catch the steam train back to Swanage.

By boat

A charming **chain ferry** (*www.sandbanksferry.co.uk*), which takes cars, buses and foot passengers, connects Studland and Sandbanks and has been operating since 1926. An area highlight in itself, it neatly avoids heavy traffic around Poole and Bournemouth. Crossings are every 20 minutes in the day, with the first leaving from the Sandbanks side at 07.00 and the last from the Studland side at 23.10. Cars can spend over an hour queuing to get onto the ferry at busy times but foot and bus passengers and cyclists can usually board straight away. From Sandbanks you can hop on another ferry to Brownsea Island (see page 206).

You can hardly miss the crowds of **sailing** enthusiasts who teem in the waters around the Isle of Purbeck. An idyllic way to arrive in the peninsula is to sail from Poole Harbour along the River Frome to Wareham Quay; Wareham has a public slipway and there is right of navigation on both the Frome and Piddle rivers. The Environment Agency controls over a hundred moorings on the river Frome; call the agency to check availability (*01392 352223*). If you don't have your own boat but want to get out on the river, you can **hire small craft** at Wareham Quay or take a cruise from Wareham or Poole Quay.

Short cruises operate from Swanage to Brownsea Island and Poole, providing magnificent views of the Jurassic Coast, including Old Harry Rocks. Specific **Jurassic Coast cruises** allow you spend more time taking in the views of the cliffs and pinnacles, which are particularly impressive from sea level as their true size becomes apparent.

Boat hire

Wareham Boat Hire Abbots Quay, Wareham BH20 4LW ℗ 01929 550688
Ⓦ www.warehamboathire.co.uk. Hires canoes, kayaks, rowing boats and self-drive motorboats, as well as a wheelchair-friendly self-drive motorboat. Daily from Easter to Oct.

Cruise operators

Brownsea Island Ferries Poole Quay BH15 1HE ℗ 01929 462383. Operates cruises from Poole along the River Frome to Wareham Quay.

Dorset Cruises Swanage Pier ℗ 01202 724910 Ⓦ www.dorsetcruises.co.uk. Offers cruises from Swanage to Brownsea Island or Poole Quay. Also Jurassic Coast and Old Harry Rocks cruises with a commentary on the area's geology. An evening cruise operates from Poole Quay to Wareham Quay on board a 1938 wooden ship, with time to stop in Wareham for fish and chips.

Marsh's Boats The Stone Quay, Swanage BH19 2LN ℗ 01929 427309
Ⓦ www.marshsboats.co.uk. Offers cruises along the Jurassic Coast from Swanage and fishing trips.

Studland Sea School Middle Beach, Studland BH19 3AP Ⓜ 07977 179941
Ⓦ www.studlandseaschool.co.uk. Situated on the beach at Studland. Offers canoeing courses and hire of kayaks, wetsuits, snorkelling equipment, fishing tackle and body boards. They also run kayaking tours, including a half-day tour to Old Harry Rocks and a full-day tour to Brownsea Island.

Cycling

If you are arriving by train you can hop straight into the saddle at Wareham station, where bikes are available for hire. The Isle of Purbeck's roads get pretty busy in summer but there are some good **off-road** options, such as the Sika Cycle Trail (seven miles) at Wareham Forest (see page 164) and the Rempstone Ride (12 miles) between Norden and Studland or Shell Bay. Local tourist information centres stock leaflets showing the Isle of Purbeck's cycle routes.

Bikes can be taken on the **chain ferry** between Studland and Sandbanks for a small fee, and also on the Swanage Railway.

Cycle hire

Cyclexperience Wareham station ⓣ 01929 556601 Ⓦ www.purbeckcyclehire.
co.uk. Bikes are available from Wareham station and, if booked 24hrs in advance,
Norden Park and Ride. Rucksacks, helmets and maps are provided free of charge.
Open daily 10.00–17.00.

A mountain bike ride on the Isle of Purbeck

Paul Connor

Length: About 15 miles; moderate fitness required. **Maps**: OS Explorer 1:25,000
sheet OL15 Purbeck & South Dorset.

❶ Jump the traffic queue at Sandbanks by taking your bike on the chain
ferry (*www.sandbanksferry.co.uk*) to the Isle of Purbeck (current fees for bikes
are £1). Breathe in the sea air and take in the views during the quick crossing
before hopping on your bike along a straight stretch of road for two miles.
Half a mile after the road curves to the left take a sharp right turn. Don't go
through the gate but take the gravel track towards Greenlands Farm. Turn left

as you approach the farm (which is to your right) and the track soon bends to the right and fords a stream.

❷ Stay on the bridleway through Newton and Newton Copse, towards Game Copse (all marked on the OS map) and you will see views of Newton Bay in Poole Harbour. After Game Copse the track gradually curves to the left, joining another track (leading you away from Ower Farm) before meeting a crossroad. Turn left and follow this track south for one mile and then take a short dog leg turn to continue southeast to follow the track towards Kingswood Farm.

❸ Turn left onto the B3351 for a few hundred yards of tarmac riding. Pause at the lay-by on your left for great views across the harbour before turning sharp right off the road up the bridleway. (If you wish to cut the ride short and avoid the steepest hills you can continue along the B3351 from here to Studland.)

❹ The bridleway goes through a gate and up through woodland thick with the smell of wild garlic in spring. Gird your loins as the track steepens before emerging on the ridgeway to the song of skylarks.

❺ Turn left, heading east along the top of Nine Barrow Down and soak up the amazing views – small wonder this was chosen as a burial site in Neolithic times. The bridleway soon heads down Godlingston Hill. Be sure your brakes are in good order for this fast and at times bumpy descent. Turn left when you reach the road and after 500 yards on the tarmac turn right for the last steep climb, up a bridleway.

❻ The ride from Ballard Down to Old Harry Rocks is a joy – a gentle sweeping ride downhill with panoramic views all around and The Needles just off the Isle of Wight in the distance. Pause a while at Old Harry Rocks before following the track to Studland. Where the track joins a lane, turn right. You pass the Bankes Arms, a tempting spot for a break, before continuing along the lane, turning left onto Rectory Lane, left onto Beach Road and then right (signposted Poole, Bournemouth) to join the road back to the ferry. A pause at the Shell Bay Café just before the ferry is recommended – you've earned it.

Walking

The Isle of Purbeck offers the nearest really challenging coastal walking to London; a microcosm with extraordinary variety in a small area – within miles you can be walking through remote-feeling heathland around Agglestone Rock, past prehistoric burial mounds on Nine Barrows Down and up onto Ballard Down for views of Old Harry Rocks and Swanage. The landscape is startlingly diverse and seems to change in character at every turn.

Studland is the starting point of the **South West Coast Path**, which traces the outline of the peninsula and runs all the way to Minehead in Somerset (a total of 630 miles). The **Purbeck Ridge**, which forms the spine of the peninsula, provides far-reaching views of the surrounding countryside and the coastline. **Swanage to Corfe Castle** along the Purbeck Ridge is a classic walk, and if you run out of steam you can switch to another form of steam and catch the Swanage Railway heritage train on the way back. Even a short walk, such as the one to **Old Harry Rocks**, will reward you with an exhilarating panorama of Studland Bay, Poole Harbour and the Jurassic Coast towards Swanage (see page 175). The walk from Worth Matravers to the cliff-top **St Aldhelm's Chapel** has a stunning coastline as well as an air of mystery (see page 183).For a short coastal walk you can't beat the stretch between **Lulworth Cove** and **Durdle Door**, with sweeping views of the undulating coastline. The **Range Walks** through the military firing ranges around Lulworth and **Tyneham** offer some very well-preserved countryside. They are open when the ranges are not in use, which is most weekends of the year; opening times are available at www.dorsetforyou.com and are well signed at the entrance.

Horseriding

The Isle of Purbeck is blessed with a network of outstanding **bridleways**. Trails through **Wareham Forest** allow horse and rider to explore the heathland and mingle with wildlife (see page 164). **Studland Beach and Nature Reserve** are criss-crossed with bridleways and provide a rare opportunity to ride along a sandy beach. A permit from the National Trust is required to ride your own horse on the beach, or you can head out on a ride with the team from Studland Stables (see page 172).

For **hacking** in the Lulworth area, try Lulworth Equestrian Centre (*Kennel Farm, Coombe Keynes BH20 5QR; 01929 400396; www.lulworthequestriancentre. co.uk*), which caters for all abilities.

Accommodation

For many visitors to the Isle of Purbeck, **Wareham** will be their first stop but not necessarily their base, because it doesn't feel as if it's in the Isle of Purbeck proper. **Corfe Castle** is a peaceful and picturesque place to stay, right in the centre of the peninsula and allowing easy access to all the local attractions. **Swanage**, like many British seaside towns, is crammed with guesthouses and hotels of varying quality, but is a handy place to stay if you are travelling by public transport. **Studland** is a quieter option and within easy reach of the Sandbanks ferry, although accommodation is limited. The whole of the Dorset coast is busy in summer, but in **Lulworth Cove** the overcrowding is exacerbated by the single road in and out. As well as the enormous campsite at Durdle Door (see page 158), the Lulworth Estate has cottages for rent (*01929 400100; cottages@lulworth.com; www.lulworth.com*).

><><><

Bindon Bottom Main Rd, West Lulworth BH20 5RL ① 01929 400256 ⓔ stay@ bindonbotom.com ⓦ www.bindonbottom.com. An imposing Victorian stone house with 5 elegantly furnished en-suite rooms, each with their own character and some with lovely countryside views. Nice touches include the organic toiletries in the bathrooms and the owners' efforts to run an environmentally sustainable business; a ground floor room is suitable for those with limited mobility. An upmarket B&B option but realistically priced.

Challow Farmhouse B&B Sandy Hill Lane, Corfe Castle BH20 5JF ℗ 01929 480052 Ⓔ info@challowfarmhouse.co.uk Ⓦ www.challowfarmhouse.co.uk. This luxurious B&B opened in 2011. It is in a quiet location on the edge of the village and within walking distance of Corfe Castle. Accommodation is either in the main house or in one of 2 attic rooms in the converted barn. The rooms are finished to a very high standard, their elegance perhaps reflecting owner Kate's years living in London. Breakfast and afternoon tea can be taken in the very pretty garden. Good value for money.

Clare House 1 Park Rd, Swanage BH19 2AA ℗ 01929 422855 Ⓔ info@clare-house.com Ⓦ www.clare-house.com. Swanage's most upmarket guesthouse is at the pier end of town, one street back from the seafront. The 6 rooms (including one family room) are extremely comfortable and are given a homely feel by the ornaments that decorate them. The prices are reasonable and it has a refined atmosphere.

Clavell Tower Kimmeridge ℗ 01628 825925 Ⓔ bookings@landmarktrust.org.uk Ⓦ www.landmarktrust.org.uk. You get astonishing views from this pretty, circular tower, right on the South West Coast Path and overlooking the Kimmeridge Coast. Dating from 1830 and managed by the Landmark Trust, it is available to let as a romantic retreat for 2, for short breaks or a week. Parking is 180 yards away, at the foot of the cliff. Book well in advance; it isn't cheap.

Cove House Main Rd, West Lulworth BH20 5RL ℗ 01929 400137 Ⓔ info@cove house.net Ⓦ www.covehouse.net. A Victorian stone house on the edge of the village with 3 clean and comfortable en-suite B&B rooms, and soothing countryside views; the welcome is friendly and the breakfasts good. Reasonable value for money.

Durdle Door Holiday Park Lulworth Cove BH20 5PU ℗ 01929 400200 Ⓔ webmaster@lulworth.com Ⓦ www.lulworth.com. A huge and very popular campsite on the Lulworth Estate above Durdle Door, with direct access to the coast. Uninterrupted sea views and easy access to coastal walks. Cabins, touring sites and tent pitches are all available. Dogs are allowed. It may be a little dearer than some campsites but the location is hard to beat.

Gatton House West Lulworth BH20 5RL ℗ 01929 400252 Ⓔ avril@gattonhouse. co.uk Ⓦ www.lulworthcovebedandbreakfast.com. A very comfortable B&B with 8 spacious rooms with a country-style décor, a 10-minute walk to the South West Coast Path. One of the more upmarket B&Bs, and the prices reflect this.

Kimmeridge Farmhouse Kimmeridge BH20 5PE ℗ 01929 481503 Ⓔ kimmeridgefarmhouse@hotmail.com Ⓦ www.kimmeridgefarmhouse.co.uk. This B&B is tucked away in a very tranquil spot on a 700-acre working farm, in the heart of some great walking country. The farmhouse, which offers 3 pretty

en-suite rooms, dates from the 14th century and is full of character, while just
a few hundred yards away are the family's farm shop and restaurant (see page
185). Good quality accommodation at a reasonable price.

Lulworth Cove Inn Main Rd, West Lulworth BH20 5RQ ℗ 01929 400333
Ⓔ lulworthcoveinn@hall-woodhouse.co.uk Ⓦ www.lulworth-cove.co.uk. It can
get a little noisy in summer, but the location is key – just a few hundred yards
from the cove. The 13 en-suite rooms are clean and comfortable; some have
access to a balcony with sea views. There is no parking but you can park at the
main car park for free.

Manor House Hotel Ferry Rd, Studland Bay BH19 3AU ℗ 01929 450288
Ⓔ info@themanorhousehotel.com Ⓦ www.themanorhousehotel.com. A 21-room
hotel in an 18th-century house overlooking the bay and Old Harry Rocks, this has
a homely feel, like staying at a wealthy friend's seaside escape. One can take tea
or luncheon on the lawn, which runs down to the water and resembles the kind
of spot where Miss Marple might have pondered a particularly baffling mystery
over a cream tea. The rooms in the coach house were very nicely refurbished in
2011, while the Westminster room in the main house is the grandest, with wood
panelling dating from 1636 and a four-poster bed. Pets are welcome and the
room rates are reasonable.

Mortons House Hotel 45 East St, Corfe Castle BH20 5EE ℗ 01929 480988
Ⓔ stay@mortonshouse.co.uk Ⓦ www.mortonshouse.co.uk. An impressive 16th-
century manor house in the centre of the village, which has been converted into
a cosy 21-room hotel. The hotel's atmosphere is nicely old-fashioned, with plenty
of character features, including an elegant wood-panelled drawing room. The
highly regarded restaurant serves a good breakfast, and the hotel is accessible to
those with limited mobility.

The Priory Church Green, Wareham BH20 4ND ℗ 01929 551666
Ⓔ reservations@theprioryhotel.co.uk Ⓦ www.theprioryhotel.co.uk. Upmarket
accommodation, with manicured gardens running down to the River Frome. The
house dates from the 16th century, and is packed with history and character,
especially the cellar restaurant where dinner is served. Its 18 rooms have a
romantic feel, particularly those with ceiling beams and four-poster beds.

Purbeck House Hotel 91 High St, Swanage BH19 2LZ ℗ 01929 422872
Ⓔ reservations@purbeckhousehotel.co.uk Ⓦ www.purbeckhousehotel.co.uk.
A 38-bedroom 3-star hotel within the castle-like building George Burt built as
his home in 1875. Rooms are either in the original Victorian building or Louisa
Lodge, which was built in 2003. The prices are mid-range, consistent with the
hotel's 3-star rating.

Purbeck Vineyard Valley Rd, Harman's Cross BH20 5HU ℗ 01929 481525
Ⓔ info@vineyard.uk.com Ⓦ www.vineyard.uk.com. Quietly tucked away, the
vineyard has 9 very well-appointed en-suite rooms (including 3 family suites),
some with views of the surrounding countryside. The Swanage Railway steam
and diesel trains chug through the fields behind the house (the station is just
8 minutes' walk away). The restaurant here has a great reputation (see page 169),

and room rates are reasonable for a hotel of this standard but, as one would expect, more expensive than a B&B.

Smedmore House Kimmeridge BH20 5PG ① 01929 480719 ⓦ www.smedmore house.co.uk. An imposing country house sleeping up to 14 and offering a range of optional extras commensurate with its grandeur, such as butler, chauffeur and personal chef. It is expensive, so best reserved for a special occasion.

Swanage Haven B&B 3 Victoria Rd, Swanage BH19 1LY ① 01929 423088 ⓔ info@swanagehaven.com ⓦ www.swanagehaven.com. Just 300 yards from the beach and a pleasant 800-yard walk along the seafront to the town centre, this is not your average suburban B&B. Thoughtful touches like contemporary décor and complimentary Chococo chocolates (see page 179) make the 7 en-suite rooms feel a little bit special, plus you can luxuriate in a hot tub in the garden or indulge in spa treatments. Breakfast is homemade and locally sourced, right down to the eggs produced by the hens in the garden, and has earned the B&B a 'Direct from Dorset' accreditation: there is even a licensed bar. No children. Prices are reasonable.

Wareham Forest Tourist Park North Trigon, Wareham BH20 7NZ ① 01929 551393 ⓔ holiday@warehamforest.co.uk ⓦ www.warehamforest.co.uk. A popular campsite on 55 acres within Wareham Forest. The park is open all year, has a heated swimming pool and easy access to the forest's walking and cycling trails.

Tourist information centres

General information ⓦ www.visitswanageandpurbeck.co.uk.
Swanage White House, Shore Rd, BH19 1LB ① 01929 422885.
Wareham Holy Trinity Church, South St, BH20 4LU ① 01929 552740.

Wareham to Swanage and north of the A351

The A351 cuts through the centre of the Isle of Purbeck peninsula, linking Wareham to the coastal town of **Swanage** and passing through **Corfe Castle** *en route*. The area north of the A351 is unspoilt, much of it being heathland, and is bordered to the north by the sheltered waters of Poole Harbour. It is here that you will find Arne RSPB Reserve, a wildlife-rich pocket of heathland and old oak woodland (see page 164). The Purbeck Ridge stretches to the sea at Handfast Point, near Studland, where the chalk stacks known as **Old Harry Rocks** stand proudly in the water.

An alternative to arriving on the peninsula via the A351 is to take the **chain ferry** from Sandbanks to Studland (see page 153). As you cross from the hectic, glamorous side of the harbour, it seems as if you are venturing to another country as the wild heathland and Purbeck Ridge rise up before you.

① Wareham

Although north of the River Frome and so not strictly in the Isle of Purbeck, Wareham dons the role of the gateway to the area. It is an ancient market town on the watershed of the Frome and Piddle rivers, surrounded on three sides by Saxon earthen defences; its fourth side is protected by the River Frome. Known as the **Town Walls**, these were a Saxon solution to the problem of Viking raids and were likely built in the 9th century as part of Alfred the Great's series of 'burh' (fortified) towns across Wessex. It seems Alfred was on to something, as the walls have lasted extraordinarily well, despite being tinkered with over the years. They were variously beefed up by the Normans, halved in size by Cromwell's troops during the Civil War and heightened on the west side during World War II to protect against tank attacks.

The Town Walls aside, Wareham may not strike you as particularly ancient. That is because much of the town centre was rebuilt in the Georgian style following a ferocious fire in 1762. However, the strict grid pattern of the streets following the points of the compass was laid out in Roman times, and some notable early buildings have survived, including medieval almshouses and one of Dorset's finest Saxon churches.

St Martin's on the Walls

If closed, you can borrow the key during shop hours from A F Joy Outfitters at 35 North St.

As you enter Wareham by road from the north, you cross the River Piddle then pass through a gap in the Town Walls and it is at this point that the history of the place resonates. Up on the walls to the left is the church of St Martin's on the Walls. If the church is open, there will be a steward on hand to guide you around. Most visitors to the church come to see the life-sized effigy of Lawrence of Arabia, but the church is enchanting in its own right. Dating from 1030 and the best-preserved Saxon church in Dorset, it contains fragments of **murals** of various ages. Painted above the chancel is the coat of arms of Queen Anne and the Ten Commandments, dated 1713.

To the left of the altar a remarkable 12th-century mural depicts the **story of St Martin**, who was born to pagan parents in AD316 and joined the Roman army at around 15 years of age. He is shown giving half of his cloak to a naked beggar; as the story goes, he later saw Christ wearing the cloak in a vision and converted to Christianity. One of the reasons for its survival is that the mural was made by fixing crushed stone into plaster, rather than painted. The Portland Stone **effigy of Lawrence of Arabia** is the work of Eric Kennington and was installed in the church in 1939. The effigy was homeless for some time after its completion. Kennington had designed it as a national memorial for Westminster Abbey but as there was already a Kennington bust of Lawrence in St Paul's crypt it was not accepted. Lawrence's brother bought the effigy, which eventually ended up at St Martin's, an appropriate choice because Lawrence, who lived locally at Clouds Hill (see page 84), had contributed to the church's restoration. He had reportedly wanted to be buried here but is instead buried at nearby Moreton (see page 83).

Around the Walls and quay

St Martin's Church is a logical point to begin **The Walls Walk**. This well-signed 1½-mile walk leads you around the town atop the grassy Saxon defences. A leaflet showing the points of interest along the route is available from the well-stocked **Wareham Information and Heritage Centre** on South Street. Highlights include passing along Wareham Quay and the views of the River Piddle, the water meadows and, in the distance, Wareham Forest. The walk also takes you through some rather unexciting modern housing estates, providing a rather disappointing backdrop to the romantic Saxon walls. Nowadays, one imagines the only Scandinavian invaders here are of the flat-packed furniture variety. As you walk around the town, don't get too excited about the signs to Wareham Castle in the southwest quarter of the town. All that remains of the Norman castle is a mound, on which stands a Victorian house.

Wareham was an important port until the 14th century, when Poole, with its much larger harbour, replaced Wareham in that role. The **quay** remains a focal point of the town but it is understated and has in no way suffered from overdevelopment. It is here that you can **hire a boat** to potter along the River Frome (see page 154). On the other side of the river, near the bridge, is a board explaining the history of Wareham. This is also the starting point for a very pleasant walk along the river, which is usually lined with an impressive array of private craft.

Wareham Town Museum

East St, in the Town Hall building ℗ 01929 553448 Ⓦ www.wtm.org.uk. Open Apr–Oct Mon–Sat 10.00–16.00; admission by donation.

This small museum tells the story of the local area and its inhabitants through the ages. It has archaeology, geology and local history exhibits but the most detailed exhibit is that on Lawrence of Arabia. The **almshouses** opposite the museum date from 1741.

The venerable Rex

Rex Cinema 14 West St, BH20 4JX ℗ 01929 552778 Ⓦ www.therex.co.uk.

Wareham's cinema is something of an institution. It began life in 1889 as the Oddfellows Hall, providing a venue for travelling theatre shows, concerts and banquets, and has operated as a cinema since 1920. In 2009, following a period of uncertainty about its future, the Rex was bought by the Purbeck Film Charitable Trust.

Full of character, the Rex still has its original gas lights and although they are no longer used, as you walk up the stairs you can see the black marks where the lights used to burn. The Rex holds a lot of memories for a lot of local people. Julie Sharman, one of the organisers of The Purbeck Film Festival (see box below) told me, 'I remember the smell of gas from the lights as I walked into the cinema years ago, long before I worked for the festival.' Dougal Dixon, who has long been involved with the cinema (including as a projectionist) talks of an elderly lady working in the box office in the Rex's early days, who recalled that T E Lawrence (Lawrence of Arabia) used to come into Wareham from Bovington Camp on a Thursday afternoon and, if it was wet, he would go to the Rex to see a film. Another familiar face at the Rex is Jocelyn Barnard, a former actress, who has worked in the box office for the last 20 years. There can be no doubt that the Purbeck Film Charitable Trust is performing a valuable service by keeping this unusual little cinema open for the enjoyment of locals and visitors.

⋊⋉⋊⋉⋊

Food and drink

There is a small farmers' market in The Corn Exchange on North Street on the second and fourth Thursday of the month from 09.00 to 13.00. A larger market operates on Saturdays at the quay.

The Purbeck Film Festival

Julie Sharman, Administrator, The Purbeck Film Festival (www.purbeckfilm.com)

The Purbeck Film Festival is run by the Purbeck Film Charitable Trust Ltd and is the largest rural film festival in the UK.

In October each year the festival puts on around a hundred performances at venues throughout Purbeck and at the Lighthouse in Poole. The main cinema is the historic Rex in Wareham but films are also shown at local village halls and other more unusual venues, such as Bovington Tank Museum. Wherever we can find a 13-amp plug and an enthusiastic local organizer, we can show a film.

The festival was originally set up as an initiative to increase tourism outside the main season and to celebrate a hundred years of cinema. The first event was so successful that the festival continued, and in due course the Purbeck Film Festival committee was formed. A lottery grant gave the stability that was needed. We feel the Purbeck Film Festival serves an essential purpose – to bring the community together to celebrate film and to take film to rural venues.

Over the years, the Rex Cinema remained at the centre of the festival, so it was with great delight that after a lot of hard work by all the volunteers involved, the Purbeck Film Charitable Trust managed to raise the funds to purchase the Rex Cinema in April 2009, and turn it into a community, not-for-profit venue.

Holme for Gardens West Holme Farm BH20 6AQ ① 01929 554716 Ⓦ www. holmeforgardens.co.uk. On the B3070 Lulworth road is this garden centre with a farm shop stocking local produce and a café serving cream teas and light lunches. Nearby is Holme Fruit Farm, which offers pick-your-own fruit and vegetables from Jun to Oct.

Old Granary The Quay BH20 4LP ① 01929 552010 Ⓦ www.theoldgranary wareham.co.uk. A Hall and Woodhouse pub-restaurant within an attractive former granary overlooking the River Frome. The deck is a great spot to sit and watch the river traffic. Local produce is used to create unfussy meals: the traditional roast lunch on Sunday is very popular. Open from 09.00 Mon–Sat and 10.00 Sun, until late.

The Priory Church Green, BH20 4ND ① 01929 551666 Ⓦ www.theprioryhotel. co.uk. An atmospheric cellar restaurant within this upmarket hotel, where locals go to celebrate a special occasion.

Salt Pig 6 North St, ① 01929 550673 Ⓦ www.thesaltpig.co.uk. An urban farm shop selling a tempting selection of Dorset produce, including fresh local fish. The popular café serves good, simple food, such as pies and quiches. The owner, James, has a farming background (he previously worked as a shepherd) and a passion for local produce. He accurately describes the food as not frilly, not chefy. It can get busy at lunch times, so a good option is to get a take-away meal and eat it down at the quay. Open daily 08.30–19.00.

② Wareham Forest

A remote-feeling and surprisingly large heathy and pinewood expanse north of Wareham, Wareham Forest is dominated by commercial forestry but varied enough for some pleasant walks and bike rides; horse riders need a permit from the Forestry Commission (*02380 286838*). The **Sika Trail** runs for seven miles (mostly level) around the forest, and takes its name from the Sika deer, which you may well spot along the way. Roe deer are also present in the forest, as are Dartford warblers, nightjars and all six native species of reptile. The corrugated iron sheets which you may see lying around are refuges installed for the reptiles. You can camp within the forest (see page 160).

③ Arne RSPB Reserve

RSPB Arne, Wareham BH20 5BJ ① 01929 553360 Ⓔ arne@rspb.org.uk Ⓦ www.rspb. org.uk/arne.

Strikingly remote and peaceful, despite its proximity to Poole, Arne is a peninsula jutting out into Poole Harbour east of Wareham. The RSPB reserve, comprising heathland and old oak woodland, provides a habitat for wildlife, including Sika deer, and rare birds, such as the Dartford warbler and the nightjar. A very pleasant few hours can be spent wildlife spotting along the trails (guided or unguided) and then relaxing on the beach, which is usually delightfully uncrowded. The visitor centre shows footage from cameras, which have been installed in the nesting boxes around the reserve. Dogs are allowed but must be kept on a lead.

Arne's glories

Paul Morton, warden, Arne RSPB Reserve

I am lucky enough to be a warden on the Arne RSPB Reserve. Being a local lad, I have been visiting the site since I was five years old. Yes, I am a keen birdwatcher and am fascinated with bird migration and behaviour, but the true spirit of Arne isn't just the birds, it's the sheer range of biodiversity.

Come to Arne at any time of the year, and you will be treated to some real wildlife spectacles. Visit in spring and all six native British reptiles can be seen emerging from their winter lairs, while our iconic Dartford warblers will be singing their scratchy song from the top of a gorse bush. When summer arrives the reserve explodes with life as hundreds of dragonflies emerge from our heathland ponds, many of them World War II bomb craters. The rare silver-studded blue butterflies carpet the illuminated purple bell heather, hobby can be seen dashing about in their aerial display and magical sunsets are elevated by the sound of the churring nightjars. Autumn is my favourite time of year, only because it hosts my favourite bird – the osprey. Poole Harbour is a magnet for these majestic 'fish eagles', which can be seen carrying large mullet to favourite eating posts. Migration is also in full swing and birds you wouldn't normally see, such as redstarts, pied flycatchers and wrynecks, can be found. Autumn is also the time when all manner of fungi appear on the reserve. If you think winter is a quiet time of year, then think again. Poole Harbour and Arne host some of the largest winter wader flocks in the UK. We are lucky enough to have the UK's largest winter avocet flock, thousands of brent geese and a multitude of wildfowl.

I hope you will agree there are plenty of reasons to visit this tranquil oasis nestled at the bottom of the Purbeck Hills.

④ The Blue Pool

BH20 5AR ① 01929 551408 ⓦ www.bluepooltearooms.co.uk. Open Mar–Nov.

Between Wareham and Corfe Castle, the Blue Pool and Tea House opened as a tourist attraction in the 1930s. What everyone got excited about was the extraordinary turquoise-blue hue of the pool, a former clay pit: it is the fine clay particles in suspension in the water that give it its characteristic colour. Walking through the 25 acres of heath and woodland which surround it, it is hard to imagine this was once an industrial site, as the plants have done such a good job of colonising the area. The original 1935 tearoom remains, and has been joined by a gift shop, a plant centre and a museum showing the history of clay mining in the area. Dogs are welcome but the water is not safe for swimming, either for dogs or for humans.

⑤ Corfe Castle

The hill-top ruins of Corfe Castle are magnificent from every angle (see page 166). Nestled at their base is the village of the same name, built in local grey limestone, some of which was salvaged from the ruins of the castle. The village thrived between the 12th and 14th centuries thanks to the Purbeck marble quarries. Stone was brought to the village to be worked and they made good use of it – many of the stone houses also have stone roofs.

Aside from the road running through it, the village has a tremendous sense of history commensurate with its position at the foot of the castle. Some curious traditions survive here. On Shrove Tuesday the **annual meeting of the Ancient Order of The Purbeck Marblers and Stonecutters** is held at Corfe Town Hall. Following the meeting, members kick a football three miles from the Town Hall to Ower Quay on Poole Harbour to preserve the right of way along which the quarried stone was transported. The tradition dates from 1695, when the company agreed to pay landowner, John Collins, a pound of pepper and a football in exchange for the right of way. Today the football is kicked into the sea and has pepper tipped over it, symbolising the peppercorn rent.

The **Town Hall** is on West Street and is reputed to be the smallest in England. It houses a tiny, one-room **museum** (*admission by donation*). One of the strangest objects on display is the Poole punt and wildfowling gun, a contraption which allowed the hunter to lie flat on a narrow boat fitted with an enormous gun capable of killing 20 to 30 ducks with one shot.

In the centre of the village is the **Church of St Edward the Martyr**, dedicated to a Saxon King who is said to have been murdered at Corfe Castle in 978 (see box opposite). On the east gable of the church is a statue of the martyr. During the Civil War, Cromwell's men occupied, vandalised and stabled their horses in the church. They used the 14th-century Purbeck marble font with its carved octagonal bowl and stem as a horse trough. Thankfully it has now reverted to its original purpose.

Corfe Castle: the castle itself

① 01929 481294 ⓦ www.nationaltrust.org. Open daily; National Trust.

Corfe Castle is everything you want a ruined castle to be: built of moody grey stone, towering high on a conical mound and reached across a stone bridge. So it is unsurprising that its image adorns countless calendars, postcards and book covers. It was also reputed to be the inspiration for Kirrin Castle, which featured in Enid Blyton's *The Famous Five* series of children's books, although this claim has been challenged by numerous other castles. The building oozes history and drama and a wander around the ruins cannot help but stimulate the imagination. Just thinking of the characters who have lived and died here, and the momentous events that have taken place here, can induce the odd shiver.

The castle's location is no accident – it guards the only break in the Purbeck Ridge. The Domesday Book records a castle at this site and attributes its construction to William the Conqueror. Later kings, including Henry I, John and Henry III put their own stamp on the place, modifying and fortifying as they went. By the 13th century, the castle was being used as a treasure storehouse and prison. High-ranking, wealthy prisoners were held in the keep (the highest tower of the ruin), but the less privileged died a slow and miserable death in the dungeon under the Butavant Tower. In 1635, ownership of the castle passed to the Bankes family.

During the Civil War the castle was courageously held for the king by Lady Mary Bankes, who became known as 'Brave Dame Mary'. She, along with her daughters, servants and a garrison of five men, successfully defended it for three years. Corfe Castle eventually fell victim to betrayal in 1646 when one of her ladyship's own men smuggled in Parliamentarian troops.

The murder of Edward the Martyr

Saxon King Edward, great-grandson of Alfred the Great, was murdered at Corfe Castle in AD978. Legend has it that his stepmother was responsible for his killing. Edward's father, King Edgar, died suddenly in AD975 leaving two sons, Edward by his first marriage and Ethelred by his third. England's ruling nobles chose 13-year-old Edward as king, much to the disgruntlement of his stepmother who would have much rather seen her own son, Ethelred, on the throne. She formed an alliance with anti-monastic noblemen who opposed Edward's close relationship with the church. Since Ethelred was too young to replace Edward as ruler, she would rule as regent until he was ready to take over, so she devised a plan to get Edward out of the way for good.

Edward, who was hunting in the area, accepted an invitation from his stepmother to visit her at Corfe Castle, unaware of her plans for his demise. According to the 12th-century chronicler, William of Malmesbury he was still on horseback when she:

allured him to her with female blandishment and made him lean forward, and after saluting him, while he was eagerly drinking from the cup which had been presented, the dagger of an attendant pierced him through ...

Edward fled on his horse but fell. His foot caught in the stirrup and he was dragged through the woods until he died.

He was initially buried at Wareham Priory but following a series of miracles and a growing number of pilgrims his body was moved to Shaftesbury Abbey. The first miracle is said to have occurred the night Edward died, when the blind woman in whose house the body was laid regained her sight. Circa 1008 Edward was canonised and became St Edward the Martyr.

Later that year the castle was blown up by order of the House of Commons so that it could never again stand as a Royalist stronghold. A combination of undermining and explosives left the previously impregnable fortress in the ruined state in which it remains today. It is astounding that the gatehouse and outer towers have not tumbled down the hills during the intervening years, as their remains seem to be leaning out at impossible angles over the mound's steep slopes. While it may have been reduced to a skeletal impression of its former self, the castle, clinging tenaciously to the hilltop, maintains an air of majesty and enduring strength.

I could go on and on about Corfe Castle because I find it tremendously evocative. My mother tells me that my great-aunt, Elsie, was less impressed. Elsie was visiting from Australia, which, through no fault of its own, is devoid of splendid castles like Corfe. My parents decided to show Elsie the highlights of our beloved Dorset and took her to Corfe Castle, which at the time had some scaffolding on one side. My father explained that the structure had been reduced to a ruin some 400 years earlier, to which Elsie responded in disgust, 'I can't believe they took this long to get around to fixing it up!'

The Model Village

The Square, BH20 5EZ ① 01929 481234 ⓦ www.corfecastlemodelvillage.co.uk. Open Apr–Oct Sat–Thu, Nov–Mar Fri–Sun, and daily in school holidays.

If you find it hard to imagine what Corfe Castle would have looked like before Cromwell's troops got their hands on it, or if like Great Aunt Elsie you prefer your castles in one piece, then you may want to head to the Model Village. The model recreates the castle and the village as they would have been before the events of 1646. Being in the shadow of the real castle, it allows for an intriguing visual comparison of the two. The 1:20 scale model was built by Eddie Holland in 1966 in Purbeck stone and its detail is extraordinary, especially the 17th-century residents and the music playing in the miniature church. A delightful (normal-sized) garden on the site is complete with bird-watching hide, several original village stocks and a courtyard café.

The Olive Tree Cookery School

The Old Barn, Cat's Eye Cottage, Norden BH20 5DT ① 01929 477260 ⓦ www.olivetreecookeryschool.com.

Just north of Corfe Castle, on the A351, you will find the Old Barn, where Giuseppe and Sara offer a range of cookery courses, lasting from a few hours to three days. Class sizes are reassuringly small, around six, and their cosy converted barn is a great venue. Giuseppe's Sicilian background means that many of the courses have an Italian theme, but there are also plenty of courses on seafood, game, preserving and baking. I rather fancy the picnic course, where you spend the morning making a delicious picnic and then take it to your favourite spot for lunch. The course schedule varies, so check the website for details.

Food and drink

Castle Inn 63 East St, BH20 5EE ① 01929 480208. This pub on the road towards Swanage is highly recommended by locals. It has plenty of character and there is a pleasant outdoor area. Friday is fish day and the traditional Sunday lunches are very popular. Open for lunch and dinner daily.

Clealls of Corfe 25 East St ① 01929 480170 ⓦ www.clealls.co.uk. If the name of this village shop rings a bell, that may be because it was featured on the BBC's shop makeover programme, *Mary Queen of Shops*. It seems Mary Portas's advice has paid off – the shop is thriving. As per Mary's instructions, a good range of Dorset produce is on sale, including a variety of local beer and wine. Open Mon–Sat 08.00–18.00, Sun 09.00–16.00.

Greyhound The Square, BH20 5EZ ① 01929 480205 ⓦ www.greyhoundcorfe. co.uk. This pub sits beneath the castle, and its beer garden looks up to the ruins. Local produce is used and there are good vegetarian and gluten-free options.

Purbeck Vineyard Valley Rd, Harman's Cross BH20 5HU ① 01929 481525 ⓦ www.vineyard.uk.com. The vineyard, established in 2000, cultivates Pinot Noir and Chardonnay grapes as well as lesser-known English varieties such as Regent, Rondo and Phoenix. Wine produced on site is on sale daily and vineyard tours are available. Its accomplished restaurant overlooks the vineyard and surrounding countryside; the menu is sophisticated and you can choose a Purbeck Vineyard wine to accompany your meal.

⑥ Margaret Green Animal Sanctuary

Church Knowle BH20 5NQ ① 01929 480474 ⓦ www.margaretgreenanimalrescue.org. uk. Open daily 10.00–16.00; admission by donation.

Margaret Green Animal Rescue is a charity with three sanctuaries in Devon and Dorset. They do exemplary work caring for domestic and farm animals in need – cats, rabbits, goats, chickens and ponies among them – finding new homes for them where possible. They rescue and re-home over 1,000 animals each year. The sanctuary at Church Knowle is open to the public and visitors can walk around between the animal enclosures. When I visited, children seemed to be enjoying this almost as much as a zoo, and parents have the satisfaction of knowing their donation goes to a very worthy cause.

Food and drink

New Inn Church Knowle BH20 5NQ ① 01929 480357 ⓦ www.newinn-churchknowle.co.uk. Maurice Estop and his family have run the New Inn since 1985. Licensee records for the pub date back to 1881 and, amazingly, Estop is only the fourth name on the licence in over 160 years. Maurice prides himself on serving reasonably priced traditional pub food and seafood, such as the delicious cottage pie made to his grandmother's recipe. Maurice's Blue Vinny (Dorset blue cheese) and crab soups are so popular that they are now available in take-away containers. A small number of camping spots are available in the field behind the

New Inn and campers can enjoy breakfast at the pub. You can choose a bottle of wine to go with your meal at the well-stocked walk-in wine store. Open for lunch and dinner daily.

⑦ Studland

Much of the area around Studland is owned by the National Trust, bequeathed by Ralph Bankes in 1981 and one of the largest gifts the trust has ever received. Each year Studland attracts great numbers of visitors who come to enjoy its unspoilt beach.

My Australian friends are always teasing me that British beaches are ugly, covered in lumpy puddles and utterly devoid of sand. Studland is one beach to prove them wrong. A four-mile, sheltered stretch of sand with views of Old Harry Rocks and the Isle of Wight, Studland Beach really is beautiful. The water here is shallow a long way out, so is ideal for families, and there are plenty of watersports available. The beach is divided into four areas: South Beach, Middle Beach, Knoll Beach and Shell Bay. At Shell Bay a chain ferry covers the short distance to Sandbanks (see page 153).

Studland Beach and Nature Reserve is run by the National Trust, and beach hut hire can be arranged through the National Trust office (*01929 450259*). A large area of protected heathland, woodland and sand dunes behind the beach adds greatly to its appeal and provides for walking, cycling and horseriding. In summer, when the heather is flowering, **Godlingston Heath** is glorious. The mass of yellow gorse flowers in spring is equally spectacular. From a mound in the midst of the heathland **Agglestone Rock** proudly surveys its surroundings. Also known as 'Devil's Nightcap', this 400-ton sandstone rock gets geologists excited. Local legend has it that the Devil was sitting on The Needles off the coast of the Isle of Wight and, in a characteristically demonic temper tantrum, threw his cap at the mainland. Its intended target was Corfe Castle but it fell short and landed in its current position. The geologists' explanation for its presence is less colourful – it is a natural rock outcrop made of Agglestone Grit, which was left behind when softer layers of rock around it eroded. The reserve around it is a haven for rare wildlife, including Dartford warblers, nightjars and all six British reptile species (adders, grass snakes, smooth snakes, slow worms, common lizards and sand lizards).

Little Sea Lagoon behind Knoll Beach was closed to the sea by the dunes around 1880 and now contains fresh water, being stream fed. Over 3,000 waterfowl spend the winter in this 79-acre body of water, including tufted ducks, pintails and pochards. Little egrets and teal are present all year round. Three bird hides are strategically positioned around the lagoon. It is hard to believe that just a short distance away is Wytch Farm, western Europe's largest onshore oil field; thankfully, the refinery is well hidden in a pine forest on Wytch Heath.

The beaches at Studland have been popular with **naturists** since the 1920s. According to the British Naturism website (*www.bn.org.uk*), Studland is the most popular naturist beach in the UK. Those pioneering 1920s naturists were taking a risk greater than sand in places where sand shouldn't be because in those days exposure was illegal. Naturists can now relax on the right side of the law in a designated zone on **Knoll Beach**. Signs clearly mark the naturist area, including the instruction 'naturists please dress before passing this point'. I've always found this request strangely immaterial because it is not as if there is a giant curtain across the beach shielding the naturists from the view of the 'textiles' (the term naturists use to refer to the clothed masses).

Most people bypass Studland village in favour of the beach. The houses are spread over a wide area, although the centre of the village is tiny and consists mostly of Edwardian buildings. Studland village was apparently the inspiration for Toy Town in Enid Blyton's *Noddy*. The **Church of St Nicholas** dates from the 11th century; it blends Saxon and Norman architecture and is featured in Simon Jenkins's excellent book *England's Thousand Best English Churches*. The original building was almost entirely destroyed by the Vikings but was later rebuilt by the Normans. The short, squat tower is the most striking architectural feature; it is thought the foundations could not support a full-sized one.

During World War II Studland was used as a training ground for the D-Day Landings. A relic from this time is **Fort Henry**, a bunker on top of Redend Point, near the Manor House Hotel. It was from here in April 1944 that King George VI, Winston Churchill, General Montgomery and General Eisenhower watched troops training for the landings. Sadly, during the exercise the sea became rough and six tanks sank, killing six crew members.

To the west of Studland is the **Isle of Purbeck Golf Club** (*BH19 3AB; 01929 450354; www.purbeckgolf.co.uk*), which was once owned by Enid Blyton and her husband. There is a nine-hole course for golfers of all abilities and an 18-hole course for more accomplished players. The courses wind through the heathland and have expansive views over both the nature reserve and the sea.

Studland is the starting point for walks to **Old Harry Rocks**, the stark white chalk stacks which stand in the water just off the cliffs at Handfast Point. Carved by millions of years of erosion by the sea, Old Harry Rocks mark the most easterly point of the Jurassic Coast, which is also the youngest. They are said to take their name from a 15th-century pirate, Harry Paye, who regularly attacked ships leaving Poole Harbour. Standing at Handfast Point on a clear day you can see a similar chalk formation off the coast of the Isle of Wight, called **The Needles**. They serve as a physical reminder that the Isle of Wight was once joined to the mainland at this point by a chalk seam, of which both Old Harry Rocks and The Needles were part. A further reminder is visible at **Redend Point**, at the northern end of Studland's South Beach. This small headland of brown, reddish and yellow sandstone bears a striking resemblance to the multi-coloured sand cliffs at Alum Bay on the Isle of Wight.

A walk from Studland Village to Old Harry Rocks

Although the beaches at Studland provide a view of **Old Harry Rocks**, the chalk stacks are much more impressive viewed up close. This can either be done by boat from the sea or by walking out along the chalk ridge towards the cliffs along a section of the South West Coast Path. The walk from the Bankes Arms Inn to Old Harry Rocks is about a mile and there is National Trust car park next to the pub, where you can leave your car.

I did the walk early in the morning, in time to see the first rays of sunshine hitting the cliff faces. This is a beautiful time of day, when the waters are at their calmest and the views towards the Isle of Wight are at their clearest. After a short descent and climb at the start, it is a mostly level walk along the chalk ridge. There are opportunities for bird and butterfly watching on the way, as well as views of Studland Bay and Poole.

Rather than return the same way, you can extend the walk by heading up the hill following the coastline to the summit of Ballard Down. As you approach Ballard Point, the South West Coast Path continues on towards Swanage. To walk back to Studland you need to head through the gate on the right. After the descent past the Glebeland Estate, you arrive at the edge of Studland. The **Manor Farm Tearooms** (*01929 450311*), within converted farm buildings, is a good spot to reward yourself with a Dorset cream tea. A detailed description of the two-mile walk is available at www.nationaltrail.co.uk/southwestcoastpath. There are many other longer variants, such as walking through Studland Heath, past the prominent Agglestone Rock, then on a path southwest over the heath before climbing up onto the western end of Ballard Down and following the ridge to the cliff top, for a grand coast-path finale past Old Harry Rocks and back to Studland.

Horseriding at Studland

A National Trust permit is required to ride your own horse on the beach at Studland and the relevant forms can be downloaded from the National Trust website (*www.nationaltrust.org.uk*). It is advisable to contact the National Trust's Purbeck office (*01929 450259*) before applying to discuss availability. Only five permits are issued per day and you will need to allow a few days for processing.

If you don't have access to your own horse, never fear because **Studland Stables** has a yard full of horses and ponies to suit all abilities.

It was a warm afternoon in May when my Australian travelling companion, Neal Sullivan, and I set off to Studland Stables, eager to view the surrounding countryside on horseback. Neal and I have very different levels of riding experience. Although he fancies himself as a jackaroo and dreams of droving 2,000 head of cattle across the Australian Outback, Neal is a beginner. Studland

Stables went out of their way to accommodate our different levels of ability. They organised two rides for us, the first suitable for beginners, like Neal, and the second allowing me to fulfil my dream of a good canter along the beach.

We were welcomed by Helen and Stuart Spreadborough, the owners of Studland Stables, who are extremely friendly and professional. They took care to discuss our requirements and select suitable horses for us. Neal, like most men, always wants to have the biggest horse, so he was delighted with his mount – a handsome 18hh Shire cross named Tom.

Helen, Neal and I rode out of the yard and were soon on **Godlingston Heath**, which was flushed with a springtime show of yellow gorse flowers. Their strong coconut scent prompted us to nickname it the 'piña colada ride'. The smell was irresistible for Tom, who carefully peeled back his lips in expert fashion to pluck a few gorse flowers from the prickly bushes.

Having climbed to the top of a rise, we were rewarded with views over Studland Beach and Nature Reserve, Old Harry Rocks, Sandbanks and Poole Harbour. As we admired the scenery, we spotted something that looked quite out of place – a large boulder protruding from the heath – it was the unmistakeable **Agglestone Rock**.

We headed back to the stables without even setting hoof on a road, making this ride ideal for beginners. The ride boosted Neal's already healthy confidence and as we were unsaddling our steeds he began to talk of joining the mounted police. The following day, when the soreness kicked in, he fell remarkably silent on his mounted police plans.

My list of things to do in my lifetime includes 'ride along a deserted beach'. I never expected to fulfil that wish in Dorset, so I was delighted when Helen and I saddled up fresh horses and set off for the sand. I had half expected to have to dodge naturists as we cantered along the beach, but a cool evening must have caused them to retire early. We rode along the deserted sand as the setting sun cast a golden glow on Old Harry Rocks, pausing to allow the horses to splash in the water, much to their delight and mine. We reached **Shell Bay** and the chain ferry, then turned and cut back through the dunes towards the stables.

As we rode, Helen explained to me how she, Stuart and their two daughters had ended up at Studland Stables. Helen and Stuart had busy careers in London and often discussed their dream of one day moving to their favourite area, the Dorset coast. Horse-lover Helen had heard that there was a place in Studland where you could ride on the beach. For years she had planned to experience it for herself but never got around to it. In 2007, Helen learned that the stables were on the market and, out of curiosity, sent off for details. She showed Stuart the brochure and was surprised by his lukewarm reaction. It turned out Stuart had bought Helen a voucher for a beach ride at Studland Stables as a birthday present and when he saw the brochure he feared his surprise had been discovered. They headed down to Dorset for the birthday ride. Helen had never ridden anywhere so beautiful or with such a variety of scenery. Both fell in love with the area and made the bold decision to give up their busy city lives and take on the stables. Their courage in making the lifestyle change so many of us talk about is inspirational. Earlier that day, as we rode to the top of the hill above Agglestone Rock and the spectacular views opened up in front of us, Helen proclaimed with a broad smile 'this is my office!'. And what a beautiful office it is.

Riding with Studland Stables

Studland Stables Ferry Rd, BH19 3AQ ℗ 01929 450273 ℗ www.studlandstables.com. For riders of **all abilities**: 90-minute heathland rides. For **able riders**: two-hour beach, forest or Old Harry Ride. **Full-day** Corfe Castle and Rempstone Farm rides. The Rempstone Ride starts with a morning trek across Godlingston Heath, with its views of Poole Harbour. You then ride through the forest to Rempstone Farm, where Andrew and Claire Head of Cedar Organic (*01929 481393*) provide a delicious lunch of organic produce from their farm. Studland Stables can arrange for your ride to be captured by a local photographer.

Watersports around Studland

The waters off Studland offer some great opportunities for the watersports enthusiast, from boat cruises along the coast to windsurfing and waterskiing.

Watersports operators

Shell Bay Sailing Ferry Rd, BH19 3BA ℗ 01258 880512 ℗ 07853 986345 ℗ www.shellbaysailing.co.uk. A small family-run sailing school with courses for adults and children. Open Apr–Oct daily 10.00–17.00.
Studland Sea School Middle Beach, BH19 3AP ℗ 07977 179941 ℗ www.studlandseaschool.co.uk. Offers canoeing courses and hire of kayaks, wetsuits, snorkelling equipment, fishing tackle and body boards. They also run kayaking tours, including a half-day tour to Old Harry Rocks and a full-day tour to Brownsea Island.
Studland Watersports Knoll Beach, Ferry Rd, BH19 3AX ℗ 01202 759087. Offers a wide range of watersports, including waterskiing, sailing, windsurfing and kayaking.

Food and drink

Manor Farm Tearooms Church Rd ℗ 01929 450311. Delightful tearooms in converted farm buildings. Light lunches, cakes and cream teas are on offer at reasonable prices. Opening times vary, so call ahead to check.
Manor House Hotel Studland Bay BH19 3AU ℗ 01929 450288 ℗ www.themanorhousehotel.com. Dining is in a cosy, oak-panelled dining room, in the conservatory or on the lawn overlooking the bay. The menu is unpretentious and varied, with plenty of seafood and non-seafood options. Reservations recommended.

Shell Bay Seafood Restaurant Ferry Rd ① 01929 450363 ⓦ www.shellbay.net. This restaurant has a fantastic location, right on the water overlooking Brownsea Island and Poole Harbour, and just 250 yards from the Sandbanks ferry. Diners from the Sandbanks side of the harbour can catch the last ferry back at around 23.10. The menu features some creative seafood dishes and a few options for non-seafood eaters. The menu is very reasonably priced, given the location and the quality of the food. The bistro is open from 09.30, and the restaurant serves lunch and dinner daily Mar–Oct. Shell Bay is closed Nov–Mar.

⑧ Swanage

If you have spent some time enjoying the slow pace of rural Dorset you may need to be prepared for a change of gear as Swanage's atmosphere of seaside-holiday jollity can come as a bit of a shock. Swanage is a typical British seaside town, complete with amusement arcades and beach crowds. Take some time to get to know Swanage, however, and the deeper aspects of its personality emerge.

With this in mind, I took time to wander the town's out-of-the-way places, as well as the seafront, and found there is much to like about Swanage. For a start, there is a lovely sandy **beach**, which is where the British seaside town bit comes in. It has everything you would expect – deckchairs, beach huts, a Punch and Judy show and tacky souvenir shops. It is a wide sweeping bay, with chalk cliffs at the northern end leading out to Old Harry Rocks, and on a clear day you can see the Isle of Wight from the beach.

At the southern end of the beach is the typically ornate **Victorian pier**, which was constructed in 1896 for shipping stone from local quarries. Horses were used to pull carts of stone along the narrow-gauge tramway which ran along the seafront and onto the pier. In 1994, the Swanage Pier Trust took control of the structure, which was by then in a sorry state, organised extensive repairs and has since managed to keep it open. Today, you can walk out along the pier for a small charge, which goes towards its upkeep. Above the pier, **Prince Albert Gardens**, a hillside park, makes a very pleasant spot for a picnic overlooking the bay.

Beyond the pier, at Peverill Point, is the **Swanage Lifeboat Station** (*01929 423237; www.swanagelifeboat.org.uk*), opened in 1875 at the request of local residents. Consisting of a boathouse and slipway, it is open to visitors from April to October.

As you head northwards along the seafront from the pier, you pass the **Mowlem Theatre** (*01929 422239; www.mowlemtheatre.co.uk*), a venue for theatre and film since 1967. It is by no means a handsome building but has become one of the town's landmarks, and the upstairs bar has views of the bay.

Before it was a seaside resort, Swanage was a quarrying and fishing town. Stone and building contractor John Mowlem (1788–1868) and his nephew George Burt (1816–94) were highly influential in the town's development – so much so that George Burt is referred to as 'the king of Swanage', a nickname supposedly bestowed by Thomas Hardy. The town owes its most interesting architectural features to Mowlem and Burt, who scavenged them from London when they delivered their stone there. The elaborate façade of **Swanage Town Hall** once adorned the Mercers' Hall in London and looks rather out of place in Swanage High Street. It dates from 1670 and was brought to Swanage in 1883. The **Wellington Clock Tower** at **Peverill Point** came from the old London Bridge. The clock tower was erected at one end of London Bridge in 1854, but apparently caused traffic chaos so was removed and brought to Swanage in 1863. **Purbeck House** (now a hotel) in the High Street, which has obvious castle aspirations, was the house George Burt built for himself using marble chippings from the Albert Memorial. The house also includes a bollard from Millbank Prison, an archway from Hyde Park Corner and floor tiles from the Palace of Westminster.

Behind Swanage Town Hall is a small, stone **lock-up** inscribed 'Erected for the Prevention of Vice and Immorality by Friends of Religion and Good Order – 1803'. It used to stand in the St Mary's churchyard and was considered a necessary measure for dealing with the town's rowdy revellers. It looks to me as if it would have served as a powerful deterrent. **St Mary's Church** is near to the pretty, spring-fed millpond. Apart from the 14th century tower, the church is largely 19th and 20th century.

The High Street is lined with tempting shops and eateries, such as the **Mulberry Tree Gallery** (*57 High St*), selling local and locally themed art and ceramics. The **Tilly Mead** area on Commercial Road is a complex of small, independent shops, including local handmade chocolate company **Chococo** (see box, page 179). It is a pleasant area to wander and, if you need to buy a gift for the cat-sitter, dog-sitter or house-sitter, you are likely to find one here.

Swanage Museum and Heritage Centre

The Square, BH19 2LJ ① 01929 423850 ⓦ www.swanagemuseum.co.uk. Open daily.
Well worth a look, this has an informative film on the Isle of Purbeck shown throughout the day, along with museum displays showing the local shops as they may have looked in the early 1900s; on sale is a range of publications on the area. A good way to get to know Swanage is to take one of the **guided walks** offered by two local historians. There is no charge but voluntary contributions are gratefully received. The walks are available from Easter to the end of September, and it is advisable to book. Groups meet outside the Heritage Centre at 14.30 on Wednesdays and Thursdays.

Water-based activities around Swanage

For those who tire of lying on the beach and wandering the shops, there are plenty of water-based activities. If you fancy a spot of fishing, the **Swanage**

Swanage Carnival and Regatta

Swanage comes into its own at the end of July/early August each year, when it holds the annual Swanage Carnival and Regatta. The week's events include various sporting competitions (including a half marathon, swimming and sailing), a carnival procession, sand sculpture competition and spectacular fireworks on the main beach. Swanage is even busier than usual during carnival week, so be prepared.

Angling Centre (*01929 424989*) at the pier end of the High Street can arrange bait, tackle, and a skipper. The waters around Swanage, in particular beneath the pier and the local shipwrecks, are popular with divers.

Watersports providers

All Marine Watersports Unit 8, 2 Ulwell Rd, BH19 1LH Ⓜ 07551 263434 Ⓦ www.allmarinewatersports.com. Specialises in boating and watersports courses, including power-boating and jet-skiing. Also offers high-speed boat rides, jet-skiing, waterskiing and doughnut rides.

Ocean Bay Waterports North Beach, Ulwell Rd, BH19 1LH Ⓜ 07721 938949 Ⓦ www.oceanbaywatersports.co.uk. Offers jet-ski, pedalo and kayak hire, as well as deckchair and beach hut hire. You can launch your own vessel using their concrete slipway and you can even hire a bouncy castle for children's parties on the beach.

Dive operators

Divers Down The Pier BH19 2AR Ⓣ 01929 423565 (Apr–Oct) Ⓦ www.diversdownswange.co.uk. Established in 1958, this is reputed to be the oldest dive school in England.

Swanage Boat Charters Larks Rise, 279b High St, BH19 2NH Ⓣ 01929 427064 Ⓦ www.kyarra.com.

Swanage Diving 64 Ulwell Rd, BH19 3DG Ⓜ 07917 794075 Ⓦ www.swanagediving.co.uk.

The Swanage Railway

Station House, BH19 1HB Ⓣ 01929 425800 Ⓦ www.swanagerailway.co.uk.

You don't need to be a train buff to be charmed by the lovingly restored steam and diesel trains of the Swanage Railway. The railway operates over almost six miles between Swanage and Norden, which is just northwest of Corfe Castle and four miles from Wareham. Trains first ran to Swanage in 1885 and continued until 1972, when the line closed. The painstaking restoration, re-opening and maintenance of the railway is the work of the Swanage Railway Trust.

Every summer thousands of families use the railway to travel to and from the beach at Swanage. You can leave your car at the Norden Park and Ride (off the A351) and take the train to Swanage via Corfe Castle, Harman's Cross and Herston. The train travels at no more than 25mph and provides expansive views of Corfe Castle and the surrounding countryside (keep your eyes peeled – on some days deer, pheasants and other wildlife can be seen in the fields). The railway stations and the uniforms of the staff are those of a bygone age and add to the romanticism of the journey. Once you arrive in Swanage, the beach is just 100 yards from the station.

Martin Payne of the Swanage Railway Company, which is responsible for the day-to-day running of the railway, explained to me that around 450 volunteers work to keep the railway functioning, and it has to be said they do a fantastic job. The railway holds a series of special events throughout the year. One of Martin's favourites is the December Santa Special, when families clamber aboard and eagerly await Santa, who passes through the train handing out presents to the children.

><><><

Food and drink

Swanage has a good selection of eateries, from casual fish bars to smart restaurants. Swanage market, including a farmers' market, is held every Tuesday in the main beach car park. The Isle of Purbeck produces some wonderful food, such as St Aldhelm Blue cheese from The Windswept Cow Cheese Company at Worth Matravers, Robert Field honey and Isle of Purbeck beer. These and other local delicacies are available from **The Purbeck Deli** (*26 Institute Rd, BH19 1BX; 01929 422344; www.thepurbeckdeli.co.uk*) where you can pick up a selection and head to Prince Albert Gardens or Durlston Park for a picnic.

Cauldron Bistro 5 High St, BH19 2LN ① 01929 422671. What a find! Terry and Margaret Flenley have been here for 22 years and could have retired by now, but instead they chose to open their restaurant 'just for fun'. They only serve 5 tables per night and it is almost like eating in someone's home. The menu is created daily, with specials handwritten on individual cards, and all the food is homemade to order using local ingredients. I tried coquilles St Jacques, one of my favourite dishes, and it was splendid; I washed it down with delicious homemade lemonade. Other dishes on the menu sounded tasty too, such as the pan-roasted quail and the wild boar sausages. Opening hours vary and space is limited so it is best to book in advance.

Chococo Central Commercial Rd, BH19 1DF ① 01929 421777 ⓦ chococo.co.uk. The Chococo chocolate shop has a café attached, which serves homemade cakes and, of course, superb hot chocolate.

The Corner 1 Institute Rd ① 01929 424969 ⓦ www.thecornerrestaurant.co.uk. It may not have sea views, but this restaurant scores on the merits of its cuisine. The menu is contemporary and creative, using local ingredients where possible.

Chococo

Commercial Rd, BH19 1DF ℗ 01929 421777 ℗ www.chococo.co.uk.

Husband and wife team, Claire and Andy Burnet, have been making delicious, fresh chocolates in the Isle of Purbeck since 2002.

I met up with Claire at the Chococo café in Swanage to learn more about this creative company (where, appropriately, I had one of the finest hot chocolates I have ever tasted). Chococo's philosophy and techniques are groundbreaking. Claire explained that they are one of the first, if not the first UK chocolate maker, to produce a truly fresh product, using cream from a local farm blended with chocolate direct from the country where it was grown, and seasonal, natural flavours. What they do not use are artificial additives and preservatives.

I was staggered by the range of flavours, such as 'Bob's Bees' (made with honey from Swanage beekeeper, Robert Field), 'Mellow Mint' (made with fresh mint from a Swanage garden) and 'Piddle Beer' (made with beer from the Piddle Brewery). They even create edible chocolate boxes – a brilliant way to reduce packaging waste.

So how do a husband and wife come to set up a chocolate-making company in Swanage? Claire and Andy were both working in high-pressure jobs for large companies in London, when they decided they wanted a 'slower' lifestyle. Connections to Swanage drew them to this part of the world: Andy's family was from Swanage, Claire and Andy were regular visitors to the area and they were married in the town. Claire told me that she had always known that if she was going to survive as Andy's wife, she needed to like both Swanage and sailing; thankfully she liked both.

When discussing how they would make a living in Swanage, Claire suggested, almost flippantly, that they make chocolates. Her parents had lived in Brussels for a time and Claire and her family relished the fine chocolates available there and lamented that they couldn't find anything comparable in England. Andy laughed at Claire's suggestion, pointing out their total lack of expertise, but he agreed to go on a chocolate-making course with her and see what it was all about. Making chocolate is a highly scientific process and Andy, who has a science background, was in his element. He was won over by the course and their business began.

As I talked to Claire I was baffled at how she could stay so slim while working with temptation on a daily basis. She explained that good quality dark chocolate is low in sugar and low GI (glycemic index), and in fact many of the Chococo staff have lost weight since joining.

Claire and Andy are proud of their ethical approach. They care about the provenance of their ingredients and about the people who produce them, and make every effort to minimise their carbon footprint.

If you fancy having a go at making chocolate yourself, Chococo offers workshops at their Swanage premises. Their delicious goodies can be bought in their Swanage shop, in premium retailers and online.

Crows Nest Inn 11 Ulwell Rd, BH19 1LE ① 01929 422651 ⓦ www.crowsnestinn. co.uk. Locals rate this as the best of the pubs in Swanage, with dishes like locally sourced wild boar and apple faggots and slow-roasted rack of Dorset lamb. Carvery Sun lunch, no Sun dinner.

Fish Plaice 14 The Square, BH19 2LJ ① 01929 423668. One of the town's favourite spots for take-away fish. Good fish cakes.

Gee Whites 1 High St, BH19 2LN ① 01929 425720 ⓦ www.geewhites.co.uk. Popular open-air fish bar and ice cream parlour near Swanage pier.

Lobster Pot Café ⓜ 07958 554067 ⓦ www.lobsterpotswanage.co.uk. At the northern end of the beach, though not much more than a modest shack ensconced beneath the cliffs, it serves good light meals and delicious homemade cakes throughout the day. You can also hire beach huts and other beach equipment (deckchairs, umbrellas, toys, etc) here.

Ocean Bay 2 Ulwell Rd, BH19 1LH ① 01929 422222 ⓦ www.oceanbayrestaurant. com. At the Studland end of the seafront overlooking the water, this enjoys the best restaurant views in Swanage; you can even moor your boat here. The décor is contemporary, as is the food. Bar and restaurant open daily 09.00 until late.

⑨ Durlston Country Park

Lighthouse Rd, Swanage BH19 2JL ① 01929 424443 ⓦ www.durlston.co.uk.

Within a few hundred yards of the hilly, southern fringes of Swanage, Durlston Country Park has 280 acres of countryside overlooking Purbeck's Marine Research Area, with meadows and coastline ideal for walking, wildlife-watching and picnics. The logical starting point is the **visitor centre**, where you can watch Durlston's nationally important guillemot colony via a live video feed and listen to sounds from the seabed picked up by an underwater microphone. The website lists ranger-led guided walks and events run throughout the summer.

I was lucky enough to meet ranger Ben Wallbridge, a descendant of the Wallbridges who farmed at Kingcombe before it became a nature reserve (see page 128). Ben and I chatted about Durlston as he sat with a snoozy black labrador lying across his lap. Ben's enthusiasm for the place was obvious as he told me that Durlston was one of the newest of England's 224 National Nature Reserves: 'It is rare because of the diverse habitats and geology it contains: sea cliffs, coastal limestone downland, haymeadows, hedgerows and woodland'. The dog had clearly heard it all before as it began to snore but, undeterred, Ben went on to tell me that Durlston has been owned by Dorset County Council since the 1970s and at one point narrowly escaped being turned into a housing estate. Parking at Durlston is expensive but the money goes towards maintaining the park and, as Ben explained, that is quite a job for the team of rangers, estate workers and volunteers.

The walks along Durlston's cliffs take you past **Anvil Point Lighthouse** and disused **quarries**, which once supplied John Mowlem and George Burt's stone company. You also pass **Durlston Castle** (more of a seaside villa than a castle), another of George Burt's legacies. In 2011, the villa was being developed to provide additional facilities for visitors, including a gallery and a café. Walking along the cliffs between Swanage and the park you will pass the **Great Globe**, a handcrafted Portland limestone representation of the world decorated with astronomical facts and quotations. Burt had it created to attract people to the area; at ten feet in diameter it is one of the largest stone spheres in the world. As you walk, look out to sea for **bottle-nosed dolphins**; according to Ben Wallbridge, Durlston is one of the best places in Britain for spotting them.

Beyond Swanage to Lulworth Cove

Some of the most exciting walking in southern England can be found on this stretch of coast, with its demanding hilly cliff paths and intriguing military ranges inland.

The area between Swanage and St Aldhelm's Head is known for its Purbeck stone quarries and the coast here has an irrepressible bleakness.

Lulworth Cove and Durdle Door are, justifiably, both tourist magnets and very busy in the summer months. Large tranches of the countryside around East Lulworth are within the army ranges, including the atmospherically deserted village of Tyneham, empty since its compulsory evacuation in 1943. Although the warning signs look forbidding, military occupation has preserved the landscape in time, making for some hugely rewarding walks within the ranges (the Range Walks), obviously only open when the firing ranges are not in use (most weekends and at certain times during school holidays).

⑩ Langton Matravers, Worth Matravers and St Aldhelm's Head

The area around Langton Matravers and Worth Matravers has long been the heart of Purbeck's quarrying industry. These two appealing villages are a living illustration of the uses of Purbeck stone, being constructed largely of that material.

There are around a dozen different types of Purbeck stone but by far the best known is **Purbeck marble**. Just as the Isle of Purbeck isn't really an island, Purbeck marble isn't really a marble, but a hard limestone made up of river mud and packed with the shells of millions of freshwater snails which lived in the great river that once flowed through the south of the peninsula. It takes its name from the fact that it can be polished. Purbeck marble is usually blue-grey but can have a green or reddish tint. It has been quarried from this area since Roman times, when it was the material of choice for tombstones. Widely used in the Middle Ages, Purbeck marble can still be seen in churches, abbeys and cathedrals throughout England, as fonts, altar tables, flooring and columns. Some of its most notable appearances are in Durham Cathedral, Westminster Abbey, Lincoln Cathedral and Salisbury Cathedral.

In a former coach house behind the church in Langton Matravers, the **Purbeck Stone Museum** (*St George Close; 01929 423168; www.langtonia. org.uk*) tells the story of the local geology, stone and quarries. Following World War II, three local men (Jim Bradford, John Dean and Reg Saville) began separate collections of items relating to the history and geology of the area. Their combined collections now form the bulk of the exhibits in the museum, which also has a reconstruction of a section of an underground quarry. Reg Saville, now in his nineties, explained to me that the museum was created in response to local demand when, in 1960, the tradition of underground quarry-mines (begun in the late 17th century) was stopped by order of the Privy Council for reasons of safety. The local community was eager to ensure that the hardships of the past should not be forgotten.

If you are inspired to unleash your creativity on a slab of Purbeck stone, **Burngate Stone Carving Centre** (*Kingston Rd, Langton Matravers BH19 3BE; 01929 439405; www.burngatestonecentre.co.uk*), offers stone-carving courses from beginner to advanced. A have-a-go course takes just two hours. Details of the courses are on the website; book in advance.

Also in Langton Matravers is **Putlake Adventure Farm** (*01929 422917; www.putlakeadventurefarm.com*), where as well as farm animals and the usual opportunities to feed and groom the patient creatures, there is an indoor play area for Purbeck's inclement days. On the second Saturday of every month, **Purbeck Products** (*www.purbeckproducts.co.uk*), a co-operative of local food producers, holds a **market** at Putlake Farm. There you can buy vegetables, eggs, meat, fish, game, cheese, preserves and cakes produced in the Isle of Purbeck.

From Langton Matravers fields lined with grey stone walls lead you to **Worth Matravers**, the last settlement before the coast. The village is more beautiful than Langton Matravers, with stone cottages huddled around a duck pond that was formerly part of Worth Manor Farm. Not far from the duck pond is the well-known and highly idiosyncratic **Square and Compass pub** (see page 184). The Newman family has held the licence here since 1907 and current licensee, Charlie Newman III, represents the fourth generation. Charlie is passionate about palaeontology and attached to the pub is a small museum showing off fossils found in the area. Charlie told me that his mother's family has lived in the village since 1660. Sadly, long-term residents like Charlie's family have become a rare breed in this village, where over 60% of the houses are now holiday homes.

In the graveyard of the **Church of St Nicholas** is the tombstone of Benjamin Jesty, who in 1774 became the first person to inoculate against smallpox when he administered a low dose of the milder cowpox to his family. Jesty's ground-breaking move is yet another in Dorset's long list of bizarre claims to fame.

A walk to St Aldhelm's Head and Chapel

Worth Matravers is the starting point for walks to St Aldhelm's Head, for sweeping views of the coast and a visit to the cliff-top **St Aldhelm's Chapel**. Note there are some vertigo-inducing sections along the coast; this walk is around 3½ miles, though there are many ways of extending it.

From the car park at Renscombe Farm, west of Worth Matravers, it is around one mile to St Aldhelm's Head. Next to the map displayed in the car park is a pedestrian gate. Head through the gate and diagonally across the field in the direction of **Chapman's Pool**. When you reach the coast (after about a quarter of a mile), you will be looking down (from around 400 feet) over Chapman's Pool, a brilliantly clear bay with a jumble of fishing huts on one side. Low rumblings from the Lulworth army range can often be heard echoing around the hills.

Turn left and head along the **cliff-top path**, bordered by a dry-stone wall. The farmland here runs almost to the edge of the cliffs, it seems not an inch of land is wasted. You may well encounter some very contented cows along the way, as I did. You will come to a memorial to members of the Royal Marines killed between 1945 and 1990, and which includes stone benches and a table, where you are invited to sit and take in the scene.

The cliffs are steep and dramatic here and care needs to be taken. You will come to a long set of steps that run down and up a deep 'v' between hills. The part heading up the hill is extremely steep and has no hand rail – if you don't like heights you probably won't enjoy this section.

At the top of the hill you will see white coastguard's cottages built in 1834 and the tiny **St Aldhelm's Chapel**, dedicated to the first Bishop of Sherborne, St Aldhelm. The chapel has a mystical quality, perched on the cliff and often shrouded in sea mist. The square, squat shape is very unusual for an ecclesiastical building, which is one of the reasons why many people, including Reg Saville of the Purbeck Stone Museum, believe its original purpose was not as a place of worship. As Reg points out, there is no tradition of ecclesiastic buildings being square in England and the corners point to the cardinal points of the compass, which is unheard of in a medieval sacred building. Although little is known about the chapel's origins, it is possible that it was built as a look-out for Corfe Castle. The mounds around the chapel suggest it is on the site of a pre-Conquest Christian enclosure and that it probably rests on an earlier timber building. The vaulting is 12th century and there are medieval graves outside. Look out for the **17th-century graffiti**, where dates and initials are carved into the stonework. The central column has for many years been used as a wishing pillar and pins inserted into it, mostly by young ladies wishing for a suitable husband. A local legend has evolved to explain the chapel's presence: when in 1140 a bride and groom were sailing around the headland watched by the bride's father, their boat capsized and they were drowned; the father is said to have built the chapel in their memory.

Near the chapel is a modern coastguard station and a **memorial to the radar research station** at Worth Matravers. The station's work in developing radar was crucial to turning the tide of World War II and was critical to the development of modern telecommunications.

To head back to the car park without retracing your steps take the track that runs between the chapel and the line of coastguard's cottages. When the track divides, bear left. You will pass a small working quarry *en route* to the car park.

You can extend the walk to five miles by carrying on along the coast from the chapel for another mile and then turning inland up **Winspit Bottom**, a steep-sided dry valley with its slopes etched in outstanding examples of medieval terracing known as lynchets. At the road at Worth Matravers turn left to Renscombe Farm.

Food and drink

Ship Inn Langton Matravers BH19 3EU ☏ 01929 426910 ⓦ www.shipinnlangton. co.uk. Traditional, unfussy pub food.

Square and Compass Worth Matravers BH19 3LF ☏ 01929 439229 ⓦ www.squareandcompasspub.co.uk. A supremely idiosyncratic pub run by Charlie, the fourth generation of the Newman family to hold the licence here. Charlie is keen on palaeontology and there is a collection of fossils on display.

Food is limited to homemade pasties and pies, which you can wash down with the pub's homemade cider. The pub is popular with locals and has regular live music.

⑪ Kimmeridge

The small village of Kimmeridge lies about a mile from the bay of the same name and consists of a clutch of stone and thatched cottages in the midst of some fine farmland. The bay is part of a privately owned estate and you pay a toll to drive on the road from the village to the bay, where there is plenty of parking. The bay lies within the **Purbeck Marine Wildlife Reserve**, one of the first underwater reserves in the country. It is wide and sheltered, backed by dark shale cliffs and with calm waters for swimming: the shallow waters mean this is fine rock-pooling country. The **Marine Centre** has displays on the marine life and organises events for children.

Archaeological evidence indicates that Iron Age residents of the area manufactured and exported jewellery, such as rings and bangles, made from Kimmeridge shale on rudimentary lathes.

The oil field at Kimmeridge is part of BP's Wytch Farm operation; its 'nodding donkey' has been pumping continuously since 1961, making it the UK's oldest working oil pump.

On top of the cliff to the east of Kimmeridge is **Clavell Tower**, its soft pink-and-cream colouring and its Tuscan colonnade combining to give it a certain wedding-cake quality. It was built as a folly in 1830–31 by Reverend John Richards, who took the name Clavell when he inherited the Smedmore Estate. The three-storey tower fell into disrepair and due to coastal erosion ended up perilously close to falling into the sea. The Landmark Trust dismantled the tower and repositioned it 82 feet further back from the cliff. It was fully restored and since 2008 has been available to rent as luxury holiday accommodation (see page 158).

Seen from the road to the east of the village is **Smedmore House** (*BH20 5PG; 01929 480719; www.smedmorehouse.co.uk*), an impressive country home constructed of Portland stone and set in the midst of an 18,000-acre estate. It is available for rent (see page 160).

Food and drink

Clavell's Village Café and Farm Shop BH20 5PE ① 01929 480701
Ⓦ www.clavellscafe.co.uk. Part of the 2,000 acres of farmland owned by the Hole family, in a quiet location on the lane to Kimmeridge Bay. Much of the produce is grown on the farm and the food served in the café is excellent. The portions are farmer's portions – large. Open Apr–Oct 09.00–17.00 daily and evenings Jul–Sep, plus some evenings at weekends in spring and autumn, Nov–Mar closed Mon.

⑫ Tyneham

Ministry of Defence Ranges, East Lulworth BH20 5QF ① 01929 404819 ⓦ www.visit-dorset.com. Tyneham village and the footpaths through the surrounding firing ranges (the Range Walks) are open to the public on certain weekends, when not being used by the army.

The village of Tyneham was evacuated in 1943 to be used as an army training facility. It was meant to be a temporary arrangement but in 1948 the village was compulsorily purchased by the British Army. Most of its buildings are now ruined, although the schoolhouse and church are preserved as museums showing what life was like in the village prior to the evacuation. The Tyneham Valley has escaped any form of development and is essentially frozen in time. It has become a haven for wildlife living among the ruined buildings.

A visit to Tyneham is a fascinating and moving experience, showing how the villagers lived and how their lives were thrown into disarray by World War II. Each of the ruined dwellings contains a board with a description and photographs of the family who lived there. The **schoolhouse**, built in 1856, is as it was when the villagers left, right down to the children's names on the coat hooks. Being such a small community, the school catered for children aged four to 14 in the same classroom: a school photo from 1928 and children's school work bring the history to life. The phone box in front of the post office was installed a few weeks before the evacuation and would have seemed very modern at the time.

When the villagers left they pinned a note to the door of the church: 'Please treat the church and houses with care; we have given up our homes where many of us have lived for generations to help win the war to keep men free. We will return one day and thank you for treating the village kindly.'

The **church** contains the names and photographs of local inhabitants at the time of the evacuation. In the gallery is the restored Bible that was last used in the church and a list of the parishioners. There is also a touching memorial to an Elizabeth Tennant, who died in 1769 and was a servant to the lady of the manor house: 'servant to Mrs Bond of Tyneham in which station she continued 34 years. To the memory of her prudence, honesty and industry this monument is erected'.

On the other side of the car park from the main part of the village is a barn in which is displayed vintage agricultural machinery. From there it is a three-quarter mile walk to **Worbarrow Bay**. On a sunny day the water here can be so clear and blue that it could almost be in the Mediterranean.

Above Tyneham, **Whiteway Viewpoint** provides far-reaching views towards Poole and Studland. From here it is a short drive to East Lulworth; the 'tank crossing' signs you pass *en route* are a reminder of this area's primary use.

⑬ Lulworth Castle

East Lulworth BH20 5QS ① 01929 400352 ⓦ www.lulworthcastle.com. Open Sun–Fri 10.30–17.00; Lulworth Castle House opens Wed afternoons in summer.

Square with round towers in each corner, this large house was built in 1608 as a hunting lodge in the form of a stylised castle. The property was bought by Humphrey Weld in 1641 and has remained in the family, at the centre of a 12,000-acre estate, ever since. The castle was gutted by fire in 1929 and what you see today is the result of extensive restoration work completed in 1998. Nevertheless, the castle is really just a shell and the only rooms inside are a cellar and kitchen.

Visitors can climb the **tower** to take in spectacular views of the surrounding estate, walk around the park and woodland and enjoy a picnic in the grounds. The best time to visit is when there are jousting displays – very exciting for children. In the grounds of the castle, the **chapel of St Mary** (1786) was the first free-standing Roman Catholic church to be built in England after the Reformation. George III approved the building on condition that it did not look like a chapel. He is reputed to have said, 'build a mausoleum and you may furnish it inside as you wish'. It certainly doesn't look like a chapel from the outside but the inside is more ecclesiastical with a large, painted dome.

Also open to the public is **Lulworth Castle House**, the modern (1977) home of the Weld family. It contains paintings and furnishings from the old castle.

⑭ Lulworth Cove and Durdle Door

The Lulworth Estate covers some 20 square miles and includes Lulworth Cove and Durdle Door, two of the most spectacular and best-known features of the Jurassic Coast World Heritage Site. Lulworth Cove is scallop-shell shape (almost a full circle) sculpted by the sea, which broke through a fault in the limestone beds at the mouth of the cove and ate away at the soft clay inland. Durdle Door, an impressive limestone arch eroded by waves, lies half a mile to the west.

The hilly coastline and looping bays backed by pale-coloured cliffs are topped with grassland and colourful flowers; if you walk only one small section of the South West Coast Path, let it be this one. The stretch west from Lulworth Cove over Hambury Tout to **Man o' War Bay** and Durdle Door is only half a mile. It is steep in parts but at the top of those climbs you are rewarded with almost aerial views of the coastline. You can park either in the car park above Durdle Door or at Lulworth Cove but bear in mind that the refreshments are at the Lulworth Cove end. Another popular walk from Lulworth Cove is the one eastwards to the **Fossil Forest**, which can be done only when the Lulworth Range Walks are open (see page 157). The 'forest' is a ledge in the Purbeck limestone cliff made up of doughnut-shaped layers of mud and algae, in the centre of which trees once grew.

The approach to West Lulworth and Lulworth Cove is via a narrow lane. The **Lulworth Heritage Centre** next to the car park in Lulworth Cove makes a handy starting point. Jo Ferris who works at the centre told me, 'we hope that by providing information about what a special place Lulworth is, our visitors will help us to take care of it for future generations to enjoy'. The free exhibition contains information on the geology, geography and social history of the area, including its long farming and smuggling traditions. You won't be surprised to learn, given the shape of the cove, that it was a popular haunt for smugglers, who exploited its seclusion. The heritage centre stocks local maps, walking guides and wildlife identification guides, which can come in handy when exploring the area.

From the Heritage Centre it is a short stroll to **Lulworth Cove** along a narrow street lined with the usual trappings of a seaside touristy spot – guesthouses, tearooms, and shops selling brightly-coloured buckets, spades and rock-pooling nets. Thankfully, however, it lacks that slick, smarmy, touristy feel and instead retains the scruffy charm of a fishing village enhanced by the presence of rickety rowing boats lying at odd angles beside the street. Running down one side of the street is a stone wall and on the other side a stream, one of the many springs which feed the cove and make its waters some of the coldest in Dorset. The water pools in a pond part way down the hill, where families of ducks go about their daily business apparently oblivious to the steady stream of visitors pounding up and down the street.

As you walk down the hill you will see a mint-coloured cottage, the **Dolls House** (*01929 400587*), which is said to have been brought from Canada and re-built here in 1860. Within is a delightfully old-fashioned sweet shop. The cottage was once home to a fishing family and one room is set out as a Victorian kitchen, showing what their life would have been like. In the 1920s and 1930s, the cottage was reportedly home to one Jimmy Carter, not the former US President but a fisherman renowned for smearing his boat with dripping to keep tourists from sitting on it. Tourists are given a much warmer welcome today and can take tea in the courtyard here.

At the cove, boats lie scattered around the slipway and moored in the calm water, reinforcing that fishing village feel. Beside the slipway is a small café (The Old Boat House), which attracts a crowd of eager ice cream hunters on sunny days. The cove is ringed by a well-sheltered shingle beach and the waters are popular with snorkellers. Lulworth Marine (*The Coach House, Main Rd, West Lulworth BH20 5RQ; 01929 400560*) offers **boat trips** and **boat hire** from the cove.

The bulk of the village of **West Lulworth** lies a mile back from the sea and contains a mixture of architectural styles, including thatched cottages and grand Victorian stone villas. It has some good bed and breakfast accommodation, as well as a village shop.

The car park above **Durdle Door** is reached by driving through the large Durdle Door Holiday Park (see page 158). It is a steep walk down (and back up!) to Durdle Door, where there is a pebbly beach. The sea washes back and forth through the arch, making a washboard of the rocks below. Adventurous visitors can be seen swimming or kayaking through the arch, but it is a risky pastime. On the way down to the beach is a lookout point with views of

Durdle Door in one direction and **Man o' War Bay** in the other. The beach at
Man o' War Bay is accessible only at low tide.

Before you head to Lulworth Cove and Durdle Door it is useful to be aware
that when the army ranges are in use, firing may be heard.

Food and drink

Cafés on the street down to the cove include a **Purbeck Ice Cream** shop. Like many
dairy farmers, Peter and Hazel were driven to diversify when milk quotas were
introduced; Purbeck Ice Cream was the result. It is made down the road at Kingston.

Castle Inn Main Rd, West Lulworth BH20 5RN ① 01929 400311
Ⓦ www.thecastleinn-lulworthcove.co.uk. A traditional thatched pub near
Lulworth Castle. The pub is known for its food and variety of local beers and
ciders. Extremely dog-friendly – there are dog treats at the bar.
Lulworth Cove Inn Main Rd, West Lulworth BH20 5RQ ① 01929 400333
Ⓦ www.lulworth-cove.co.uk. Just a few hundred yards from Lulworth Cove.
Popular restaurant specialising in seafood.
Weld Arms East Lulworth BH20 5QQ ① 01929 400211 Ⓦ www.weldarms.co.uk.
A 17th-century thatched pub believed to have been popular with the local
smugglers. Serves traditional pub meals and some more upmarket dishes. There
is a large garden with a children's play area. Dogs are welcome.

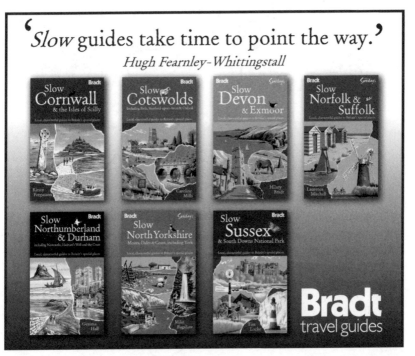

POOLE, BOURNEMOUTH AND THE EAST

Highcliffe Castle

Mudeford

Hengistbury Head ④

Avon Heath Country Park

River Avon

A35

A338

A3060

A338

CHRISTCHURCH

Southbourne

Boscombe ⑤

BOURNEMOUTH ③

RINGWOOD

⑥

A31

Holt Heath ⑫

Holt

Ferndown

A348

Canford Cliffs

A341

Sandbanks

Hinton Martell ⑪

Stanbridge

WIMBORNE MINSTER ⑦

A349

Brownsea Island ②

Pamphill ⑧

Badbury Rings

Kingston Lacy

⑩

A31

Upton

POOLE ①

Shapwick ⑨

A350

WAREHAM

River Stour

4 miles

5km

A35

0

0

6. POOLE, BOURNEMOUTH AND THE EAST

Poole and Bournemouth, Dorset's two largest towns, virtually combine into one large conurbation, with Christchurch as an appendage to make this by far the most densely populated part of Dorset. Although heavily urbanised, it has Slow corners to be discovered and I hope to help you find them.

The historic town of **Poole** sits on the second largest natural harbour in the world, after Sydney, and its sheltered waters offer ideal conditions for all manner of watersports. Eight islands are dotted around the harbour, most of them privately owned, but the National Trust's **Brownsea Island** is open to the public and provides an unspoilt, car-free sanctuary and a vantage point to watch the harbour's abundant birdlife. Many visitors, however, are drawn to the island by the possibility of catching a glimpse of the red squirrel as this is one of the few places in Britain where it remains.

Seven miles of sandy beaches stretch around Poole Bay from Sandbanks to Hengistbury Head near Bournemouth. **Sandbanks** is a small spit jutting out across the mouth of Poole Harbour, mirroring Studland on the Isle of Purbeck; a useful chain ferry links the two and replaces a long drive around the harbour. Sandbanks is the pick of the Poole Bay beaches: glamorous and well known for its exclusive real estate.

Bournemouth and Christchurch are relative newcomers to Dorset – until 1974, when the county boundary was moved, they were part of Hampshire. It is said that in Dorset terms it takes around 40 years to be accepted as a local, so they should be feeling just about settled by now. **Bournemouth** was created as recently as the 19th century and quickly developed all the accoutrements of a British seaside town: the pier, beach huts and souvenir shops.

Christchurch has a very different feel as it dates from Saxon times, lies on the sedate rivers Stour and Avon and has as its focal point the magnificent Priory Church.

Rural East Dorset offers a pleasing mix of open rolling countryside, cherished heathland and forest, while just over the border into Hampshire is the unspoilt New Forest National Park. **Wimborne Minster** is a pleasing historic town with a minster church dating from the 8th century.

A short distance from Wimborne Minster is the National Trust's **Kingston Lacy Estate** with one of Dorset's most imposing houses at its centre. **Badbury Rings**, an Iron Age hillfort, lies on the estate and offers some pleasant walking; a popular point-to-point course is nearby.

Getting there and around

Bournemouth International Airport lies north of Christchurch and links Dorset to other UK and European cities; an airport shuttle operates to Bournemouth town centre. Dorset Flying Club (*0800 0837320; www.dorsetflyingclub.co.uk*) is based at the airport and offers trial lessons flying over the Dorset coast, Solent and the Isle of Wight.

The A35 links Poole, Bournemouth and Christchurch but traffic can be frustratingly heavy in the area, particularly during summer, so you may wish to consider some car-free options to get around the coastal area.

Public transport

South West Trains connect London Waterloo to Christchurch, Bournemouth, Poole and Weymouth. If you arrive in Poole by **train**, a **Plus Bus** ticket gives you unlimited bus travel on most local bus services around the urban area of Poole, Bournemouth and Christchurch.

The **Getting About Card** allows unlimited travel for a day on buses across Poole, Bournemouth and Christchurch; it can be purchased on the bus. Poole's distinctive sky-blue **town-centre bus** (*route 1; Mon–Sat 07.30–18.20*) loops around the major attractions. From April to October an open-top **sightseeing bus** runs through Christchurch, Bournemouth and Poole, allowing you to hop on and off at any of the 22 stops (*01202 557007; www.city-seeing.com*). Parking in Sandbanks in summer can be troublesome but buses 150 from Bournemouth or 152 from Poole will get you there. Regular buses link Poole and Bournemouth to Wimborne Minster, and to Swanage on the Isle of Purbeck, although the **chain ferry** from Sandbanks to Studland is a more memorable way of reaching the Isle of Purbeck.

By boat

If you are arriving in your **own boat**, Poole Quay Boat Haven (*01202 649488; www.poolequayboathaven.co.uk*) has 125 serviced pontoon berths for visitor use and is within walking distance of the town centre. Permanent berths are also available. The harbour master can answer any queries about navigation and regulations (*01202 440210; www.phc.co.uk*). Further east, mooring is available at the Christchurch Sailing Club (*01202 483150; www.christchurchsailingclub. co.uk*).

Sailing is part of the area's identity and regattas are held throughout the summer. At the heart of it all are Poole Yacht Club (*www.pooleyc.co.uk*), Parkstone Yacht Club (*www.parkstoneyachtclub.com*), Royal Motor Yacht Club (*www.rmyc.co.uk*) and Christchurch Sailing Club.

Small **ferries** provide a time-saving and enjoyable way to get around the Poole and Christchurch harbours; bikes and dogs are usually welcome on board. From Sandbanks you can hop on a chain ferry to the quieter side of the harbour, Studland, in the Isle of Purbeck (see page 153). Poole Quay is the departure point for ferry cruises around the harbour and along the Jurassic Coast. You can reach Brownsea Island via ferry from Sandbanks or Poole Quay. A short ferry ride from Christchurch Quay or Mudeford Quay to Mudeford Sandbank allows you to avoid the drive around the harbour, and from the sandbank you can walk up onto Hengistbury Head.

Boat operators

The following offer ferries to Brownsea Island and/or boat cruises.

Blue Line Cruises Poole Quay BH15 1HJ ① 01202 467882 Ⓦ www. bluelinecruises.co.uk. Jurassic Coast cruises, Swanage day cruises and Isle of Wight day trips. Private hire.

Brownsea Island Ferries Poole Quay and Sandbanks ① 01929 462383 Ⓦ www.brownseaislandferries.com. Provides ferries half hourly from Poole Quay and Sandbanks to Brownsea Island. Also harbour cruises, Jurassic Coast cruises and trips to Swanage. A Wareham River cruise from Poole Quay takes around 75 minutes. In winter they operate RSPB-guided birding trips.

Dorset Cruises Poole Quay BH15 1HJ ① 0845 4684640 Ⓦ www.dorsetcruises. co.uk. Brownsea Island, Harbour and Jurassic Coast cruises. River cruises to Wareham.

Greenslade Pleasure Boats Poole Quay BH15 1HJ ① 01202 669955 Ⓦ www.greensladepleasureboats.co.uk. Brownsea Island ferries. Harbour cruises, river cruises to Wareham. Private hire.

Poole Sea Safari Poole Quay BH15 1HJ Ⓜ 07792 820245 Ⓦ www.pooleseasafari. com. A 12-seater rib zooms up and down the Jurassic Coast, giving you striking (albeit fleeting) views of the geology and wildlife. Departing from Poole Quay, you can expect to see Brownsea Island, Sandbanks, Old Harry Rocks, Swanage Bay and Durlston Country Park.

Boat hire and watersports providers

Watersports are big business in Poole Harbour and there are plenty of companies offering everything from windsurfing to waterskiing. Hiring a boat or kayak is a relaxing way to explore Poole Harbour and get up close to the birdlife.

Castaway Boat Charters Poole Quay BH15 4EL Ⓜ 07860 793450 Ⓦ www.castawaycharters.co.uk. Full-day, half-day and evening charters exploring the harbour.

Poole Harbour Watersports School 284 Sandbanks Rd, Poole BH14 8HU ① 01202 700503 Ⓦ www.pooleharbour.co.uk. Kayak and stand-up paddle harbour tours, windsurfing and kitesurfing.

Purple Pelican Self-drive Boat Hire Cobbs Quay Marina, Poole BH15 4EL ① 01202 687778 Ⓦ www.pooleboathire.co.uk. Powerboat hire; no experience necessary.

Rockley Watersports Rockley Point, Poole BH15 4LZ ① 01202 677272
Ⓦ www.rockleywatersports.com. Based at Poole Park, and offers sailing,
windsurfing and powerboating courses.
Superhawk Marine Charters Cobbs Quay Marina, Poole BH15 4EL ① 01202
694427 Ⓦ www.superhawkmarine.com. Sunseeker Superhawk 48-foot luxury
powerboat charters. Experienced skipper provided for up to 12 passengers.
Watersports Academy Banks Rd, Sandbanks BH13 7PS ① 01202 708283
Ⓦ www.thewatersportsacademy.com. Dinghy lessons and hire, kayak hire,
windsurfing, wakeboarding and waterskiing.

Cycling

You may think that the built-up area along the coast would be unsuitable
for riding but there are off-road cycle routes and cycling does present the
opportunity to avoid the traffic. Poole has around 48 miles of cycle network
and the town is well equipped with bike stands. A 7½-mile **Heritage Cycle
Route**, part of National Cycle Route 25, takes you around places of historical
interest in Poole and alongside the harbour to Upton Country Park. The
Castleman Trailway runs almost 17 miles along the route of the defunct
Southampton to Dorchester railway, linking three country parks: Avon Heath,
Moors Valley and Upton. It also allows you to ride from Upton Country Park
to Wimborne Minster. The trailway is open to walkers and cyclists and part of
it to horseriders. The **Bourne Valley Greenway** for walkers and cyclists runs
4½ miles from Canford Heath in Poole to Bournemouth seafront, taking you
through heathland and past the Alder Hills Nature Reserve, run by the Dorset
Wildlife Trust.

Bournemouth has a good **promenade** for cycling, although you can't ride
on it between 10.00 and 18.00 in July and August due to the high volume
of pedestrians. You can cycle from Bournemouth Gardens to Hengistbury
Head along the seafront, and extend it by continuing down Harbour Road
and through Wick to Tuckton Gardens on the River Stour. Alternatively, you
and your bike can catch the **ferry** from Mudeford Sandbank to Christchurch.

For a full day out, you can take bikes on the train from Bournemouth to
Brockenhurst for riding the hundred miles of cycle paths around the **New
Forest National Park**.

Cycle hire

The Bicycle Company 2 Grand Parade, High St, Poole BH15 1AD ① 01202 671611
Ⓦ www.thebicycleco.com. Offers guided rides as well as bike hire.
Front Bike Hire The seafront, Bournemouth ① 01202 557007 Ⓦ www.front-
bike-hire.co.uk. A few hundred yards from the pier. A good range of bikes and
accessories, including children's trailers.
On yer bike 88–90 Charminster Rd, Bournemouth BH8 8US ① 01202 315855
Ⓦ www.onyerbike.co.uk.

Walking

This bit of Dorset is by no means as rich in great walks as the county is further west, with most of the coast built up – but the waterside provides plenty of interest, notably around Poole Harbour, which can be explored by a series of scenic trails (*www.pooleharbourtrails.org.uk*). A leaflet detailing the routes is available from the Poole tourist information centre. One of these, the **Cockle Trail**, helps you uncover the town's heritage with points of interests marked and explained.

A stroll around **Brownsea Island**, perhaps followed by a picnic, is a memorable way to spend a day and provides the opportunity for wildlife watching and views of Poole Harbour from a different perspective.

The **Stour Valley Way** follows the river 64 miles from its source in Stourhead to the sea at Christchurch, with some rewarding sections at the Christchurch end of the walk. The path ends at **Hengistbury Head**, which provides pleasant walking and excellent views of Christchurch Harbour and along the Bournemouth coastline. If you park at the base of the head you can walk over the headland to **Mudeford Sandbank** and catch the land train along the harbour on the way back. From Mudeford Sandbank you can catch a ferry either to Christchurch Quay or to Mudeford Quay, where local fishermen sell their daily catch (see page 212).

The Stour Valley Way runs through the village of Shapwick, from where a short detour leads to the Iron Age hillfort of **Badbury Rings**; the site is imprinted with history and atmosphere and provides good views of the surrounding countryside. The nearby **Kingston Lacy Estate** is criss-crossed with footpaths and bridleways and offers some very pleasant walking country.

Horseriding

Rural East Dorset offers some decent riding, including the opportunity for beach rides; horseriding is allowed on **Highcliffe and Mudeford beaches** between September and Easter but not between Easter and October from 10.00 to 21.00.

Ringwood, which lies near the Dorset/Hampshire border, is the gateway to the **New Forest**'s superb riding (itself not in Dorset and therefore outside the scope of this book), and there are no restrictions for riding across New Forest District-covered beaches (Barton on Sea, Calshot, Milford on Sea or Hordle Cliffs). Between April and July, New Forest stallions are let out into the forest to breed with the mares and it is best to keep your distance from them. Another thing to be aware of is that the New Forest Hounds drag hunt on Tuesday and Saturday from November until the end of February, so unless you are content to join the chase involuntarily, those days may be best avoided. The Forestry Commission has produced a code of conduct for riding in the forest, available online (*www.thenewforest.co.uk*).

The **Kingston Lacy Estate** near Wimborne Minster has 22 miles of pleasant public bridleways with shared access for cyclists.

Riding stables

Arniss Farm Godshill, Fordingbridge SP6 2JX ℡ 01425 654114 ⓦ www.arniss equestrian.co.uk. Set in 50 acres, with 2 all-weather arenas and hacking in the New Forest without having to venture onto roads. Runs summer camps for children.

Bagnum Riding Stables Charles Lane, Ringwood BH24 3BZ ℡ 01425 203902 ⓦ www.bagnumridingstables.co.uk. Well positioned for rides in the New Forest. Open Tue–Sun.

Fir Tree Farm Equestrian Centre Ogdens, Fordingbridge SP6 2PY ℡ 01425 654744 ⓦ www.fir-tree-farm.org.uk. Direct New Forest access.

Stocks Farm Equestrian Centre Christchurch Rd, West Parley BH22 8SQ ℡ 01202 570288. In countryside near Bournemouth International Airport and Ferndown.

Sweetlands Riding School Flowers Drove, Lytchett Matravers, Poole BH16 6BX ℡ 01202 630180 ⓦ www.sweetlandsridingschool.co.uk. Offers hacking, including 3-hour pub rides incorporating a pub lunch.

Accommodation

Poole, **Bournemouth** and **Christchurch** have an extensive range of accommodation from self-catering apartments and cottages to upmarket hotels. The coastal region is very busy in summer, although Christchurch is slightly quieter than the Poole and Bournemouth conurbation. **Brownsea Island** is a very special place and a National Trust cottage is available for rent there. Staying in rural East Dorset allows you to be within easy reach of the coast without being in the thick of it.

Antelope 8 High St, Poole BH15 1BP ℡ 01202 672029 ⒺNED 6603@greeneking. co.uk ⓦ www.antelopeinn-poole.co.uk. A former coaching inn close to the quay, the oldest hotel in Poole. It has 23 en-suite rooms and a restaurant; free Wi-Fi; pet-friendly. Prices are average for pub accommodation.

Balincourt 58 Christchurch Rd, Bournemouth BH1 3PT ℡ 01202 552962 Ⓔ rooms@balincourt.co.uk ⓦ www.balincourt.co.uk. An upmarket guesthouse close to the seafront with thoughtfully decorated rooms. This is designed to be a couples' retreat, so children, stags and hens are not allowed. It has a restaurant open for dinner and breakfast. A relaxing refuge from the busy beaches. Reasonably priced.

Black House Hengistbury Head BH6 4EW Ⓜ 07855 280191 Ⓔ enquiries@ theblackhouse.co.uk ⓦ www.theblackhouse.co.uk. Simple, self-catering accommodation on the water. The house has apartments with 1, 2 or 3 bedrooms. Not cheap but you are paying for the location.

Grove Farm Meadow Holiday Park Stour Way, Christchurch BH23 2PQ ℡ 01202 483597 Ⓔ enquiries@meadowbank-holidays.co.uk ⓦ www.meadowbank-holidays.co.uk. On the river and the main road into the town centre, this offers touring pitches and very good quality on-site vans with modern interiors and everything you could need. Coarse fishing is available for a small fee. There is a shop, a launderette and a games room. Good value for money.

Haven Hotel Sandbanks BH13 7QL ℗ 0844 8806551 Ⓔ reservations@fjbhotels. co.uk Ⓦ www.havenhotel.co.uk. This hotel's best features are its location on the Sandbanks peninsula and the presence of a spa. The 82 rooms are modern and most have a balcony with sea view. Expensive, especially in summer.

Hotel du Vin Thames St, Poole BH15 1JN ℗ 0845 3654438 Ⓦ www.hotelduvin. com. A boutique hotel in a handsome Georgian building in Poole Old Town, offering 38 elegant en-suite rooms finished to a high standard. Priced at the expensive end.

Langtree Manor Derby Rd, East Cliff, Bournemouth BH1 3QB ℗ 01202 553887 Ⓔ Lillie@langtrymanor.co.uk Ⓦ www.langtrymanor.co.uk. Reputedly built in 1877 by the Prince of Wales, the future Edward VII, for his mistress, Lillie Langtry, this is now one of the most upmarket hotels in the area. The rooms are elegantly furnished and have a luxurious and romantic air. This is a couples' retreat rather than a family hotel. Rooms with four-poster bed and spa bath cost considerably more than standard rooms.

Les Bouviers Arrowsmith Rd, Canford Magna, Wimborne BH21 3BD ℗ 01202 889555 Ⓦ www.lesbouviers.co.uk. Boutique hotel with a good restaurant near Wimborne Minster. The 6 en-suite rooms are individually designed and spacious. On the expensive side.

The Old George 2 Cornmarket, Wimborne Minster BH21 1JL ℗ 01202 888510 Ⓔ chrissie_oldgeorge@yahoo.co.uk; Ⓦ www.theoldgeorge.net. This former inn is in a small, pedestrianised square in the town centre. It has 2 spacious rooms, one en suite and the other with private bathroom. Reasonably priced.

524 Pamphill Green Cottage Little Pamphill Green BH21 4EE ℗ 0844 8002070 Ⓔ cottages@nationaltrust.org.uk Ⓦ www.nationaltrustcottages.co.uk. A delightful semi-detached 2-bedroom thatched cottage tucked away in a quiet part of the Kingston Lacy Estate. There is a cosy sitting room with wood-burning stove, dining room and kitchen. Reasonably priced, but the cost rises steeply in summer.

Quay Cottage Brownsea Island, Poole Harbour ℗ 0844 8002070 Ⓔ cottages@ nationaltrust.org.uk Ⓦ www.nationaltrustcottages.co.uk. The only holiday cottage on Brownsea Island is on the sea, has 3 bedrooms and a private garden. There is parking for one car at the National Trust car park in Sandbanks and although there are regular ferries during the day, there are none in the evening. The cottage is closed over Christmas and the New Year. Expensive for self-catering but certainly memorable.

Riverbank House 5 Swan Green, Christchurch BH23 1JJ Ⓜ 07796 402912 Ⓔ enquiries@riverbankholidays.co.uk Ⓦ www.riverbankholidays.co.uk. A luxurious, 3-storey house with a garden fronting the River Stour, complete with jacuzzi. It sleeps 8, has beautiful water views and is an easy 10-minute walk from the town centre. Prices are surprisingly affordable.

Round Island Cottages Poole Harbour ℗ 01202 882885 Ⓔ info@roundisland. co.uk Ⓦ www.roundisland.co.uk. Self-catering accommodation in a special location, on a privately owned island in Poole Harbour. The 2 cottages are simple but fully equipped, one sleeps 8 and the other 6. No pets. Reasonably priced given its location.

Royal Exeter Hotel Exeter Rd, Bournemouth BH2 5AG ℗ 01202 438000 Ⓔ enquiries@royalexeterhotel.com Ⓦ www.royalexeterhotel.co.uk. One of the oldest buildings in Bournemouth provides 54 en-suite rooms, including family rooms and suites with four-poster bed and spa bath. Facilities include a restaurant, gym and sauna. One of the more upmarket options and the prices reflect this.

The Saltings 5 Salterns Way, Lilliput BH14 8JR ℗ 01202 707 349 Ⓔ saltings_ poole@yahoo.co.uk Ⓦ www.the-saltings.com. An elegant, marine-themed B&B 100 yards from Salterns Marine and a 20-minute walk from Sandbanks Beach. Free Wi-Fi; no children or pets. Reasonably priced for a B&B of such a high standard and so close to Sandbanks.

Thatch Cottage Guesthouse Ringwood Rd, Three Legged Cross BH21 6QY ℗ 01202 822042 Ⓔ thatchcottage@aol.com Ⓦ www.thatch-cottage.co.uk. A charming thatched cottage in rural East Dorset with 2 double rooms and a family suite. There is a heated swimming pool in the grounds and the owners will provide a picnic basket for lunch on request. One of the more expensive guesthouses.

Wilksworth Farm Caravan Park Cranborne Rd, Wimborne BH21 4HW ℗ 01202 885467 Ⓔ rayandwendy@wilksworthfarmcaravanpark.co.uk Ⓦ www. wilksworthfarmcaravanpark.co.uk. An exceptional caravan park in the grounds of a Grade II-listed building recorded in the Domesday Book and once owned by Henry VIII. In a quiet setting, it offers pitches for tents and caravans, and the Olde Cart Shed serves meals and snacks. Other facilities include a pool, games room, tennis court and children's play area. Pet-friendly. Good value for money.

Tourist information centres

Bournemouth Westover Rd, BH1 2BU ℗ 0845 0511700 Ⓦ www.bournemouth. co.uk.
Christchurch High St, BH23 1AS ℗ 01202 471780 Ⓦ www.visitchristchurch.info.
Poole 19 The Quay BH13 1HJ ℗ 01202 253253 Ⓦ www.pooletourism.com.
Wimborne Minster 29 High St, BH21 1HR ℗ 01202 886116.

Poole and surrounds

Poole Quay and **Poole Old Town** offer some good pottering territory – historic buildings, numerous eateries, independent shops and the chance to gaze with envy at the fabulous Sunseeker motorboats under construction there.

Poole Harbour's 110 miles of coastline, shallow waters and eight islands are a haven for wildlife, in particular birds. The best place to appreciate the area's flora and fauna is **Brownsea Island**, where the Dorset Wildlife Trust manages a conservation area with hides overlooking the lagoon. The harbour draws almost as many watersports enthusiasts as it does wildfowl and plays host to events throughout the year, including windsurfing and kitesurfing championships.

The **beaches**, in particular Sandbanks, attract people to the area but if they get too busy there are some waterside parks where you can relax and admire the harbour. Perhaps the best of these is **Upton Country Park**, a great spot for a picnic in front of the 18th-century manor house.

① Poole

Although modern development dominates Poole, a historic core remains around the quay and Poole Old Town, testament to the town's long seafaring history. The earliest evidence of that history was discovered in 1964: a 33-foot boat hollowed from an oak tree found preserved in mud off Brownsea Island and dated to around 295BC; it is now on display in Poole Museum. While being on the sea has its advantages, it has also meant the town had its fair share of seaborne invasions – both the Romans and the Vikings landed here. The Romans took over an Iron Age settlement at Hamworthy on the western side of the harbour and built a road between it and their settlement at Badbury Rings, near Wimborne Minster. In 1015 Canute used Poole Harbour as a convenient base from which to attack Wessex. Poole began to emerge as an important port in the 12th century and, gradually taking over from Wareham, was the biggest port in Dorset by 1433. In the 18th century it was the main British port trading with North America, bringing great wealth to its merchants. It was central to the Newfoundland trade, whereby Poole's ships sailed to Newfoundland laden with salt and provisions, collected salted cod caught off Newfoundland and delivered it the West Indies and southern Europe, and then returned with wine, salt and olive oil. More recently, Poole played an important role as one of the principal departure points for the World War II D-Day landings.

Today, an easy and sedate way to get around is the **Poole Land Train**, which runs every 15 minutes past the hour from Poole Quay and travels for 45 minutes around the town; stops include the High Street and Poole Park. Look out for Poole's **town crier**, David Squire – he took on the role in 1958 and is reputed to be the longest-serving town crier in the world. The **tourist information centre** on Poole Quay is helpful and has leaflets on various trails around the town, including the **Cockle Trail**, which leads you around the older parts of Poole – shells inlaid in the pavement mark significant points with background provided in the leaflet, which you can also download (*www.pooletourism.com*). Cyclists can pick up a leaflet on a 7½-mile heritage cycle route around the town.

Poole suffered some bombing during World War II, and in the 1950s and 1960s over half the buildings dating from before 1850 were demolished. In 1975 a conservation area was established around the southwest end of High Street and across to West Street, in order to preserve the remaining old buildings. Within this zone, known as **Poole Old Town**, some medieval buildings survive but the predominant style is Georgian. Church, Market and Thames streets in particular have some fine Georgian buildings, many of which were houses built in the 18th century to accommodate the town's prosperous middle class, made wealthy by sea trading. **Poole House** in Thames Street has a typically flamboyant façade, while another highly decorative example sporting Baroque decoration is **West End House** in St James Close; built in the early 18th century for Newfoundland merchant, John Slade, it was in the late 19th century home to the Carter family, founders of Poole Pottery.

At the end of Market Street, the **guildhall** dates from 1761, with twin exterior flights of steps curving up to the first floor, which once housed the courtroom; the ground floor was originally open and occupied by market stalls. Behind the guildhall in 1886, Alderman Horatio Hamilton, once mayor of Poole, was shot repeatedly by John King, a disgruntled harbour pilot following a dispute over a boat; you may be able to spot the bullet holes.

The large **St James's Church** (*open May–Sep Tue–Fri 11.00–16.00*) was built in 1820 from Purbeck stone, although there has been a church here since the 13th century. The interior has a nautical feel; its grainy wooden pillars, which arrived on ships from Newfoundland, are reminiscent of the masts of

sailing ships, and galleried seating extends all around. **St George's Almshouses** in Church Street have been restored but a plaque erected in 1904 reveals that they were built in the time of Henry V (reigned 1413–22) and 'have been devoted to the use of the poor for 500 years'. A niche in the wall was used for Poole's first street lamp.

The quay

A colourful variety of fishing boats are moored in this lively, industrious part of town, and early risers will see the daily catch of crabs and flat fish. Mussels are also regularly farmed and clams are racked within the harbour. Poole still has a thriving fishing industry with a strong fleet of some 80 to 90 professional fishermen.

The quay is also the departure point for **boat trips** around the harbour, to Brownsea Island and along the coast. A statue of Baden-Powell gazes out from the quay towards Brownsea Island, where he held the first scout camp, and the distant Purbeck Hills.

At the western end of the quay is the **Town Bridge**, a lifting bridge built in 1927 and sporting green copper cladding, which gives access to Hamworthy, where Sunseeker builds its luxury powerboats and the ferry port operates services to France and the Channel Islands. **Hamworthy Park** (*Lulworth Av, BH15 4DH*) is on the waterfront and has views of the harbour, a small sandy beach, promenade, tennis courts, paddling pool (*open during summer*), playground facilities and a café. It is lesser known than Poole Park (see page 202) and tends to be quieter in busy periods.

On the oldest part of the quay, at the edge of Poole Old Town, stands the **Custom House**, which now houses a restaurant. It was rebuilt in 1813 in the style of the original building of 1747 that was later destroyed by fire. In front of it is the beam that was once used to weigh goods for customs duty. In 1747, following the seizure of one of their shipments, the notorious Hawkhurst Gang of smugglers raided the Custom House to retrieve their contraband. The shipment from Guernsey contained about 30 hundredweight of tea, 39 casks of brandy and rum, and a bag of coffee; it had been destined to land at Christchurch Bay when it was intercepted off the coast. About 30 members of the gang broke into the Custom House and escaped on horseback with the tea; several of them were later captured and hanged.

Nearby, in one of the 18th-century warehouses that once served the busy port, **Poole Museum** (*4 High St, BH15 1BW; 01202 262600; open Oct–Apr Tue–Sat; free admission*) displays over four floors exhibits on the area's history and prehistory, plus a colourful collection of Poole Pottery. Poole's seafaring history features prominently, including its murkier side – smuggling and piracy. The museum's star attraction is the log boat dating from 295BC found off Brownsea Island in 1964 (see page 199). The boat is thought to have been based at Green Island in Poole Harbour and used for continental trade. From the museum's terrace you get expansive views of the harbour and Poole Old Town; the museum is accessible to those with limited mobility and is child friendly. Attached to it is a local history centre where people researching the area or their family tree can draw on local archives.

Behind Poole Museum is **Scaplens Court Museum and Garden** (*free admission*), used during school term time as a learning centre for local children but open to the public during August. The building dates from around 1500 and contains exhibits of Poole's domestic life; around the stone fireplace are initials believed to have been scratched by troops during the Civil War when it was known as the George Inn. There is also a carefully restored walled herb garden. Scaplens Court is the starting point for **ghost walks** around the town with Granny Cousins (*07977 969080; Jul–Sep Mon & Wed 20.00*) or Inner Sanctum (*01202 914377; Tue & Thu 19.45 in summer, 20.00 in winter*).

Heading eastwards along the quay you pass a series of historic pubs that have served Poole's thirsty seafarers for centuries, and the old seaman's mission, now the Oriel Restaurant. The front of the Poole Arms is covered with tiles made a little further along the quay by the forerunners of Poole Pottery, 'Carter's Industrial Tile Manufactory'. **Poole Pottery's factory shop** (*The Quay BH15 1HJ; 01202 668681; www.poolepottery.co.uk*) stands on the site of Carter's original factory, which opened in 1873 and where many of the tiles used in London underground stations were made. Production ceased when the company went into administration in 2006 but it was subsequently taken over and the pottery is now produced in Stoke-on-Trent. Live demonstrations at the shop allow you to watch distinctive pieces being created and for a few pounds you can even paint your own pottery; the café specialises in local produce.

Next to Poole Pottery, **Ginger Pop Shop** (*Old Orchard, BH15 1SD;* ① *01202 670504; www.gingerpop.co.uk; open daily from 10.00*) is dedicated to the work of Enid Blyton, who spent much time in Dorset, the places and landscapes of which inspired many of her writings. The shop stocks every Enid Blyton book currently in print, around 150 titles, and has a second-hand section for those elusive out-of-print titles you wish you hadn't thrown away. A range of items from the Blyton era are on sale, such as old-fashioned toys and a jolly (if not entirely pc) assortment of golliwogs. Behind the shop, **Eileen Soper's Illustrated Worlds** is essentially a museum of Blyton's work. Soper illustrated Blyton's books for over 20 years and the displays take you back to the days of *The Famous Five* and the *Secret Seven*; the young at heart can enjoy solving mysteries within the exhibition. Exhibits provide an insight into life at the time Blyton was writing, focusing on World War II and the work of the Land Girls.

At the eastern end of the quay, **Poole Old Lifeboat Museum and Shop** (*Fisherman's Dock BH15 1RA; 01202 666046; www.poole-lifeboats.org.uk; open Apr–Dec 10.00–16.00; free admission*), in a lifeboat station established in 1882 tells the story of the Royal National Lifeboat Institution (RNLI) and has a shop selling RNLI memorabilia. The centrepiece at the museum is the *Thomas Kirk Wright*, one of the first lifeboats to reach Dunkirk on 30 May 1940. She was one of the flotilla referred to as 'Dunkirk's Little Ships', sent to rescue members of the British Expeditionary Force from the beaches. On her third and final rescue voyage she was hit by German gunfire but managed to limp back to Poole on one engine; she returned to service at Poole until 1962. The RNLI has its headquarters in Poole at West Quay Road (*BH15 1HZ; 01202 662228*) and maintains a library and archive on its work, which you can visit by appointment.

Poole Park, to the east of the town centre off Parkstone Road, is a green open space which snakes around a large saltwater lake separated from the sea by a thin strip of land where the railway runs. The park was opened in 1890 on land given by Lord Wimborne of Canford Manor, near Wimborne Minster, now Canford School. The lake has plenty of wildfowl, including some very friendly Canada geese, and is also suitable for watersports. Rockley Watersports (*01202 677272*) has a boathouse here offering all manner of water-based activities, including sailing, windsurfing, pedalo and kayaking. For landlubbers there are tennis courts, a bowling green, indoor and outdoor children's play areas and an ice-skating rink. A miniature railway runs from one end of the lake to the other, and you'll also find a restaurant and café.

Harry Paye

One particularly lively event on Poole's calendar takes place in June when the Harry Paye Charity Fun Day brings assorted crowds of sightseers and 'pirates' to the quay, with various forms of re-enactments and children's entertainment. It gives a nod to local boy Harry Paye, a colourful privateer and pirate who led naval raids along the coasts of France and Spain in the late 14th and early 15th centuries. He caused a fair amount of mayhem along the way, capturing ships, rasing cities and holding prisoners to ransom. In 1406 he captured 120 French and Spanish vessels in an expedition, brought them back to Poole and distributed the booty to the residents. It is said that the wine from one of the ships kept the people of Poole happy for a whole month.

Poole's beaches

Poole is blessed with some fine, golden sand beaches that wouldn't look out of place on a tropical island.

Heading east from the town the first beach you come to, **Shore Road**, lies within the harbour and has a dedicated launch zone for kitesurfers and windsurfers. The next beach along is Poole's best-known, **Sandbanks**, a sandy peninsula stretching across the harbour mouth and connected to Studland on the Purbeck side of the harbour by a chain ferry (see page 153). Sandbanks is well known for its luxurious homes and is reputed to have the fourth highest land value in the world by area. While it may exude an air of exclusivity, it is packed in summer. The beach ranks among the finest on the South Coast; the water is clean and shallow for around 200 yards offshore. In July the beach plays host to the **British Beach Polo Championships**, which draws top national and international teams, and is coupled with music events in the evening. When the inaugural tournament was held in 2008, it was the first of its kind in the UK – the sport was more usually seen on the beaches of Dubai and Miami. The polo is played in an arena with an oversized orange ball, designed not to get lost in the sand; spectators are pretty close to the action and get a real appreciation of the speed, agility and skill involved.

The stretch of sand continues from Sandbanks in the direction of Bournemouth and includes the beaches of **Canford Cliffs**, **Branksome Chine** and **Branksome Dene Chine**. They have views towards the Isle of Purbeck and Old Harry Rocks, and Canford Cliffs has the area's oldest beach huts, dating from 1927. Although officially belonging to Poole, the Branksome beaches seem more part of Bournemouth because of their location; the surrounding area is largely residential, with wooded hills running down to the beaches.

If you are looking for a **dog-friendly beach**, note that the main beaches are closed to dogs between May and September but you can always take your dog to Rockley Point at Hamworthy, the beach at Hamworthy Park, Branksome Dene Chine or the western end of Sandbanks.

Upton Country Park

BH17 7BJ ① 01202 261306 ⑩ www.uptoncountrypark.com. Park open daily 09.00–
dusk; house open certain Sundays – see website for details.

A quiet escape with views of the harbour, just four miles from Poole town
centre: walk or cycle through the hundred acres or so of gardens, parkland,
woodland and coastline, or simply have a picnic and enjoy the views. You can
download a nature trail map of the park from the website, and there's a hide
for watching birds on the harbour. Orienteering, segway and boules pitches
are available and above the Peacock Tearooms the **Peacock Gallery** (*www.
peacockgallery.org.uk*) shows works by professional and non-professional artists.
A plant centre sells plants that grow in the park (*open daily 12.00–16.00*).
Upton House, built in 1816 and now a venue for learning and events, is usually
closed to the public but guided tours are available on certain Sundays. The
house was built for Christopher Spurrier, one of the many Poole merchants
made wealthy by the Newfoundland trade. He was declared bankrupt in 1830
after trade plummeted and things didn't get better – he reputedly managed to
gamble away the family silver by losing a bet on a maggot race.

Compton Acres

164 Canford Cliffs Rd, BH13 7ES ① 01292 700778 ⑩ www.comptonacres.co.uk. Open
daily Mar–Oct 10.00–18.00, Nov–Feb 10.00–16.00.

Between Poole and Bournemouth and covering ten acres, this garden displays
over 3,000 species and is enhanced by views of Poole Harbour, Brownsea
Island and the distant Purbeck Hills. A margarine entrepreneur bought the
property as a seaside residence in 1920 and four years later created a garden
to reflect his worldwide travels and interest in horticulture. It is divided into
seven distinctly themed areas, including Italian, Japanese and heather gardens;
the wooded valley area is at its best in spring, when the bluebells and other
bulbs are in flower. Plants and gifts are on sale and there are two cafés, a deli
and a children's play area.

Farmer Palmer's Farm Park

Wareham Rd, Organford BH16 6EU ① 01202 622022 ⑩ www.farmerpalmers.co.uk.
Open daily from 10.00.

Off the A35 between Poole and Bere Regis, this farm park evolved from a
working farm and is aimed at children under eight. The barn has farm animals
and pets and there is the opportunity for interactive experiences. Each day at
13.45 a milking demonstration shows the children where milk comes from;
trailer rides, woodland walks, play areas and a bouncy castle are also on offer.

The Courtyard Craft Centre

Huntick Rd, Lytchett Minster BH16 6BA ⑩ www.thecourtyardcraftcentre.co.uk.

Just west of Poole near the A35, this complex of converted farm buildings
houses a variety of small, independent shops. Many are craft-related and

include a pottery, where you can often see the potter at work, old-fashioned sweet shop and a card-making shop. The centre runs a programme of classes and events. Pet-friendly.

Food and drink

Poole general market takes place in the High Street on Thursday and Saturday, while a farmers' market is held in Falkland Square (outside the Dolphin Shopping Centre) on Thursday (*09.00–14.00*). Unsurprisingly, Poole does seafood very well; **Frank Greenslades** (*New Quay Rd, BH15 4AF* ℗ *01202 672199*) has been selling freshly caught seafood since 1884, including local crab, lobster and scallops. A string of eateries along Poole Quay features casual cafés, pubs and restaurants.

Branksome Beach Restaurant & Terrace Bar Branksome Chine BH13 6LP ℗ 01202 767235. On the beach, the restaurant has impressive sea views, which are amplified in the upstairs terrace bar. Serves modern British cuisine made using locally sourced, seasonal produce. Open daily for breakfast, lunch and afternoon tea; and evenings in summer. One of the area's more expensive dining options.
Canteen 18 High St, BH15 1BP ℗ 01202 680014 Ⓦ www.thecanteenpoole. co.uk. An intimate, family-run restaurant serving unpretentious and exceptionally good value homemade food. The menu varies according to the season, with the emphasis in summer being on fish and in autumn and winter, meat and game, as well as Dorset specialities such as the excellent Blue Vinney-stuffed chicken. Chef Mike butchers his own organic lamb, beef and Purbeck deer and uses all cuts of the meat to prevent wastage. Open Mon–Sat for dinner only.
Courtyard Tearooms 48a High St, BH15 1BT ℗ 01202 670358. Tearooms in a 16th-century building with plenty of character, tucked away in the Old Orchard Plaza. Serves a huge range of teas, homemade cakes and light lunches. Free Wi-Fi. Open Mon–Fri 11.00–16.00, Sat 10.00–16.30.
Custom House The Quay BH15 1HP ℗ 01202 676767 Ⓦ www.customhouse. co.uk. An à la carte restaurant upstairs and a more casual café/bar downstairs. Serves modern English and French cuisine and seafood specialities. Good views of the quay and the Georgian building has an elegant atmosphere. Open daily for breakfast, lunch and dinner.
Fishy Fishy 18 Dolphin Quay BH15 1HH ℗ 01202 680793. Modern seafood restaurant on the quay serving fresh local fish. Open daily 12.00–23.00.
Guildhall Tavern 15 Market St, BH15 1NB ℗ 01202 671717. In the Old Town, an upmarket French seafood restaurant. Open Tue–Sat for lunch and dinner.
Lakeside Fish & Chips Lifeboat Quay BH15 1LS ℗ 01202 914336. Eat-in and take-away fish and chips said to be among the best in the South West. Open Mon–Sat 12.00–22.00, Sun 12.00–21.00.
Sandbanks Beach Café Banks Rd, BH13 7QQ ℗ 01202 708621. Large, casual café on the beach. Has a bit of a school canteen feel but is well positioned and the homemade cakes are good. Open daily.

South Deep Café Parkstone Bay Marina, Turks Lane, BH14 8EW ℗ 01202 724915.
A hidden gem: an informal café tucked away in a quiet spot at the marina,
overlooking the water. Open daily.

Storm 16 High St, BH15 1BP ℗ 01202 674970 ⓦ www.stormfish.co.uk. A fish
restaurant owned by a fisherman – which indeed sounds like a recipe for success.
Pete Miles still goes out fishing and ensures the fish that ends up on your plate is
as fresh as it can be, and he adheres to sustainable fishing principles. Everything
is made from scratch, using as much local produce as possible. Cookery courses
are also available. Open daily for dinner in summer, lunch Mon–Sat; dinner Tue–
Sat in winter; best to ring to confirm lunch opening.

② Brownsea Island

℗ 01202 707744 ⓦ www.nationaltrust.org.uk/brownsea. Open Mar–Oct; landing fee
payable on arrival; foot-passenger ferry from either Poole Quay or Sandbanks (see
page 193); limited dedicated car parking at Sandbanks; National Trust.

A car-free haven for wildlife as well as the starting point of the Boy Scout
movement, Brownsea is the largest of the islands in Poole Harbour and one
of Dorset's treasures. The journey to the island gives the impression you are
travelling to a magical, faraway land; arriving by boat, the first thing you see
is the island's few stone houses and the castle, with a backdrop of woodland.
The first castle on Brownsea was built in the time of Henry VIII as one of a
string of defences; in the 18th century it was rebuilt as a residence. In the late

19th century it burnt down and was
again rebuilt; today the John Lewis
Partnership rents it as a hotel for its
employees and it is not open to the
public.

The **visitor centre** is a good
starting point and provides
information on the island's history,
flora and fauna. Exploring the island independently is straightforward
and rewarding, or you can take a **guided walk** or **tractor-trailer tour**. There
really is great pleasure in walking around an island where there are no roads
and no traffic, and absorbing sea views. Around the quay and visitor centre are
traces of the communities that have lived here, including **St Mary's Church**,
built in 1853 by the island's then owner, Colonel Waugh. The church remains
virtually unchanged since its construction, there is no electricity and no water
supply, but its services are often well attended.

The island was the site of Major-General Robert Baden-Powell's original
experimental scout camp in 1907, which gave rise to the international scouting
movement. A **memorial** commemorates the first camp and a permanent scout
campsite now exists on the island.

The island has plenty of space for picnics, or there is a National Trust
tearoom near the ferry. In summer the **Brownsea Island Theatre Company**

(01202 251987; www.brownsea-theatre.co.uk) puts on open-air productions in the atmospheric location. If you would like to prolong your stay at Brownsea, you can rent the National Trust cottage (see page 197).

Wildlife on the island

Indications are that the island was inhabited as early as the 5th century BC. Until the 16th century it was mostly heathland but successive owners farmed the island, planted deciduous and coniferous woodlands, reclaimed marshland from the harbour, created meadows and excavated peat bogs to form two large lakes. The National Trust acquired Brownsea Island in 1963, after the last owner, Mrs Bonham-Christie died in 1961. She had owned the island since 1921 and virtually lived as a recluse, she ordered almost everyone off the island, reducing its population from 70 to six. She let the island run wild, free from farming and forestry, and in part that is what preserved it.

The whole island, with its combination of woodland, heathland, wetland, seashore and lagoon, is rich in wildlife. Over 60 native and introduced species of trees grow on Brownsea, providing a shady canopy for walks around the island. Pheasants roam the woodland, the descendants of those introduced for shooting parties, while the pine forest is the domain of goldcrests, woodpeckers, nuthatches and treecreepers. The open heath supports diverse butterfly species, common lizards and nightjars.

The northern half of the island, including the lagoon, is managed by the Dorset Wildlife Trust (DWT) and you can enter this area for a small fee, which goes towards the trust's conservation work. Chris Thain, DWT reserve manager, who lives on the island and is devoted to conservation work here, told me a large part of their work has been the removal of the rhododendrons that have spread invasively throughout the island. A trail leads around the DWT part of the island, where you can watch wildlife and admire the views of the harbour. This area is where you are most likely to catch a glimpse of **red squirrels**, a key attraction for many visitors. Food is put out for them at The Villa, which serves as the DWT's visitor centre providing detailed information on the wildlife.

Brownsea Island and the Isle of Wight are the only natural locations in southern Britain where red squirrels live. At the time of writing the population of red squirrels here was 200. They flourish on the island because the 50-year-old pines provide an ideal habitat and their competitor, the grey squirrel, has never been introduced here. The squirrels are most active at sunrise and sunset for about three hours, they sleep during the day and shelter when the weather is inclement or very hot.

You may also see **Sika deer** – they were introduced to the island from Japan in 1896 and were one of the first populations in the country. They lived alongside the roe and fallow deer until a severe fire swept the island in 1934, when the deer swam to the mainland. Only small numbers were returned in the 1970s but their population has thrived.

A series of hides allows you to watch the lagoon's abundant and diverse **bird population**. The lagoon was reclaimed from the harbour in the 1850s to create 70 acres of farmland; from the 1930s it was rarely drained, creating a rich non-tidal wetland. In spring, and autumn waders stop off during their migration, including little stint, curlew sandpiper, ringed plover, spotted redshank and ruff. In spring common and sandwich terns return from overwintering off the western coast of Africa and nest on gravel islands in the lagoon. Each pair usually rears two chicks and from May to September you can see them diligently feeding their young. From autumn to early spring large flocks of waders, including avocets and black-tailed godwits, make their home here, as do spoonbills. Colourful shelducks are present all year.

A freshwater marsh is home to an entirely different array of bird species, including water rail, reed bunting and red warbler, an African migrant which spends the summer here. The marsh also supports many insects, including 24 species of dragonflies.

Bournemouth and Christchurch

Colourful, vivacious, even shameless, **Bournemouth** is what you may have come to expect from a British seaside resort; what you may not expect is the high quality of the beaches, which draw crowds of eager sunworshippers in summer. **Christchurch** is more refined, imprinted with history spanning generations and with the elegant **Christchurch Priory** at its heart. The River Stour meets the sea here and you can spend a very sedate afternoon pottering along the river in a boat hired from the quay. Small ferries cross the harbour, providing plenty of opportunity for relaxing, car-free travel.

The area is within easy reach of the peaceful and beautiful New Forest National Park, with its excellent walking and horseriding, although as it is in Hampshire I don't discuss it in detail here.

③ Bournemouth

There is little truly 'Slow' about Bournemouth, a large and relatively new settlement that has exploded around the coastal resort but I have endeavoured to uncover the elements that give Bournemouth its distinctive character.

Prior to 1810, the area where Bournemouth now stands was little more than rugged heathland leading down to a deserted coastline. Smugglers landed their contraband here and took advantage of the chines (small ravines running down to the sea, carved into the cliffs by streams) to hide their illicit goods. The smuggling activity and threat of invasion by Napoleon's forces prompted the government to authorise the protection of the coast by Dorset Volunteer Rangers. The commander of the local Cranborne troop was Captain Lewis Tregonwell, who is credited with founding Bournemouth. Tregonwell took a liking to the area he was charged with protecting, built a summer residence here and planted the valleys with pine trees. The Victorians considered the sea air scented with pine to be therapeutic, in particular for those suffering with tuberculosis, and a series of villas sprung up in the area to cater for wealthy, ailing, visitors. The villas are still visible at the southern end of Tregonwell Road and Tregonwell's house has been incorporated into the Royal Exeter Hotel.

Hotels specialising in seawater treatments followed, such as the Mont Dore, built in the 1880s and now part of the town hall. One of those who came for rehabilitation was **Robert Louis Stevenson**, who wrote *Kidnapped* while living in Alum Chine Road. As well as creating grand villas, the prosperous Victorians added expansive parks and gardens, which, along with the pine trees, are characteristic of Bournemouth. The Lower, Central and Upper Gardens break up the urban sprawl and maintain a Victorian feel, while Alum Chine has tropical gardens by the sea.

For many years, Bournemouth was considered a retirement town but the council has taken steps to attract other demographics. The university and a large number of schools teaching English as a foreign language have brought young people but it lacks that seat of learning atmosphere, perhaps because the institutions are relatively new and have not yet become an integral part of the town's identity. With students and youngsters comes a lively **nightlife** and in summer stag and hen parties invade the town. It also has a strong **gay scene**, similar to Brighton but on a smaller scale. Bournemouth is subject to incessant entertainment, with events running throughout the year; one of the best known is **Bournemouth Air Festival** (*www.bournemouthair.co.uk*), held over four days in August when aircraft display teams provide an exciting spectacle, and there is live music, fireworks and outdoor films.

The seafront

Bournemouth's main draw card is its sandy **beaches**, with views across the bay towards the Isle of Wight. The beaches referred to as Bournemouth's (as opposed to Poole's) lie at the centre of the seven-mile stretch of sand that runs from Sandbanks to Hengistbury Head. As a general rule, the further you head east (towards Hengistbury Head) from Bournemouth, the quieter the beach. For the full English-seaside experience, you can hire **beach huts** by the day, week or month, or even buy one (*0845 0550968; www.bournemouthbeachhuts. co.uk; book online at www.bournemouth.co.uk/abc*). Over 250 beach huts stretch across the seafront from Alum Chine to Southbourne and come equipped with four chairs, a gas ring and curtains. Boscombe Beach has a modern take on the beach hut: beach pods designed by fashion guru, Wayne Hemingway, come complete with kitchenette, French doors and private balcony. Between May and September, **dog-friendly beaches** are at Alum Chine, Middle Chine, Fisherman's Walk and Hengistbury Head, near Christchurch.

A **land train** runs along the seafront – westwards from Bournemouth Pier to Alum Chine and eastwards to Boscombe Pier, via Boscombe Precinct and Gardens. Bournemouth's **pier** provides a good vantage point over the bay and coastline. It has a cheap-and-cheerful, British-seaside flavour and is crammed with souvenir shops, sweet shops, a fun fair, cafés and a restaurant. At the end of the pier is the Pier Theatre, built in 1960 and designed to resemble a paddle-steamer. The pier began life in 1855 as a retractable jetty to accommodate the Weymouth paddle-steamer, *Princess*, but was rebuilt and expanded over the years. In 1940, for security reasons, a gap was blown in it that remained for the duration of World War II and the repaired pier re-opened in 1946.

The town centre

The busy commercial centre of the town is slightly inland, around **The Square**. If you enjoy Victorian churches, have a look in **St Stephen's**, north of The Square and widely recognised as Bournemouth's most interesting. It was designed by renowned architect John Loughborough Pearson and built in 1881–98. According to John Betjeman in 1952, 'it was worth travelling 200 miles and being sick in the coach' to view the interior. Light and airy, it features towering columns, dramatic stone vaulting and a decorative wrought-iron screen, which separates the chancel from the main body of the church. The floors of the choir, sanctuary and lady chapel contain around 60 different types of coloured marble. The stained glass is reputed to be the best in Bournemouth; the life and death of St Stephen are depicted in the west window and a rose window in the north transept commemorates the first vicar here.

To see the town from a different perspective, you can head into the air in the **Bournemouth Balloon** (*BH1 2AQ; 01202 313649; www.bournemouthballoon. com*). The hot-air balloon is tethered by a steel cable and hovers at 500 feet; day and night flights operate when weather conditions allow. It takes off from the Lower Gardens, between The Square and the seafront. Also in the gardens are bungee trampolines and Victorian kiosks, where you can hire a deckchair and buy refreshments.

Boscombe and Southbourne

To the east of Bournemouth, **Boscombe** developed from the middle of the 19th century and has a neat seafront and some pleasant gardens, including the Italianate Gardens, Boscombe Cliff and Boscombe Chine. It is trying to shake off its long-held reputation as the seedy end of Bournemouth through a series of initiatives, such as Boscombe Spa Village, the redevelopment of the once run-down seafront to create a modern, surfy vibe. Key to this is **Boscombe Surf Reef** (*www.thesurfreef.co.uk*), an artificial reef designed to create waves for fans of surfing. When it was built in 2009, it was a European first, made up of 55 giant sandbags placed 240 yards offshore on the seabed over an area the size of a football pitch. The reef has attracted a good deal of controversy; it cost three million pounds to install but has been plagued by technical problems and at the time of writing it was closed for repair.

East of Boscombe towards Hengistbury Head is **Southbourne**, where Southbourne Grove provides some inviting, independent shops. A funicular railway, **Fisherman's Walk Cliff Railway**, runs the 128 feet between the coastal road on top of the cliffs and the promenade, and was built in 1935. Similar railways operate at West Cliff and East Cliff, and opened in 1908. All three railways operate between April and October, labouring up their respective hills and looking as if they are about to run out of energy before they reach the top.

The Oceanarium

Pier Approach, West Beach BH2 5AA ℗ 01202 311993 ℗ www.oceanarium.co.uk. Open daily 10.00–17.00.

The oceanarium takes a high-tech approach to displaying aquatic creatures. A virtual interactive dive cage creates the experience of being face to face with a great white shark, blue whale, dolphin and manta ray. A walk-through tunnel passes underwater allowing you to see sharks, turtles and other fish found on the Great Barrier Reef, while in a recreated bamboo forest the oriental small-clawed otters are enchantingly mischievous. You may wish to time your visit around daily feeding presentations, details of which are on the website.

Russell-Cotes Art Gallery and Museum

East Cliff Promenade, BH1 3AA ℗ 01202 451858 ℗ www.russell-cotes.bournemouth. gov.uk. Open Tue–Sun and Bank Holiday Mon 10.00–17.00.

Sir Merton Russell-Cotes was a mayor of Bournemouth (1894–95) and a local philanthropist. Built for him in 1901, this grand Victorian house contains artwork and souvenirs collected by the Russell-Cotes family during their worldwide travels in the late Victorian era. The abundance of statues, paintings and gold paint gives an effect somewhere between grand and gaudy. Regular exhibitions provide the opportunity to purchase artwork by local and other artists.

Food and drink

Bournemouth is packed with bars, restaurants and nightclubs, concentrated around the town centre and along the seafront.

All Fired Up 35–37 Bourne Av, BH2 6DT ℗ 01202 558030. Just off The Square, a café where you can paint your own ceramics. Open Mon–Wed & Fri–Sat 09.30–18.00, Thu 09.30–22.00, Sun 11.00–17.00.

Aruba Pier Approach, BH2 5AA ℗ 01202 554211. A light, airy bar/restaurant with sea views. The menu is extensive and relatively inexpensive. Open daily 09.00–23.00.

Chez Fred 10 Seamoor Rd, Westbourne BH4 98N ℗ 01202 761023. Serves ethically sourced fish and chips; eat-in or take-away. Open Mon–Sat for lunch and dinner, Sun for dinner.

Goat and Tricycle 27–29 Westhill Rd, BH2 5PF ℗ 01202 314220. A real ale pub serving home-cooked food. Goat curry is a speciality. Pet-friendly. Open daily for lunch and dinner.

Kayla 42 Holdenhurst Rd, BH8 8AD ℗ 01202 554300. Trendy, contemporary Italian restaurant and bar in the town centre. Open daily 10.00–late.

Key West Bournemouth Pier BH2 5AA ℗ 01202 306155. On the pier with views of the beaches. Simple décor and food, such as local fish and chips, pizzas and pies. Open Mon–Tue 10.00–19.00, Wed–Sun 10.00–20.00 .

Larder House 4 Southbourne Grove, BH6 3QZ ℗ 01202 424687 Ⓦ www.thelarderhouse.co.uk. A wood-fired oven is at the heart of things here, producing artisan breads and pizzas. Open Mon–Sat 11.00–late, Sun lunch.

L'Assiette 141 Belle Vue Rd, Southbourne BH6 3EN ℗ 01202 420537. French and British cuisine, made using locally sourced ingredients. Open Tue–Sat for lunch and dinner, Sun for lunch.

West Beach Pier Approach, BH2 5AA ℗ 01202 587785. A modern, upmarket seafood restaurant and bar near the pier with sea views. Open daily 09.00–22.00.

④ Hengistbury Head and Mudeford Sandbank

One of the few uninhabited parts of this built-up coastline, the sandstone promontory known as **Hengistbury Head**, a nature reserve, offers a quiet retreat for walking, cycling and wildlife watching.

The headland and the long sand spit trailing from the end of it (Mudeford Sandbank) provide natural protection for Christchurch Harbour. The unspoilt sandbank has a spine of colourful beach huts running along it and is a good vantage point for watching the harbour's birdlife. Facilities are limited but there is a good restaurant, **The Beach House** (see page 219), with a small shop adjoining it.

The headland and sandbank are easily reached from both the Christchurch and Bournemouth sides. A ferry shuttles visitors the short distance to the sandbank from Mudeford Quay on the northeastern side of Christchurch Harbour (*Mudeford Ferry 07968 334441; www.mudefordferry. co.uk; Easter–Oct 10.00–17.00,weekends in winter weather permitting; bikes and dogs allowed*). Bournemouth Boating Services (*01202 429119; www. bournemouthboating.co.uk*) operates a ferry between Christchurch Quay and Mudeford Sandbank.

From the large car park at the base of Hengistbury Head at the Bournemouth end, you can walk or catch the land train to **Mudeford Sandbank**. The car park has a helpfully positioned café (*Hiker Café; Hengistbury Head BH6 4EN; 01202 428552*) and is the departure point for the **land train** (*01202 425517; 10.00–17.00*), which runs 1½ miles around the harbour to the sandbank. The train has been running since 1968 and provides a scenic, atmospheric and fun way to get to the beach at Mudeford (dogs also carried); it is great value for money.

A pleasant walk extends from the headland to the sandbank and the views from the top over Christchurch, Bournemouth and the Isle of Wight make it worth the climb. Heath, grassland, woodland, reed beds and water meadow are all present on the headland, which supports 500 plant species and over 300 bird species, including Dartford warbler and sky lark. In 1989 the endangered natterjack toad was reintroduced to Hengistbury Head, where temporary pools near sand dunes and heathland are ideal for breeding. At dusk you may hear the call of the male natterjack, so loud it can be heard from over a mile away. Human activity in the 19th century left acidic ponds on the head, now a significant element of the nature reserve and home to 16 species of dragonflies.

Archaeological investigations of the headland have revealed a wealth of activity from at least 10,500BC. Its visible lumps and bumps include Bronze Age barrows and Iron Age earthworks dating from its time as a busy cross-Channel trading centre. Italian amphorae, Breton pots and raw purple glass are among the imports that have been unearthed here; a planned new visitor centre at the head will display some of the many finds from the area.

⑤ Christchurch and surrounds

Although a close neighbour, the delightful, historic town of Christchurch, on the rivers Stour and Avon, is a world away from the bustle and modernity of Bournemouth. It is certainly worth visiting for its attractive riparian scenery and historic buildings, the most notable of which is its medieval church, Christchurch Priory.

Christchurch Priory (see page 215) lies in a park-like area on the River Avon and the town's key historic features are conveniently clustered around it. Christchurch's bowling green must surely have the best outlook of any of its kind, for it stands next to the ruins of **Christchurch Castle**, probably built by the Normans around 1100 to protect the town's river access. The castle was taken by Cromwell's troops during the Civil War and when hostilities ended Cromwell had it torn down, leaving it in the ruined state in which it remains. Steps lead to the top of the motte on which the castle was built and it is worth the short climb to see the remaining stonework and for the views over the town. Within the castle precinct beside the river are the roofless remains of **Constable's House**, a 12th-century chamber block with a rare surviving Norman chimney. From here you can walk along the mill stream (Convent Walk) past the priory and onwards to the point where the stream meets the River Stour, near Place Mill. In the **Priory Gardens** is a handsome mausoleum for a Mrs Perkins, who died in 1783. She reportedly had a horror of being buried alive and so asked that she be laid to rest in the mausoleum at the entrance to the school so she could be heard if she revived. She left instructions that the coffin should not be sealed and she should be able to unlock the door of the mausoleum from the inside. Her wishes were carried out but when her husband died in 1803, her body was removed, the mausoleum sold and re-erected here.

A sculpture by Jonathan Sells in the gardens has a humorous take on the history of the priory; the images include one monk climbing on the shoulders of another to feed birds. It was erected in 1994 to commemorate the priory's 900th anniversary.

Place Mill (*BH23 1BY; 01202 487626; open Apr–Oct Tue–Sun & bank holidays 11.00–17.30*) was used to grind corn until 1908 and, although no longer in working order, it has been restored and opens in spring and summer as an art gallery.

Near Place Mill is the quay, where you can **hire small boats** and potter upstream along the River Stour. I spent a very relaxing hour taking a boat up the river, which flows gently at this point, passing carefree swans, ducks and moorhens drifting in and out of the reeds and golden waterlilies. The river gives you a totally different perspective on the town and you can't help but covet the houses with gardens running down to the water and private moorings. You can also hire a boat further upstream from **Tuckton Tea Gardens** (*01202 429119; open Feb–Dec*), a riverside café. The **Wick Ferry** (*01202 429119; Easter–Oct 10.00–17.00*) runs across the River Stour between Wick Village (on the Hengistbury Head side of the harbour) and Christchurch. Simply beckon to Tony, the lively Italian skipper, and he will gladly pick you up. At the time of writing the fee was 90p one way. A **vintage ferry service** (*01202 429119; Easter–Oct 10.00–17.00*) operates boats built in 1934–35 between Tuckton Tea Gardens, Wick Ferry, Christchurch Quay and Mudeford Sandbank.

From the quay you can often see ponies or cattle grazing on the meadows almost surrounded by water, creating the illusion of an island inhabited by marooned livestock. Behind the meadows, **Stanpit Marsh Nature Reserve** juts out into the harbour on the northern side, giving the waterway its narrow appearance. A visitor centre fleshes out detail on the resident wildlife of this habitat, made up of salt marsh with creeks and salt pans, reed beds, freshwater marsh, gravel estuarine banks and sandy scrub. Although it is boggy in parts, you can walk through the reserve. In the 18th century Stanpit Marsh was a favourite haunt of smugglers, who landed their contraband at Mudeford Quay and brought it across the harbour and up the narrow channels that cut across the marsh.

Christchurch town centre is a pleasing blend of Georgian and older buildings, such as that containing the **New Forest Perfumery Gift Shop and Tearooms** (*11 Church St*), which dates from the 13th century. Full of character inside and out, it is distinguishable by its medieval timber frame and thatched roof.

It is worth popping into the **Red House Museum and Gardens** (*Quay Rd,*

BH23 1BU; 0845 6035635; open Tue–Fri 10.00–17.00, Sat 10.00–16.00; free admission) for an insight into the archaeology and social history of the area. The building was constructed in 1764 as a workhouse; upstairs is a collection of finds excavated during the building of Bournemouth, while the ground floor has an array of more recent items and changing art and photography exhibitions. In a barn at the back of the house is a Royal Horse Artillery fire engine of 1795; the pretty garden is brimming with heritage plants (ones that were grown in earlier times but which are now rare) and there is a small café.

A pleasant coastal walk leads from **Mudeford Quay**, a working quay piled high with lobster pots, to **Highcliffe Beach**. The beach stretches for four miles and is divided into areas known as Avon, Friars Cliff, Steamer Point and Highcliffe Castle. You will pass colourful beach huts and have views across to the Isle of Wight and The Needles; a couple of cafés along the way provide handy stopping-off points. Avon Beach offers excellent windsurfing and plays host to the national championships.

St Catherine's Hill Nature Reserve lies north of the town and provides commanding views of the town and surrounding area. It has probably served as a look-out point since prehistoric times and there is evidence of Bronze Age and Iron Age settlement here. The heathland and coniferous forest provide a habitat for smooth snakes, sand lizards, Dartford warblers, nightjars and abundant butterflies. You can leave your car in the small car park at the bottom of St Catherine's Hill Lane, or on surrounding residential roads, and walk up from there. A suggested walk is available online at www.dorsetforyou.com.

Christchurch Priory

℡ 01202 485804. Open Mon–Sat 09.30–17.00, Sun 14.15–17.30; free recitals Thu 12.30–13.15.

A characterful cobbled street lined with shops and restaurants leads to the longest parish church in England – it is so long it looks almost as if it has been stretched lengthways. There is so much to see within that it is just as well there are hugely knowledgeable volunteer guides on hand to point you in the right direction. The church has been considerably added to since it was first built in the 11th century and therefore displays a catalogue of architectural styles from Norman to Renaissance. Thankfully, during the Dissolution Henry VIII abandoned his plans to pull down the church in a merciful response to a plea from the townspeople, instead giving permission for it to be used as the parish church.

At the end of the 11th century Ranulf Flambard (later Bishop of Durham) decided to build a church to replace the 7th-century Saxon one that existed on the site of the current priory but he elected to build it on St Catherine's Hill, about two miles away, so the new Norman church would be visible for miles around. The townspeople objected – they wanted the church built in the town on the same spot as the Saxon one. Flambard ignored their wishes and in 1094 preparations began to build the church on St Catherine's Hill. After the stones that were laid out on the hill were repeatedly moved overnight to the site of the Saxon church, Flambard conceded to build the church there, citing divine intervention.

Talk of miraculous happenings continued throughout the construction. It is said that a mysterious carpenter helped with the building and was never present for meals or to collect wages. Then there is the **miraculous beam**, still visible at the rear of the lady chapel – a large beam was cut from the New Forest for the roof but when it was brought to the church it was found to be too short. The workers returned the following morning to find it was the perfect length and already installed in its intended position. The mysterious carpenter was not seen again and was assumed to be Jesus. Until that point the intended name was Church of the Holy Trinity but because of the miracles it became known as Christchurch.

The **lady chapel** was completed and vaulted early in the 15th century, and features what is thought to have been the first pendant vault (a decorative pendant hanging from the vaulted ceiling) in England. Above the lady chapel, reached by climbing 75 steps, is St Michael's Loft, originally a school for novice monks and later for local boys; it now contains a **museum** on the history of the priory (*open May–Oct*).

The absorbing **reredos** behind the high altar is essentially Jesus's family tree caricatured – it illustrates the prophecy in the book of Isaiah, 'And there shall come forth a shoot out of the stem of Jesse, and a branch shall grow out of his roots'. It dates from around 1350 and is remarkably well preserved.

The oak **misericords** are mostly from the 1520s, although four date from the early 13th century and are thought to be the oldest in England. Misericords are seats designed to prevent monks falling asleep during services – if they did so, the seats fell forward with a loud crash. Each seat has a carving, either human or animal or a blend of the two. Look out for the depiction of a fox in the pulpit and geese underneath, a cheeky ecclesiastical metaphor.

The large **memorial** of 1500 to Margaret, Countess of Salisbury, is ornately carved and exquisite but tells a chilling tale. The countess was punished for the sins of her son, when Henry VIII had her beheaded at the age of 74 because her son had published criticisms of the king. Henry VIII refused to allow her to be buried in her chantry in Christchurch and she was interred in the Tower of London's cemetery for traitors.

For a small fee, you can climb the 176 steps to the top of the 15th-century **tower** accompanied by a steward; you are rewarded with memorable views over the town, harbour and surrounding countryside.

Boating around Christchurch

The boating companies at the quay provide boat hire for pottering along the River Stour and some also offer cruises in the area. Alternatively, you can opt for a high-speed rigid inflatable boat trip around the bay or across to the Isle of Wight. Most boat-hire companies only operate between Easter and October.

Boat hire and cruises

Adventure Voyages Mudeford Quay BH23 4AB ℡ 01202 488662
Ⓦ www.adventurevoyages.co.uk. Offers 20-minute blasts around the bay in a RIB, or longer trips across the Solent to the Isle of Wight.

Messing about on the River Stour Christchurch Quay ℡ 01202 429119
Ⓦ www.bournemouthboating.co.uk. Hires self-drive motorboats and rowing boats for exploring the River Stour. Also operates boat cruises.

Mudeford Ferry Mudeford Quay Ⓜ 07968 334441 Ⓦ www.mudefordferry.co.uk. As well as the ferry to Mudeford Sandbank, offers daytime and evening harbour cruises.

Quay Leisure Hire Christchurch Quay Ⓜ 07813 278698. Hires self-drive boats and operates the wheelyboat (wheelchair accessible).

(Re)Discover Christchurch Quay Ⓜ 07788 131735 Ⓦ www.re-discover.co.uk. Guided canoe trips along the River Stour.

Tuckton Tea Gardens ℡ 01202 429119; open Feb–Dec. A riverside café offering boat hire and hour-long barbecue cruises on Saturday evenings in summer.

Wick Ferry 323 Belle Vue Rd, BH6 3BA ℡ 01202 429119. As well as a ferry service across the River Stour, also offers self-drive motor boats and rowing boats.

Fishing around Christchurch

Anglers are well catered for, with opportunities for excellent sea, coarse and fly fishing in the waters in and around Christchurch. The harbour is good for bass and mullet during spring and summer, while Mudeford and Hengistbury Head yield mackerel, sea bream, wrasse and the occasional cod. Some of the best river fishing in England is available at the acclaimed Royalty Fishery on the River Avon and the Throop Fishery on the Stour, where you can expect to hook barbel, chub, roach, carp and pike. Permits are available from Davis Tackle (*75 Bargates, BH23 1QE; 01202 485169; www.davistackle.co.uk*) and you can pick up a leaflet on fishing from the tourist information centre.

Highcliffe Castle

Rothesay Drive, Highcliffe BH23 4LE ℡ 01425 278807 Ⓦ www.highcliffecastle.co.uk. Open Feb–Dec 11.00–17.00.

There can be few stately homes with a better location than Highcliffe, which stands looking out to sea from its cliff top. The house was built in the 1830s by Lord Stuart de Rothesay, an eminent diplomat, using materials salvaged from medieval French buildings, including gargoyles and coloured glass windows. It is this Norman and Renaissance carved stone, along with the castle's Gothic revival features, that make it appear older than it is. It remained a family home until the 1950s but was severely damaged by fire in the following decade, and it is only the shell of the building that remains. Nevertheless, it is widely recognised as one of the best surviving houses in the Romantic and Picturesque styles of architecture. Highcliffe was bought and renovated by Christchurch Borough Council and now hosts a range of events throughout the year, from concerts to murder mystery suppers. The interior has not been restored but each room has information and a photograph showing what it would have looked like in its prime; visiting the inside doesn't take long (low admission fees reflect this) but every Tuesday and Sunday at 14.00 you can take a volunteer-led hour-long tour of the unrestored parts of the building not normally open to visitors, including the wine cellars, kitchens and servants' areas. You can linger in the 14-acre cliff-top grounds (a good spot for a picnic), and wander down to the beach below.

The tearooms serve Dorset cream teas, cakes and light lunches and there is a gift shop.

Museum of Electricity

The Old Power Station, Bargates BH23 1QE ☎ 01202 480467. Open Easter–Sep Mon–Thu 12.00–16.30; free admission.

Set in an Edwardian power station built in 1903 to supply the trams that ran between Poole and Christchurch, this Scottish and Southern Energy initiative opened in 1981 and is the only museum in the country dedicated to the history of electricity. Interactive displays explain how electricity works and the museum is packed with over 700 early electrical appliances, like a grandfather's shed full of defunct gadgets. A romantic-looking Bournemouth tramcar dating from 1914 is one of the key exhibits. The museum has an educational bent, is geared up for children and regularly receives school groups.

Bournemouth Aviation Museum

Merritown Lane, Hurn BH23 6BA ☎ 01202 473141 ⓦ www.aviation-museum.co.uk. Open daily.

On the B3073 Bournemouth International Airport perimeter road, this is emphatically a hands-on museum, run as a charity and staffed by enthusiastic and knowledgeable volunteers. You are encouraged to climb into aircraft and twiddle the knobs; a flight simulator allows you to play pilot. I saw plenty of excited children clambering into the helicopter, fighter planes and double-decker bus and wrestling with the controls. The aircraft are scattered in a field, rather than in a hangar, and the planes taking off and landing at the airport add to the atmosphere.

Food and drink

A farmers' market takes place on the first Friday of the month in Saxon Square (*09.00–13.00*); while the regular weekly market is on Mondays. An annual food festival in May (*www.christchurchfoodfest.co.uk*) features demonstrations and special offers in the town's eateries.

A Taste of Dorset 18A Church St, BH23 1BW ☎ 01202 477374. Near the Priory, this wonderful little shop opened in 2011 and sells a delightfully tempting range of Dorset produce, all of which can be tasted. It is a reminder of how bountiful Dorset's food and drink is, and is great for present shopping. Open daily 10.00–18.00.

Beach House Mudeford Sandbank, Hengistbury Head BH6 4EN ℗ 01202 423474 Ⓦ www.beachhousecafé.co.uk. An excellent casual restaurant among the beach huts on Mudeford Sandbank, with views across Christchurch Harbour to the Priory. Not surprisingly, the restaurant specialises in fresh seafood. Adjacent, a small shop sells essentials. If you arrive in your own boat, you can moor outside the restaurant. Opening times are dependent on the weather but usually 09.00–17.00 and evenings at the weekend, plus additional evenings in summer. Pet-friendly.

Boat House 9 Quay Rd, BH23 1BU ℗ 01202 480033 Ⓦ www.theboathouse. co.uk. A trendy restaurant and bar in an enviable position on the quay. Italian chef Maurizio conjures up wood-fired pizzas and breads, while the Creole chef has added a range of exotic dishes to the menu, like drunk Barbados chicken with rum, lime and Caribbean spices. The live music in the bar on Friday evenings attracts a good crowd. There is outdoor seating and a crazy golf course for entertainment. Open daily 09.00–late.

Cheese & Alfies 10 Church St, BH23 1BW ℗ 01202 487000 Ⓦ www.cheeseandalfies.com. A popular restaurant close to the Priory. Its name honours the owners' 2 sons, Charlie (AKA Cheese) and Alfie. There is a good supply of books tucked into the backs of the chairs if you fancy a read while eating, and it is very child friendly. Serves a decent breakfast, a delicious hot chocolate and plenty of vegetarian dishes. Open Mon–Sat 08.00–17.00, Sun 09.00–16.00 and Tue–Sat for dinner. Cookery classes are held here on Mon evenings.

New Forest Perfumery Giftshop & Tearooms 11 Church St, BH23 1DP ℗ 01202 482893 Ⓦ www.newforestperfumery.co.uk. In a 14th-century thatched building with oodles of character; there is also a pleasant courtyard. Homemade lunches, cakes (including gluten free) and, of course, perfumes. Open Mon–Sat 09.00–16.30, Sun 10.00–16.30.

Old Mill Tearooms The Quay BH23 1BY ℗ 01202 474942. Small, unpretentious tearooms on Christchurch Quay. A good spot to stop off after taking a boat up the River Stour. Open daily 10.00–16.30.

The Ship 48 High St, BH23 1BN ℗ 01202 474799. A fancy pub, restaurant and piano bar. Dishes use fresh ingredients from a range of local suppliers wherever possible.

Splinters 12 Church St, BH23 1BW ℗ 01202 483454 Ⓦ www.splinters.uk.com. A well-regarded restaurant near the Priory, which serves creative international cuisine. Open Tue–Sat for lunch and dinner.

Tuckton Tea Gardens 323 Belle Vue Rd, Tuckton BH6 3BA ℗ 01202 429119. A riverside café with extensive gardens, mini-golf and boat hire. During the summer they offer Sat-night barbecue cruises, when a 1-hour river cruise is followed by a barbecue in the gardens. Open Feb–Dec.

⑥ Avon Heath Country Park

BH24 2DA ℗ 01425 478470. Open 08.00–dusk; admission is free but parking is charged.
Two miles west of Ringwood off the A31, Avon Heath is an important
area of lowland and wet heath, acid grassland and heather. It is managed in
conjunction with the RSPB and is home to various rare species, including
Dartford warblers, nightjars and woodlarks; grazing by livestock is part of its
conservation strategy.

You can walk or cycle along marked trails, and for families there are activity
trails and play equipment. A visitor centre provides information on the park
and there's a hide for watching the wildlife visiting the feeders. It's dog-friendly,
and you can picnic or use the café.

Wimborne Minster and surrounds

Wimborne Minster is an appealing riverside town with an impressive minster
church. Nearby is the National Trust **Kingston Lacy Estate** with its manor
house, parkland and **Badbury Rings**, an Iron Age hillfort in an appealing
countryside setting. Kingston Lacy has the distinction of being the National
Trust's largest lowland property, with a working estate encompassing three
villages, a dozen farms, a farm shop and an extensive network of footpaths and
bridleways.

⑦ Wimborne Minster

If you're arriving from the north, Wimborne Minster, often shortened to
Wimborne, is the last pleasantly sized Dorset town before you hit the heavily
populated area around Poole and Bournemouth. Although just five miles north
of Poole, it retains a rural flavour and streets full of character, which make for
pleasant wandering. Bright floral displays heighten the overall impression of
a well cared for town. For its size, Wimborne has a very well stocked and
equipped **tourist information centre**; it sells a booklet containing a town trail,
which leads you around some of the less obvious places of historical interest,
marked with green plaques.

The town stands on the confluence of the rivers Stour and Allen and dates
back to the early 8th century. It became an important market town although
trade had slowed by the 18th century when John Hutchins noted in his *History
of Dorset*, 'the town of Wimborne is much more remarkable for what it was
formerly than for what it is now'.

Whatever the changing fortunes of the town, its principal feature has
remained constant through the ages, the **minster** of **St Cuthburga** (see page
222), the two towers of which dominate the town's skyline.

Narrow streets following medieval lines lead away from the minster to the
well preserved town centre with its abundance of historic buildings. One of
them, a town house dating from the 16th century, contains the **Priest's House**

Museum and Garden (*23–27 High St, BH21 1HR; 01202 882533; www. priest-house.co.uk; open Apr–Oct Mon–Sat 10.00–16.30*). A series of rooms shows the area through various eras, including finds from the excavation of a nearby Roman site, a representation of a Victorian kitchen and an elegant Georgian room. A childhood gallery has a colourful array of toys and games, which might hold a few surprises for today's children, and a long, narrow garden running down to a stream behind the house is dotted with historical agricultural and horticultural implements and is also where you will find the tearoom. This is a child-friendly museum with interactive displays, quizzes and trails to follow; children can even dress up in Victorian or Roman dress.

To the northwest of the minster, the **Cornmarket** with its market house of 1738 is the original market place. The **markets** have now moved to Mill Lane, where they take place every Friday (*07.30–13.30*), Saturday (*07.30–13.00*) and Sunday (*08.00–15.00*) and a farmers' market is held on the second Saturday of the month (*09.00–13.00*). Friday features a renowned antique bazaar, which draws bargain-hunters from quite a distance. Erected as a corn mill in 1771, the **Town Mill** at the end of Mill Lane now houses a café overlooking the River Allen. Nearby is **Dreamboats** (*Station Rd, Riverside Point; 07794 507001; www.dream-boats.org.uk; open Apr–Sep weekends, public holidays & school holidays*), where you can hire a rowing boat and mess about on the River Stour. It is a registered charity staffed by volunteers and was created in 2000 to promote enjoyment of the river, in particular for children.

The town is blessed with some good **independent shops**, such as Gullivers Bookshop (*47 High St, BH21 1HS; 01202 882667; open Mon–Sat 09.00–17.30*), which has been selling books on Dorset, maps, jigsaw puzzles and stationery since 1969.

Wimborne always seems to have plenty going on. The **Tivoli Theatre** (*West Borough BH21 1LT; 01202 885566*) is a very active Art Deco cinema and theatre built in 1936 in a Georgian town house. It fell into disrepair and was closed in 1980 but thanks to a committed band of volunteers, known as the Friends of the Tivoli, was restored and re-opened in 1993. A highlight on the local calendar is the annual **Wimborne Folk Festival** (*www. wimbornefolkfestival.co.uk*) in June, one of the largest folk-dancing and music events in the country. Wimborne also hosts the longest fireworks display in Dorset, as part of its 5 November Guy Fawkes celebrations. Held in the grounds of St Michael's Church of England Middle School, it draws a good crowd from the surrounding area.

Wimborne has a rather grim skeleton in its closet: it was the birthplace of one of the chief suspects in the Jack the Ripper murders. **Montague John Druitt** was born in Wimborne in 1857 into a medical family – his father William was the town's leading surgeon. They lived at the substantial Westfield House, which has now been converted into flats; he was educated at Winchester College and New College, Oxford and went on to become a schoolmaster and a barrister. Druitt was found drowned in the River Thames on 31 December 1888, believed to have committed suicide; his death coincided with the cessation of the Jack the Ripper murders. Druitt is buried in Wimborne Cemetery, now something of a macabre tourist attraction.

Just north of Wimborne on the River Allen, **Walford Mill Craft Centre** (*Stone Lane, BH21 1NL; 01202 841400; www.walfordmillcrafts.co.uk; open Mon–Sat 10.00–17.00, Sun 11.00–16.00; free admission*) has exhibitions of crafts, plus a craft shop and restaurant. Some of the artisans have studios on site and you can see them at work. The centre also runs craft classes.

The minster

Open Mon–Sat 09.30–17.30, Sun 14.30–17.30; guides available in summer.

As you approach the minster church in summer, pink flowering chestnuts provide a decorative surround. Its foundations date back to around AD705, when Cuthburga, sister of Ine, king of the West Saxons, founded a nunnery here. In its heyday it housed around 500 nuns (there was also a monastery) but it was destroyed by the Danes in 1013 and never rebuilt. The Saxons obviously considered the church significant as King Alfred buried his brother Ethelred here in AD871 after he was mortally wounded in a battle near Cranborne.

The largely Norman building dates from around 1120 to 1180, although the transepts are 14th century and the western end is from 1500. On the northern exterior of the west tower a **quarter jack** strikes his bells every quarter of an hour. He was created in 1612 and reportedly began life as a monk but during the Napoleonic Wars was given a makeover to create the appearance of a grenadier. Attached to the quarter jack on the inside of the tower is a colourful **astronomical clock** built in the 14th-century by a monk at Glastonbury in Somerset. Its rudimentary depiction of the solar system is rather beautiful and resembles a drawing from a children's storybook in its simplicity but its operation is remarkably clever. The sun points to the time of day and the gold-and-black sphere represents the moon; both move around the face of the clock. The sphere shows the moon's phases with appropriate portions showing black and gold: when there is a full moon it is completely golden and when there is an eclipse it is completely black.

Opposite the clock is the simple memorial to **Isaac Gulliver**, better known as 'the King of the Smugglers': in 1782 the government offered a pardon to smugglers who joined the navy, or who could find substitutes to undertake military service on their behalf. For a man of Gulliver's means, buying a substitute was no problem and thus he cleared his name and became a respected member of Wimborne society. It is also said that he uncovered a French plot to kill King George III and this contributed to his receiving a pardon.

The minster contains other fascinating tombs, such as that of **Anthony Ettricke**, known as 'the man in the wall', whose plans to be interred in Wimborne Minster on his death were scuppered when he fell out with church authorities and announced he would not be buried either in the church or outside it. He subsequently relented but to save face was buried in the wall. All in all his demise was rather farcical: he had predicted he would die in 1693 and had that date engraved on his memorial but ended up living until 1703 and so the date had to be altered. In the north chapel is an ornate and colourful monument of 1606 to **Sir Edmund Uvedale**, whose effigy is lying on his side in full armour and appears to have two left feet. While it would nice to think this was a hint that he was an appalling dancer, it is believed to have been the result of a restoration by a sculptor who was having a bad day.

Above the choir vestry, reached via a spiral staircase is the **chained library** (*open Easter–Oct 10.30– 12.30 & 14.00–16.00, Oct–Easter Sat 10.00–12.30*), established in 1686. With over 400 leather-bound books it is the second largest of its kind in England and was one of the earliest public libraries. It holds some literary treasures, including the *Regimen Animarum* written in 1343 on vellum (lambskin) with a quill pen and ink made from oak apples. Only two other copies survive and this one is believed to be the finest of the three. Also in the library are the collected works of St Anselm of 1495, some of the earliest printings of the Gospels, Bibles in Hebrew, Greek and Latin, and a book bound for the court of Henry VIII.

Wimborne Model Town

16 King St, BH21 1DY ① 01202 881924 ⑩ www.wimborne-modeltown.com. Open Apr–Oct daily 10.00–17.00.

This intricately detailed 1:10 scale model of Wimborne Minster was begun in the 1940s and finished in 1951 yet it still bears a striking resemblance to the town today, aside perhaps from the goods on sale in the shops. Seeing what was on offer in a rural town centre in the post-war years will be quite a revelation for many. Children may enjoy the model railway based on Thomas the Tank Engine and there is also a mini-golf course and giant outdoor games. The model is surrounded by beautiful gardens and the tearooms are good value. In the mid-1980s the model town had fallen into disrepair and a group of townsfolk managed to save it from developers; they found a new site for it and it re-opened here in 1991.

Food and drink

Angels 10 East St, BH21 1DS ① 01202 849922. Unfussy café serving homemade food prepared with locally sourced ingredients. Open Mon–Sat 08.00–16.00.

Barley Mow Inn Long Lane, Colehill BH21 7AH ① 01202 882140. In the nearby village of Colehill, an inn dating from the 16th century with plenty of character and a cosy log fire in winter. Traditional pub food and some more creative dishes. Open daily for lunch and dinner.

Kings Head The Square, BH21 1JG ① 01202 880101. A large 18th-century inn in the town centre, serving traditional pub food. Open daily for lunch and dinner.
Les Bouviers Arrowsmith Rd, Canford Magna BH21 3BD ① 01202 889555 Ⓦ www.lesbouviers.co.uk. Fine dining restaurant at this boutique hotel. Locally sourced ingredients wherever possible. Open for lunch daily, dinner Mon–Sat.
Long Crichel Shop and Tearooms 7 Cook Row ① 01202 887765. Opposite Wimborne Minster is the shop and tearooms of the excellent Long Crichel Bakery, selling goodies from the bakery. Open Mon–Sat 09.00–16.30.
Olive Branch East Borough BH21 1PF ① 01202 884686. A pub/restaurant/bar run by Hall and Woodhouse Brewery of Blandford Forum. Riverside beer garden.
Pick More Daisies 11 Leigh Rd, BH21 1AB ① 01202 887557. Simply prepared local produce is on offer here. Plenty of healthy options, including vegetarian dishes, as well as tempting cakes. Open Mon–Fri 09.00–16.00, Sat 09.00–17.00 and Fri evening. Cookery courses are also available. Reservation recommended.
Riverside Café 10a The Old Mill, Mill Lane, BH21 1JQ Ⓜ 07930 951508. An informal café on the River Allen, with indoor and outdoor seating. Open Mon–Sat 09.30–16.30.

⑧ Pamphill

Around a rambling green in this delightfully unspoilt village of the Kingston Lacy Estate huddles a group of 17th- and 18th-century cottages, many of them thatched. **St Stephen's Church** at the northern end of the green was built in 1907 in Arts and Crafts Gothic style as a memorial to Walter Ralph Bankes, who left £5,000 in his will for the purpose of 'building and endowing a church at Kingston Lacy'. The interior is simple with fine carved oak from the Kingston Lacy Estate. The nearby Pamphill First School and Nursery began life as an almshouse and school in 1698, and the 17th-century manor house was built by a steward to the Bankes family. **Abbott Street Forge** served the estate from the 19th century until 1945, when it closed. It swung into operation again in 1997, when Giles Stuart fired up the old brick forges to produce fine, handcrafted ironwork (*01202 888573; www.abbottstreetforge. co.uk*). He receives a steady flow of commissions for interior and exterior restoration work, particularly from the National Trust. In December he and his wife hold an exhibition and open up the forge to visitors, who can see Giles in action. In spring, Pamphill's **Abbott Street Copse** is awash with bluebells, offering up an unmistakably English scene.

It is a short stroll along quiet lanes from the village to the **River Stour** (or you can drive and leave your car in the parking area just off Cowgrove Road), where there is an inviting picnic spot, and a footpath leading along the river and through farmland towards Cowgrove, another small, unspoilt village on the Kingston Lacy Estate.

Food and drink

Barford Ice Cream Barford Farm, BH21 4BY ① 01258 857969 Ⓦ www.barfordicecream.co.uk. West of Pamphill towards Sturminster Marshall, this is is the home of Barford Ice Cream, made on the Kingston Lacy Estate using milk from a small Jersey herd in the village. You can drop in and sample their wares during the summer months at the farm's Ice Cream Garden, and there is a shop. Garden open Mar–Oct Tue–Sun 11.30–17.30, weather permitting.

Pamphill Dairy Farm Shop and Restaurant Pamphill BH21 4ED ℗ 01202 880618 Ⓦ www.pamphilldairy.co.uk. Close to the church in a converted dairy and milking parlour, this complex comprises a farm shop, butcher, florist, cosmetics shop, gift shop, restaurant and animal feed store. Products on sale at the butcher include Kingston Lacy's Red Devon beef. The restaurant serves wholesome, farmhouse cooking. Open daily 08.30–17.30.

Vine Inn Pamphill BH21 4EE ℗ 01202 882259. A classic unspoilt country pub owned by the National Trust but run by the same family for generations. Local cider, simple food and 2 tiny, characterful bars.

Kingston Lacy House and Estate

Wimborne Minster BH21 4EA ℗ 01202 883402 Ⓦ www.nationaltrust.org.uk. House open Mar–Oct Wed–Sun 11.00–17.00; garden open daily.

One of Dorset's grandest houses, Kingston Lacy was the home of the Bankes family from 1665 until 1981, when Ralph Bankes bequeathed the magnificent 8,500-acre estate to the National Trust. Today it draws a steady flow of visitors for its sumptuous interior, outstanding collections of art and Egyptian artefacts, and serene grounds.

The house was built in 1665 for Sir Ralph Bankes after the family's original home, Corfe Castle, was destroyed by Cromwell's troops during the Civil War. It was significantly altered in 1835 at the behest of William Bankes, who employed the noted architect Sir Charles Barry (whose other projects included work on the Houses of Parliament and Westminster Bridge) to refurbish it in flamboyant Italian-Renaissance style. The house's lavish interior is in large part the legacy of William Bankes, who was an avid traveller, collector and Egyptologist and enjoyed displaying his trinkets at the family home. From 1841 he lived in Italy, where he had fled to avoid prosecution for homosexual acts, but he continued to collect and send back furniture and fittings for the house, and may have made the occasional clandestine visit to his beloved Kingston Lacy.

A grand marble staircase leads from the entrance hall; William Bankes bought it in Italy and it was part of Barry's brief in the refurbishment that he alter the house to accommodate it. Perched in niches in the walls on the first floor loggia are bronze statues of King Charles I, Sir John Bankes and Dame Mary Bankes. Dame Mary is depicted holding the keys to Corfe Castle, which she successfully defended during the Civil War until Cromwell's men gained access via subterfuge and destroyed the building (see page 166). The real keys to Corfe Castle hang over the fireplace in the library, which is adorned with family portraits and Guido Reni's ceiling fresco, *The Separation of Night and Day.* Still sporting their 18th-century design are the library and saloon, created when Henry Bankes (William's father) renovated the house in the 1780s. The saloon contains some of the house's exceptional art collection, including paintings by Rubens and Titian. William Bankes built the oppressively flamboyant Spanish room to display his Spanish art collection; the room is a monument to opulence, with gilded leather wall hangings and a gilded ceiling taken from a Venetian palace. The Egyptian room contains objects Bankes collected while on expeditions in Egypt and represents the largest private collection of Egyptian artefacts in the UK. The Egyptian theme extends to the grounds of the house, where an obelisk from the 2nd century BC has stood since 1827. Its journey from Egypt to Kingston Lacy reportedly took 20 years and a team of 19 horses was needed to haul it into place.

The house is surrounded by formal gardens and 250 acres of landscaped parkland, grazed by Red Devon cattle. The garden features an Edwardian Japanese area and a Victorian fernery, which contains over 20 varieties of ferns. Paths lead from the formal gardens through the park and woodland, awash with daffodils and bluebells in spring. Longer walks, bridleways and cycleways lead around the estate, and are mapped in a leaflet available at Kingston Lacy. The red-brick stables of 1880 house a restaurant which serves a wealth of local food, including the estate's Red Devon beef and Barford Ice Cream.

White Mill

Open Apr–Oct Sat–Sun & bank holidays; National Trust.

Just over half a mile west of Pamphill, White Mill was last rebuilt in 1776 and was worked by tenants of the Kingston Lacy Estate until the late 19th century. The National Trust took over the mill when it was given the estate but it was not until the early 1990s that efforts were made to conserve it, using a photograph from 1900 to assist in the accurate restoration of the exterior of the mill; even the dovecotes on the wall are copies of those seen in the photograph. Although some restoration work has been done on the interior, the wooden drive gear, which dates from the 1776 rebuilding, is too fragile to work. The wheels are thought to be elm, which is resistant to water and to vibration, while the teeth are likely made of apple wood. Apple was traditionally used to make the teeth as it is more fragile than elm and should anything go wrong the teeth will shear off before more substantial parts are damaged. Local legend tells that the bells from the ruined church at Knowlton were stolen and dropped into the mill pond by the thieves, and that they can still be heard ringing.

Near the mill is a statuesque eight-arch **stone bridge**; while the current bridge is thought to date from the 16th century its predecessor is referenced in documents from 1175 as 'a bridge on the River Stour adjacent to the White Mill'. Carbon dating of the wooden pilings on which it stands indicate they are 12th century, making this the oldest bridge site in Dorset. A plaque warns: 'any person wilfully damaging any part of this county bridge will be guilty of felony and upon conviction liable to be transported for life by the court'.

⑨ Shapwick

Across the B3082 from Badbury Rings is the turning to the small village of Shapwick, which lies just over a mile down the lane. On the River Stour, it is an ideal spot to stop off during a walk along the **Stour Valley Way**. At its centre, opposite the Anchor pub is the village cross, believed to be of Saxon origin. In 1880 it was destroyed in a brawl and in 1920 the remains were converted into a war memorial. **St Bartholomew's Church** was originally built in the 11th and 12th centuries near an old Roman ford, where the Dorchester to Old Sarum road crossed the river. It is remarkably close to the river and has been known to flood, including during a funeral in 1870 when a torrent of water carried the coffin off down the river, never to be seen again. Little did the unsuspecting occupant know that they were going to receive an impromptu burial at sea. The tower, with its heathstone and flint banding, is thought to have been added in the 14th century, when the height of the roof was raised: coffin lids from that period can be seen supporting the north wall of the nave. Much restored in the late 19th century, the church was until the Reformation connecred with a priory. Henry VIII expelled the prior and gave the land and houses to 'my belovit cousin Hussey, the little man but a great General'. The Commissioners of Henry VIII left 'ye one silver cuppe'; this is probably the chalice still used in the church today, which dates from 1527, and is one of the finest of its type in England. In the floor of the church, near the altar, is a gravestone bearing the inscription, 'Anne Butler here beneath is laid, a pious prudent modest maid – 1659': an epitaph of which any girl could be proud.

〰〰〰

Food and drink

The Anchor at Shapwick West St, DT11 9LB ℡ 01258 857269. A newly refurbished pub with a sophisticated modern British menu. Local produce is used and the meat comes from a nearby RSPCA Freedom Farm. It is a great place to stop for those walking the Stour Valley Way. Open Mon-Sat for lunch and dinner, Sun 12.00–16.00.

⑩ Badbury Rings

The road to Badbury Rings announces that you are in for something special, with the stately avenue of beech trees along the B3082 providing a fitting approach. It stretches for over two miles and is made up of 731 trees planted in 1835. Sadly, the trees are nearing the end of their natural lives and gaps in the avenue are starting to appear.

Badbury Rings is a memorable spot for a stroll, with far-reaching views from the ramparts of the surrounding countryside, and an abundance of wildflowers, including 14 species of orchid. The Iron Age hillfort was built on a site that was occupied much earlier, as evidenced by the four Bronze Age (2200–800BC) round barrows, the most notable of which are the three that lie just to your right as you travel up the track to the car park. The hillfort itself consists of three concentric, circular ditches with high walls that protect a large central area where the settlement would have been. From the bottom of the ditch to the top of the rampart would have reached a height of some 40 feet and, even accounting for 2,000 years of erosion, the ditches are still formidable today. Above the rampart a timber palisade would have been constructed to further protect the settlement on top of the hill, now covered by a small wood. The circular depressions visible in the ground, roughly ten feet in diameter, are evidence of the wattle-and-daub roundhouses.

Badbury Rings is believed to have been one of several settlements in the area belonging to an ancient Dorset tribe known as the Durotriges. It would almost certainly have fallen to the invading Romans, and was probably taken by the Second Legion Augusta, led by Vespasian under Emperor Claudius. Evidence of the important Roman road from Old Sarum to Dorchester can be seen running to the west of the hillfort; the 22-mile portion of the road from Old Sarum to Badbury Rings is known as Ackling Dyke and is visible as an embankment. To the north this crosses a north–south road, which probably ran from Bath to Poole. The Romans are thought to have built a town just outside the rings, which they called Vindocladia – the place of white walls. It has been suggested that Badbury Rings could be the *Mons Badonicus*, where King Arthur and his army defeated the invading pagan hordes of the early 5th century, the Jutes, Angles and Saxons. Ravens, which have always been associated with Arthur, bred here until the late 19th century.

Just below the rings is the **point-to-point** racecourse, the scene of much drama and excitement during the season. I have fond memories of going point-to-pointing there as a child – it was usually freezing cold, wet and muddy but nothing could detract from the enjoyment of the day.

⑪ Stanbridge and Hinton Martell

North of Wimborne Minster on the B3078 are the hamlets of Stanbridge, also known as Hinton Parva, and Hinton Martell. Visible from the road between the two is an irrepressibly quaint, thatched, Hansel-and-Gretel-esque gate lodge built in 1809. To complete the picture, roses in pastel shades climb the walls of the lodge. It was built as the gate lodge to the substantial Gaunts House, which is now run as a personal development centre.

Sir Richard Glyn of Gaunts House had the now redundant **church of St Kenelm** built in 1860 as his estate church. It is a dainty building of banded stone and flint and nearby is a string of almshouses in the same style. The dedication of the church to St Kenelm is unusual, it is thought there are only seven other examples in the country. St Kenelm was an Anglo-Saxon boy saint, murdered when he was only seven years old. He was chosen to succeed his father as King of Mercia but when his father died in AD819, his jealous sister had him killed so that she could reign.

Tucked away on a side road is **Hinton Martell**, with an unusual fountain at its centre that Frederick Treves found quite out of keeping; he described it in his 1906 *Highways and Byways of Dorset* as 'just such a fountain to be found in a suburban tea garden, or in front of a gaudy Italian villa'. It was originally built for sheep but is far more elaborate than your average trough. Damaged by severe weather in 1963, it was rebuilt in 1965 and re-opened by Miss World 1965, a Dorset girl named Ann Sidney.

Honeybrook Farm and Country Park

Stanbridge BH21 4JD Ⓣ 01202 881120 ⓦ www.honeybrook.org. Open Tue–Sun 09.30–17.00; entry fee per car payable.

Honeybrook Farm lies 1½ miles north of Wimborne Minster on the B3078 and is part of the Gaunts Estate. The working farm offers fun and learning for children, who can interact with farm animals, and it has three play areas as well as a programme of nature-based outdoor activities. You can buy produce from the farm's butcher, baker, dairy and vegetable garden in the shop, sample it in the café, or tuck into it at the picnic area.

⑫ Holt and Holt Heath

Holt was originally the centre of the Royal Forest of Wimborne, mentioned in the Domesday Book. The area is still well wooded and has scattered 18th- and 19th-century cottages and houses. The **church of St James** is unusual for Dorset, being of red brick. It was completely rebuilt in 1836 but records show a church was repaired here in 1493 so that inhabitants would not have to walk to Wimborne Minster for services, which was particularly troublesome during the winter months.

At 1,200 acres, **Holt National Nature Reserve** is one of Dorset's largest areas of lowland heathland and has to its northwest two areas of ancient woodland (Holt Forest and Holt Wood); the National Trust owns the area and manages it in association with Natural England. It is best to keep to the paths as the heathland can be very boggy in parts. The reserve offers a quiet retreat from the busy East Dorset coast and is particularly fine in July and August when wildflowers are prolific. The heath is home to large populations of Dartford warbler, stonechat and nightjar and it is Dorset's only site for breeding curlew. All six British species of reptile (adder, grass snake, smooth snake, slow worm, sand lizard and common lizard) are present. The heath had traditionally been maintained by grazing but this ceased following World War II. In 2010 grazing was reintroduced in the form of a small number of cattle and New Forest ponies, which hopefully will help to reverse the deterioration by reducing the invasive scrub.

Index

Main entries in **bold**, map pages in *italics*.